W9-BGU-791

IRON MAN

Also by Lawrence Martin

The Presidents and the Prime Ministers

Breaking with History: The Gorbachev Revolution

The Red Machine: The Soviet Quest to Dominate Canada's Game

Behind the Red Line:
An American Hockey Player in Russia (co-author)

Pledge of Allegiance

Mario (a biography of Mario Lemieux)

Chrétien: The Will to Win (Volume 1)

The Antagonist

Harry Thode (co-author)

IRON MAN

THE DEFIANT REIGN OF
JEAN CHRÉTIEN

VOLUME TWO

LAWRENCE
MARTIN

VIKING
CANADA

VIKING CANADA

Penguin Group (Canada), a division of Pearson Penguin Canada Inc.,
10 Alcorn Avenue, Toronto, Ontario M4V 3B2

Penguin Group (U.K.), 80 Strand, London WC2R 0RL, England
Penguin Group (U.S.), 375 Hudson Street, New York, New York 10014, U.S.A.
Penguin Group (Australia) Inc., 250 Camberwell Road, Camberwell, Victoria 3124, Australia
Penguin Group (Ireland), 25 St. Stephen's Green, Dublin 2, Ireland
Penguin Books India (P) Ltd, 11, Community Centre, Panchsheel Park,
New Delhi – 110 017, India
Penguin Group (New Zealand), cnr Rosedale and Airborne Roads, Albany, Auckland 1310,
New Zealand
Penguin Books (South Africa) (Pty) Ltd, 24 Sturdee Avenue, Rosebank 2196, South Africa

Penguin Group, Registered Offices: 80 Strand, London WC2R 0RL, England

First published 2003

1 2 3 4 5 6 7 8 9 10   (FR)

The author wishes to thank Jean-Marc Carisse and Diana Murphy,
both of the Office of the Prime Minister, for use of their photographs in this book.

Manufactured in Canada.

NATIONAL LIBRARY OF CANADA CATALOGUING IN PUBLICATION

Martin, Lawrence, 1947–
Iron man : the defiant reign of Jean Chrétien / Lawrence Martin.

Sequel to: Chrétien : the will to win.
Includes index.

ISBN 0-670-04310-9

1. Chrétien, Jean, 1934–. 2. Canada—Politics and government—1984–1993.
3. Canada—Politics and government—1993–. 4. Prime ministers—Canada—Biography.
I. Martin, Lawrence Chrétien. II. Title.

FC636.C47M373 2003   971.064'8'092   C2003-904909-4

Visit the Penguin Group (Canada) website at **www.penguin.ca**

In memory of Frances Martin
The heart of our family
1918–2001

CONTENTS

AUTHOR'S NOTE

THE FIRST VOLUME of this biography, *Chrétien: The Will to Win,* took the story from his birth in 1934 to the beginning of his second run for the Liberal Party leadership in 1990. The second volume, *Iron Man: The Defiant Reign of Jean Chrétien,* begins with the leadership campaign, follows his three years as Opposition leader, and charts his ten years as prime minister.

Iron Man uses the same interview-intensive technique as the first volume. Mr. Chrétien, Paul Martin, Eddie Goldenberg, Jean Pelletier, and so many others were kind enough to grant on-the-record interviews for the book and their co-operation is most appreciated.

A government in power for a decade is a lot to cover. Some parts of the story are worthy of books of their own, and indeed some have been written on subjects like the Airbus affair, the Somalia debacle, the crushing of dissent at APEC, and the over-concentration of power in the prime minister's office. Shockingly, no book has been written on one of the more dramatic events in the nation's history: the 1995 Quebec referendum. Foreign policy in the Chrétien government also merits a detailed examination, as does the abuse of power that was apparent in the many ethics controversies that arose over the last ten years.

Though *Iron Man* obviously cannot cover all the drama, it attempts to draw the various themes into a cohesive portrait of Jean Chrétien in power. After completing the first book in 1995, I kept a close watch in anticipation of a second volume. My work as a national columnist for Southam News from 1998 to 2001, and for *The Globe and Mail* in the two years following, gave me a close-up view of Chrétien's government in action. Like other journalists, my relations with the prime minister's office were good or bad depending on the latest articles I had written. For one long stretch of time, when I was reporting on ethics abuses and the Shawinigate story, relations chilled to the point where communications were infrequent.

Through the course of researching the book, much conflicting evidence was gathered from differing sources. I have tried to sort out the wheat from the chaff, but no one has a claim on the truth—certainly not this author.

The key person on the project was Diane Turbide, the savvy editorial director at Penguin Canada. As a former journalist herself, Ms. Turbide knows that journalists only get moving when the deadline confronts them. As I kept getting later and later on the manuscript, she showed remarkable patience and diplomacy. In maintaining her equilibrium, she allowed the author to maintain his. Her broad knowledge of history, the arts, and politics, combined with the essential ingredient of good judgment, make her a prize catch for the publishing business.

My tardiness caused headaches for many of her able colleagues at Penguin and I owe them a debt of gratitude. I most appreciate the forbearance of senior production editor Joe Zingrone who, while benefiting from my grasp of the latest computer technologies, had so much to juggle in so little time—and managed to pull it off. Janice Weaver was the copy editor for the first volume and took on the task for *Iron Man,* too. I was forever surprised and humbled by the number of errors in syntax she found. Penguin's formatter extraordinaire, Christine Gambin, somehow turned the pages around with amazing speed and precision. Their efforts are much appreciated.

I was helped immensely by some important research from Marc Nadeau. He is a history buff, a bright and energetic young man who is destined to write an important book of history himself some day. While some researchers go about their work lugubriously, Mr. Nadeau had a diligence and spark that made the task at hand much easier.

The around-the-clock schedule resulted in neglect of duties around the household and an empty fridge on many a day. My wife, Maureen, who has had to live through the trials of book writing on nine other occasions, was most understanding, as were our delightful girls, Katie and Kristina. My thanks to them and all others who helped in any way in putting *Iron Man* between the hard covers.

—*Lawrence Martin*
Ottawa, October 2003.

"THE TERRIBLE KID"

C HARACTER, IT IS SAID, is formed early in life, takes firm hold, and will inevitably return to reassert itself.

Never perhaps was the adage more applicable than in the case of Joseph Jacques Jean Chrétien. To know him in his raucous, desperate youth was to have a sense of what he would be like when there was a country to run and when he was the unlikely one chosen to run it.

In the summer of 2003 when his stewardship of Canada was nearing its end, he told of playing golf with a couple of Shawinigan locals, one a teacher, the other a retired mechanic. They knew Chrétien when he was a teenager, back in the days when he was "breaking every rule in the book," and they informed him that he had remained profoundly unchanged.

Chrétien reported that he liked hearing that. He enjoyed relating the story because he was comfortable with the notion that he was still the same: that his beliefs and values, anchored in the pre-television era, had not changed, that he was still the anti-establishment man.

As he sat in his elegant living room at 24 Sussex Drive, Chrétien still looked as if he didn't belong. He'd been there a decade, but he was still the misfit. It was as if he'd been taken straight from the factory floor and plunked down under the chandeliers.

He still had the demeanour of the tough guy. His eyes were well-hooded and there was a hard look in them. The deluxe sofa he rested on might just as well have been a stool in the corner of the boxing ring, its occupant, age 69, ready to go a few rounds with anyone dumb enough to take him on.

His conversation had a "me against them" tone to it. He talked about how satisfied he felt with his record as prime minister, but he did so in a defensive way, as if he knew the elites of the country still looked down upon him.

Their attitude was something that had always got under his skin. On that very June day, for instance, he was putting out a story saying he had fewer problems with the United States than Brian Mulroney did at the end of his term in office. Everyone knew this was a ridiculous claim—that while Mulroney may have faced some bilateral problems, he was America's Man. But Chrétien, berated by the establishment for his record with Washington, felt compelled to challenge the belief. His pride wouldn't allow it to be otherwise.

It is what had driven him since his days as "the terrible kid," as he once described himself, on the streets of his hometown. Self-esteem was the motivating force of many politicians, but for Chrétien it was more than that. It was a narcotic.

He had so many infirmities as a youth and suffered so many indignities as a result that his frenzied search for acceptance could hardly be surprising. The eighteenth of nineteen children, Chrétien grew up in a town where shift work at the paper mill was the culmination of ambition. He was born not with a silver spoon in his mouth but, judging from the way he talked, a cement mixer. He was physically small, which gave him a complex and he was disfigured at the corner of his mouth, which gave him another complex, and he was deaf in one ear and partly dyslexic which gave him a third.

On the streets of Shawinigan, young kids mocked him. "Hey, crooked face," they'd yell. Young Jean would fight back, but the street scenes were only a harbinger of the calumnies he would confront throughout his life—charges that he was lowbrow, a backwoods hick, or, in the words of Jacques Parizeau, "a cretin." The insults gnawed at him. Even in victory he had trouble rejoicing for long.

But while others succumb to their weaknesses and the attendant humiliations, Chrétien wasn't one to yield. He was a believer in the dictum of the novelist Fitzgerald, who said that "Life is something that can be dominated if you're any good." Chrétien set out on a mission to affirm that. As a friend put it, "He had to prove the elitist bastards wrong."

At school, his best grades were in troublemaking. Chippy, unruly, the young Chrétien preferred the pool hall to the classroom because that was where those who had the least respect for authority hung out. In that era in Quebec, students were sequestered almost ten months a year in boarding schools run by the clergy. "To be contained like that," recalled Chrétien's friend Pierre Garceau, "it just wasn't normal."

So Chrétien rebelled. At one such school in Trois-Rivières he got hold of the master key and would sneak out classmates in the middle of the night for some carousing at the Blue Bird Café. The priests were none the wiser, and just to thumb his nose even more at the authorities, Chrétien hid the master key right outside the principal's door in the firehose box.

That was one way of gaining self-respect. Another was brute force. "Street fighting, I was the best at that," Chrétien claimed. When anyone got in his way, he had a simple method of solving the problem: he'd knock the guy over. It didn't matter if he was bigger. In one famous encounter, a bruiser named Georges Trepannier came at him in the school gym. Chrétien begged off, leaning over to nurse a leg he had previously injured. Then he flew up at Trepannier and levelled him with a haymaker that was even celebrated in the school yearbook.

Near the end of one school year at a seminary college in Trois-Rivières, he was expelled. Terrified to go home and face severe punishment from his father, he displayed a degree of stealth and cunning rather noteworthy for his age. Instead of returning to Shawinigan, Chrétien sneaked away to a friend's Montreal apartment, where he hid out. Then, when the final day of school came, he returned home to his father's doorstep—like nothing had happened.

If the young Chrétien had a first commandment, it was the one that Canadians would see often throughout his decade as prime minister. Never get caught. But don't give in—even if it means losing a body part.

Of course, for all the brass his other tricks took, none could match the time he faked appendicitis to get out of boarding school in Joliette, then went home and carried on with the sham until he was told he would have to go in for surgery. Faced with a choice between owning up to the truth or going under the knife, Jean Chrétien went under the knife. His tiny, perfect appendix was removed.

The appendix caper summed up Chrétien's fierce determination better than any. As someone who worked for him put it, Chrétien had "balls of steel." Nothing was going to stop him from winning. In his early teens, while coaching a hockey team, he tinkered with birth certificates so that an outstanding player—but a player who was over the age limit—could remain on his squad. He spoke often of "the thrill to be outside the rules." There was "nothing like it," he said.

When the girl, Aline, came along, things began to change. She was the prettiest girl in town, classy and ambitious, and to win her over, Chrétien had to start behaving. No more punch-ups at the pool hall. His father began pushing him towards a career in politics. The corrupt patronage system of Maurice Duplessis's Union Nationale was then the order of the day in Quebec and, as Liberals, the Chrétiens saw all the favours and opportunities going to those with Duplessis connections. The terrible kid was getting used to being on the side of the disadvantaged and tended to favour those of similar station. As a student delegate from Laval University, where he attended law school, he supported the hapless cause of Paul Martin, Sr., in the 1958 Liberal leadership race against Lester Pearson. He had intended to vote for Pearson, but when he arrived at the convention, he saw how lonely Paul Martin looked in the lobby of the Château Laurier. "When I saw that he was the underdog," Chrétien recalled, "I said, 'Goddamn it, I'm going with him.'"

He played golf, but the posh club in the Shawinigan area, the Grand-Mère Golf Club, was run by the Anglos, and Chrétien and other ordinary francophones weren't allowed in unless they had fantastic connections. It was something that stuck in Chrétien's craw. The "big shots," as he called them, would be hearing from him.

He was becoming more refined and serious. He listened to classical music and read books, and Aline, who married him in his third year of law school, worked on his wardrobe and presentation. But—whether it was because of his handicaps, his small-town heritage, or the fractured, guttural tone of his speech—there was something irretrievably rural about him, something for the upper classes to frown on.

The image might have changed had it not been for a chance meeting in Quebec City with Louis St. Laurent. Chrétien was about to graduate from Laval law school, and he, like several classmates, was thinking of going off to an English environment to get a post-graduate degree at a prestigious school. But when he met St. Laurent, who had then completed his years as prime minister, they talked about careers. "What do you want to do, young man?" St. Laurent asked. The young man said he wanted to be a lawyer. Well, no need to waste time on other pursuits, the former prime minister told him. You want to be a lawyer? "Go practise law."

Chrétien decided not only to go straight into law but to bypass the big, polished Montreal firms and return home to practise law in Shawinigan. Aiming for a career in politics, he wanted to nurture the riding base. He thus became a small-town lawyer without a big academic degree or the name of a big firm behind him.

They were critical moments. Had he followed the big-degree and the big-city route, he would have been stripped of his vital political selling card. He would have been unable to cast himself as the anti-establishment man, the scorn of the intellectuals of Quebec. For his story to be written, he needed their disdain.

He never wanted to be smooth—or at least, that's what he claimed. "I could have become a snob," he said in 1990, "and talked *à la française*. I didn't want to. I wanted to remain what I am."

In his first campaign, he was the underdog, running against a
Social Credit Party that had trounced the Liberals in the last election,
only the year before. The twenty-nine-year-old Chrétien pummelled
his opponent, taking out newspaper ads displaying photos of the
penury of 1922 Germany—when it took a wheelbarrow of money
to purchase a loaf of bread—to decry his economic platform. Chrétien
had his own official campaign biography doctored to leave out his
embarrassing scholastic performance at Joliette. As for his opponent,
Gérard Lamy, Chrétien labelled him "a buffoon" and prevailed in a
close fight.

Arriving in Ottawa in 1963, he was surprised to find so little talent
and quickly concluded that he could do well. But the sceptics in
Montreal started in on him early. After the novice MP's first speech to
Parliament, a journalist belittled his pedestrian effort. "No intellectual
meteor" here, he wrote. There was soon broad consensus on that. But
Chrétien, raw and relentless, got himself noticed and was appointed
parliamentary secretary to Lester Pearson. He had to lower his sights a
bit when Pearson brought in star recruits from Quebec, including
Jesus Christ himself, the guy in sandals. With Pierre Trudeau, and the
others in the lineup, the opportunities for a commoner like him
appeared to shrink. But there was something irrepressible about
Chrétien—a primitive, driving imperative. His palpable weaknesses
endeared him to average Canadians, as did his starkly etched home-
spun values.

Under Trudeau, he served five years as minister of Indian and
northern affairs, enjoying the assignment more than any other Cabinet
posting. He was in his element, at home with the underdogs, the
outsider representing outsiders. He and Aline adopted a Native boy,
and as he travelled through Canada's North, Chrétien was seized by its
great expanse and wonders and developed a roaring pan-Canadian
patriotism that aroused suspicion in his home province.

As Trudeau's main campaigner on the unity file—leading the way
against special status for Quebec, leading the charge in the 1980

referendum, leading the push to patriate the Constitution in 1982—he was seen by Quebec nationalists as not only lacking in style and intellect but also as someone who was promoting his popularity in English Canada at the expense of Quebec's interests.

He had set his sights on becoming the first francophone finance minister of Canada, not because he had any prevailing sense of what he wanted to do in that position but because of the prestige it brought. At that point in his career, in the late 1970s, many who knew Chrétien began to notice that he would talk endlessly about himself while rarely asking a question about those around him. They found it peculiar. They wondered how a guy who, in the words of the late Tory strategist Dalton Camp, looked like "the driver of the getaway car" could be so narcissistic.

By this time Chrétien had become pathologically political, less concerned about issues and substance than with his own advancement, and in finance it caught up with him. On issues like monetary policy, he was out of his depth. Trudeau excluded him from a major economic decision and Chrétien was hurt, the suggestion being that he still wasn't good enough for high intellectual company. Nothing had changed.

Instead of backing down, he plowed ahead, and when Trudeau departed in 1984, the little guy from Shawinigan faced off against the establishment man himself, John Turner, to succeed him. But the moment the campaign gun went off, everyone who owned a good suit ran to Turner. Chrétien, the guy who had to win, took the loss so hard that he went home and cried in a friend's living room. He was convinced that he, the better man, had been overlooked because the elites didn't want him. The people seemed to agree. When Chrétien found he couldn't work under Turner, he left politics and wrote a book about himself, *Straight from the Heart,* which became a Canadian political bestseller.

Chrétien had struck a chord. It didn't matter that he hadn't worked a blue-collar job since his days as a summer student in the Shawinigan paper mills. He *was* the working-class man. He was the symbol of the masses against the classes.

For a while, he made himself a member of the club. He joined a Bay Street law firm and a Montreal investment firm, and he sat on boards and watched the money pour in. His flirtation with the establishment was a way of both making money and, as he said himself, proving that he could run in those circles. But while his daughter, France, married a Desmarais, scion of the Power Corporation family, Chrétien could never become a bona fide member of the boardroom. He was the outsider and the outsider, could never be happy inside. For Mulroney, who was also of humble, small-town origins, the opposite was the case; the Tory crooner oozed boardroom tastes. But Chrétien never liked "big shots." A great moment for him came when, with a couple of partners, he was able to purchase the golf club that had barred him as a youth. He had vowed to get back at them—and he did.

As for John Turner, he'd get back at him too. Chrétien wasn't about to let the verdict of 1984 stand. Calling on some of his schoolboy skulduggery, he did his part to bring down Turner, and by 1990, he was in a position to take control of the Liberal Party and the country.

He still had demons to fight. He could now set his sights on others—separatists, right wingers, intellectuals, the monied class—who looked down on him, who thought of him as peasant stock, a man who would be an embarrassment as the leader of the country.

Canada was in dire condition. It was racked by recession, unemployment, massive deficits, and in Quebec, the momentum was ominously building toward another appointment with destiny.

It was hardly the right time to be turning over the country to a leader who was frowned upon in his native Quebec and who was viewed as lacking the right stuff in big-money circles. It was hardly the time be turning over the country to a politician who was mocked for never having uttered an original thought and who showed signs of being burdened by an inferiority complex.

After the Mulroney years, surely Canada needed more promising leadership.

But with the stakes so high and the expectations so low, Jean Chrétien was making his way to the top. He had a lifelong mission to fulfill. The tough guy had to vanquish his legions of upper-echelon doubters.

He had to show them that the average man was just as good as they were; and that the average man's values—streets of Shawinigan values circa 1953—were just as worthy as well.

.

CHAPTER ONE

WELCOME TO THE 1990s

C HRÉTIEN HAD WATCHED a decade earlier as Pierre Trudeau, under the chandeliers of the Château Laurier hotel in Ottawa, delighted the Liberal flock with the election-night proclamation "Welcome to the 1980s." Now a new decade, the nervous nineties, had begun, and it was Chrétien who had a message for the Liberals gathered in the capital. "It's the arrival of the Chrétien era!" he announced. "I will be my own man."

It was January 23, 1990, and he was kicking off his second campaign for the leadership of the Liberal Party. While he was the favourite, his words had an extravagant ring. No one had ever equated "era" with this floor scrubber.

He didn't convey that day any measure of intoxicating possibilities. He had been around so long as a political careerist that he could more readily be viewed as a relic of a bygone era, an echo of decades past, a 1970s carnival barker.

Throughout the century, Canadians had looked to Liberal men of higher station to lead the nation. There was Pierre Trudeau, cut from the intellectual aristocracy; Lester Pearson, an academic turned lofty mandarin; Louis St. Laurent, an upper-crust, old-money lawyer; Mackenzie King, a bookwormish Harvard man; Wilfrid Laurier, a nobleman in silk. None of them had come from so low on the rung as Jean Chrétien.

Chrétien's stature, or rather, lack of it, had been a factor in the 1984 campaign. He had not anticipated that party members, including so many from his native Quebec, would turn so frontally to their rusting prince, John Napier Turner. But Liberals felt that Turner was a better fit for prime ministerial garb—or, as the class-conscious Chrétien saw it, the more sophisticated man. In the 1990 campaign, he was pitted against another establishment figure in Paul Martin, and there were indications that the business of pedigree was weighing on Chrétien once again. In trying to recruit caucus members to support him, he called Albina Guarnieri, who had backed him in the 1984 race, into his office to give her the sales pitch. Guarnieri admired him as the guy who struggled against adversity, so she wasn't prepared for the Chrétien she saw on this day. He told her first that the train was leaving the station and she better get on quick. Then, in reference to one of the other candidates, he said, "My suit is more expensive than Paul Martin's." Guarnieri was shocked. That he would think she would be impressed by that kind of thing was enough to make her forget about the idea of supporting him this time. "My God," she recalled thinking, "After all these years, the inferiority complex is still there."

It was still there and it would factor into the corrosive Chrétien–Martin feud. Chrétien saw Martin in the same mould as Turner. An establishment big shot. And he could see the unofficial alliance that had been fashioned between Martin supporters and the old Turner crowd. For Chrétien, the new leadership campaign would be a continuance of the Turner wars.

Fractious internal combat wasn't something that normally plagued the Liberals, but the ascent of the forever-combative Chrétien to the leadership circle brought to the party a new culture of conflict, a culture that had been the reserve of the other great party of federal politics, the Progressive Conservatives. Liberals, as the old saying went, didn't wash their dirty laundry in public. Lester Pearson, a disaster in his first year as leader of the party, was trounced by John Diefenbaker in the 1958 election. But Paul Martin, Sr., who lost the leadership race to Pearson, didn't seek to foment any kind of caucus revolt. Similarly, no one openly challenged Pierre Trudeau after his poor performance in the 1972 election or after his loss to Joe Clark in 1979.

But Chrétien came at Turner again and again—and sometimes he wasn't terribly subtle about it. Ed Broadbent, the New Democratic Party leader, admired the spunk and spark, if not the depth, of Jean Chrétien. But when it came to Turner, he saw a nasty streak in Chrétien that he hadn't anticipated. "I noticed that any negative comment Chrétien could make about John Turner in the lobbies, he would do it. I didn't like it."

David Collenette, a Chrétien man, was director of the Liberal Party in the late 1980s and bore witness to all the scheming. Collenette was a tough guy. He had a direct "I'll peel your face off" approach to politics, and Chrétien liked that about him. But for all his toughness and his bias in favour of Chrétien, Collenette didn't appreciate his friend's behaviour towards Turner in those years. "A lot of things were going on which I don't even want to talk about."

A succession of backroom insurrections undermined Turner, but none of it diminished the popularity of Jean Chrétien. While he was out of politics, his ratings, in fact rose. He didn't have to work hard at it because he was simply maintaining something that he had had since coming to Ottawa—his bond with the people. It was, as his adviser David Zussman was coming to appreciate, the rarest of political gifts. In his natural state, Jean Chrétien was "closely allied with the masses," noted Zussman. He was at one with the mythical creature called "the average Canadian." No one could take that magic away.

During the 1988 election, Chrétien was ostensibly stumping for John Turner, but he knew that if Turner got whipped again, the leadership prize would come open. He noted during a stopover in Winnipeg that he had been on the CBC national news four times in the previous ten days. "I lost the leadership, but I fought the establishment—and now I'm more popular than ever." With Turner's second loss to Mulroney in 1988, Liberals were impatient in their lust for a new leader. At one unruly caucus meeting, Turner tried to put his foot down. "Listen," he shouted, "we're going to do it this way as long as I am leader of this party." From the back rows came the mocking voices of the Chrétien supporters: "You won't be leader for long!"

Chrétien was popular across the country. It was a francophone's turn to head the party, and he had a track record as a good campaigner. But while he was the clear favourite, doubts simmered. John Turner had come out of the past and in from the sidelines to lead the party to nowhere, and what some now feared was that another old warhorse was about to do the same.

Among Chrétien's challengers—who included Sheila Copps, John Nunziata, and Tom Wappel—Paul Martin was the only one with a hope of winning. In large part because of his famous father, he had been viewed as a potential political star for a long time. He had chosen first, however, to earn his fortune in business, and had done so, purchasing Canada Steamship Lines from Power Corporation, then turning it into a great money-maker. All the while, he kept an eye on the political arena. He bumped into the national columnist Allan Fotheringham in Montreal one evening in the mid-1980s. In short order, they were over at Martin's office emptying a bottle of Scotch. He told the journalist that he couldn't decide between politics or mission-ary work in Africa. But in the way Martin spoke, Fotheringham wasn't betting on him being in Liberia any time soon. The shipping magnate continued to cultivate journalists, some of whom he'd invite to his beautiful home atop Mount Royal. It sat on a higher plateau than Brian Mulroney's, though Mulroney wasn't one who liked to admit it. Once when someone asked him where he lived, Mulroney piped up, "You know the mountain? . . . Right at the fucking top!"

Chrétien had got to know his prime challenger when Martin worked for Power Corporation. John Rae, Chrétien's political fixer, also worked at Power, and the three of them had the occasional golf outing—which Chrétien enjoyed because he was a better player than Paul Martin. But once the leadership quarrels started, any possibility of friendship was quickly washed away. It was galling to Chrétien that this newcomer, elected for the first time in 1988, would presume to think he could become leader. All he had was the name of his father. Chrétien had been beating the bushes for the Liberal Party since 1963. A dozen Cabinet portfolios. Martin had yet to sniff the government benches.

When the 1990 race began, the constitutional crisis was the issue of the day. Canadians groaned. There was no subject more tedious. Most would rather read a telephone book. Quebec's place in the federation had preoccupied governments since the October Crisis of 1970. There had followed the separatist victory in the 1976 election, the 1980 referendum, and the extended debate over the question of bringing the Constitution home from Great Britain. Just as the issue seemed mercifully to be receding, the Mulroney government reignited the debate with its attempt to gain approval for the Meech Lake Accord. And now, the same government was careening towards cliff's edge with the foundering accord strapped to its back.

The Quebec fixation was debilitating. Other national priorities languished. The French problem was certainly not the foremost cause, but some viewed it as no coincidence that during the same period that it was paramount, Canada's economic growth stalled, living standards levelled off, and the country fell further and further behind the economic standards of the United States.

Mulroney had reached the Meech agreement with the premiers in 1987. It was followed by a three-year ratification process, and as Chrétien took to the podium to announce his leadership candidacy, there remained six months until the ratification deadline. The deadline, in fact, was the very same day, June 23, that the Liberals were to hold their leadership convention in Calgary.

Martin supported Meech Lake, Chrétien didn't. As the leadership campaign began, the issue was a potential trigger point. Chrétien had long shared Trudeau's harder-line philosophy of no special status for the province. Mulroney knew that as the next likely Liberal leader, Chrétien would play a decisive role in the accord's fate. There were already signals that the deal was headed for oblivion. It had received the approval of all premiers in 1987, but new premiers had been elected since that time. One was Clyde Wells of Newfoundland; he stood squarely against the accord, prompting John Crosbie, the tart tongued Tory, to quip, "All's well that ends Wells."

At the University of Ottawa, Chrétien gave a much-anticipated speech on his constitutional position just a few days before he declared his leadership candidacy. Vetted by Trudeau, the speech put forward a compromise. In its present form, the Meech Lake Accord was totally deficient, Chrétien stated, but with amendments, he could support it. For him, the chief sticking point was the distinct society clause. He was willing to recognize Quebec as a distinct society in a preamble to the accord, but not in the Constitution itself. He feared that the larger enshrinement would allow Quebec to use the claim to refuse to adhere to a variety of federal requirements.

"I came back into politics for one reason: I want Canada to stay together," Chrétien declared. "The tragedy of our land is that we have become more British Columbian, more Albertan, more Québécois, and more Ontarian. This is a problem. We have to become Canadian. Otherwise we won't survive."

Another vital problem was that under Mulroney, he claimed, the country had become more American. Chrétien wasn't promising, like Turner had done, to tear up Mulroney's free trade pact, but he maintained that the deal might have to be abrogated if the Americans declined to make changes. Mulroney, he charged, was in bed with the provinces, in bed with the Americans, in bed with big business. "Canada was built on subsidies," Chrétien said. "We have a duty to keep Canada Canadian." He pitched his campaign as a return to traditional Canadian values. Martin's was more an agenda of change. His vision, Martin was quick to point out, wasn't rooted in the past, like that of another leadership contender. "Canada," said Martin, "now needs a new vision that combines a coherent policy on nationhood and brings forward a decade's worth of new ideas on the economy and social policy." He condemned the Free Trade Agreement as "a terrible,

terrible deal that is in the process of coming apart at the seams." But, at the same time, he opposed the centralism that characterized much of Trudeau's policy-making, and that, he charged, marked Jean Chrétien's thinking as well.

While Chrétien was criticized for operating in an idea-free zone, Martin had a mind that pitched forward. He wrestled with new concepts and theories about where the world was going. He wanted to keep up with the latest books and the useful ideas they might offer. He listened well; one could feel his mind roaming the terrain, looking for the nuggets to pounce on and explore. He was always on high alert.

But Martin soon discovered that after the tumult of the Mulroney years, raucous debates about changing the country were not what the people wanted. There was an appetite instead for peace and quiet. One of the Paul Martin slogans was "PM," as in "Policy matters." It was shelved quickly.

Since innovative policy was low on Chrétien's list of priorities, the mood of the times favoured him. David Zussman had joined him as his executive assistant in the early 1980s, when Chrétien was energy minister. He took on the not-so-easy task of being his personal policy trainer. When it became apparent that his man could well ascend to the Liberal throne, Zussman felt it necessary to set up educational sessions for Chrétien, about a dozen of them. It was odd. Though he had served in all those Cabinet portfolios, maybe more than anyone in Canadian history, Chrétien was effectively being sent back to high school. He wasn't keen about the lessons, Zussman recalled, but didn't go to the extent of faking appendicitis to get out of them.

It wasn't that he suffered from a lack of intelligence, Zussman found. On the contrary, he was very bright and very shrewd. But Chrétien didn't view expertise in policy areas as fundamental to getting elected. He could absorb policy detail, if so inclined. But he was not often so inclined. Questions on, say, the effect of a social policy on a family of four didn't interest him. "That really distinguished him from people like Paul Martin and Lloyd Axworthy," recalled Zussman.

"They get far more deeply into the nitty-gritty of the details of policy. It makes them very different people."

With Chrétien, it was all about values. Shortly after Zussman went to work for him in 1982, Chrétien asked, "Have you ever been to Shawinigan?" Zussman hadn't. A week later, Chrétien said, "Come on, we're going." He took Zussman all over town—to the small home where he grew up, to his schools, to the pool halls, to the factory where he had worked as a summer student. Zussman was struck by the experience. Chrétien was telling him, This is who I am. You want to know my policies? Here they are.

His family home sat against a big hillside that cascaded into the old paper mill. Chrétien's house was near the bottom of the hill, and he liked to point out that it was the bosses who lived, to borrow a Mulroney phrase, right at the fucking top.

Zussman liked the words "value-based pragmatist" to describe Jean Chrétien. His values ran so deep—were so cemented, so anchored in his mind—that new concepts barely made a dent. He admired Canada the way he had found it in the 1950s. He wanted to change things, but he didn't want to change them very much.

He differed from Paul Martin in style, intellect, background, party experience. Patrick Lavelle, a long-time friend who was co-chair of his leadership campaign in Ontario, could sense the animosity Chrétien felt towards his chief rival from the outset. "I don't think Chrétien had any warm feelings about Martin—ever!" That animosity set the stage for an unusual leadership war. Until 1968, the party's leadership races, the ones anointing King, St. Laurent, and Pearson, had been coronations. The fights in 1968 and 1984 featured some discord, but not of the intensity of the 1990 rivalry.

Joe Comuzzi, a towering MP from Thunder Bay, Ontario, was a Martin guy, fairly new to politics. He had a big, Tony Bennett–like smile and an easygoing manner, and while he knew politics could be a rough game, he wasn't prepared for the backlash he received simply for stating a preference for Paul Martin. It was one thing to be told he would never get a Cabinet post if he supported Martin. But "how about not even getting your nomination papers signed to run in the next election? That was a real eye-opener."

Many of the collisions between the two camps occurred at the delegate-selection meetings. The trick in winning those tilts often lay in signing up new Canadians as party members and stacking the meetings with them. It quickly became apparent that the Martin side was paying the ten-dollar membership fees for the ethnics and winning some early victories as a result. Chrétien had to respond. "I needed a tough guy," recalled Lavelle, his Ontario manager. "A guy who could go on a search-and-destroy [mission], who could do a kamikaze [raid] for our side." Jimmy Karygiannis, the MP for Scarborough-Agincourt, was his pick. Jimmy K became the most hard-ass Chrétien campaigner on the team. A Greek immigrant, he was a specialist in herding in new ethnic members. He signed up 9,500. "We were getting Greeked," complained one Martin campaigner. "And if we weren't getting Greeked, we were getting Sikhed."

Jimmy K had a couple of tough-guy helpers. One was called Heavy Stick, the other Two-by-Four. "I signed up anything that moved back then," Karygiannis recalled. Near Peterborough, Ontario, he heard of a family of about fifteen Sikhs living in a shack out in the middle of nowhere. With a Sikh friend, he and Heavy Stick went out at one o'clock in the morning and signed them all up for Chrétien.

At a delegate-selection meeting in Kitchener-Waterloo, Martin organizers were using public phones to call in last-minute recruits before the vote. Karygiannis ran around sticking bubble gum in the pay-phone slots. Martin supporters tried to have him expelled from meetings. Jimmy K's response was "Get the hell out of my face." At one meeting, he sensed that a returning officer was playing tricks with the ballots and came down on the fellow with such rage that the Martin supporter was later hospitalized for angina. He told Albina Guarnieri, who had become an effective organizer for Martin, that by the time he was finished with her, she would be "toast." After his forces defeated hers in a delegate-selection square-off, he sent her over an order of toast—burnt to a crisp.

Karygiannis had thought Chrétien might be a little annoyed when he heard of some of his tactics. Instead, he got the opposite message. "Whatever it takes to win, Jimmy," Chrétien told him. "Whatever it takes to win."

"Did we go over the line?" asked David Collenette. "Sure." But it wasn't all that dirty, he added. "When we found out about it, we cracked down on a lot of people. I mean, I remember one guy, I ripped the shit out of him."

Chrétien kept his own charts of the proceedings. He phoned Lavelle at seven every morning for an update on the delegate-selection meetings. Trying to keep the boss happy, Lavelle tended to inflate the numbers. But Chrétien had other sources and often caught him out. "Don't give me that crap," he'd say. "I want the real numbers." He was tough and demanding, recalled Lavelle. "It got so I hated those calls."

By comparison, Martin was the greenhorn campaigner. His senior strategist, David Herle, pushed him to call potential convention delegates. "What'll I talk about?" Martin asked. "Talk about the weather, anything. It doesn't matter," he was told. "So he'd call up," recalled Herle, "and say, 'How's your weather?' then hang up!"

Herle's plan was to build early momentum in Ontario, then have Quebec kick in to give the campaign the look that it could score a big upset. Because Paul Martin favoured the Meech Lake Accord, he was confident of doing well in *la belle province*. But he misread the situation. While the intelligentsia supported Martin and Meech, the party's rank and file were more inclined to back Chrétien's federalist position. Martin didn't get a Quebec bump. Chrétien did.

By late April 1990, the power of the Chrétien machine had become apparent. With more than two-thirds of the 5,200 delegates chosen, estimates were that he had 1,500 delegates and Martin 500. Sheila Copps had captured about 150, while the other candidates were below 100. "Jean did two things," said Martin, trashing his rival at an all-candidates meeting in Halifax. "He simply repeated his support for government policies established in the 1970s, most of which have now proven to be dated. And he refused to commit himself to any kind of agenda as to where he would take the country."

Chrétien was the perceived front-runner and therefore the recipient of the enormous benefits that accrue to those with such status. Ironically, this time around he had the support of most of the party establishment, not because they viewed him as one of their own, but mainly because it was in their interests to be on the side of the victor. He also had had an organization in place since 1984, and as Martin was discovering, these campaigns were won with on-the-ground muscle.

Martin grew enormously frustrated at not being able to drag Chrétien out from behind his vague statements. Chrétien was using the classic front-runner's strategy of sticking to generalities. His vagueness was bothering not only Martin but some of his own supporters as well. One was the Toronto MP Dennis Mills. He told the media, "I think Chrétien needs more than an 'I love Canada' speech to run the country. I think we have to put some ideas in the system." The next day, when his critique appeared in headlines, Mills's phone lines started heating up. Headquarters was calling. "The shit had hit the fan," recalled Mills. "You couldn't imagine the calls I got."

As convention day approached, the unity of the party had become a bigger question mark than the identity of the new leader. Internecine warfare had plagued the party since 1984, and the Chrétien–Martin clash had the potential to prolong it. At a leadership debate in Manitoba, Sharon Carstairs, the provincial Liberal leader who was a fervent opponent of Meech Lake, was seated in the audience with Aline Chrétien. At one point, Martin looked over at Chrétien and then pointed at Carstairs. He said that she was going overboard on Quebec, and that Chrétien had better get her in line. Aline turned to Carstairs and said, "Nobody is going to force you to get in line."

With his anti-Meech pitch, Chrétien was being pilloried in Quebec as willing to do anything to curry favour with the Anglos and get their votes. Few Canadians knew the essentials of the pact: the distinct society clause, the right of veto, the provincial say in the selection of Supreme Court judges, and the rest. The general view in English Canada, though, was that Quebec was being favoured, and that Chrétien was the guy who was saying "Down with the deal."

He had no easy options on the issue. To keep this support outside Quebec, to keep the support of the Trudeau wing of the party, to be consistent with his history, he had to maintain a negative stance. But the unity package had backing from a broad segment of the media, large numbers in caucus, nationalists in Quebec, and four Liberal premiers, including Robert Bourassa of Quebec. Chrétien did not want to be seen as the great spoiler of the unity pact. His image in Quebec was bad enough. Guy Pratte, a Montreal lawyer who worked on Chrétien's campaign, found that "as a Quebecer, there was almost a stigma attached to being associated with Mr. Chrétien precisely because he was not perceived, even by staunch federalists, as a particularly sophisticated person." Pratte found this offensive. "I always thought snobbery was at the root of such criticism."

Chrétien had his strategists secretly meeting with Mulroney representatives in search of a compromise that could help him out of the jam. That bid was unsuccessful, but Mulroney appointed a special committee, headed by Jean Charest, to try to come up with changes acceptable to all parties. The report's recommendations, tabled in May, had hardly become public before Lucien Bouchard, then Mulroney's environment minister, resigned in a great fit of torment over them. His high-voltage exit was cheered by nationalists throughout Quebec. He had been in quiet talks with sovereigntists over the idea of forming a separatist party in Ottawa. In short order, he would do so.

As Bouchard lapped up his hero's welcome on his home turf, he targeted Chrétien as the politician responsible for derailing progress on the accord. "Jean Chrétien has come back to haunt us like an old ghost dragging his chains," he told an audience in Alma, Quebec. Chrétien, he predicted, would never form a government in Ottawa because

Quebecers would remember how he had denied them their dreams. The shots stung Chrétien. Mulroney was wrong-headed for having taken a sovereigntist into his Cabinet in the first place, he argued. It's what can happen, he said in a veiled shot at Martin, when an inexperienced politician becomes prime minister.

Three weeks remained until the June 23 convention. Though Martin's hopes appeared doomed, he maintained that he could still push the vote to a second ballot, where he might have a chance. He arrived at an all-candidates debate in Montreal, where the constitutional accord was certain to be an explosive issue. He wasn't prepared to play down the rift with Chrétien over it. He decided that he was going to shove it right down his throat. That decision was one that Jean Chrétien—who was capable of carrying grudges—would never forget. The campaign had been hotly contested, but until this moment, there was little to suggest it would leave a permanent scar. As Paul Martin's supporters prepared to tear open a gash, that was about to change.

In the Liberal Party, there was no group more vocal than the Liberal youth wing, whose members in this campaign were rallying around Paul Martin. In Quebec, the youth of the party were particularly incensed because Chrétien, their native son, was against the Meech Lake Accord. As the candidates' debate began, Martin pressed for a clear statement of his position. "Don't give us a great speech," he demanded of Chrétien. "Just answer the question. What is your bottom line on Meech Lake?" When Chrétien started to respond, he was drowned out by shouts of "Yes or no? Yes or no?"

Martin kept at him. "Those who reject the new Quebec will transform nationalists into separatists," he charged. "I will keep them Canadian. . . . Jean, for the love of God, you want to become prime minister of Canada, but you give us no indication where you are going."

When it became obvious that Chrétien, who was trying to put forth a nuanced position, would not make a categorical endorsement of the accord, the demonstrators began pumping their fists. They madly waved placards and began shouting *"Vendu! Vendu!"* You're a sellout to the Anglos, they were telling Chrétien, using a word even most separatists were reluctant to employ. You're a sellout to the Anglos.

Then came chants of "Judas! Judas!"

Supporters for Sheila Copps were among the demonstrators. She, too, blasted Chrétien. "You have not understood Quebec, and you are gambling dangerously with the survival of Canada."

Chrétien tried to explain his position. "I couldn't be clearer," he said of his Meech stance. "If the Charter of Rights is not protected, it's no." He had always maintained that the charter had to have priority over a clause in the accord that would define Quebec as a distinct society. If that was made clear with amendments, he could support the accord. It was a hedged, but, in fact, clear position. The rancour in the hall, however, would not subside. *"Vendu! Vendu!"* they cried again.

In the wings, the president of the Liberal Party, Michel Robert, was trying to contain himself. This was an embarrassment for the party, and he suspected that the Martin campaign had plotted it. He got on his walkie-talkie and demanded that Martin's representative get his "ass over" to see him right away. When Mark Resnick, who had previously run John Turner's office, made his way backstage, he faced a raging bull. Robert accused Resnick of deliberately orchestrating the cheap, mudslinging tactics. "No one planned it," Resnick shot back. The Quebec youth were hotheads. "We can't control them."

"Well, get the fuck out there and do something," cried Robert.

Sure, thought Resnick. "Here I am, a white boy from Brantford, and I am to tell these nationalist Quebecers to cool it." He tried, and got the expected result: they told him to go fuck himself and kept on chanting.

Chrétien had stared on blankly and coldly as the insults flew at him. It was as if his mind were ticking back in time to insults past, and he was trying to suppress his inner rage. To be levelled by this kind of attack from Lucien Bouchard was one thing. To get it from his own federalist party members at a televised leadership forum was too much to tolerate. "I don't attack anyone personally in the campaign," he told reporters afterwards. "It's the tradition in the party [not to do so], and there are some who didn't follow it today."

Martin wasn't apologetic. "I'm living in the Quebec of today, not the Quebec of fifty years ago. Quebec will not accept being put in its place." Many years later, he would still insist that the demonstrations were spontaneous, that he hadn't even noticed them. "To be quite honest I didn't realize it took place. . . . When you're a candidate, you have a lot of other things going on. You're not looking at demonstrations." The outrage from the Chrétien crowd was over the top, Martin claimed. "A lot of things happen in leadership races. They happen, and you just forget about them and get on with the job."

There was a tone to Martin's voice that suggested that those in the Chrétien camp should have been the last to complain about tough tactics. Mark Resnick could go along with that. As John Turner's assistant, he had sat and watched as the little guy from Shawinigan and his friends stuck the knife in Turner through the late 1980s— and left it there. Still, he could understand why the Chrétien contingent was steamed on that day in Montreal. "Here's a guy who thinks in his own mind that he has spent his whole career fighting for Quebec, and a bunch of kids are yelling at him that he is a traitor."

From Chrétien's perspective, the leadership race was more or less locked up at the time of the debate. Martin was simply showing the desperate behaviour of a sore loser. Chrétien knew it was anglophones shouting out the insults, because they couldn't pronounce the word *vendu* properly. "They were coming from Toronto to call me '*vendu*,'" he said, looking back on that time. "You know, I could handle the lies that were in my own language. But coming from Toronto to shout that at me . . . You have the right to be annoyed." How could the Martin camp claim it was not involved, Chrétien wondered, when this kind of thing was happening?

Describing the turn of events as "awful," Eddie Goldenberg, a Chrétien adviser, maintained that Martin, or Big Suit, as another

Chrétien aide derisively described him, had inflicted lasting damage on the party. "What they did, which was for very short-term gain, was to make it very hard to bring people together afterwards," Goldenberg said. "That's a lesson in politics. You have to be very careful, particularly when you aren't going to win."

Two weeks before the Liberal leadership convention, Mulroney appeared to have won agreement from all premiers on a revised constitutional pact. The amended agreement was closer to Chrétien's position, and some of his advisers, Goldenberg included, were now pushing for him to endorse it. In effect, they wanted him to agree with Paul Martin. The backlash against Chrétien in Quebec if he didn't do so, they feared, would be crippling to his future as leader of the party.

As Chrétien prepared to board a plane to Calgary, where the convention was being held, debate raged in his camp. Never mind the backlash in Quebec, Pat Lavelle told him. What about English Canada? That's where his delegates were. What about a backlash from there? "You sold the delegates a position on Meech Lake, and you just can't go in and say 'Screw it' at the convention," Lavelle told him. He was at war with Goldenberg and thought Chrétien was going to capitulate. In the end, however, Chrétien's long-time mentor, Mitchell Sharp, advised that he just stay quiet in Calgary. That was the course he followed. When he arrived in Cowtown, Chrétien maintained that he had said "everything I have to say on Meech Lake."

Meanwhile, Mulroney's new arrangement was unravelling because Newfoundland and Manitoba refused to come on board. The convention was gripped by that drama more than the one on the floor, where the outcome, as anticipated, came on the first ballot. Jean Chrétien— winner in a walk.

When the verdict was announced he stood with Aline, his expression in stark contrast to the tormented look he had worn six years earlier, when Turner defeated him. It was not so much an expression of joy and goodwill as one of vindication, the look of someone who had successfully taken a measure of revenge on his opponents—party adversaries or demons of other kinds—after endless years of struggle against them.

But it was a bittersweet triumph. The collapse of the constitutional accord on the same day had cast an ugly pall over the convention, "a spectre," said Goldenberg, "which was haunting us." Many Quebecers in the Calgary Saddledome greeted Chrétien wearing black arm bands. Jean Lapierre, the incendiary Quebec MP who was co-chair of Martin's campaign, bolted the Liberal Party to sit as an independent with Lucien Bouchard. "I would not want to have an association of one minute with that individual who is now the shame of most Quebecers," he said.

After Paul Martin, Sr., who had lost two leadership campaigns himself, kissed him on the lips and said, "Sorry, son," the losing candidate proceeded to the podium to give a concession speech that was better than Chrétien's winning one. "We can unite this party that we all love," Martin said. He felt he had won the convention week itself. It was perhaps true, in that momentum seemed to be leaving Chrétien at the very time he took the prize.

On the convention floor, the new leader of the Liberal Party was caught by the cameras embracing Clyde Wells. The Newfoundland premier, along with Manitoba's Elijah Harper, had blocked passage of the Meech Lake Accord, which Wells had initially appeared to support. Now Chrétien, who had been advised to stay as quiet as possible on Meech at the convention, was embracing its killer, hugging Clyde Wells in front of the nation. He would later say it was just to thank Wells for bringing delegates to him from his province, but few saw it that way. Many Meech supporters viewed it as Chrétien rubbing their noses in it. "We were extremely disappointed. Furious, furious," said Liza Frulla, a leading Quebec provincial Liberal. "And the hug he gave to Clyde Wells the same night—this was a symbol. A terrible symbol."

Eddie Goldenberg would still claim years later that it wasn't a premeditated gesture, that Chrétien probably embraced 150 people that night. "I think if you were to have asked Mr. Chrétien that night, 'Did you hug Clyde Wells tonight?' he probably would have said no."

Did you regret hugging Clyde Wells? Chrétien was asked in 2003. "But you know it had nothing to do with Meech," he claimed. "It had everything to do with the vote I had received from Newfoundland. His son was organizing for me." But as a shrewd, experienced politician, Chrétien must surely have known how such a gesture would be viewed. He must surely have known that people would think he was sending a message to Quebec nationalists, to Paul Martin, to Brian Mulroney, to those who had opposed him for so long. More than likely he was showing the defiance of which he had been capable since the age of ten, when he first started staring down anyone who got in his way.

The proof that this was no innocent gesture had come with his red-carpet treatment of Sharon Carstairs. The Manitoba legislature had defeated the Meech deal on Friday, June 22. Sharon Carstairs flew to Calgary for the convention on Saturday, and the first thing Chrétien did when he saw her was to invite her—one of the leading enemies of the accord—right into his open arms in his booth. Even Carstairs was stunned at this. "The last [person] he needed sitting next to him on national TV during the convention was me," she would later explain. "After all, I, along with Clyde Wells, had just torpedoed Meech."

Among the many who noticed was Iona Campagnolo. The former party president had stood on the podium at the close of the 1984 leadership race and delivered the oft-quoted line about Jean Chrétien's being number one in everyone's heart. She wasn't so sure any more. As she viewed the divisions on the floor, her message at this convention stood in cold contrast. "I am uneasy, concerned, worried," she said.

After the vote, Patrick Lavelle was walking with Chrétien outside the Saddledome and they came upon Martin. The two titans coldly sized up one another. They weren't even capable of summoning up phony smiles and phony small talk—private rage, public duty—for the smallest moment. A tense and brief exchange ensued, with Lavelle noticing the chill beneath each man's words.

Rarely had the party been less enthused about handing over the leadership prize. Jean Chrétien had come in as a figure out of the past, promising little, stirring no great dreams. He had come in in the crush of a searing debate that divided the party and the country, and that again had the effect of spurning Quebec. He had come in on the heels of a campaign that created deep divisions between him and the party's man of the future. He had chased the prize for so long. He had won, and winning was always what mattered most to him. But this victory came with many doubts.

His era, the Chrétien era, had begun. But not many were excited about it—not even, it seemed, the winner himself.

CHAPTER TWO

THE WRONG JOB

Victories normally imbue winners, at least for a short period, with a rush of self-confidence that makes them perform at a higher level. It was assumed that once installed as Liberal leader, Jean Chrétien, having pursued the ambition for so long, would move ahead at a gallop. He was, as he told one journalist, "a doer, a person who loves action, a patriot." At the Calgary convention, he kept repeating the phrase "We have work to do. We have work to do."

But after the victory, work stopped. What followed was a long, lugubrious period during which Chrétien's confidence deserted him, inertia replaced passion, and he looked like a lost man, a man of a different time. It was as if, having spent a lifetime fighting to get to the top of the Liberal Party, he didn't know what to do once he'd arrived.

One embarrassment followed another, leaving many to believe that their earlier suspicions about Chrétien's capabilities were well-founded. He lacked the stuff of leadership. He was a grunt, not a general. It got so bad that Brian Mulroney, plummeting to unparalleled depths in public esteem, was licking his chops, believing there was still hope of a resurgence. It got so bad that they started comparing Chrétien to Chauncey Gardiner, the dunce who became a major political player in the Jerzy Kosinski novel *Being There*. It got so bad that there were calls for Chrétien to step down before he had even contested one election.

His performance was all the more odd because, given his rugged history, given the way he had cut down opponents in his youth, the way he had stood up to authority, many thought he would have made the ideal Opposition leader. But he hated the job—and it showed.

In the summer of 1990, fresh in the Opposition leader's chair, he put off a decision about running in a by-election to get a seat in the House of Commons. He rarely appeared before the media and when he did, he tripped over his words. On policy, he was vague. He equivocated on the question of Mulroney's proposed GST, and on whether free trade talks should be extended to Mexico. When several Mohawks set up a blockade at Oka, near Montreal, because of a land dispute with the community, he remained silent until the tensions had almost escalated out of control. For someone who had served in the Indian affairs portfolio for five years under Trudeau, and who had an abiding interest in the subject, it seemed strange indeed.

In September, his friend Sharon Carstairs and her Manitoba Liberals were relegated to third place in the election there. In Ontario, the Liberal premier, David Peterson, was thrown out of office after calling an election two years before it was necessary. In Quebec, the Liberals got a taste of the impact of Chrétien's handling of the Meech Lake Accord. Denis Coderre, his hand-picked candidate for a by-election in the Montreal riding of Laurier–Ste-Marie, was crushed by the insurgent Bloc Québécois. The Bloc ended the riding's seventy-three-year history of sending Liberals to Ottawa.

The drubbing he was taking in the media—"Chrétien is the invisible man, the man who stands for nothing," wrote Geoffrey Stevens—finally led him to call a press conference three months after his leadership victory. Chrétien had confidently pounded his way through hundreds of press conferences, but at this one he came across as a first-timer. He kept looking over to his advisers, as if he were about to get trapped. He criticized Mulroney for his poor attendance in the Commons, though he, Chrétien, was backing off from even running for a seat. He had promised to return integrity to government but came off sounding as if he were excusing Pierre Trudeau's much-condemned patronage splurge in 1984. He again dodged questions on whether he would kill the GST.

Then came a strange moment, a tiny, perfect pratfall that was to become part of the Chrétien lore. Chrétien was asked a technical legal question on the Oka issue. In responding, he went blank on his past and declared—this despite having worked as a member of the legal profession in Shawinigan for several years—"I'm not a lawyer." Raised eyebrows filled the press theatre. They kept rising. Finally Dan Dugas, who posed the question, had the temerity to recall the leader of the Opposition's past to him.

Concerns about the effect his performance might be having on voters were soon confirmed by autumn opinion polls. The Liberals had dropped eleven points since his election as leader in June. They were at 39 percent; the NDP, fresh off Bob Rae's startling victory in Ontario, was at 33 percent; and the governing Tories stood at 18. "We didn't have a good summer, but now that it's fall we're going to do better," said Chrétien.

He kept stalling on the question of running for a seat in a by-election, prompting Herb Gray, the Liberal elder statesman, to make a special appeal. Gray was in Parliament in 1963 when Chrétien was first elected. He remembered the day the young Chrétien brought his father, Wellie—the same Wellie Chrétien who had harboured so many doubts about his misbehaving son—to Ottawa. Now his wayward son had become an MP, and the look of pride on his father's face as he stood with Jean under the Gothic spires of the Centre Block was something Gray never forgot.

"To have credibility, you've got to be in the House," Gray told Chrétien that fall. "You can't afford to wait two years until a general election." With the publication of more bad polls, Chrétien finally agreed and changed course, announcing he was running in the New Brunswick riding of Beauséjour, a predominantly francophone area that had voted Liberal for fifty-five years and was certainly a safer option than a fight against Bouchard's surging Bloc in a Quebec riding.

In Beauséjour, Mulroney, following the charitable route of allowing a new leader to run uncontested, put up no opposition to Chrétien, who was expected to win easily. As evidence of his difficulties, however, he faced a strong challenge from the NDP. Chrétien, who declined to participate in the candidates' debate, moved into the riding two weeks before the election but got a lukewarm reception. In the final days, some polling suggested a huge upset was possible. It looked so bleak that the PMO's George Radwanski was sent down to the riding the day before the vote. When he arrived, he had a message for stunned campaign workers. "I'm here to put a spin on the defeat," he said.

That same day, Chrétien attended a brunch in a local village where the NDP candidate was popular. People turned away from the Liberal leader, leaving him worried, especially when some early voting results came in and had him trailing. Then the tide turned. He moved comfortably ahead and emerged the winner in the December 10 by-election by a healthy 4,500-vote margin.

He won. But it didn't solve much. The issue of the GST was starting to confound him, the Persian Gulf War was about to become a source of embarrassment, and his own health, normally reliable, failed him.

IN THE LEADERSHIP CAMPAIGN, following his own instincts, Chrétien had judiciously announced that it would be irresponsible to call for a scrapping of the GST without telling Canadians what the alternative might be. Once he was leader, however, his caucus wanted him to kill it outright, and reluctantly following its will, he announced that the Liberal-dominated Senate would block passage of the GST on behalf of the Canadian people. Mulroney responded quickly by resorting to a rarely invoked clause in the Constitution that allowed for the appointment of new senators in the case of a deadlock. To cries from Chrétien that he was abusing his powers, the prime minister appointed eight new senators, giving his Conservatives a majority in the chamber.

The rhetoric heated up. This, said Chrétien, was a "dying and discredited" government foisting its right-wing policies on the people. "Privatization, deregulation, cutbacks. Handouts for the rich and heartaches for the poor," he charged. Biting off a big chunk, he declared that the Mulroney administration was "the worst government in our history" and should resign. "A government in a society as rich as Canada's forfeits the right to hold office when people in Canada cannot put food on their table and a roof over their heads."

Mulroney moved the focus to an area that had never been one of Chrétien's strengths: foreign affairs. As 1990 neared its close, an invasion of Iraq by a Washington-led coalition to repel Saddam Hussein's occupation of Kuwait seemed certain. Despite all his years in government, including many trips abroad as minister of trade and minister of finance, Chrétien had never developed a deep interest in the world outside his own country. As the party's critic for external affairs for a short period under John Turner, he was decidedly lacklustre. At the end of the 1980s, the Soviet Union collapsed and the Cold War was brought to an end, but these seismic shifts barely caught his attention. An expert on those developments recalled briefing Chrétien and coming away appalled by his lack of interest and knowledge. During the forty-five-minute session, Chrétien asked only one question: "Can you give me one story I can tell to illustrate what's going on?"

Long an opponent of Mulroney's cozy relations with the White House, Chrétien reflexively opposed the prime minister's "Aye aye, Uncle Sam" response to Washington. When Mulroney pledged to join the coalition to invade Iraq, the Liberal leader stood in strong opposition. "At the moment, we in Canada are looking more belligerent than the Americans. . . . The international reputation of our country has never been so low. The prime minister is a Bush-leaguer," he said.

Chrétien could get away with that. But when he tried to forge the ultimate middle ground, when he tried to find the saw-off that would please all concerned, he got caught. Setting out his position, the Liberal leader said, "Military action . . . is very dangerous for the long-term security in the Middle East. It is very dangerous even for the survival of the United Nations. Of course, our force, if there is no war, should stay there, because our forces are present to enforce the embargo and the sanctions." He then added, "If there is war, our troops should be called back."

By the time the media was finished parsing his words, he came out sounding as if he was pledging Canadian co-operation in the war—so long as there was no war. He was mocked mercilessly. Mulroney had the proverbial field day, excoriating the Grits for their weak-kneed anti-Americanism. When the shooting starts, he said, they run.

Defence spending had hardly fared well under the Tory government, given the budgetary constraints, but Mulroney always found the Liberals to be an easy target on military matters. He reserved a special disdain for Pierre Trudeau and his lifelong peacenik tendencies. A favourite line was one he shared with friends. "When Canadians were off fighting in the Second World War," Mulroney told them, "Trudeau was back home swatting blackflies in Outremont."

Like Trudeau, Chrétien never saw the need for a big military. His top aide, Eddie Goldenberg, was vigorously opposed. In a memo he wrote to Chrétien in 1976, he described himself as having "a strong anti-military bias." He told Chrétien that being a soldier is not "that demanding a task," that the country did not need an army of maximum efficiency, and that "if there is a war, it will be over before our troops have time to do anything about it."

John Turner, meanwhile, still held his seat in the House of Commons. Unable to countenance Chrétien's opposition to the war, he asked the leader's office for speaking time. When he was denied, he appealed the decision to the Commons. With the support of the Tories, who knew what he was up to, Turner was granted all the time he wanted and used it to take apart Chrétien's position.

As a reward, Turner soon found himself occupying a smaller office in the House of Commons. Under Turner's leadership, Chrétien had suffered similar indignities. Now the new leader was able to pay them back in kind. Turner was ostracized to the point that he often found himself sitting alone in Question Period, with all of Chrétien's allies keeping their distance. Feeling that this constituted shameful treatment of a former prime minister, Joe Comuzzi, the Thunder Bay MP, made a vow. "I made up my mind that he was never going to sit alone again as long as I was a member." Comuzzi, whose support for Paul Martin was growing, took a seat next to Turner every time.

With his performance on Iraq another embarrassment, Chrétien continued his tumble in the polls; the party fell below even the New Democrats. Colleagues like Herb Gray and David Collenette speculated that he was suffering from the Turner syndrome: Leave politics for a few years and the instincts get rusty, the confidence disappears, the mistakes pile up. The fallout from Meech Lake had also hit him hard. Being bludgeoned in his home province, as he was in the press on a daily basis, shook his confidence. He felt alone, and he wasn't sure he was up to the job. All the calumnies he had heard throughout his career about his lack of sophistication and polish, his lack of intellectual depth, preyed on him. It was as if he were starting to believe the whispers in the corridors. Brian Tobin, the Newfoundland MP, had never seen Chrétien like this. "He looked," said Tobin, "absolutely defeated."

It was one thing to be an able-bodied lieutenant to Pierre Trudeau—a Cabinet minister reporting to the boss—but another to run the show himself. When journalists asked what had happened to the old Chrétien, he candidly explained that he couldn't be the same as he used to be. "For me, it is a new job. I am adjusting to a new role after being in politics so long as number two or three or four. I had a different perspective there because I had a safety net. There was always my boss to tell me I was wrong, and there was so much more freedom in a way."

He had derived his freedom from his status as the underdog, the outsider. That status, by definition, was now gone. He was the boss himself, and he thought that this meant he had to be different. His brothers and sisters had worried about his difficulty with language and had told him that, as leader, he would be expected to perform at a higher level. They had images, as Quebecers did generally, of highly articulate, erudite leaders like Trudeau and François Mitterand. They forgot that there were also more ordinary models like Harry Truman, whom Chrétien admired, and Ronald Reagan, who was never accused of being burdened by intellectual depth. There was also the current occupant of the Oval Office, George Bush. His syntax was frequently as deplorable as Chrétien's, and sometimes he didn't make much sense. "I have opinions of my own, strong opinions," Bush once observed. "But I don't always agree with them."

To work on Chrétien's presentation, the Liberals had previously brought in an image consultant, André Morrow of Morrow Communications. He felt that in the 1984 campaign, Chrétien had gone overboard with the "ordinary man," populist approach and now needed some refinement. Work began on Chrétien's speech, his hair, his teeth. Work began on trying to turn a blacksmith into a slick Madison Avenue politician. Language pronunciation was part of the mix. His handlers even went to work on teaching him how to say the word "the." Chrétien had been plying his trade in Ottawa since 1963. Twenty-seven years later, he was being tutored on the "the" word.

Chrétien was bemused. He met with a group of Toronto supporters who were urging him to be the old Chrétien. He explained to them that while he tended to agree, he was being given different instructions from those supposedly in the know. "You know what they were teaching me today?" he told them. "They taught me for twenty minutes how to say the word 'the.'" His supporters were laughing as their leader dismissively went on about it. "The," he scoffed. "Well, you know, it's one of the bigger issues facing the nation."

In the end, the tutoring served only to make him more self-conscious. One of Chrétien's great gifts—the reason he appealed to so many voters—was that he was the antithesis of the self-conscious man.

Like André Morrow, Eddie Goldenberg, who was running Chrétien's office, wanted him more programmed so he would be less prone to mistakes. Brian Tobin disagreed with Goldenberg on this. Known for his communication skills, Tobin had been brought in during the leadership campaign to rev up Chrétien's dry speeches, speeches that Goldenberg had had a hand in. The two men clashed and soon entered into a protracted conflict.

Goldenberg was under the gun for Chrétien's poor early performance. While regarded as a superior policy man with a high-calibre, lawyerly mind, Goldenberg lacked people skills and organizational skills. The office, insiders complained, was falling into near chaos.

Policy strategy wasn't clicking either. Jean Chrétien hadn't changed his fundamental policy outlook since the Trudeau era. "The country does not need either very left wing or very right wing policies," he explained. "This country has always grown socially and economically by being in the middle of the road." But he had searched for the middle road on the Meech Lake Accord, and it had bitten him. He had sought the middle ground on the Persian Gulf War and been ridiculed. He was seeking, while shifting positions, some kind of middle ground on the GST, and this would prove very difficult.

THE GOOD NEWS, his Liberal colleagues thought, was that he was returning to the Commons. After a five-year absence, he was ready, having won the by-election, to take his seat. He would be back in the centre of the action, loosened up, feeling at home on the benches where he had put in twenty-three years.

In late February, before his first day back, he went in for a routine medical checkup. He wasn't expecting any surprises. His last extended period of hospitalization was two decades earlier, when, as Indian affairs minister, he was sent in for several days because of stress. The only surgery in his life was of an idiotic, volunteer kind—when he'd had his healthy appendix removed. This checkup, however, revealed a growth on his lung, one that looked potentially cancerous. Doctors got him quickly to the National Defence Medical Centre for surgery. He kept the news hidden from his party and the media, but the night before going in, he phoned Sharon Carstairs, who could sense that he was worried. "He didn't know it was going to be okay," she recalled. "They had done some tests and didn't like the results."

Doctors had to break some of his ribs and make a twelve-inch incision. The growth turned out to be benign, but the convalescence was long and painful. He lost so much weight he looked deathly. He was also hearing stories that would stick in his craw for a long time. Over in the Martin camp, he was told, they were hoping his recovery would not go well. Chrétien went so far as to tell his friends that Martin and his crowd were praying that the growth was malignant. "They hoped I had cancer."

Years after the health trauma, he was still repeating this story to colleagues as an indication of the opposition he faced from within his own Liberal Party. Of Martin, Chrétien said, "From day one, he was after me."

After a few weeks in hospital, he was eager to get back to his job and tried to do so too soon. He travelled to Winnipeg for a fundraiser, but in the middle of his speech, he started shaking and had to sit down. Convalescing in Florida, he took long walks on the beach with Aline and took stock of his endless run of bad luck. Aline had often been the one to turn him around when he was off course. As a member of the cottage industry trying to deconstruct what had happened to him, she concluded—as did dozens of others—that he was best left to his own instincts. No makeovers were possible. They only made him self-conscious. She advised that he dispense with the coaching, the teleprompters, the written texts—and go with his raw self.

Having recuperated from his health trauma, he returned to the Commons—"I was scared a little," he said at the time, "but I am back to fight for my convictions"—but before long, he was hearing from someone who had been watching the proceedings with an uncommon degree of interest. Paul Martin was starting to feel it was time to speak out.

Back in the summer of 1990, after the leadership convention, Eddie Goldenberg had travelled to Martin's estate in the Eastern Townships of Quebec to spend a weekend. He wanted to test the waters with Martin, to say, "How do we work together?" He found him clearly still wounded from the harshness of the leadership fight, but went away from the weekend thinking that a working arrangement could be put in place between the two men.

Martin had made no sustained effort to keep his forces intact after the leadership loss. But as he would later explain, he and his friends had "come through fire," and "I came out of that leadership race with some of the best friends of my life, and they remained friends." It wasn't a question of working to keep the organization together, he said. The bond was already there, and then, explained Martin, using an economics term, "the multiplier effect" took hold. Those friends told other friends, and "everyone had this common interest in politics, and that brought us together."

Loyalties had been formed that could not be shaken. They were loyalties that made it unlikely that Jean Chrétien would ever feel he had the whole party supporting him. Though it was far from formalized, it was already becoming clear that the party had two wings. Shortly after the convention, some had begun spreading the word around Chrétien's office that Martin could not be trusted, that he was out to undermine the new leader. One such hawk was Warren Kinsella, a lawyer and Chrétien devotee straight out of the Lee Atwater school of politics. Atwater was George Bush's attack dog, the strategist who took down Michael Dukakis in the 1988 presidential campaign by accusing the Massachusetts governor of granting furloughs to murderers and rapists. The late Atwater would have appreciated Kinsella's take on governing. "In politics, one half of the job . . . is trying to do some good," Kinsella wrote in his 2001 book *Kicking Ass in Canadian Politics*. "The other half is kicking the living shit out of the other guy."

Kinsella spent most of his time on the latter half. When he began raising red flags about Martin, Goldenberg told him he was being an alarmist. "Eddie and I had been very close but he just refused to see that this stuff was going on," he recalled. "That was the breaking point with Eddie." Kinsella, feeling unwelcome, would leave Chrétien's office before long. But he would be back.

During Chrétien's early stumbles as Opposition leader, Martin was reasonably restrained. Party members were coming to him with messages. "Paul, it looks like we made the wrong choice." Or, "Paul, be ready, you might have to take over sooner than you think." In deciding to apply some pressure, he chose to focus on the unity issue, saying at the opening of a three-day caucus in the spring of 1991 that the party was missing a big opportunity. There was a vacuum to be filled on Quebec, "but we are not filling it now," he asserted, leaving no doubt that he was taking a shot at the leader.

Chrétien loyalists responded. "I think Mr. Martin's position reeks of division," said Sheila Copps, who was now strongly supporting the leader. Chrétien himself took aim. "We have a party position. The party position will remain the same until I change it."

Martin soon found more to get exercised about. In Quebec City, seemingly caught off guard at the end of a press conference, the Liberal leader committed yet another blunder. He said a new constitutional deal for Canada could be put in place without the approval of Quebec, referring to the possibility that a referendum might have to be held. If the rest of Canada approved it and Quebec didn't, it still could be implemented.

Quebec politicians and the media pounced. This was the very thing, they reminded one and all, that Chrétien had allowed to happen ten years earlier during the so-called Night of the Long Knives, when the patriated Constitution was approved without Quebec's signature. A strong argument could be made that the separatist leader of the time, René Lévesque, had not wanted to sign any unity deal anyway. But the "long knives" story, true or not, endured. Responding to Chrétien's latest remark, Quebec's premier, Robert Bourassa, was flat-out insulting. "It's not only a mistake, it's political stupidity. And I would say the worst threat now to national unity is precisely political stupidity."

Bourassa and other Quebec politicians rarely employed such belittling vocabulary against others. But this was Jean Chrétien. With him, they felt comfortable in levelling the lowest of blows. The Bloc leader, Lucien Bouchard, never one to soft-pedal an argument, went a step further than Bourassa. Chrétien's approach to constitutional reform was "literally fascism," he charged.

The battered Chrétien tried to explain that he had only been speaking legally and technically. But even outside Quebec, the frustrations with his leadership were reaching a crisis point. The blows, the shocks, the setbacks accumulated to the extent that there were calls for his head. Chrétien hadn't even contested a general election as leader yet, and many in the party wanted him out. A headline in the *Toronto Star,* the country's big Liberal newspaper, captured the mood: "Liberal Strategists Hope Chrétien Will Quit."

Trying to plug some holes, he came forward with a new plan for constitutional reform. It would give Quebec distinct society recognition in its preamble. It also called for an elected Senate, the right of aboriginal self-government, greater involvement by the provinces in the appointment of Supreme Court judges, and a region-based constitutional amending formula. The new package, which was to be put to the people in a national referendum, was quite similar in many ways to a plan Mulroney was laying out as a successor to Meech Lake.

In part because of his misstatement in Quebec City, Chrétien returned to a more scripted approach for a major speech on foreign policy to the Canadian Institute for International Affairs. Chrétien had great difficulty with the text, stumbling over words and syntax, leaving a top Liberal to grumble, "He can barely read it. This is very discouraging." His staffers were left shaking their heads in dismay. They vowed never again to let him appear before an audience with an academic text. An embarrassed Chrétien tried to explain. "Everyone knows my language problem. I am always putting my emphasis on the wrong syllable."

People knew he demolished the language, but they didn't know there was a good reason for it, something he couldn't help—something that escaped the notice of intellectuals who dismissed him. He had a form of dyslexia, an affliction shared by his younger brother, Michel, a pioneering medical researcher. Sometimes Chrétien could see a word on a page and not be able to say it. Sometimes, explained Michel, he could be looking at an apple but would be unable to say that word. He'd have to use a lame substitute, like "red fruit." At other times, it was Chrétien's pronunciation that got in the way. Once, he was trying to tell a joke about a Conservative and a Liberal adrift in a boat in shark-infested waters. The problem, Chrétien said, was that they had "no whores to get them ashore."

Eager to get beyond the advice of his own staff, he had dispatched a half-dozen caucus members to tour the country and sound out Liberals on where things were going wrong. Joe Fontana, the London, Ontario MP, put together the resulting report and delivered the bad news. "It was pretty damn blunt," he recalled, but Chrétien knew most of what was coming. He put up his hands when Fontana entered his office and said, "I know exactly what you're going to say." Fontana's recommendations? Hire better staff. Get a think-tank going to develop policy. Be himself, the old Jean Chrétien.

He finally moved, starting with what Joe Volpe, a Martin supporter, called "the bunch of gadflies in his office who didn't know whether they were coming or going." One morning, Eddie Goldenberg and other staffers were sitting around the table leafing through the morning news-papers. They hit upon a story in *The Montreal Gazette* by Joan Bryden. It said that Jean Pelletier was Chrétien's new chief of staff. Goldenberg saw it, Kinsella recalled, "and he just stood up and walked out. Dave Dingwall looked at me, and we chased out after him across to the Plaza restaurant." Sensing that Goldenberg was thinking of quitting the team entirely, they tried to reason with him. They were shocked that, given his dedicated service to Chrétien over two decades, Goldenberg was finding out through the newspapers that he had been removed from the top job.

Chrétien had been holding back the news because Jean Pelletier had yet to give his final word on whether he would accept the post. In the meantime, the news leaked. Chrétien had met with Pelletier a couple of months earlier. While in Quebec City, he asked the unsuspecting former mayor up to his hotel suite to say hello. He then made the offer. The two of them had attended both university in Trois-Rivières and Laval law school together. Pelletier moved on to broadcast journalism, then jumped into the political arena as press secretary to Paul Sauvé, the one-time leader of the Union Nationale. He published a little Quebec paper, *L'Action catholique,* did some real-estate work, administered a theatre, then spent a successful dozen years as mayor of Quebec.

He and Chrétien were good friends, but they hadn't seen each other often in recent years. Pelletier, who was a smooth and authoritative operator, one who commanded respect, defined himself politically as "a man of the centre," just like Chrétien. He decided to take the job of running the office of a leader who was on the skids because "I had confidence in him. He was a good campaigner. I made the analysis that the birth of the Reform Party and the Bloc Québécois had killed the chances of the Conservatives. I couldn't see the NDP coming [on strong]. So I said that if the Liberals have a good platform, if Chrétien performs well, he's got all the chances to be the next prime minister." He had noticed his friend's dismal start, "but I didn't think it had damaged the situation up to the point that this could not be put back in order."

Pelletier sat down individually with all forty staffers on Chrétien's payroll and then went away on a summer vacation, coming back with colour-coded flow charts and a command system that brought order to the disorder. Chrétien had made much of the fact that throughout his political career, he had had good deputy ministers working for him in the many portfolios he'd held. Never a policy man, he needed them. In his first year as Opposition leader he was without such a deputy. But now he had one. "The minute everything was reorganized," Pelletier recalled, "I think he felt better and had his mind in a better state, so that he could look after the issues."

Goldenberg stayed on as policy adviser. He had been with Chrétien since 1972 and wasn't about to leave when the prime minister's seat was within reach. Chrétien was occasionally puzzled that Goldenberg didn't wish to do something else. "I never forced anybody to go," he said, "but I would say, you know, 'Perhaps you should do something.'" But, obviously confident that his man would make it, Goldenberg stayed. "We became extremely comfortable with him," Chrétien said. He knows me very well. He knows how I will react very well. If you talk with Eddie, he will say what Chrétien will say."

For the vital position of communications director, Chrétien brought in Peter Donolo, a young man who had caught the political bug early, working as a fourteen-year-old on Pierre Trudeau's campaign in the 1974 election in Mount Royal. He was a former president of the Young Liberals of Ontario and head of the Liberal Club at Carleton University. Putting his keen sense of humour and eye for the one-liner to use, he worked a couple of years as a copywriter for an ad agency, then became press secretary to Toronto's mayor Art Eggleton. Eggleton also knew Pelletier. Chrétien consulted with him on both Donolo and Pelletier before hiring them.

Donolo soon discovered that, temperamentally, Chrétien was not an Opposition politician. He had served on the governing side for more than twenty years. He didn't like criticizing for the sake of criticizing. For Question Period, Donolo would suggest a line of attack, only to have Chrétien complain about how easy it would be for the minister in question to bat it down. Donolo had to explain that the idea was to get a good television clip. The networks wouldn't show the whole answer anyway.

Occasionally, however, Chrétien had the better argument. One day, Donolo advised him to go hard at Mulroney for not doing anything about a rash of bankruptcies across the country. Well aware of Mulroney's sumptuous personal tastes, Donolo suggested that Chrétien get up and, with a tone of indignation, demand, "Are Canadians going to have to wait for Holt Renfrew to go bankrupt before the prime minister is finally going to act?"

Chrétien responded, "No, Peter, I can't do that."

Donolo asked why, whereupon the little guy from Shawinigan opened his suit jacket to reveal a Holt Renfrew label on the inside pocket. As he had once explained to Albina Guarnieri, his suit was as good as Paul Martin's.

To bone up on foreign affairs, Chrétien set off on a ten-day tour through Europe, where he met with François Mitterand. Family members and friends had often cited the French president when trying to explain to Chrétien how a leader of a nation needed to comport himself. The two men swapped stories. Mitterand had become a Cabinet minister at age twenty-seven and spent the next thirty-seven years plying the trade, before becoming president at sixty-four. Chrétien had become a Cabinet minister at thirty-three. In Canada, Chrétien complained, his long experience was not regarded as advantageous; instead, it prompted references to him as "yesterday's man." Mitterand sighed. "I've had that problem for forty years."

DESPITE HIS OWN WEAK POLLS, Chrétien remained highly confident that the political winds were shifting in his direction. During a car trip with Donolo to Stratford, Ontario, in late 1991, Chrétien analyzed the country, region by region, riding by riding, opinion poll by opinion poll. He had it all down to a science, and though the election was still more than a year away, he was sure, given the state of the Tories, that a Liberal majority was in the making. "This is the only way it can add up," he said.

He had outlined his constitutional plan and, while continuing to counter charges of vagueness, delivered an economic package. It included a fairer tax system without the GST, a reduction in interest rates, a lower-valued Canadian dollar, employment adjustment and job programs, and a move away from the single-minded, anti-inflation mania of the Bank of Canada's governor, John Crow.

Most of this was standard fare for Liberals. They needed, as the caucus group that travelled across the country had recommended, a modernization of their playbook, something more dramatic. The world had moved beyond the Trudeau years of nationalization. Now the buzzword was globalization. The party's ideology had to be cast forward, and to do it, a policy conclave was organized for Aylmer, Quebec, in November 1991. David Zussman and Eddie Goldenberg lined up a list of speakers, including some of the more innovative thinkers of the period. They could perhaps shake the old Grits out of the collective lethargy that Paul Martin had complained about during the leadership campaign.

Chrétien's main problem, Goldenberg had concluded, was not that he felt uncomfortable in the role of attack dog against the government, having served on the governing side all his career, but that there was a lack of consensus within the party on the major issues of the day. "The problem with the Opposition party is that they got elected for what they stood for—this when their party was actually defeated for what it stood for." It was not an easy task for Chrétien to move the party on free trade, the GST, globalization, and the Constitution, since members had been elected for opposing such change.

"There were a series of things that were difficult for me," recalled Chrétien, listing his illness and the constitutional battles as two developments that plagued him as Opposition leader. "The media was very tough on me because I had opposed Meech. . . . And you know, I had to change many views of the party. The party was officially opposed to free trade, and I thought that we had to be with free trade. It was the right thing.

"[The Tories] had a book on me, about my precedent," he went on to say. "I had proposed a free trade agreement between Mexico and the United States in 1972. So they were using it against me. I was minister of Indian affairs then. I was not minding my own business when I said that."

Every Liberal leader was different, he noted. "I had different approaches than Trudeau and Turner. But I was always more in line with the Trudeau type. I never hid it. I never ran away from what I consider traditional Liberalism. I was very centrist, anti-establishment."

A conference like Aylmer's could build a new consensus, however. On the economy, for example, most of the speakers were proponents of a deficit-free, open-border ethos. Their argument was that since globalization was inevitable, there was no use trying to hide behind old-fashioned protectionism.

Chrétien came to the conference prepared to accept the new thinking. Open-border commerce wasn't a quantum leap for him, or, given its history, for the Liberal Party. In the 1911 election and through most of the first half of the century, the Grits, under Laurier and King, tended to favour more open trade with the United States, especially since natural forces inclined the Canadian economy in that direction anyway. But by 1960, dependence had swung so far over from Britain to the United States that a counter-trend set in. At the Kingston conference in 1960, the Liberals, responding to fears that the Canadian economy was being swallowed up, moved to more protectionist precepts, as advocated by Walter Gordon, then finance minister. Jean Chrétien, just coming to political prominence then, initially subscribed to a good deal of Gordon's nationalist gospel. In seconding the Speech from the Throne in 1965, when he was thirty-one years old, he left few doubts as to where he stood. He told the Commons that Canadians had to build a country "totally different from the United States." It had to be different, he asserted, in its mindset, its culture, its educational and social security systems.

But after coming under the influence of Mitchell Sharp in the late 1960s, Chrétien began tacking towards a more moderate position. In the 1970s, his experience in the trade portfolio impressed upon him the need for Canada to do more business abroad, though preferably not all in the United States. In Chrétien's view, Mulroney had gone too far in that direction with the free trade pact. But even though free trade wasn't paying off initially, Chrétien was keeping an open mind. He appointed Roy MacLaren, a Liberal with a distinctly conservative bent, to be the party's trade critic. To balance the ledger, he made

Lloyd Axworthy, a Winnipegger who was very much of opposite tendencies, his foreign affairs critic.

At the Aylmer conference, people immediately noticed that Chrétien was seated with MacLaren. In the run-up to Aylmer, MacLaren had distributed an internal discussion paper called "Wide Open." It mirrored Chrétien's view that the mistake the Mulroneyites had made was not in opening the doors wider to the United States, but in doing so "to the exclusion of the rest of the world." At the conference, the globalization guru Lester Thurow, no fan of the Trudeau tradition of economic nationalism, was a keynote speaker. "The role of government," he said, "is to represent the future to the present." Though he showed a different side at this conference, Chrétien was considered a politician more inclined to represent the past than the present.

Applauding Thurow's words was Paul Martin. With his background in international business, Martin strongly opposed much of the interventionism of the Trudeau years, in particular the National Energy Program. "Trudeau tried to isolate us by claiming we could withdraw into ourselves and operate on oil prices lower than [those in] the rest of the world," he said. "From then on, we stopped evolving."

Martin's close friend Peter Nicholson, an academic, banker, and policy wonk, was also on the conference's featured speaker list. He reflected the Martin view that societies that lose out in the global investment fight "can, at best, look forward to a life of genteel decline and, at worst, a descent into social chaos."

When Chrétien took the stage, he delivered a line—much to the chagrin of the social Liberals present—that sounded the death knell for protectionism. "Protectionism is not left wing or right wing," he declared. "It is simply passé. Globalization is not right wing or left wing. It is simply a fact of life."

The Lloyd Axworthys of the party were not at all convinced. "All this talk about globalization," Axworthy told a reporter on the way out, "is just a cover for right-wing ideology." Roy MacLaren's response, picked up on an open microphone, was pointed. "Eat your heart out, Lloyd Axworthy."

It was a tough day for the old guard but a big moment for the party. "A very big leap," said Goldenberg, who could take a good deal of credit for it. Never leaving Chrétien's side through the tough times since the leadership convention, he had worked hard to persuade the leader to make the bold move. As he noted, this was the party that had run against free trade only three years earlier. Now the nostalgic and defensive economic nationalism of the 1988 campaign was being buried.

Having been credible on social issues and sometimes unity issues, the Liberal Party, with the success of the Aylmer conference, would at last start to become credible in an area where it had long been a laggard—the modern economy. And with Aylmer, Jean Chrétien, a laggard as Opposition leader, would start to become credible as well.

CHAPTER THREE

THE ONLY ONE
LEFT STANDING

THE DISAVOWAL OF ECONOMIC NATIONALISM at Aylmer was a major moment for the party and marked Chrétien's first real triumph as leader of the Opposition. For all the gaffes and bad polls, for all the talk of his mind being cemented in times past, he had shown he was capable of moving himself and his party into the future. Around the office, some levity of spirit returned. "Politics," a Chrétien staffer had once remarked, "is the most fun you can have with your clothes on." But it hadn't been that way on this Liberal team, not while the leader was in his Chauncey Gardner phase.

That he was gaining confidence was obvious from his reaction to another jolt—an Uncle Tom attack—from his own province. The Quebec elite was after him again. But Chrétien didn't sit quietly this time, as he had on other occasions.

He had been pilloried earlier by the influential commentator Lise Bissonnette. Chrétien's use of language, she wrote, "indicates clearly to his compatriots the extent of the contempt he feels for them, how he would like to see them forever confined to the past. . . . It is good that people should know that for years he has with simply stupefying success been parading around English Canada doing this number of the ill-spoken Quebecer, the happy slave who asks his master for more punishment."

After Bissonnette, it was the turn of the highly respected Alain Dubuc of Montreal's *La Presse*. Dubuc also periodically wrote a column for the pages of the *Toronto Star*. In December 1991, he published a frontal assault on Chrétien in that paper, listing the leader's flaws before concluding that this "is not the stuff you make a prime minister with."

"We often feel that there is an Uncle Tom quality in your relationship with Chrétien," Dubuc told English Canada. "You seem to be touched by this modest but grateful French Canadian." But "that doesn't wash here. We are not swept along by his basic drive or his pride in having succeeded in this Anglo-Saxon world that is Canada, a little like a first-generation immigrant grateful for being able to go to the top in his country of adoption."

Canada had changed, Dubuc said, and Quebec had changed. "In short, he is an anachronism." He pointed to Chrétien's simplistic approach to problems, citing as an example his comment that the constitutional crisis was like a car stuck in a snowbank. "Then ask yourself if this guy can lead the eighth power of the world, if you want him to represent you around the globe. We think not."

For Chrétien, this was enough. Here was proof in big, bold letters of the snobbery towards him. Here was proof that he had not been exaggerating the classism he had had to fight all his life. His normal response to this type of criticism was to curse the matter privately. But this time, he took up the pen. In a response to the *Star* article, which made headlines in other papers, he wrote: "Let's recognize this for what it is: outright, if thinly veiled, snobbery. I'm sure pundits in other countries have, at one time or another, said the same things about Harry Truman, or John Major, or Helmut Kohl, or Lech Walesa, or Boris Yeltsin.

"No, I didn't go to finishing school. No, I wasn't raised in a cosmopolitan city like Montreal or Toronto. But I guess I'm a little naive. I always thought that substance was more important than form . . . that competence, ideas and conviction counted for more than expensive suits and pretty words."

One of the qualities that made Dubuc a first-rate journalist was that he didn't hide behind words. But his attack was still surprising. The insulting notion that Jean Chrétien wasn't sophisticated enough to be prime minister was something repeated over meals in fancy Montreal restaurants, not printed in major newspapers.

Was it Chrétien's fault, wondered Peter Donolo, who wrote his letter of response, that he had been born with impediments and handicaps? Wasn't it a mark of his strength that he had come this far? And wasn't it a mark of the strength of Canadian democracy that it could happen? These types of insults, Donolo knew, tended to give Chrétien back his edge as the outsider hurling thunderbolts against the high and mighty. Some good could come of them, he reasoned. Had he been able to foresee what would happen in the coming election campaign, when his leader's image became the subject of an odious television attack, he would have been all the more convinced of that fact.

Jean Pelletier viewed Chrétien's straightforwardness as a strength. "One of the greatest assets of Chrétien is his simplicity. He's a simple man, and Canadians like him like that. His character is very much liked because people in Canada have the impression he is one of them." But this analysis generally applied to Canadians other than Quebecers. Many in Quebec preferred more stylish leaders, like Trudeau, to show off to the rest of Canada. They didn't want a leader from the lower echelons, or a leader who could be seen as kowtowing to the Anglo majority to gain favour. The elites in Quebec liked Mulroney over Chrétien because the Tory was debonair and articulate, and also more inclined to accommodate the province's nationalistic urges.

For Chrétien what was more important, however, was the national political picture. Mulroney's approval ratings had dropped so low that historians were pulling out the record books to find a precedent. The Tory crooner's personal style grated on Canadians outside Quebec. His unity plan had collapsed. His Free Trade Agreement was off to an inauspicious start. The economy, staggering under a gigantic debt load, was in deep recession.

Mulroney's old Tory coalition, the one he had used to defeat the Liberals in the two previous elections, was fracturing to a degree that would have profound ramifications for Canadians. In winning elections in the past, the Conservatives had corralled the right-wing vote in the West and the nationalist vote in Quebec. But now each territory was deserting the Tories in favour of new regional parties. In Quebec, Lucien Bouchard's newly formed Bloc Québécois was an instant hit, gobbling up huge segments of the nationalist vote that had gone Tory in 1984 and 1988. In the West, Preston Manning had given birth to the Reform Party, making the case that with their lax approach to tax cutting and the deficit, the Conservatives were failing to heed Western interests. Mulroney could well argue the opposite case. He had dismantled the hated National Energy Program and the Foreign Investment Review Agency. He had championed other Western policy priorities, like deregulation and privatization. He introduced free trade, which Westerners welcomed, and put many of the West's demands on the table in constitutional negotiations. But none of these considerations could stop the rise of the Reform Party.

The political trend-lines could hardly have been more favourable for the Liberals. For all his own troubles, Jean Chrétien was getting an early sampling of a run of good fortune that few other Canadian leaders ever enjoyed. Unlike John Turner, who'd caught the Tories on the rise when he became Liberal leader, Chrétien had won the leadership at the ideal time. His chief opponent was in such a destitute state that all Chrétien had to do to become prime minister was keep breathing. Even that modest assignment had appeared burdensome in his first year as Opposition chief. But he was starting to find his feet.

To beef up his credibility on the foreign stage, he went to Washington in February 1992 to visit President George Bush. The trip occasioned a sarcastic blast from Mulroney. "Mr. Chrétien is meeting with George Bush?" he asked incredulously. "He went to Washington to see the enemy!" Then, more seriously, "You just look back at the anti-Americanism that has dominated the Liberal Party. It's viscerally anti-American."

Eight years earlier, Mulroney, as Opposition leader, had beamed with excitement at the prospect of going to the White House for a private audience with President Ronald Reagan. The two of them formed the basis of a companionship at that meeting, and Mulroney, delighted by the Gipper's reception, announced that Canada and the U.S. were at the dawn of new possibilities.

Chrétien showed no comparable exhilaration at the prospect of sitting down with George Bush. Though Aylmer signalled a shift in big policy lines, he was still vowing to renegotiate the Free Trade Agreement. He knew the Americans would not agree. His staff was apprehensive about this trip for other reasons. The media would be ready to pounce if, as Dubuc suggested, Chrétien demonstrated in any way that he didn't belong in the big company.

But the visit went smoothly. Chrétien didn't show up in sackcloth, or declare "I am not a politician," or stir his coffee with a fork. "Friendship is friendship and business is business," he told Bush, restating his position that the Free Trade Agreement had to be changed to clarify the issue of subsidies and to protect Canadian energy supplies. As expected, Bush didn't respond favourably. But the Liberal leader got his picture taken in the Oval Office, which was the primary purpose of the visit.

Kept out of the public eye through this period was the family crisis Chrétien was facing. His son Michel, the troubled Native-Canadian boy he adopted two decades earlier, was on trial in Montreal on charges of sexual assault, sodomy, and illegal confinement. Chrétien sat through the proceedings as the complainant, a twenty-nine-year-old woman, testified that after a night of drinking with Michel in May 1990, she woke up nude and bound at the wrists and ankles. Michel claimed that the woman had consented to have sex with him. He explained that he'd heard of people having sex while bound and wanted to try it. As the details got more difficult for Michel—and his father sat watching—the young man's lawyer applied to have testimony made behind closed doors.

Friends had never seen Chrétien so distraught. He wouldn't talk about the assault case with the media. He appeared on *Canada AM* to discuss other matters but was rambling and disconnected. A staffer described him as "hyper." In the Commons, Aline showed up one day wearing large dark sunglasses to hide her eyes. The media was understanding and chose not to dramatize the tragedy. It helped, but staff members detected through this period a profound change in their leader—as they would every time the subject of the troubled Michel arose.

Soon, there were other preoccupations. With only a year or so to go before an election, Mulroney brought the Constitution back to the centre of the national agenda. With Joe Clark now his unity minister, Mulroney searched for a successor to the Meech Lake Accord, one they planned to put before the public in a referendum. The Liberals wanted to keep the focus on the collapsing economy. The resurrected constitutional fights would dominate headlines and put Chrétien on the defensive again, especially in his home province.

Soon, there were other preoccupations. The Charlottetown Accord contained many of the elements Chrétien had put forward in his Liberal plan a year earlier. He had some reservations about the new pact but gave it his support. He wanted to show a more conciliatory attitude towards Quebec and get the issue settled because "it's bleeding the nation to death."

As he had with the Meech Lake Accord, Pierre Trudeau came out boldly against the Charlottetown plan. Chrétien campaigned for it across the country, but in Quebec the federalists didn't want him, so he stayed away. A poll released three weeks before the vote asked Quebecers which politicians they had the most confidence in. Chrétien finished last, at just 2 percent. He was more popular in the Liberal wasteland of Alberta than in his home province. When Joe Clark invited him to his Alberta constituency to promote the accord, Chrétien he noticed how warmly he was received. It was hard to fathom. It would be like Clark polling better in Quebec than in his native Alberta.

Clark was puzzled by the Liberal leader throughout the Charlottetown debate. He thought that since Chrétien had helped author the patriation deal of 1982, he would be much engaged in any proposals for constitutional reform. "We were trying to bring everybody into the tent on it, and I made a practice of taking proposals to the other party leaders, particularly Chrétien," recalled Clark. But he could barely interest him in talking about it. "I just didn't think he was following the issue. . . . I don't know what it was. Maybe it was a bad time in his life. But what it left me with was the belief that here was a guy for whom the substance of things doesn't matter much."

The accord, though overwhelmingly supported by the country's elites, the media, politicians, and the business community, suffered a resounding defeat at the hands of ordinary Canadians. The loss didn't worry the Liberals, as their leader wasn't blamed. Most regarded the Mulroney government's unpopularity as the prime cause. The only drawback for the Grits was that Mulroney was now so battered that he couldn't possibly run in the next election.

WHEN HE WON the leadership, Chrétien made a remark in casual conversation that struck the listener, a former Liberal MP, as rather ominous. He said that throughout his career, he had "taken a lot of shit" from a lot of people. "From now on," the new leader said, "they will be doing the listening." He told another MP, "I don't owe anyone anything."

In preparing for the coming campaign, Chrétien pushed for and won the right to have final say over riding nominations. The decision touched off an angry backlash from party stalwarts, who felt that democracy was being cheated. But the new rule, Chrétien argued, would mean that well-organized special interest groups like pro-lifers could not sign up instant Liberals and install the nominees of their choice. He also needed to show that he was a strong enough leader to attract big names to run under his leadership—and one way to do that was to guarantee them a nomination. Art Eggleton, the former

Toronto mayor, was handed a nomination, as were Douglas Peters, the vice-president of the Toronto-Dominion bank, Marcel Massé, once the top civil servant in the land, and Alberta's Robert Blair, the president of NOVA Corporation.

John Nunziata, a bullheaded Grit who under Turner was a member of the Liberal attack squad known as the Rat Pack, criticized the decision to have Eggleton run in Toronto York Centre, prompting Chrétien to strip the MP of his caucus duties. Nunziata wasn't one to back off Chrétien. "The backroom boys have taken over control of the party," he protested. "I guess they think they can muzzle us all." A splinter group called Liberals for Democracy was formed. It included John Munro, the hard-working health and Indian affairs minister from the Trudeau era; he had designs on running in the Hamilton area but was getting negative signals from Chrétien's office. "I predicted this would happen," said Munro. "When backroom people make decisions not subject to fundamental democratic principles, it leads to rampant nepotism."

Hec Cloutier was a party activist in the riding of Lanark–Carleton, outside Ottawa. He had challenged Len Hopkins, the long-time incumbent, for the nomination in 1988 and lost. He was preparing to make another big try for it in the coming campaign, so he thought he should visit Chrétien and make himself known. But the reception was not what he had anticipated. The diminutive, hard-nosed Cloutier excitedly told the Opposition leader of his near certainty of winning the nomination, whereupon Chrétien interjected, "Well, you might. But you're not going to get the chance." Cloutier had a hard time believing what he was hearing. This was a democracy, after all. He had worked the constituency like a dog to be able to run for a Liberal nomination. How could he be ordered to step aside?

Chrétien explained his reasoning. As Cloutier recalled it, he said, "I am the boss. I have the right to make this decision. I have an agenda for the country. I want to become prime minister and do great things, and I've got to put people in place who I know can win." Chrétien knew Hopkins could win, he added, because he had done so eight times.

The talk got heated. When Chrétien said he was going to stop Cloutier's bid, Cloutier came back at him. "The hell you are!" Chrétien banged his fist on his desk as the two men traded expletives. The Liberal leader wasn't backing down, nor was his visitor. Now Chrétien went a step further. He said that if Cloutier put his name up for the nomination, he'd be kicked out of the party. Cloutier, who had had enough, countered, "You do that, you son of a bitch. I'll run as an independent, and I'll beat your ass."

Two days later, Cloutier received notice that he was being expelled from the Liberal Party. Keeping his word, he ran in the election as an independent, but he lost to Hopkins.

Chrétien's heavy-handedness was countered by his promises to provide a more transparent government that would give MPs greater clout. For example, he would allow members to participate in pre-budget hearings to make recommendations on financial decisions, rather than just having them handed down to them. There would be more free votes in Parliament. "Canadians," he said, "have had enough of the abuses of Parliament and the arrogance of government." In keeping with that statement, he promised to cut down on patronage. He would give no jobs to his hairdresser or favourite hotel owner, as Mulroney had done. Liberals would be there not to serve themselves but to serve Canadians. They were high-sounding promises of the type made by many leaders in the past—the type that come back one day to haunt them.

Almost a year before the election had to be called, Chrétien had become so confident of victory that he asked David Zussman to start preparing transition documents for his takeover of power. Zussman occasionally consulted with Chrétien on the type of government he wanted—the Cabinet structure, the committee structure, the size of the PMO, and so on. "He saw a more targeted government," recalled Zussman, a government that was not into everything. "But he saw government playing a huge role on the social side. To be responsible for the less fortunate was very much a large part of his thinking."

Though Zussman favoured a more decentralized federation, he couldn't engage the Opposition leader on that theme. Chrétien didn't want money transferred to the provinces unless the federal side had a good say in how it was to be spent. "I think he's a centralizer," Zussman concluded. "He sees a very vigorous role for the federal government." He wanted the feds to have "a physical presence as well as a fiscal one."

Zussman followed the traditional mechanics of a transition, but a departure from times past came with the preparation of a heavily detailed policy book, a meaty volume that, coming from a generalist with a reputation for being thin on policy, would serve good purpose. The idea of preparing what became known as the Red Book did not come from Chrétien's inner circle, however. It originated with Paul Martin, who went to Goldenberg and Chrétien. "I asked for it and nobody else," Martin recalled. "It wasn't as if there was competition for the job. Party platforms for the election campaigns up until that point had been very much done at the last minute."

Because it was a new way of doing things, there was some resistance. In the past, Martin explained, the government would rely on proposals put forward by the civil service. But Martin "really felt that the basic responsibility of a political party coming into government . . . was to tell the public service that this is what we want to do now, so you go ahead and figure out the mechanics."

At the PMO, they liked the idea. They readily recalled John Turner's 1988 election campaign. During one of his early stops, he was asked about his child-care program, couldn't come up with a cost estimate, and got slaughtered in the media as a result. Better to be prepared this time, Chrétien's advisers concluded.

Martin did the heavy spadework, with the help of Goldenberg and the brainy Chaviva Hosek, the former Ontario Cabinet minister who was now a policy wonk in the PMO. Martin barely talked to Chrétien throughout the whole exercise. At this early stage, the two men were defining their working relationship, which involved staying as far apart as possible and letting intermediaries communicate for them. "My involvement with him," Martin recalled, "was effectively to present it to him at the end. I'm sure that Eddie discussed it with him."

The reason many Liberals favoured having Martin prepare the Red Book was that he sought out their views. He had an inordinate degree of natural curiosity, and asked more questions in a day than some self-centred politicians would ask in a month. "I think that's why I adore Paul Martin," MP Carolyn Bennett would say. "He never thinks he's the smartest person in the room. He always knows there is somebody who knows more about something than he does. And he will go and seek them out and ask them."

One of the few areas where Chrétien did get involved in the Red Book concerned Martin's plan to promise to erase the burgeoning government deficit. Chrétien, as Zussman was discovering, wanted to shy away from creating big expectations. Better to deliver on smaller stuff than fail on larger, he thought. So he told his policy book authors to follow the route of several European countries, where they were setting deficit targets at 3 percent of gross domestic product.

MULRONEY RESIGNED ON FEBRUARY 24, 1993. Rather than stepping down earlier to give a successor more time to prepare, he had lingered in office, hoping the tide of public opinion would somehow turn. Chrétien's weak performance in his first year in Opposition had given him some hope. But the deep recession, combined with the defeat of the Charlottetown Accord, killed off any chance of recovery. With his resignation, he had at least avoided personal defeat at the polls. He could walk away having captured two successive majority election victories, something no other Tory had done in the century.

From the day of his decision, it was clear that his successor would be Kim Campbell, the perky neophyte from British Columbia who was quickly capturing the imagination of Tories across the land. Other hopefuls, including Michael Wilson, Don Mazankowski,

Barbara McDougall, and Perrin Beatty, could read the trend lines. Some of them nudged their way to the starting line, only to pull back, leaving the youthful Jean Charest as the only well-known challenger.

Chrétien had reason to fear Campbell. What a modern-day contrast to him! For a while, Liberals worried that she could be the equivalent of another former justice minister, Pierre Trudeau. She had a fresh, contrarian style, and she projected intellectual and sexual appeal. She was already registering—before she even won the leadership race— higher personal favourability ratings than Chrétien. Some of that lustre dimmed when she ran a safe and uninspiring leadership campaign that was almost overtaken by the late-charging Charest. But then she hit the summer barbecue circuit, charming the masses as Canada's first female prime minister, and she was on the upswing again.

Chrétien responded, saying, "New Tory, same story. Campbell is a temporary prime minister. She got a summer job." He knew about pre-election bubbles. He used an example from his own party, which had been far behind the Tories in 1984, then chose John Turner and drew even. Then, of course, the bubble burst and the Grits were trounced. "We don't need to get excited because they're changing the label on the product," he said of the Campbell Tories. "As someone said the other day, if you have a can of tainted tuna and you change the label, it doesn't change the product."

Liberal caucus members fretted as their lead disappeared. Instead of trying to ease their concerns behind closed doors, Chrétien took them on publicly. "There are always nervous Nellies in any organization," he said. "If they cry, they will be seen as crybabies—and the people don't vote for crybabies." Give me the names of the tremblers, he demanded, "so that I can put some backbone in their back." In private he made it clear that if he lost to Campbell, there wouldn't be a Chrétien to kick around any more. While some greeted these words sceptically, Chrétien disliked being Opposition leader so much that he likely would not have put up with four more years of it.

He went on a bus tour of Alberta, during which he savaged the Mulroneyites for planning to spend $5.8 billion for new helicopters. Didn't they know that the Cold War was over? Were they mad? Spending billions on whirlybirds when the country had more food banks than McDonald's restaurants! In Medicine Hat, where his reception was rousing, Chrétien hit them with another sledgehammer. "They were elected to reduce the debt. They made a promise to balance the books. They started with $160 billion, and they reduced it to $440 billion. What a reduction!" The Tories and Preston Manning's Reformers were promising to wipe away the deficit in quick order, two or three years. Sure, said Chrétien, anyone can do that, "but you would have 25-percent unemployment. And when you have 25-percent unemployment, you will have a revolution on your hands."

At this juncture, Chrétien was no deficit hawk. The modest targeting that he wanted spelled out in his Red Book meant that the deficit would still be over $20 billion after his first term in office. He would be adding more than $100 billion to the national debt. Herb Dhaliwal, a businessman from British Columbia's Sikh community who was preparing to run for the Liberals, talked to Chrétien before the campaign and came away worried. He could see that there was still a lot of the red-ink mentality in Chrétien, and that much pressure would be required to get him to change his ways. "His attitude was that the deficit is okay," Dhaliwal recalled, "as long as you can manage it."

As the day of the election call approached, Campbell's press reviews got even better. After visiting Bob Rae, the Ontario premier, at Queen's Park, she sent away the limousines and hopped a subway back to her hotel. The populist turn created a media frenzy of Trudeau-ish proportions. A poll showed that 37 percent of Canadians thought Kim Campbell would make the best prime minister, compared with 29 percent for Chrétien. While he hadn't recovered from his early woes and he was still running behind his party, she was well ahead of hers.

"I remember I was with Eddie Goldenberg," recalled Peter Donolo, "and we were wondering, 'Shit, you know, is this 1968 all over again? Is our guy Stanfield and the other one Trudeau?'" Jean Pelletier was pushing a different line, comparing the phenomenon to a balloon. "And you know a balloon. You just need a little needle and 'Boom!'" Warren Kinsella did some checking into Campbell's political history. "I went back to her high school, every goddamn thing she ever said." He told Chrétien she was highly vulnerable. She was undisciplined, he explained, and she somehow equated this with being refreshingly new and candid. But it wouldn't work in a campaign.

Chrétien went to northeastern Newfoundland, to Fogo Island, the most eastern part of the country, the end of Canadian earth. George Baker, a long-time Newfoundland MP with a bullhorn voice, was escorting him, and they made a stop at the Fogo Island Motel, where there were two pool tables and ten dartboards. Chrétien beat a local in billiards and then was challenged in darts.

"Well, for me, you know, I don't play the game too well," Chrétien told the guy. "I hardly ever play."

"First dart," Baker recounted, "Chrétien puts right in the twenty-five circle, just outside the bull's eye. "

"Good," the local says, "but the big number you want to hit is the triple-twenty. That's worth the most."

"Chrétien takes another dart," Baker explained, "fires it, and damn if it doesn't go right into the triple-twenty! They're still talking about it on Fogo Island today."

It was a sign of things to come. In the 1993 campaign, Jean Chrétien fired bull's eyes while Kim Campbell missed the board entirely.

Senator Joyce Fairbairn, a co-chair of the election campaign, had been involved in most Liberal battles since the 1960s. Never had she seen the level of preparedness she did for this campaign. They had the 112-page policy book; they had the trains, buses, and planes running on time; they had a well-rested leader with low expectations in a blue denim shirt. Fairbairn had been telling people not to worry—the

Chrétien she had known for so long would show up. Now she was beginning to see that Chrétien.

On a trip through Shawinigan, she wandered off with him into the river valley for a short break. Away from the political maelstrom, he talked about how his father and grandfather grew up in this place, and how he still felt the presence of them. Fairbairn got the sense that day that the essence of Chrétien hadn't changed. He was still a man who had "a very real understanding of what ordinary people need to have to live a life—and the odds so many of them are up against."

On the campaign's very first day, Campbell offered the jaw-dropping message that the unemployment rate wouldn't dip into the single digits until the turn of the century. She was trying to be refreshingly honest and cool. She wanted to do politics differently. "I can say how many jobs I'd like to create, but that's old politics," she explained. With her new politics, however, she offered no hope to Canadians who were worried about their future.

The driver of the Tory campaign bus, a veteran of many election wars, was known for his down-home political acumen. On hearing Campbell's remark, he was astonished. When the party brass piled onto the bus, he told them, "That's it. Over. We're done."

Someone responded, "Oh, relax. It's only the first day."

"Doesn't matter," said the driver. "It's over."

Campbell had forgotten that what Brian Mulroney won on in 1984 was "jobs, jobs, jobs." She was campaigning on "No jobs, no jobs, no jobs."

Chrétien's debut was hardly spectacular itself. In the opening moments, he talked about a return to the good old days, an image well suited to yesterday's man. The good old days of the Liberals' last stretch in power featured the stagflation of the late 1970s and the deep recession of the early 1980s. But the crowds were warm, and he got a special lift when he arrived late that first night in Prince Edward Island. Though it was about two o'clock in the morning, some three hundred people had waited up to greet him. Fairbairn said she went to her room thinking, "This is going to work."

Campbell made a second controversial declaration. She said she couldn't tell voters how she would eliminate the deficit until a couple of months after the campaign. The books were in too big of a mess. But it was her party and she was in power and they were her books! Chrétien was in Kingston. "Ridiculous! . . . What a statement!" he told reporters. "This has got to be the easiest campaign any politician has ever had to run. All I have to do is read her statements from the day before."

Soon he was reading yet another chapter from Campbell's book of doing politics differently. In answering questions about reforming social programs and the need for a dialogue with Canadians on it, she explained that the forty-seven-day election period was "the worst possible time to have such a dialogue." The issues, she said, were much too complex to deal with in that framework. The media responded scathingly. The Liberals had set up a quick-response task force modelled on the war room that James Carville and George Stephanopoulos ran for Bill Clinton's 1992 presidential campaign. The task force members had collected almost every quote Kim Campbell ever made, and every time she contradicted herself, the media would receive faxes of her earlier statements or other information that could be used to impugn her.

Meanwhile, Chrétien released his Red Book. He wanted to do it from the hotel where the Aylmer conference had been held, to make the connection, but it was booked. Though many of the policies had been laid out in the pre-campaign, voters now had them in a published document that they could later wave in Grit faces if their promises weren't honoured. The main plank of the book was the $6-billion infrastructure program, designed to help the economy out of the recession. Other features included a replacement tax for the GST, tighter gun-control laws, the appointment of an independent ethics counsellor, and the somewhat modest deficit-reduction package. As for the rest, analyzed the Trudeau biographer Stephen Clarkson, it might just "as easily have been expressed in the 1960s and 1970s by the Pearson–Trudeau party in its more generous moments."

But the book was a hit. "Be like Billy Graham," Donolo told his boss. "Carry it around like it's your Bible." While the original plan was to use it to show that the party had substance, something else happened. The Liberal consultant John Duffy, who worked on writing it, said it turned into "this magical weapon of accountability. It became this emblem of the new politics, a symbol of doing politics differently, which was supposedly Kim Campbell's brand."

Nonetheless, the public was slow in moving to the Liberals. Their support stayed the same, at roughly 37 percent, throughout the first month of the campaign. Voters who began losing hope in Campbell were switching to the Reform Party in the West and, in some cases, to the Bloc in Quebec. The NDP, under the diligent but plodding Audrey McLaughlin, couldn't attract much attention.

In Quebec, Chrétien, now identifying himself as the "man with a plan," was in a battle to win his own riding of St-Maurice, to which he was returning after his temporary stay in Beauséjour. Across the province, the Bloc was far out in front of the Liberals, and in the Shawinigan area, its candidate, Claude Rompré, held an early lead in the polls. Chrétien, however, was confident enough to barely set foot in the riding until the end of the campaign.

In early October, three weeks before election day, he flew into Montreal. His aides told reporters he had basically nothing on his schedule for the rest of the day. A little rest time, they said. However, a radio reporter discovered that Chrétien had been whisked away to a $1000-a-person cocktail party with the corporate elite in Westmount. They paid that much because Chrétien looked to be the future prime minister and here was a chance for some access to him. But this was hardly a good fit for Chrétien's blue-collar campaign. Worse, he had seemingly tried to do it on the sly.

Though it was a nice opening for Campbell, she was slow to pick up on it. Chrétien, meanwhile, came forward to answer the charges directly. Well, he said, it was a cocktail party for the Laurier Club, and he was a member, so why not drop in? No favours would be done for anyone there, nor would there be privileged access. "My wife is a member. She is the only one who has privileged access to me." But why, reporters pressed on, was he meeting with millionaires? "You know," said Chrétien, "millionaires vote too."

His next step was to tackle the Bank of Canada's governor, John Crow. Crow was loathed by many in the Prime Minister's Office and the Liberal caucus. They found him insufferably snooty and arrogant. Chrétien pleased his flock with the announcement that Crow's anti-inflation zealotry, which, Liberals argued, had put tens of thousands out of work, would end under a Liberal government. In the future, promised the leader, monetary policy would have to "take into account job creation as well as inflation."

Chrétien had a comfortable lead going into the televised debates. He managed to avoid most of the traps his opponents tried setting for him and turned the debates into non-events, which was exactly, given his lead, what he wanted to do. No one performed exceptionally well and no one did the opposite. Campbell needed a big lift, but she didn't prepare diligently. While she showed her zip on occasion, she wasn't able to get the boost her campaign badly needed. The Bloc's Lucien Bouchard, a man of established debating credentials, held steady but was unable to flatten Chrétien.

As election day approached, there was no doubting the outcome. Kim Campbell was smart enough, quick enough, and had that sassy edge that can be appealing in a leader. Her potential was limitless. But she had been catapulted to the leadership of her party too soon. She was too new to the leadership, too new to federal campaigns, too new to the national media. Her early mistakes had touched off a journalistic feeding frenzy, and she couldn't halt the negative momentum. Even on the good days, the spin was bad. Rumours began to circulate that she was spending more time in the evenings with her Russian partner than she was preparing for the next day's campaigning. "One day they were saying she was shacked up with her boyfriend in B.C.," recalled her adviser, Jodi White, who accompanied her for much of the campaign. "Well, I was there, and that wasn't true. She was on anti-biotics and in bed recovering. The boys who were saying that stuff wouldn't blink if one of their own was having a little fun."

Being so new to a national campaign, Campbell needed a deep and efficient support system. She didn't have it. The campaign director, John Tory, was simply not up to the task and bore heavy responsibil-ity for the party's collapse. The analytical ability of the usually capable Allan Gregg went missing in action.

The responsibility for the campaign's final calamity—the notorious Forrest Gump ad—lay more with the campaign's management team than with Kim Campbell. The decision to run the advertisement was one that would reverberate with profound consequence for the politics of the nation in many elections to come.

The Tories' advertising strategy had been lame and vacuous. One much-repeated spot featured Campbell mouthing platitudes that were followed by a voice-over saying simply, "It's time." Canadians were left wondering, Time for what? Chrétien told them what. "It's time, all right," he exclaimed. "It's time for a change! It's time to get the truth! It's time to throw them out!"

Desperate, the Tory ad men then switched course. They decided to pick up on the favourite theme of Quebec intellectuals, as illustrated by the Alain Dubuc analysis. They went after Chrétien as a man unfit to be prime minister: a hayseed. They ran a commercial with a series of unflattering photos of him. Anonymous mocking voices chipped in along the way. "Does this man look like a prime minister?" asked one. Another declared, "I would be embarrassed with this man as prime minister."

Allan Gregg didn't intend for the ad to target Chrétien's physical disability, the small disfiguration at the corner of his mouth. But he might have known, given his experience, that it would be interpreted in such a way. As soon as the ad first ran, Thursday, October 14, at 7:35 p.m., complaints began to come in. The CBC then ran a news report that drew more attention to the ad's distastefulness. As early as the next morning, Tory headquarters and Tory candidates were being deluged with calls and faxes from angry voters. The backlash had begun. Allan Gregg got a call at his hotel from John Tory. "You better get back here. . . . There's an absolute shit-storm on the telephone, and a lot of people are starting to cut and run." Even the March of Dimes was calling, asking why the Tories were making fun of people's disabilities.

By now, Tory MPs were threatening to resign if the ad wasn't pulled. One former Cabinet minister, Sinclair Stevens, telephoned Liberal headquarters to say how ashamed he was of his party. Gregg was angered by demands to pull the ad, because he knew it would amount to total surrender. He also thought the ad might work, and later claimed that a couple of tracking polls had showed the party going slightly up after it appeared. But if that was the case, the negative publicity it was generating soon would have reversed that trend. Campbell heard his arguments but announced to the media that the ad was being pulled.

When the ad ran, many in the Liberal hierarchy were appalled. At their quick-response unit—which did some nasty things but didn't stoop that low—one campaign worker, Deb Davis, burst into tears. The campaign director, John Rae, and other party officials happened to be screening their own ads at the home of the head of their advertising team, Kevin Shea. They turned on the TV and, recalled Shea, "There was the Tory ad, attacking Mr. Chrétien. We watched it. Everyone was just sick. John Rae, he was hurt. You could see it in his face."

In Winnipeg, Sharon Carstairs was worried when she saw the ad. "I thought this was going to hurt him. I hated it. I thought it was awful. But I had seen enough negative campaigning in the United States to think maybe this would work." In the morning, she went to the office of the popular radio talk-show host Peter Warren. When she saw the rate at which his fax machine was pouring out venomous reactions to the ad, she changed her mind.

Perhaps the least surprised man on the Liberal team was Jean Chrétien himself. He had told Donolo earlier in the campaign that he expected the Tories to try to smear him in this way. He had experienced it all his life. He knew it was out there. In New Brunswick the day after the ad appeared, he responded, exploiting the moment for all it was worth. "It's true that I have a physical defect," he said. "When I was a kid, people were laughing at me. But I accepted that because God gave me other qualities, and I am grateful."

Chrétien was handed many gifts throughout the campaign. With this last Tory blunder, he was guaranteed not just the major victory he was expecting, but also something invaluable to politicians—the empathy of the public. He had lost some of his blue-collar appeal when he worked on Bay Street during the late 1980s and with his weak performance as Opposition leader. With that belittling ad, however, the Tories did much to give him back his prime selling point. They made him the little guy from Shawinigan again.

Before the ads ran, the Liberal pollster Michael Marzolini had Campbell running close to Chrétien in voter preference. Three days after the ads, Canadians favoured Chrétien over Campbell by a two-to-one margin. Tory numbers went into free fall. The campaign had been careening towards a terrible result, but there had remained a chance that the party could salvage forty seats or so, thus maintaining its historic place as the prime alternative to the Liberals. With the disgust generated by the ad, however, that remaining hope was lost. It was now straight to the bottom. The ad not only killed the campaign but was quite possibly the death knell of the Progressive Conservative Party as a major force in the country's politics.

Jean Chrétien's infirmities again served as his source of strength. Opponents who sought to ridicule him became the subject of ridicule themselves. The Forrest Gump appellation belonged not to him, in the end, but to the Tory campaign.

The Conservatives had won 211 seats in the 1984 election. Now the only party in Canada ever really capable of challenging the Liberals was reduced to two seats.

The Liberals had not simply won the election. Something of far greater significance had transpired: their opposition had evaporated. The Canadian political model, the two-party-plus system, lay in ruins. The only remaining paramount political force was the one Jean Chrétien commanded.

CHAPTER FOUR

BARE-BONED PRAGMATISM

"POLITICS, FOR ME, IT'S A SPORT," Chrétien said one day. "It's sports. You know, it's a very important endeavour, but . . . it's scoring points. It is winning seats and winning votes."

Idealism was never part of the scrapper's makeup. Politics was not about the pursuit of noble ideals or the realization of high ambitions for the country. It was about the fighting man getting his way. His best moments, Chrétien would say, came not with the passage of legislation but with election-night triumphs.

When he became prime minister on October 25, 1993, nothing on a grand scale was promised. There was no invoking of a just society or a great vision of the north from him. Lower expectations had always served him well. He wanted to repair the house, not build a new one.

Chrétien had run a good and efficient campaign, but by and large, he'd only had to stand and watch the opponent fall. Peter Donolo summed it up well. "Once you have the look of a losing campaign, it gets worse and worse," he remarked. "Once you have the look of a winning campaign, it gets better and better. Mistakes that might get you in trouble are sort of glossed over."

At the moment of victory, Chrétien and Goldenberg were too busy thinking of the first things they had to do, to appreciate the ramifications of what had happened. They didn't sit down and talk about how precedent-shattering the election result had been, how the opposition had been atomized. The Reform Party had fifty-two seats, the Bloc

Québécois fifty-four, the Tories two. The three parties combined had 108 seats, which was about the number the Conservatives might normally get in a losing campaign. To pose a credible threat to the Grits, those three parties would have to miraculously return to one. Putting Humpty-Dumpty together again was unlikely to happen for a long time.

The Liberal Party stood firmly in the centre, where the Canadian voter, a non-ideological breed, usually resided. Around it now lay regional parties. Reform represented Western ideology and had a well-schooled leader in Preston Manning, who embodied prairie-preacher conservative gospel. The Bloc represented Quebec nationalist ideology and was not even in the business of trying to form a Canada-wide government. The New Democratic Party, with just nine seats, was marginalized even more than usual.

Because it seemed clear that the Bloc Québécois would win a good portion of the Quebec vote in future elections, *la belle province* was no longer such a critical player in Canadian politics. Formerly, Quebec had vied with Ontario in importance, offering national parties up to seventy-five seats. With a Quebec-only party entrenched, only about half as many seats were available for the national parties.

Now Ontario stood alone as the great battlefield of consequence, and the Grits, with all but one seat, owned Ontario. The ninety-eight constituencies they won in the election would have been enough in themselves to form a government—even if the Liberals had been shut out in every other province in the country. In many Ontario seats where the Conservatives were once strong, the vote was divided between Tories and Reformers.

Canada did not suddenly become a one-party state on October 25, 1993. But the political culture had changed so much that it could well be argued that the country had moved from a two-party-plus system to a one-party-plus system. A democracy benefited from a strong and threatening opposition party, one poised to take power. Now there was no such threat.

Instead, Chrétien faced a different kind of opposition, a threat entirely unprecedented. Had anyone predicted at the outset of the campaign that separatists would become Canada's official opposition, they would have been herded up and sent off to the nearest psychiatric ward. A few years earlier, when Chrétien had cast his eyes across the floor to the governing benches, Lucien Bouchard was Brian Mulroney's minister of the environment. Now this brilliant, brooding mass of hubris, a man "driven by forces," as the author John Ralston Saul put it, "which he himself doesn't seem to understand," sat in the same chair that was once occupied by Pearson, Diefenbaker, King, St. Laurent, and for a brief time, Pierre Trudeau.

Bouchard reserved for Chrétien every vile descriptive he could imagine. With his powder-keg eloquence, he was a daunting opponent for anyone. Few dared try to divine him. Arthur Campeau, a Montreal lawyer who had worked alongside Bouchard in the Mulroney days as a special ambassador on the environment, found him a strange, volcanic brew. "I came to think that there are about eight Lucien Bouchards living within the same body. And that he shifted from one plane of awareness to another plane of awareness without even realizing that he had. I'd start off a meeting with this guy, with one Lucien Bouchard, and end up the meeting talking to another Lucien Bouchard. It was really bloody weird."

The tumultuous nature of the man baffled and angered Chrétien. He noticed how Bouchard could inflict deep personal insults upon opponents, then forget the next day that he had ever done the deed. When someone drew it to his attention, he would be half astonished and apologetic. The prime minister agreed with Campeau. It *was* really bloody weird.

The more consistent Manning was encumbered with a squawky style of speech delivery, but he was a persistent and capable force who had a thorough knowledge of the issues and a withering way of marshalling his arguments. Kim Campbell would quickly disappear, her place taken by the allegedly promising Jean Charest. And the NDP would soldier on with the unimposing Audrey McLaughlin. The party had had its best result only five years earlier under Ed Broadbent, winning forty-three seats and 20 percent of the vote. Now, it had been reduced to its lowest vote tally ever. Only 6.9 percent of Canadians supported the NDP.

The patchwork cast descended on the nation's capital in the dreariest of times. The staggering $42-billion deficit was coupled with an unemployment rate of almost 13 percent. The West was bitter about taxes, the East was racked by joblessness, and Quebec was in foul humour over the repeated constitutional batterings.

Walt Lastewka, who had served as a senior executive with General Motors and was freshly elected under the Liberal banner in southern Ontario, recalled sucking in only bad air. "Our deficit, our debt—I mean, you couldn't walk to the corner store without somebody biting your head off. Everybody was in the dumps. The country was going to hell in a handbasket. If you looked at the auto industry, they were going down; if you looked at the steel industry, they were going down. The farmers? They were going down."

Canadians were exasperated with politicians and their promises. Their 1992 vote on the Charlottetown Accord was a big middle-finger salute to them and their supporting elites. Jean Chrétien was assuming power when the country was dispirited and expectations for him and his party were modest.

"I'M REALLY GRATEFUL to be back in the St-Maurice valley," he'd said on the eve of his election victory. "These are my roots. I'm the little guy from Shawinigan, and I'm so proud of it." On the night of the triumph, he slept four hours at his cottage near Shawinigan and was awakened by his wife, who addressed him as "prime minister." He had breakfast with four grandchildren and took a congratulatory call from Bill Clinton. The president had heard that Chrétien had worked the same theme of hope into his campaign as had Clinton, and that he had borrowed the war-room strategy from the Democrats as well.

Returning to the capital, Chrétien had to find security guards to open the doors to the governing chambers. There were no liaison people from the Tory team. Chrétien and his cohort Goldenberg walked into an empty building, the Langevin Block, and started trying to connect the wires and locate the lavatories. "All I was thinking," recalled Goldenberg, "was we have an agenda and let's get it right, let's not make a lot of mistakes. Let's try to pull the public service together. Let's make sure the public service knows we see them as friends." Chrétien and Goldenberg had seen a few incoming governments in operation. One that failed to impress was Trudeau's following its 1974 election triumph. That government didn't do anything, Goldenberg recalled. "It sort of disappeared."

Chrétien immediately launched his $6-billion program to seed employment. He fulfilled his promise to cancel the Tory government's plan to purchase military helicopters. Their cost would have been almost the equivalent of that public works program. The Cold War was over, Chrétien must have thought. The deficit was already astronomical. Why pay that much for military hardware? A third decision quickly made was to establish an inquiry into the Tories' plan to privatize Toronto's Pearson International Airport. Chrétien wanted that decision overturned.

In the aftermath of the Mulroney years, the new prime minister felt that questions of ethics and trust in government were a top priority. David Zussman recalled him saying that "the people are fed up with lies and scandals and excuses. They want integrity and good government. Integrity and good government must be the beginning, middle, and end of every policy and plan we develop." It was a tall order, and Chrétien appointed his long-time mentor, the highly prudent Mitchell Sharp, now in his early eighties, to be the ethics gatekeeper. For a token dollar a year, he took an office beside Goldenberg's and set about examining Cabinet ministers' past records for possible conflicts of interest. The appointment, the columnist Richard Gwyn reasoned, was the right one. It represented "the vanishing of the varnish of sleaze that covered Ottawa these past few years." Gordon Osbaldeston, one of the more respected senior civil servants in Ottawa and a man who had also served as a deputy minister to Chrétien, put out the word that there was one thing Canadians could rely on with this prime minister: On the ethics front, he was as straight as the day is long.

Sharp was competent and colourless. John Rae, the close confidant who managed Chrétien's campaign, was more than three decades Sharp's junior, but he was far closer to his age in terms of mindset. While highly efficient, Rae was not overly burdened by imagination or a sense of humour. Colleagues joked that they could count on him cracking a smile at least once every three months. Goldenberg, tense, brilliant, defensive, shared the caution of Rae and Sharp. In this PMO, new ideas could make their way to the wastebasket in a hurry.

If Chrétien was judged by the friends he kept, he would be termed disciplined, shrewd, and prudent. His closest confidants were duller than a dial tone. Sharp had been in Ottawa almost fifty years, Chrétien thirty, Goldenberg twenty. Experience breeds caution. The three of them had one hundred years of it. Jean Pelletier, who could enjoy a glass of wine or two, brought a touch of *élan* and *savoir vivre* to the place, but it was largely a Prussian-style PMO.

The selection of Chrétien's first Cabinet proved nettlesome because Paul Martin, everyone's pick for the finance portfolio, felt that he could make a grander impact in the department of industry. He had talked to his father at length about the power of C. D. Howe, the King-era trade and commerce minister who became the so-called "minister of everything." But while Howe was able to accumulate such powers in his day, the minister of everything in the 1990s was more likely to be found in the finance department.

The new prime minister initially appeared willing to let Martin have his wish and go to industry. David Smith, the PM's Ontario man, attended one Cabinet-making session at which the Martin issue was aired. "Martin wants industry," Chrétien said. "Don't let him have it," responded Smith. He explained that the deficit numbers would be worse than imagined, that Chrétien would have to gain the confidence of the markets, and that he wouldn't get that unless he sent in the A Team. A few days later, Smith got a call late in the evening from Paul Martin. He wanted to know what exactly Smith had been telling the prime minister. After getting the rundown, Martin conceded that they were good arguments, but he still had doubts about becoming finance minister. Given the deplorable state of the nation's treasury, why would anyone want the portfolio? The authors of brutal austerity budgets had seldom enhanced their political status in the past. Why would it change now? Ultimately, however, the pressure became so strong that Martin relented and took the post.

Chrétien put Roy MacLaren in trade and Lloyd Axworthy in human resources. He felt that he needed someone with MacLaren's right-wing reputation in trade. If the PM had to say no to Washington, it would be a much easier sell at home if it came from a well-known free trader. He felt the same about Axworthy. Given the deficit, cuts would surely be coming to unemployment insurance. Someone with Axworthy's reputation could pull it off more credibly than, as a Chrétien aide put it, "some bastard who comes in with a chainsaw."

Settling the trade issue—specifically, Chrétien's wish for some amendments to the plan to extend free trade to Mexico through NAFTA—became the first order of foreign business. Clinton's election had come as some relief to Chrétien. A Democrat with values closer to Canada's, Clinton would be easier for a Liberal to work with than Mulroney's close friend Bush.

But Clinton had no interest in making changes to NAFTA. He had spent long hours cajoling reluctant party members to get the pact through Congress, and he was not about to tell his supporters to start over again because the new Canadian government wanted renegotiations. The matter was settled at a somewhat awkward late-night session between Clinton and Chrétien at the Asia-Pacific Economic Cooperation summit in November in Seattle. When the president started off their meeting by asking what Chrétien thought about all the bloodshed in the war in Bosnia, the PM did not appear to be up to speed on the issue. The atmosphere warmed up when Clinton joked about the number of Cabinet positions Chrétien had held under Trudeau. Why couldn't he ever hold down a job? the president light-heartedly asked.

On NAFTA, the prime minister had to settle for toothless side declarations to the body of the text—including one saying that Canada would interpret NAFTA in a way that maximized energy security for Canadians. Lloyd Axworthy secured a supplementary letter stating that Washington was not intent on making a power grab for Canada's water resources. It was also agreed that panels would be created to work on subsidies and dumping issues. The add-ons to the agreement were a bit of a face-saver for Chrétien, but critics on the left were dissatisfied. He hadn't lived up to his promises to renegotiate the pact or strike it down.

On the home front, meanwhile, Chrétien made a fundamental change, one that received little public attention, in the way the government functioned. He began paring down the political apparatus Mulroney had built up to oversee the federal public service. Mulroney had come to power following many years of Liberal rule, and he'd concluded—just as Diefenbaker had done when he took over from the Liberals in 1957—that the bureaucracy had become biased towards the Grits. Therefore, more political oversight had to be exercised.

Chrétien chopped down the forest Mulroney had put up. He reduced the number of Cabinet committees from sixteen to four and did away with the powerful Priorities and Planning Committee. The number of Cabinet ministers was dropped to twenty-three from the almost forty who'd served under the Tory leader. The staffs of ministers were also slashed.

Because the bureaucracy had always served him well, Chrétien decided to place considerable faith in it. He wanted a collegial relationship with the bureaucrats, as opposed to a confrontational one. He and Mitchell Sharp called together all the deputy ministers and laid down the new operating principles. The staffs of the political ministers

would cease to wield great power over the deputies and their departments. "There's no longer any chief of staff in the government except
myself," Chrétien told them. "You deputy ministers are in charge of
legislative and administrative advice to your ministers. Political advice
is not your turf."

Some, including close supporters of the prime minister's, looked
upon the broad changes with suspicion. They worried that the bureaucrats—who elected these guys?—would set their own rules and impose
power in an unchecked way. Percy Downe, the Prince Edward Islander
who would later become Chrétien's chief of staff, was vigorously
opposed, as was Dennis Mills, the colourful Toronto MP who had
worked in Trudeau's PMO and thought the decision was just plain
dumb. "The first time I heard about what he was doing, I went to
caucus and I said, 'For God's sake, fix this!'" recalled Mills. He had
experience with bureaucrats under Trudeau. "One of Trudeau's guys
told me something about the 'crats. He said they have a system
called MAD. It stands for maximum administrative delay. If you're
a politician and you don't kiss ass, that's what you get: maximum
administrative delay."

Though the MAD term was not widely used, many agreed that
the appelation was not without merit. The problem under the Tory
system, explained Chrétien, was that "they put a layer of people
between the minister and the bureaucrats. So the minister never
benefited from the experience of the bureaucrats." The Tory minister, said Chrétien, had "twenty-six kids going and arguing with the
deputy minister and not discussing policy. They were just discussing
patronage."

In his initial months in power, Chrétien took another decision that
would later prove to be of far-reaching consequence. The prime minister quietly dropped his Red Book pledge to create an independent
ethics counsellor who would report to Parliament. No one foresaw
that ethics would become a predominant issue, so the move was barely
reported. David Zussman talked to Chrétien at length about why he

was breaching the promise, and he believed what he heard. "I think the prime minister felt that it was one of those issues where he thought—I remember the discussion clearly—that the cost of it would be way out of proportion to its value. It would be like creating a new privacy commissioner or information commissioner." Zussman did the costing for him. It would require about $10 million a year.

Of far greater visibility was the issue of the future of John Crow, the governor of the Bank of Canada. Having stated that he would likely appoint someone new, Chrétien found himself facing mounting opposition from Bay Street—but not enough to make him change his mind. While Crow's near-manic obsession with killing inflation had many positive long-range effects, his medicine was excessively painful. Leading economists had repeatedly warned that with his high-interest-rate and high-dollar policies, he would stoke the recessionary flames, hurt free trade (by keeping the dollar high), and drive up the deficit and the debt. Mulroney once had sent over an adviser, Peter White, to ask Crow if he would consider moderating his policies. True to form, Crow was recalcitrant.

By 1992, a think-tank was calculating that Crow's policies had increased unemployment by a whopping 2.1 percent, reduced economic growth by 3.1 percent, and added $25 billion to the deficit. In effect, he had been a godsend to the Liberals because he so hardened public attitudes against the Mulroney Tories. While the tackling of inflation was a vital task, it could have been done at a more moderate and far less costly pace.

In December 1993, Paul Martin met with Crow to gauge his openness to allow for some modest inflation. He was greeted with the same inflexibility that the Tory emissary had received. In the end, Martin effectively fired Crow, touching off elation in the PMO and among the many Liberal caucus members who had had to deal with the bank governor. "The beauty of it," said Peter Donolo, who was among those put off by Crow's arrogance, "was that you didn't need some [expletive deleted] like him to prove you need a tough monetary policy."

For Chrétien, a great source of pleasure was the calm reaction of the markets to the change. What was all that fear, he wanted to know, over the dumping of John Crow? The dollar, he noted, had actually risen a cent. "Look," said the prime minister, "at the collective judgment of the business community on that." Meanwhile, Crow's replacement, Gordon Thiessen, accepted the new government's slightly higher inflation targets and began to work comfortably with his political bosses.

Even though Chrétien had swung right at the Aylmer conference, Liberals like Dennis Mills never doubted his willingness to take on the rich and powerful. Mills, for example, loved his take on the banks. "I told Chrétien when we were in Opposition that we've got to kick the shit out of the banks because they are not treating small businesses properly. So when he made me parliamentary secretary to John Manley [then industry minister], he let me take the lead role in kicking the shit out of the banks. Chrétien encouraged it totally. He just let me go crazy."

Chrétien liked the reviews and approval ratings he was receiving as the New Year turned, and he spoke of having put the country in a more relaxed frame of mind. "On substance, we're different," he told the journalist Bob Fife. "We're not perceived as working for big business." Nor was he tilting too far in the other direction. "The people on the left say Chrétien is too much on the right. And the people on the right say Chrétien is too much on the left. I say fine, that's perfect for me. That's exactly where I want to be."

He boasted of a change of governing style as well. "The Cadillac is in the garage. My wife did not take up the office that existed for her in the Prime Minister's Office, and she didn't buy new furniture." Less flash is "natural for me. It's not something that I have to discipline myself to do. I'm like that." An American embassy official reported a Chrétien sighting at a movie theatre. The diplomat was waiting for *Schindler's List* to begin when down the aisle, popcorn in hand, came Jean Chrétien. His wife soon joined him, and after the film they strolled out with the other patrons.

Not everyone was sold on his apparent modest ways. Wasn't it a bit strange, asked the Quebec political columnist Lysiane Gagnon, that having worked for a Bay Street law firm and for Gordon Capital, and having made all those big dollars, Chrétien could boast about his humble lifestyle? "Coming from a man who was the well-paid darling of the Canadian financial elite during his years away from politics, this simple-folk showing-off smacks of pure demagoguery," she wrote. "It should be seen for what it is—a cheap way of catering to the country's deeply ingrained Puritanism."

The PMO wouldn't reveal his salary for the work at Gordon Capital and the law firm, but some sources put his income at close to a million a year. For Gordon Capital, he was a representative on the board of British Columbia Forest Products Ltd. Other corporate boards on which he served were those of the Toronto-Dominion Bank, Consolidated Bathurst, which was a subsidiary of Power Corporation, and the Viceroy Resource Corporation, a Vancouver gold-mining company.

But if Chrétien had done well working in the boardrooms, those who knew him were quick to point out that it didn't mean he took on a boardroom lifestyle or character. While Mulroney became a bona fide member of the club—while he oozed the lifestyle of the rich and famous, while it was clear he was out to impress high society— Chrétien was different. He liked the comforts but was never a member of the class. From the group of newly elected MPs who arrived in 1993, there were certain types he favoured. Colleagues noticed that, by and large, they were not the high rollers. "We have a certain number who you could tell when they arrived on this earth their parents thought it was the Second Coming," observed Bonnie Brown, the Oakville MP. "Nothing has happened since to disavow them of that notion." Chrétien, Brown said, "just wouldn't warm to them. He'd be kind of nervous of them."

His Cabinet, however, featured the most prominent names. One new face belonged to Art Eggleton, who was made Treasury Board president and therefore became responsible for the $6-billion infrastructure fund, which the opposition parties were already denouncing as a Liberal pork barrel. To handle the crisis brought on by the collapse of the fishing industry in the Atlantic region, Chrétien had the talented and ambitious Brian Tobin. Allan Rock, a high-gloss, bilingual star of the legal firmament from Toronto, took the justice portfolio. John Manley, first elected in 1988, became minister of industry. Though he had a staid, conservative image, he had been an Ottawa municipal activist who started a charity to fight poverty in the developing world and who opposed the 1991 Persian Gulf War.

Chrétien also gave some key slots to women. Hamilton's Sheila Copps was made environment minister and deputy prime minister. No one, Sheila Copps included, seemed to know what the DPM's duties might entail. But she had to be up to speed on a huge range of issues, which, she would acknowledge, was not easy given that it was her first time in Cabinet. In the category of powerful women, she joined Jocelyne Bourgon, a forty-three-year-old career civil servant who became the first female clerk of the Privy Council, the top bureaucratic job in the country. Anne McLellan, a former law school dean from Alberta, was a rare breed—a female Liberal from the West who could win a riding. She thus was guaranteed a seat at the Cabinet table. Chrétien called her to his office and said, "You are going to be my minister of natural resources." McLellan's response was, "Oh, but I don't know anything about that." She didn't realize that lack of expertise in a discipline was not something that traditionally got in the way of prime ministerial appointments. How about, McLellan suggested, "something in my area, like solicitor general?" No, came the reply. "I want to send a signal to your province that we understand how important this is, that we've turned a page in terms of the past, the National Energy Program."

PARLIAMENT OPENED. Jean Chrétien entered the Commons debating chamber for the first time as prime minister on January 19, 1994. More striking, however, was the appearance of Lucien Bouchard. The high priest of separatism descended into the chamber from the oak-panelled Opposition leader's quarters—the same quarters that had once served as the office of the prime minister, the same quarters where Lester Pearson had chosen the design for the Canadian flag.

It was expected, given Bouchard's agenda, given the fires that burned within him, that he would outshine the others on the first day and indeed the lava flowed throughout a thirty-six-page speech. "Take a look at the Western world," he said. "Ninety-five percent of its population lives in nation-states. And the fact is, Quebec is the only nation of more than seven million people in the Western world not to have attained political sovereignty. I invite the members of this House to reflect on this."

For his part, Chrétien lauded the multicultural dimension of Canada and spoke of the one million francophones living outside Quebec who weren't rebelling against the country and had helped make Canada a model nation for the world. He later expanded on the thought. "We have coloured people, visible minorities of different kinds," he told reporters. "But we're all in the Canadian family, and it's what I said to Bouchard. I said, 'This is modernity. This is the idea that should exist in the world, this ability that we have had in Canada to live together with our diversities.' Something that some of his supporters cannot see."

Asked a related question about ethnic confrontation in Bosnia, the prime minister offered those same reporters a profound thought. "One of the most dangerous notions in humanity is the notion that the land and the blood have to match." Some in the Parti Québécois have this problem, he added. "They talk about their blood brothers."

A month later, Paul Martin brought in his mild and tame first budget as finance minister. Though the Tory books had been worse than expected, and the Grits had been left with a $42-billion deficit, Martin stuck to the party's promised target of bringing the deficit down to $25 billion in three years. Analysts had trouble figuring out how his numbers could make even that modest goal possible. This sounded more like a continuation of Mulroney budgeting than anything else. Was Paul Martin a deficit dove? Had Chrétien been too steeped in old-fashioned Liberal spending habits to countenance bold change?

It was clear, thought David Zussman, that the PM and Martin initially had different perspectives on the deficit issue. "Martin was basing his view primarily on his experience as a private-sector owner of a large corporation. He was saying, 'Hey, if this was a company, I'd be in big trouble.' And Chrétien is coming at it from the context of a Trudeau government, where that sort of thing wasn't that big of an issue."

But Martin wasn't pushing for a big-bang first budget either. The main problem was time. Since the budget traditionally came down in February, there was not really enough of it to do a major overhaul of the nation's finances. There was no choice, Martin later explained. "Sixty days to do a budget with a brand-new government? . . . How the hell can I go to somebody who's never been in government before and say, 'Look, we really think you need to cut your spending.' The guy says, 'What do I know about my department? I'm still learning where the washrooms are.' Everybody at this point was a rookie."

While Martin didn't oppose moving gingerly at first, he would soon think differently. The Liberals, in not addressing the enormity of the fiscal crisis in their first budget, were moving close to the brink and would have to resort to extraordinary measures.

Martin did take an axe to a couple of departments. He cut $2.4 billion from unemployment insurance, tightening eligibility requirements and reducing payments. The other big loser was the defence department, where 16,500 jobs were cut and several military bases mothballed. But these changes trimmed the deficit by only $1.5 billion.

At defence, David Collenette was running the show. He had wanted transport, but the PM argued that defence was one of the best jobs, saying the military would salute him and he would get to travel the world. Collenette worried about the coming cuts. Chrétien said not to. But thirty-three existing or planned military installations were affected by Martin's first budget, among them the Collège Militaire Royal in St-Jean, Quebec. It was the only facility, as a steaming Lucien Bouchard noted, where training was done in the French language. "They'll jump on anything, the Bloc," Chrétien replied. "They want to separate, so why do they worry about Quebec institutions?" He sided with Bouchard, however, on the hit the province was taking from tobacco smuggling. Quebec demanded a major cutback in federal tobacco taxes to combat the problem, and Chrétien responded.

Reflective, perhaps, of the tendency to give new governments a honeymoon period before drawing out the knives, most media outlets gave the first budget a passing grade. The major exception was *The Globe and Mail,* which ran a stinging headline: "Martin Cowers before Debt Mountain." *The Globe* was the business paper, the paper Martin read more closely than any other—and it was only getting started with its invective. Andrew Coyne penned several clarion calls that made a compelling case—one which would soon be vindicated—for dramatic action. Finance did not respond kindly. At the newspaper's Toronto headquarters, Martin and Coyne traded heavy insults at an editorial board meeting that turned into a shouting match. "Calm down. You're going to have a heart attack," Martin said. "I'm not the one pounding the table," Coyne replied.

In the Commons, Preston Manning led the Reform Party assault, asserting on a daily basis that there was no alternative to massive spending cuts. That Chrétien didn't understand this was tantamount, he said, "to the captain of the *Titanic* not believing in icebergs. And that's bad for the passengers." Far from being swayed by any criticism, Chrétien appeared on an Alberta open-line show to vow that no big new spending cuts—none!—would be necessary for the Liberals to attain their deficit targets.

But economic conditions began to change. Interest rates in the United States rose, and there came the usual rebound effect in Canada. This meant much higher payments on the interest on the national debt, which in turn meant a larger deficit. The Liberals therefore had no chance of meeting even their limited deficit-reduction targets without further action.

Martin imposed a freeze on all new spending and began to prepare a full-scale attack on government expenditures. While it was a clear contradiction of what the prime minister had said in Alberta, Chrétien was prepared to give Martin some room. He knew what it was like to be undercut by the PMO. In 1978, he experienced one of the worst humiliations of his political career when Trudeau returned from an economic summit in Bonn and announced—without even warning his finance minister—$2 billion in budget cuts and reallocations. Though Trudeau should have been more respectful, Chrétien had brought some of the problem on himself. As his deputy minister in finance, Tommy Shoyama, would point out, Chrétien was not a student of written documents. In finance, one had to be. Street smarts couldn't get you by. It was not a portfolio for a populist like Chrétien, who, Shoyama and others suggested, was in over his head. In the wake of Bonn, many in the government thought that he had no choice but to resign—that he should do so out of self-respect. Chrétien hung in.

When Paul Martin imposed his spending freeze, it was met with opposition by some ministers. At Cabinet, one began talking about a new project he had in mind. As recounted by Edward Greenspon and Anthony Wilson-Smith in their book *Double Vision*, Chrétien slapped him down. "Didn't you just hear the minister of finance? Just ten minutes ago, he said there wouldn't be any more money." A little later, another minister piped up to demand new spending. "Didn't you hear me ten minutes ago?" Chrétien asked. The next minister who asked for money, he threatened, would get a cut instead.

The portents were dark. Even the modest cuts of the first budget were meeting concerted opposition. In talking of the dignity of work, Chrétien told reporters in Ottawa that people don't like to be staying home and receiving money. "It's better to have them at 50 percent productivity than to be sitting at home drinking beer at zero percent." He later had to apologize for implying that the jobless were a bunch of beer guzzlers. Instead of the phrase "unemployment insurance," which they believed encouraged the stay-at-home culture, the Liberals began using "employment insurance." Some of the money from the program would go to retraining, job counselling, and job-relocation expenses.

In Shawinigan, Chrétien was met by union protesters who smashed windows and called him a liar. Crowds pushed at him as he made his way from his constituency office to a press conference. When he got to the room where he was to speak, security officers slid closed some glass doors behind him. The force of the demonstrators shattered the glass. He had promised jobs, they said, and all he had done so far was cut benefits to the jobless.

He had come in the spring of 1994 to his hometown, where unemployment was 15 percent, from the East Coast, where a crowd of over a thousand marchers in Bathurst, New Brunswick, had burned him in effigy. After the trip, he told reporters there would be occasional bumps in the road. Nothing unusual, he said, looking back forty-five years. "If I recall, on my honeymoon, I had a problem with my car."

ONE OF HIS FIRST SIGNIFICANT ACTS as prime minister was a curious one. He brought forward gun-control legislation, the centrepiece being a universal firearms registry. In the wake of the 1989 Montreal massacre at École Polytechnique, the Tories, under then Justice Minister Kim Campbell, had brought in a gun-control program of their own, one featuring requirements for safe storage of firearms and tightened screening of applicants for firearms' licences. Moreover, a registry system of sorts—though not as broad as the one the Liberals were planning—was already in place in Canada.

But the Chrétien strategists had trained their sights on Campbell earlier and wanted to one-up her on the gun issue. In office, they were having to cut expenditures widely and were looking for ways, Goldenberg would later explain, to show the public they were in fact Liberals. They worked out a gun-control plan that was almost cost-free—or so they thought at the time.

Allan Rock's justice department, which wasn't used to administering massive programs involving millions of Canadians, was given jurisdiction over the plan. There were an estimated six million owners of firearms in the country, a number that surprised many urbanites who were unfamiliar with Canada's gun-oriented recreational and hunting culture, especially in the West. Handguns accounted for about 20,000 of the 100,000 new firearms sold annually.

Although polls showed that Canadians favoured the gun-control measures by a broad margin, the gun owners, supported by the Reform Party, gathered with considerable force. Chrétien was surprised at the ferocity of the counter-campaign. This was a motherhood issue for him. He had always taken great exception to American gun culture, which he considered the most uncivilized aspect of that great republic.

In Canada, levels of violent crime had been increasing by about 5 percent every year since 1977, but proponents of the new legislation had trouble tying the rise to the possession of firearms. The number of robberies, for example, had shot up substantially over the previous decade, but those involving firearms had remained about the same. The urbane Rock, new to the game of politics, was not the ideal man to sell such a program. His problem, said a PMO official, was that he thought "he could reason with these people." He made his first mistake by extending the period of public consultation on the legislation far too long. It was only the first of many errors on this file made by many ministers. A program that initially looked like a walk in the park would turn into a quagmire.

Despite his difficulties, Rock was a natural for justice. Not so André Ouellet for foreign affairs. He was a man more schooled in party intrigue in Quebec than the art of diplomacy. Only a few years earlier, it had looked like he would never get near a Chrétien Cabinet. Chrétien had expected Ouellet to support him against Turner in the 1984 leadership. Since he and Marc Lalonde, a one-time finance minister, controlled the party machinery in Quebec, his support was crucial. But Ouellet reneged, and a furious Chrétien had vowed never to forgive him. They didn't speak for years. Chrétien needed him for the 1990 leadership run, however, and this time, Ouellet helped him against Martin and was rewarded in return.

When Chrétien became leader of the Liberals, he asked his long-time acquaintance Doug Roche to brief him on defence and disarmament matters. Roche, a rare breed in that he was a leftist Albertan, served as Canada's disarmament ambassador. He viewed Chrétien as a man of peace, and he thought that, left alone, the PM would steer Canada towards the high-minded international values of less militarism, less arms spending, and more development aid. But Roche had been around long enough to know that Chrétien would not be left alone.

As disarmament ambassador, Roche got a close-up look at how heavy the pressure from Washington could be. During the Mulroney years, he was at a meeting with George Shultz, the secretary of state. Shultz got indignant at one point and made a remark that hit Roche so hard he practically had to pick himself up off the floor: "Look, let's get one thing straight," said Shultz. "That land that you people occupy up there, north of the forty-ninth parallel, geographically speaking, is part of the northern United States."

From his briefing of Chrétien, Roche came away with previous impressions confirmed. The PM was a very bright man when focused, but there were times when he was not focused at all. His foreign policy would reflect the inconsistent pattern.

The PM overshadowed the low-profile Ouellet, handling all the big international issues himself. Though he looked reasonably comfortable doing so, he could usually be counted on for the occasional blunder. Asked about the booing of the Canadian anthem at a Montreal Expos baseball game, for example, he said, "It's not polite not to respect any national anthem. Even if I'm not a Communist, I respect Russia's national anthem." Of course, Communism in Russia had died five years earlier.

One of Chrétien's first tests, a NATO summit in January 1995 in Brussels, coincided with another flare-up in the Balkans, where Serb nationalism was rampant. Canada had two thousand peacekeepers in Yugoslavia, some of whom had been beaten up by apparently inebriated Serb soldiers in Bosnia. Chrétien threatened to withdraw the troops. "In Bosnia, there is no peacekeeping because there is no peace," he said at the summit. "We're frustrated. . . . We don't know exactly what the role of our soldiers is there. . . . There is a limit sometimes to being a Boy Scout." At the meeting, he won a commitment that there would be no NATO strikes in Bosnia until his troops were out.

Canada's traditional role as peacekeeper was undergoing change. Ottawa had begun the peacekeeping tradition with the Suez Crisis in the mid-1950s. There were many times since then when missions had been clear-cut, Chrétien noted, but with the end of the Cold War, the community of nations was unsure about how to proceed. In Croatia, he saw a traditional peacekeeping mission, with the Canadians preventing the Serbs and Croats from renewing hostilities. Bosnia, however, represented something different. "It's a new concept. We're there for humanitarian reasons." The government, he said, had to make subjective decisions about human rights as they applied to many countries, one of which was Georgia, in the former Soviet Union, where there was internal strife. "Is it moral for us not to intervene in Georgia?" Chrétien asked. "That's the same type of problem, but they are far away."

As it did in domestic affairs, a bare-bones pragmatism often ruled his approach. In preparing for a trade mission to China, for example, he got caught up in the debate over Beijing's human rights abuses and whether he should be condemning the Chinese or simply doing business with them. In the end, Chrétien opted for the latter. Canada simply didn't have the clout to lecture the Chinese, he felt. Speaking of President Jiang Zemin, Chrétien said, "I'm the prime minister of a country of 28 million people. He's the president of a country with 1.2 billion. I'm not allowed to tell the premier of Saskatchewan or Quebec what to do. Am I supposed to tell the president of China what to do?" When it came to smaller countries such as Haiti or South Africa, he said, then Canada would weigh in. "You have to measure your strength. Sometimes you will have influence, and sometimes you won't."

Lucien Bouchard saw it another way. "The less the possibility of business making a profit from a country, the more severe we are with it in terms of human rights," he charged. "But the richer the country, the more lenient we are with it."

In his early foreign policy initiatives, Chrétien focused heavily on expanding trade and investment markets. He had been a go-getter trade minister in the 1970s, when the buzz around Ottawa was about finding a Third Option—alternative markets to the United States. While endorsing NAFTA, Chrétien was hoping to broaden it to include Central and South America. He wanted to pursue Team Canada missions, leading delegations of business people and politicians around the world to forge new trade links. The odds were against his achieving any kind of meaningful counterbalance to the country's growing dependence on the United States, however. Diefenbaker had hoped to divert more trade to Britain but was unsuccessful, and Trudeau's Third Option failed to make much of a dint. Mulroney put the focus back on the United States, and now Chrétien was going the globalization route.

His trade-oriented policy, which seemed to encourage Canadians to view the world as a giant shopping market at the expense of moral priorities, drew criticism from foreign policy traditionalists. After Chrétien's China speech cast doubt on Ottawa's potential for influence, they crafted an address for Ouellet that struck quite a different chord.

CHRÉTIEN'S FIRST YEAR IN OFFICE drew to a close with the Canadian people generally pleased, but with the critics wondering what he had done. Before he had a chance to take stock, his first ethics controversy broke open.

One of his Quebec ministers, Michel Dupuy, was found to have written a letter on behalf of a constituent's application to the Canadian

Radio-television and Telecommunications Commission (CRTC). As heritage minister, Dupuy had responsibility for the CRTC. The Opposition, alleging a clear conflict of interest, demanded his resignation. Chrétien claimed it was an honest mistake and refused to ask for it. Having promised a new era of integrity, he was being watched closely on his handling of this file, but he was unable to avoid missteps. He claimed, for example, that he had consulted the government's ethics counsellor, Howard Wilson, on the matter. In fact, it was a member of his staff who did the consulting, and more important, he did so only after Chrétien had already made the decision to keep Dupuy in his post. It also appeared that Chrétien had known of the Dupuy conflict three weeks before the story broke. He had tried to keep it under wraps, and then, when the story came out, gave the wrong impression about the Wilson consultation.

It was hardly a major scandal, but since the PM had been boasting about the contrast between his and the Mulroney performance on ethics, the timing was embarrassing. Moreover, the Dupuy affair spotlighted aspects of the Chrétien style that would echo most unpleasantly through much of his stewardship. It demonstrated the relative powerlessness of the new ethics office. The Red Book had promised an independent watchdog. But Chrétien had changed that—and it was clear he could easily manipulate this overseer. The Dupuy case also showed a prime minister hesitant to confront transgressions head-on. The much-maligned Mulroney had acted quickly on conflict matters, an example being his eviction of Environment Minister Jean Charest from Cabinet for a call he made to a judge about a case involving one of his constituents. When he was faced with conflicts involving his team, Chrétien would show no such decisiveness, preferring instead to dodge, dilly-dally, and stonewall.

Soon it was revealed that four other ministers had written the CRTC about licence applications. Though none of these transgressions appeared to be as serious as Dupuy's, Chrétien felt he should come forward and make a special statement to the Commons promising stricter control over the behaviour of Cabinet ministers. "I have said before that this government will make mistakes, but they will be honest mistakes and we will always move to correct them," he vowed. "All my career I have believed that honesty is the best policy, that a government and a prime minister must level with all Canadians, tell them the truth, and treat them with the respect and intelligence they deserve."

He was hardly upset by the controversy. His first-year polls showed his approval ratings up in the high 60s. One had him at 71 percent. While observers couldn't point to a significant achievement, the pollster Donna Dasko said this wasn't really the issue. Rather, she explained, it was all about persona. "People get up in the morning and the first thing they see isn't a picture of Brian Mulroney."

CHAPTER FIVE

PERILOUS TIMES

C HRÉTIEN'S FIRST YEAR in power had proceeded quietly enough. But the relative calm of 1994 was misleading. Canada was marching towards climactic confrontations in the coming twelve months on its two biggest battlefields, the economy and national unity. It was rare in the history of the country for a financial crisis and a unity crisis to converge. But 1995 brought both. The deficit crisis had become so severe that an alarmed Paul Martin worried about "hitting the wall"—turning the country into an economic cripple, a ward of the International Monetary Fund. In Quebec, sovereigntists were laying the groundwork for a new referendum campaign. In an astonishing turn of events, Lucien Bouchard lost a limb from a savage infection, the aptly named flesh-eating disease. Odds were about five million to one against contracting it, and equally slim that he could survive it. Bouchard did, and while no one wanted to talk in crass terms about the political consequences of his trauma, everyone knew what they were. The sovereignty movement had received an incalculable moral boost. Its heroic leader had defied death. The symbolism could be drawn by those who wished to draw it.

The economic and political crises moved on separate trajectories, but history was full of dark examples of the tie between ethnic liberation movements and economic woe. It was well possible that Canada's two crises could feed off each other to produce nightmarish consequences.

Chrétien's style of governance provided Canadians with little confidence that the challenges could be met. "Mr. Chrétien is extraordinarily cautious," remarked Stephen Harper, one of the Reform

Party's rising stars. "If you look at the portfolios he held over the years, he was not known for major public-policy initiatives. My reading of him is that he attributes his long survival in politics to not making mistakes by not doing a hell of a lot."

Throughout his political career, Chrétien had gained a reputation for being more a reactor than an initiator. Torrance Wylie, who worked for Lester Pearson in the 1960s and had acted as an unofficial adviser to Chrétien since then, noticed that this was a politician who rarely got out ahead of the curve on anything. He usually waited until matters reached the breaking point before he decisively engaged. "Chrétien is a counterpuncher," said Wylie. "He's like Jersey Joe Walcott. Jersey Joe won by counterpunching."

But what if he waited too long to counterpunch? The Chrétien government had idled on the deficit issue during its first year, not wanting to make the big step, and now *The Wall Street Journal* had taken to calling Canada an honorary member of the Third World. On Quebec, Chrétien had been similarly unresponsive. A proactive leader would have come forward with proposals to appease the nationalists in the province. Chrétien offered nothing. He was confident, despite what had befallen Bouchard, that he could win on the basis of the status quo.

The word "sleepwalking" was starting to appear in a lot of critiques. Chrétien was sleepwalking to a disaster in Quebec, the critics charged, and to the same at the nation's credit houses. Everyone who knew him was aware of his stubborn streak, a streak that often manifested itself when he was pitted against lifelong antagonists. Those now demanding accommodation were members of the business establishment and the sovereigntist class. Chrétien was unlikely to yield to the wishes of either. Circumstances would have to put him in a position where he felt he had no choice. There was also the question of his relations with Paul Martin. The prime minister and his minister of finance still weren't communicating much. The effect of their poor relationship on the stewardship of the country had yet to be tested in a crisis.

On the need to control the deficit, Chrétien still wasn't sold. Canada had carried large deficits before and—as the political left was constantly reminding the prime minister—got by. Chrétien had been a prominent player in the big spending days of the 1970s, and while he had earned a reputation for being tougher than some, his braking actions didn't really amount to much. In 1995, he needed more convincing that a crisis was at hand. To his good fortune and that of the country, more evidence arrived. Interest rates rose unexpectedly in the United States. That translated to higher rates in Canada and increased payments on interest on the national debt. A second surprise was the Mexican currency crisis. The plummeting peso had the side effect of putting the Canadian dollar under attack, which put even more pressure on interest rates. A third was the *Wall Street Journal* editorial "Bankrupt Canada?" It said that "Mexico isn't the only U.S. neighbor flirting with the financial abyss. Turn around and check out Canada, which has now become an honorary member of the Third World in the unmanageability of its debt problem." Chrétien didn't normally pay attention to the conservative bible of American big business, but that editorial focused much attention on the Canadian condition.

Paul Martin was ramping up the pressure. The finance minister had recently toured the financial capitals of the world, where he was given a stern message. "I had been in difficult financial situations in business before," he explained in an interview years later, "and if you get in a difficult financial situation, you basically lay out a plan to deal with it and then you go to your bankers. They would look at the plan and say, 'Okay, that makes sense,' and they would lend you the money." This time that didn't happen. Martin set off for New York, Tokyo, and elsewhere. "Here's what we're going to do," he'd say. The response? "We've been hearing that from the last five finance ministers, and they didn't do it."

That hit Martin hard. The Canadian government's projections were no longer good enough. The message was clear. To convince these institutions to keep the loans coming, Canada had to change course.

"Not by making a bunch of projections ahead," said Martin, "but by saying, 'I made the deal. I'm cutting this, this, and this.'" Hard action. Immediately.

"The important thing to understand," said Martin, "is that when people lose confidence in a country, it has a snowball effect, so you have to take a look and see where that snowball can take you. That was the problem we had to deal with at that time."

Marcel Massé, the low-key minister of intergovernmental affairs, had been heading up a program review aimed at cutting departmental budgets. In the Mulroney government, Erik Nielsen had implemented a sweeping program review, only to see it quickly forgotten. Many assumed Massé's would meet the same fate. But as the deficit situation worsened, the program review took on more and more importance. The goal became to chop no less than 20 percent in program spending from every single government department over three years. Ministers submitted business plans to the review committee. Massé made them pass muster on several fronts.

The exercise was greeted with scepticism. The bureaucracy doubted that the PMO would ever go through with such drastic cuts. One deputy minister got up at a meeting and told David Zussman straight out that he'd heard this same old song-and-dance about ten times in the past, and nothing ever happened. So why was it any different now?

The Cabinet was uneasy. Like any Cabinet, it was divided between moderates and tougher-line types. Massé's review committee had taken on such power that it was now referred to as the star chamber. Some Cabinet members—Agriculture Minister Ralph Goodale was one— didn't appreciate its haughty attitude. Goodale was usually a calm individual, but one day he lit into the star chamber with a tirade that was talked about for weeks to come. "What gives you the right to act as judges on what generations of people have decided?" he demanded to know. "The future of thousands of people is going to be decided by you nine here. From what divine right do you derive the power to decide that fifty of my scientists will be out of work tomorrow?"

Martin had been working through Goldenberg at the PMO to get his message upstairs. They had carved out a good rapport, and Martin was generally pleased with the latitude he had been given to date. Indeed, most Cabinet ministers felt the same way. "Chrétien let you run your department," said Anne McLellan, "and he only wanted to see you if there was a problem you couldn't resolve with another minister, or if there was an issue you felt uncomfortable with in terms of the way it was evolving. But, basically, it was, 'You're the minister.' In a way I liked it, but it sort of had a brutal ruthlessness to it which was, 'Okay, I've given you this job because I have confidence in you. If, in fact, you prove me wrong, you won't have your job.' But I liked that. You knew what the rules were. There was no one looking over your shoulder."

As the deficit crisis worsened, however, Martin didn't like what he was hearing from Chrétien's shop. "They were not as concerned as I was. They had not had the exposure to the market that I had." He wished Chrétien had been with him on the trip through the foreign capitals to hear what he had heard.

The finance minister had been, as always, in close contact with his father. The senior statesman told his son, "I was the father of Canada's social revolution; you will create the country's economic revolution." The son appeared to be taking the message to heart. He applied pressure, constant pressure, until the prime minister acquiesced and acceded—with one major exception—to Martin's demands for the back-breaking budget cuts.

Chrétien also had to be pushed and prodded by others, Goldenberg included. But this was not the version of the story the PM would put forward. After all was said and done and the historic budget was on the books, anyone who dared suggest to him that it was mainly Martin's doing got a cold street-fighter stare. Chrétien wanted it known that he was the main man.

The prime minister, of course, had the power to reject Martin's bold plan, but to do so could well have resulted in the resignation of his foremost minister—something that simply could not have been tolerated when the nation's financial stability was in such peril. This argument was in fact made to Chrétien. Even if he wanted to say no, he was in a very tough position to do so.

Chrétien was viewing the deficit-cutting process from a broader perspective, as was his duty. The Quebec referendum was coming. Making dramatic cuts in social spending in a province that was heavily dependent on that spending was clearly not the way to win the hearts and minds of Quebecers. That's why he blocked one of Martin's priority plans. The finance minister wanted to redesign the $20-billion old-age pension system to create big savings for the Treasury. Even though his father had introduced the universal pension plan in 1952, and even though it was one of his treasured legacies, the son felt he could not spare it. Everyone remembered that Mulroney had also attempted this. In 1985, in his first budget, he had introduced the partial de-indexation of pensions from inflation, only to be upbraided by an elderly woman, Solange Denis, in full view of the cameras on Parliament Hill. A week later, the plan had to be withdrawn.

Martin wanted to replace the pension scheme with an income-tested plan, one that gave more to those most in need. Sensitive to any tampering with the crown jewels, Chrétien didn't like it. He felt, recalled David Collenette, that Martin had already pushed him further than he wanted to go. Pension reform was too risky. He tried getting this point across to his finance minister in a couple of meetings, but Martin dug in. He visited the Quebec Liberal leader, Daniel Johnson, and he didn't state any strong objections, even with a referendum likely on the way. Martin even visited Solange Denis, to win her approval and assure the PM that he wouldn't be accosted on Parliament Hill by a grey brigade.

Chrétien still wasn't compromising. Nor was Martin, and the budget was only ten days away. Meanwhile, Canada's stock in the markets was falling. Moody's Investors Service in New York announced that it was putting $428 billion in Canadian bonds under review. Another meeting was held, and Chrétien laid down the law. No pension reform.

Martin left the meeting, returned to his office, and called in his aides. He was considering resigning.

Goldenberg stepped in to mediate, believing he saw both positions clearly. "Martin was insisting that pension reform was necessary for a successful budget. He was saying, If this budget is not well received, we're going to have a hell of a time not only economically but with the referendum in Quebec. The PM held the opposite viewpoint. He was saying, 'Paul, I think we have enough structural reform in this budget. If you touch old-age security, it may be the straw that breaks the camel's back, and we'll lose all that elderly vote in Quebec.'"

In the end, Goldenberg suggested a compromise. Martin could do pension reform in the next budget, when Quebec was no longer in the balance. To show there would be no reneging on the deal, the finance minister would be allowed to include in this budget a statement of his intent to make the change the next time around. It was enough to assuage a reluctant finance minister. The crisis was averted.

Martin found Goldenberg to be a tremendous help. "Would Eddie have cut as much as I did?" asked Martin. "Probably not." But Goldenberg, he said, helped ease the explosive tensions in the budget-making process. He became the go-between. As Martin put it, "By the time I sat down with the prime minister, I knew exactly what was going to work and what wasn't going to work."

Those were decisive days for Paul Martin. He had heard it said so often before: the finance department was the burial ground of ambition. Michael Wilson and Don Mazankowski, two Tory finance ministers with big feet, were not at the top of the list of potential successors to Brian Mulroney. The same thing happened to Marc Lalonde and Allan MacEachen, who had each been in finance before Trudeau stepped down. Chrétien himself had almost been buried when he held that job. John Turner ran afoul of Trudeau and resigned from finance, but he was able to climb the ladder later. Walter Gordon, Lester Pearson's prized lieutenant, suffered so much criticism over his 1965 nationalist budget that he was never able to get on track again.

On February 27, 1995, Martin announced the biggest federal spending cuts in Canadian history. Government spending was to be slashed by $25 billion over three years. All departments—except Indian and northern affairs—were downsized, some brutally. Transfer payments to provincial governments for health, welfare, and education were reduced by $7 billion. The payments in those areas of jurisdiction would now come in lump sum, leaving the provinces to parcel out the money according to their priorities.

Everyone felt the axe. The CBC was hit so badly that its president, Tony Manera, resigned the day after the budget came down. The business sector suddenly saw its subsidies chopped by 60 percent. The farming community lost its $560-million Crow rate subsidy. The federal public service had 14 percent of its positions eliminated, or 45,000 jobs. In addition to the savings the cuts would bring, Martin would raise $4 billion over three years in new tax levies on gasoline and aviation fuel.

Martin and Chrétien waited tensely for reactions from the markets and from journalists. They were worried, though they need not have been. The lead opinion makers knew the guts of the package before it was presented, and most had indicated they were prepared to accept it.

Martin had initiated a new and highly effective public relations ploy. In the past, much secrecy had surrounded the budget-making process. The buildup was so hush-hush that it invited overreaction. Feeling that the old practice was "archaic," Martin signalled the direction of all his budgets well in advance of their delivery. As well, his department leaked essentials to the media, sometimes as trial balloons. The result was that on budget day, there were no shocks for the journalists, no shocks for the markets, no shocks for the public.

The budget won a thumbs-up reaction, and the deficit crisis—for the time being, at least—was eased. The elites of the country, though still wondering why Martin didn't do more in his first budget, were basically in agreement with his draconian measures. The finance minister was helped by his personal stature. He was big and strong and confident in his presentation, which lent credibility to his enterprise. Chrétien looked on, thankful that he had not yielded to Martin's desire to take another portfolio. The two other men who might have stood in his place, Roy MacLaren and Doug Young, would not have attracted the faith that Bay Street accorded Paul Martin.

Peter C. Newman, who as a journalist and author chronicled a half-century of federal budgets, had never seen one this bold. He pronounced it a "watershed document," in that "it broke the back of the defeatist psychology subscribed to by the half-dozen finance ministers who served in the Trudeau and Mulroney Cabinets. They believed, or were convinced into believing, that if their budgets contained anything but marginal reductions of obvious extravagances, their government's political base would be threatened. That was why they never dared make the kind of deep cuts that would trigger the cultural revolution required before the Canadian economy could regain some semblance of reality."

But a question arose. Could such draconian measures have been avoided? After this period, the country began a sustained stretch of economic growth that was impressive enough on its own to cut sharply into the deficit without the huge spending cuts. Given the revenue increases, perhaps the country could have moved out of deficit hell with cuts of only half the severity—with cuts, for example, that didn't stagger the health care system for years to come.

In an interview years later, Martin would acknowledge that this was possible. But he explained that given the gravity of the situation in 1995, he simply could not base his projections on the happiest of assumptions. It didn't look then as if the growth spurt would be so impressive.

"What the budget had to do was to re-establish the credibility, the financial credibility, of the country," he explained. "The reason we did so much better than the budget said was because the budget more than satisfied the tests that the markets were setting for it." Another consideration was the state of the U.S. economy. "I had two great fears. One was an increase of interest rates. The second fear I had was that the U.S.

economy was going to go into a downturn. If you read all the projections of that time, everybody said that the U.S. . . . . would go into a downturn."

Paul Genest, who worked as a senior official in the health department before moving over to the PMO in 2001 to become Chrétien's policy adviser, was initially of the view that the cuts were over the top. He saw the damage being done to health services. But from the perspective of 2003, Genest was changing his mind. "As I look now at where the rest of the G-7 is in terms of deficit and not us, I'm starting to think there was wisdom in doing it aggressively and getting structural fiscal change locked in. Because now we've been able to make very substantial investments socially."

One of the side effects of the historic budget was the crippling of Lloyd Axworthy's social security review. The review was a mammoth project aimed at reconstituting the unemployment insurance system, post-secondary education funding, and social assistance, with special focus on child poverty. During the 1993 election, the Tories' human resources minister, Bernard Valcourt, had promoted a sweeping reform plan with some similarities. But it conjured images of money being taken from the poor and was deemed too risky to get off the ground. It was so risky that when Liberals got word of the plan during the election campaign, they wanted to release it. Goldenberg nixed the idea, arguing that Kim Campbell really didn't need any more tarring, and that the Liberals might soon have to be doing some of the same things themselves. Once in office, though, Goldenberg wasn't terribly keen on Axworthy's bold plan. The minister's staff, feeling stifled by the PMO, identified Goldenberg as the ringleader of what they called the Jean "Don't Act Until It's Urgent" team.

Axworthy was an idealist, a man of imagination and big ideas who adhered to the Kennedyesque notion that lofty ideals were attainable, and that government could attain them. Given that he had been in the Commons since 1979, long enough for the average mortal to grow cynical about the entire exercise, it was remarkable that he still held to this core faith. Paul Martin had a similar faith in the power of government and the power of ideas. In this sense, neither man was the right fit for Chrétien's reactive style of governance. Neither one was a counterpuncher. On the budget Martin got action from the prime minister because the deficit problem had reached critical mass. He couldn't be patient any longer. But Axworthy's hobby horse hadn't reached that level of alarm.

Axworthy had been employment and immigration minister under Trudeau, and he had sought then to reform the unemployment insurance system to encourage people to gain the skills necessary to get back to work. Under Trudeau, Canadians could collect forty-four weeks of benefits for just eight weeks of work. With such generous terms, who would ever want a real job? Many didn't. In the winters, youths took to the slopes. The UI Ski Team, as it was cynically labelled, was born. Axworthy wanted to cut the heart out of this entitlement mentality.

But Axworthy's timing, under both Trudeau and Chrétien, was unfortunate. The country was coming out of a recession in the Trudeau era, just as it was under Chrétien. Axworthy also lacked organizational and consensus-building skills.

He spent a lot of time in meetings with the prime minister, explaining the huge dependencies created by the social welfare system and why it was bad for the economy and the country. In 1992, 3.7 million Canadians had made use of the unemployment insurance program. The entitlement mentality was firmly embedded. "Maybe during the Trudeau years," Axworthy said, "this notion built up that somehow government owed everybody something." There had to be a swing back to individual initiative. To illustrate his point, he liked to use a fishing analogy. "What's better? Give a person a fish, or give them a fishing rod and teach them how to fish?"

But while some big issues engaged the attention of Jean Chrétien, on others he went missing in action. Joe Clark had discovered this with the Charlottetown Accord. It was as if Chrétien couldn't be bothered thinking about it. The same held true for the social review. "Chrétien didn't understand the file in a conceptual way," recalled

Giles Gherson, a journalist hired to coordinate the reform plan. "The PM ended up treating social security reform as some housecleaning we had to do, not as a bold way to get people back to work. He hated bold things anyway, and he hated experimentation."

Axworthy and Gherson couldn't get Goldenberg on side either. They were idealists, and Chrétien and Goldenberg were realists. In the end, said Gherson, "Goldenberg simply wasn't a believer that we could have a revolution here. That's what made him roll his eyes, I think—the notion that we were on a bit of a crusade. His view was just get it done, and just make it smallish and keep the Atlantic caucus onside. It was a managerial approach."

Goldenberg maintained it was a question of bad timing. "Axworthy was encouraged to move before people realized the severity of the fiscal situation. The department of finance was heading in different directions, so he didn't have the resources. . . . I blame myself a bit for encouraging him." Not all was lost, however. In giving UI its new name, Employment Insurance, and in tackling the issues of job training and the culture of entitlement, Axworthy made some progress.

With all the budget-cutting and retrenching, Chrétien worried about his image and that of his party. Though pleased with the public's acceptance of the budget, he told the CBC radio host Peter Gzowski that this was not what Jean Chrétien, the working-class man, was all about. He was described as being on the right of the Liberal Party—which for him was hardly a compliment. It's "not out of pleasure, sir. I have to tell you that. I've been around a long time. It's no pleasure at all. I'm not doctrinaire, a right-winger. I'm a Liberal, and I feel like a Liberal and it's painful. But it's needed." That he hadn't really thought he would have to go to such lengths was clear from his comments the previous spring, when he said, following the first budget, that no new cuts would be necessary to tackle the deficit. He could be thankful the media didn't play back the remarks, as frighteningly off-the-mark as they were, on the release of budget two.

In his caucus, he encountered a lot of panicky faces. MPs hadn't been expecting such heavy spadework. They hadn't been consulted on the giant cuts to transfer payments to the provinces. "You've got to remember," recalled Reg Alcock, a member from Winnipeg, "that this was an inexperienced group. Many had just been elected for the first time. There was a real appetite to back off on some of the stuff. People would get upset because there would be this group or that group out there yelling at us." In that atmosphere, said Alcock, who was not normally one of the PM's biggest boosters, "Chrétien was a calming influence, a guy who had been around a long time, and who could reassure all the new faces that everything would be okay."

On health care, Chrétien tried to defend the cuts, saying that medicare had mushroomed into something it was never intended to be. It was not meant to cover eyeglasses or dental care or even ambulance trips, he said, but just to protect people from huge medical bills. "You can have medicare that is functioning in Canada and you don't necessarily have to spend 10 percent of GDP." It was close to that level in Canada, he said, and "I'm of the view that we have to reduce it to under 9 [percent], to be in the range with those who have full medicare in Europe. They manage to do it with around 8 or 9 percent of GDP. So we will do it."

Experts corrected him. Of Canada's 10 percent, a good chunk—more than in Europe—was private-sector spending. Therefore, European governments were actually spending more.

Some took his comments to mean that the social safety net was indeed on the block. Critics pointed out that while they were still paying lip service to the provisions of the Canada Health Act, Chrétien and Martin were stripping the system of the means to enforce it. It could mean the end of medicare as Canadians know it, argued the Canadian Medical Association.

With the block transfer of social and health spending to the provinces, known as Canada Health and Social Transfer (CHST), Chrétien was allowing more provincial say in the disbursement of federal monies. The premiers weren't happy to be receiving less money, and they knew they would have to respond to the shortfall by slashing welfare, hiking school tuitions, and closing hospitals, among other measures. But with the smaller, untargeted amounts, they at least won the freedom to allocate the resources as they wished—a freedom they had been demanding of Ottawa for a long time.

The federal side, in turn, could more easily dodge responsibility for weaknesses in health or education delivery by citing the flexibility given the provinces in the block transfer system. Bill Fox, one of Mulroney's key advisers, saw expert political handiwork in the government's strategy. By offloading the global package, the government had ensured that "there were no hospital closures, base closures, or massive layoffs that could be laid directly at the feet of the federal finance minister."

Some believed this decentralizing approach went beyond what was called for in the ill-fated Meech Lake Accord. "Yes," the prime minister said when Gzowski asked him if he was changing the nature of federalism. "For years, the provinces said, 'Let us run these programs.' I said, 'Fine. Run them.' . . . This is changing, yeah. It's changing to respond to the requirements of the provinces that they say, 'We need more flexibility.'"

With his disarming pragmatism, he waved away the complaints. "If you're a mayor and you have a problem, what do you do? You blame the provincial government. And when you're the provincial government and you have a problem, what do you do? You blame the federal government." Then came the kicker. "And for us, we cannot blame the Queen any more, so we blame the Americans once in a while." It was a line of defence he used repeatedly, on a wide range of subjects.

Premiers voiced their disapproval. Ontario's Bob Rae was outraged. "This is truly an historic change that literally ends the Canada that we have known and sets us on a much meaner course." In Quebec, Jacques Parizeau took note of the timing of the measures. He pointed out that Quebec would hardly be touched in the first year—the

referendum year—but then would be put through the meat grinder
for the two years following. "It's as if the federal government was
telling us, 'Hurry up and get out of Canada in '95–'96 or just wait and
see what's going to happen to you after that.'"

Luckily for the Liberals, the provinces were not able to form a
unified front against the federal government. "The feds just walked
away from this responsibility and left the provinces holding the bag,"
said the Reform Party strategist Rick Anderson. "It was amazing.
You had Alberta saying one thing and Quebec another and Frank
McKenna in New Brunswick another." Chrétien benefited from
this, reasoned Anderson. Even better, for the increased revenues he
needed, he had the GST, a cash cow for which the Tories had taken
so much blame.

Remarkably, after the most severe budget ever, the Liberals were
trending upwards in the opinion polls. The party was at 63 percent
approval. The budget hadn't fried Paul Martin—it had made him.
Chrétien drew some of the credit, as well he might have. He could be
relieved as well that there was no dramatic drop of support in Quebec.
The pro-sovereignty vote stayed stable, still at below 50 percent.

Ron Graham, the author who wrote *Straight from the Heart* with
Chrétien, said that because of the PM's very nature, Canadians were
prepared to give him the benefit of the doubt. "It wasn't just that he
had none of the extravagances and pretensions of Brian Mulroney,
though that alone would have given him a hallowed place in people's
hearts," he analyzed. "[But] his populist image and flexible approach
let Canadians believe that if he cut national institutions and programs,
it must have been because he really had to." If brutal choices had to be
made, said Graham, it was "better they were made by warm guys like
Chrétien and Martin, whose values were in the right place and whose
heads were not in some ideological cuckoo-land."

Chrétien had moved away from traditional Keynesian dogma,
which viewed deficits in a rather innocent vein. As the Aylmer conference had proved, Liberalism was changing. This was the party that had

presided over the broad expansion of government from the Second World War through to 1984. It had created the welfare state. Now it was moving from expansion to contraction. Years of it were in store. Throughout the Tory era, the Grits had attacked any moves to shrink the government, just as they had attacked free trade. Only four years earlier, in 1991, they had bashed the Tories around the block for imposing cutbacks in civil service hiring. Now they had gone further than the Tories had ever dreamed of—and they were doing it with a straight face. Liberalism was changing, and one of the most hidebound Liberals of them all, Jean Chrétien, was directing that change, along with the son of the man who was Mr. Welfare State himself.

But it was not the men who were changing the party so much as the nature of the times—times brought on in part by the profligacy of the Trudeau years, when governments everywhere were more cavalier about indebtedness. The changes of 1995 didn't mean the Liberals had stopped believing in the role of big government. It meant that they were behaving just as successful Liberal governments had always behaved: pragmatically.

SOON AFTER THE TABLING of the budget, an unexpected development took the focus off the austerity measures. The timing could hardly have been better. A fish war in the North Atlantic saw Canadian boats firing on a Spanish fishing trawler, the *Estai,* sparking a row that continued to capture headlines for weeks. The Spaniards were accused of overfishing the turbot stock by using illegal nets to catch turbot far smaller than regulations permitted. The catch was outside Canada's two-hundred-mile territorial limit, but Fisheries and Oceans Minister Brian Tobin raised a great hue and cry. The British tabloids dubbed him "Terrific Tobin." He turned the drama into a proud moment for Canada, as it faced down its European counterparts and, for all intents and purposes, won the fight.

A former radio announcer and political operative with the Newfoundland Liberals, Tobin had jumped into politics early, taking a run at what was considered a safe Tory seat on the island at the age of twenty-five. He won, and entered the Commons brimming with energy and ambition. He became a Commons brawler, an irksome member of the infamous Liberal Rat Pack, and he gained national attention for antics that included getting kicked out of the House for calling Brian Mulroney a liar. Tobin always had an eye for the theatrical. During a debate over the ethical transgressions of Sinclair Stevens, Tobin took the Tory party's conflict-of-interest guidelines, ripped them to shreds in full glare of the cameras, and littered the floor with them.

In the fish war, Tobin portrayed the Spaniards as pirates and threatened to capture more boats if they dared threaten the tiny turbot again. The European Union's fisheries commissioner, Emma Bonino, accused him of launching "a wave of terror." The fight moved to the United Nations, where Tobin beat up on Bonino before delivering his decisive melodramatic blow. Standing on a barge directly across from UN headquarters he held in his hands a tiny little turbot that, he said, came from the hold of the *Estai.* "We are down to the last, lonely, unloved unattractive little turbot clinging by its fingernails to the Grand Banks of Newfoundland, saying: 'Someone, reach out and save me in this eleventh hour as I'm about to go down to extinction.'" At another point, Tobin said, "I speak for those who have no voice: the fish!"

His gunboat-cum-showboat diplomacy was a hit. The spat united Canadians as only wars—however small they may be—can unite nations. Gone for a brief moment was the self-effacement that often characterizes the country, and in vogue for a brief moment was an American word, "patriotism." A poll showed that 89 percent of Canadians supported the Tobin wars; about the same number of Americans supported the Iraq war.

The fisheries minister also had to overcome the opposition of senior bureaucrats, who cowered at the thought of being so bold. Throughout the 1980s, there had been no such Canadian bravado on the high seas. Ottawa usually shied away from such actions for fear of creating ill will among European partners. Tobin, like other Cabinet ministers, had been told by Chrétien and Sharp to pay the deputy ministers strong heed. But there would have been no triumph in the fish war had he done so.

Tobin returned to a standing ovation in the Commons and cries of "Academy Award!" from both sides of the chamber. "You're being hailed as a hero," a reporter told him. How does it feel? "The distance between a hero and a zero is about one inch, and the time frame is about one second," Tobin responded. "I'm not getting too excited about it."

But he was an excitable, blarney-filled, and talented young man and he had become a bona fide star of the party, a scrapper cut from cloth similar to Chrétien's. As the crisis intensified, Chrétien had to restrain Tobin from going after more foreign boats. "You score some goals," he advised his understudy, "then you can play defence for a while."

CHAPTER SIX

TO THE BRINK
OF DISASTER

I N PARIS, the prime minister had addressed the French Senate and been interviewed by *Le Monde* when rumours started reaching him that Lucien Bouchard might have died.

The bacteria that tore through Bouchard's body with a frenzy had taken away one of his legs and was moving towards his upper body. Bouchard, conscious enough to realize the gravity of the moment, saw images of his life flash before him: "Every second with my father, my childhood." Taking advantage of the research capacity of computer technology, physicians found a case where the progress of the disease had been halted through the injection of a special mixture of immunoglobulins. In desperation, they tried it, and the bacteria's spread was stopped. Bouchard survived. "He had the eyes," said a friend, "of someone who had returned from the dead."

The trauma turned the nation's heart towards the man who wanted to tear the nation apart. "At moments like these," said Chrétien, "we must put political differences aside to express our personal solidarity with the suffering of a fellow human being." The prime minister telephoned Bouchard during his convalescence to wish him well. Bouchard was touched by the call, but it wasn't long before he was lashing out at Chrétien as "the assassin of Meech Lake" and accusing him of planning a further assault on Quebec's aspirations. Before the trauma, Bouchard had been the most admired political figure in Quebec. Now, having defied death, he was in the vicinity of the gods.

In the PMO, advisers debated the political impact. One recalled that President Franklin Roosevelt wore leg braces after he was afflicted with polio, and that this naturally drew sympathy from the public. Prime Minister Mackenzie King, who visited FDR often, had gone so far as to say, "I think the president is reaching the people through his infirmity more than anything else." But Chrétien's attitude towards the coming referendum did not significantly change. He still held to the complacent notion that the best strategy was good government. "Some say I have no plan to resolve the problems," he said. "But I have a good and clear strategy: it's faith in Canada. If we provide a good, honest, solid working government, everybody will want to remain in Canada." There was no need to cave in to the demands of the sovereigntists or to try to meet them halfway. He was convinced that he could win the referendum with no concessions, which would make it a better victory, a more personal victory.

He had compromised at the very last moment on the deficit, but that didn't mean he was prepared to compromise on the Quebec question, even if it meant marching the country to the brink. Secession was illegal—Chrétien was saying as much. "The prime minister has a Constitution to abide by," he declared, "and there is no mechanism in the Constitution that permits the separation of any part of the Canadian territory." What then, commentators wondered, would he be prepared to do in the event of a Yes vote? Send in the troops?

The prime minister wasn't saying, but he had, in David Collenette, a defence minister who was among the hardest of hard-liners. "My view," Collenette would explain in a later interview, "was that these guys aren't going to get away with this. This is my country. I don't care what the numbers are. It's one thing to say you want to separate. But now we start playing hardball. Because we're not going to abandon all those people who want to stay in Canada."

SHORTLY BEFORE BOUCHARD'S HEALTH ORDEAL, Quebecers— while giving Daniel Johnson's Liberals almost the same numbers in the popular vote—had elected a Parti Québécois majority government under the leadership of Jacques Parizeau. There were few politicians Chrétien held in less esteem. As well as being a secessionist, Parizeau, in Chrétien's view, was an elitist snob. "All of us are made to feel that we lack sophistication and culture," Chrétien once remarked, "because we are still close to our rural roots compared to those who have made it in the cities for several generations." It was the Parizeaus of the world who made him feel this way.

The two men had begun warring with each other fifteen years earlier, when Chrétien was federal finance minister and Parizeau held the same position in the government of René Lévesque. Then came the 1980 referendum, then Meech Lake, then Charlottetown. With Parizeau in the premier's chair, they were soon duelling again. Quebec wanted Ottawa to pay the bill for the province's staging of the Charlottetown referendum of 1992. Chrétien believed Quebec should pay, but Mulroney informed him that he had given his assurance that the federal side would take care of the bill. Chrétien at first seemed to misinterpret the conversation, stating that there had been no assurance. Finally, he received one in writing from Mulroney and backed down, announcing that Ottawa would pay Quebec $34 million in expenses.

Parizeau grinned like a Cheshire cat. Then he won another one. In the fall of 1994, Chrétien planned a Team Canada trade mission to Asia with all the premiers. Parizeau, only recently elected, said he could not afford to take the two weeks out of his schedule but was willing to send his deputy premier. Chrétien said it had to be the premier or no one. The media castigated him for his intransigence.

The other half of Team Sovereignty, Lucien Bouchard, returned to the House of Commons on February 22, 1995, less than three months after his horrifying health trauma. Torrents of applause and testimonials cascaded down upon him. Standing noble in the spotlight, Bouchard put his fingers to his eyes, as if to stem a flood. Preston Manning and Jean Chrétien praised his courage, as did many on the federalist side. "I was able to observe first-hand how compassionate and generous our fellow citizens from English Canada can be," said Bouchard, who would soon be sounding radically different notes.

He was not in a hurry to call a referendum, and he favoured a much softer question than Parizeau did—one with economic association built in, and maybe political association as well, as in the European Union model. This was pure logic. Polls showed that only 40 percent of Quebecers would support sovereignty without economic association, while 55 percent would support it with that added comfort.

Chrétien travelled to Val Cartier, Quebec, where, with a crafty turn of rationale, he mocked the new soft talk. If they wanted all these associations, economic and political, he said, why bother leaving in the first place? "All of this is the Canada as we know it." He celebrated the thirty-second anniversary of his entry into Parliament with polls showing he held a reassuringly high approval rating of 70 percent nationwide. In Quebec, he rated much lower, at 43 percent, but the number was considerably better than his dismal image might have suggested.

At the start of May, he went to Trois-Rivières, which was not far from his hometown of Shawinigan. As a teen, he had travelled by bus to the city to hear the passionate political orators of the day and been seized by the prospect of a political career for himself. It's sad, he now told the Liberals there. This is "the province where there is more poverty than anywhere else in Canada, and here I am having to talk to you about the Constitution." Bouchard rebutted him in the Commons lobby. How could he possibly talk like this, the Bloc leader asked, "when his own government went after the poor and the helpless in the first two federal budgets, forcing thousands of people onto welfare?"

Throughout the spring, the two sides continued to trade calumnies. The prime minister held stubbornly to his view that there should be no appeasement of Quebec with constitutional concessions. Such offers, he felt, would ring hollow when the promises of both Meech and Charlottetown had fallen through. He showed his attitude in a debate with his Cabinet colleague Marcel Massé over the question of devolving labour-training responsibilities to the province. Chrétien argued that Ottawa wouldn't get any credit for it. He got worked up as he talked about the issue, inadvertently handing to Massé a coffee that he had prepared for himself. "If you think it's going to change any hearts and minds in Quebec, you're wrong," he told him.

Parizeau and Bouchard also feuded over referendum strategy and the control of the sovereignty movement. But they were able to widen their tent. In June, Mario Dumont and his fence-sitting third party, the Action démocratique du Québec (ADQ), signed on to campaign for the Yes side. Though small, the ADQ represented many soft nationalists who could potentially swing a tight referendum vote into a sovereigntist victory. His action was unexpected—and it was Chrétien's inflexibility that drove him to it. "Being with Jean Chrétien was basically impossible because people in Quebec wanted change," Dumont later analyzed. "The Chrétien camp was not proposing any change. . . . The offer was status quo and shut up!"

Unlike the 1980 referendum, when the separatists had one party in their camp, they now had three—the PQ, the Bloc, and the ADQ. Unlike in 1980, the separatists now had Bouchard, and the federalists had no Pierre Trudeau. And unlike in 1980 the sovereigntists had two failed accords, Meech and Charlottetown, as evidence that renewed federalism couldn't work. Moreover, they were campaigning against a federalist side that had run up a $550-billion national debt and brought in a draconian budget that slashed social programs.

But because the polls weren't changing, the Ottawa strategy wasn't changing. Chrétien, Goldenberg, and Chief of Staff Jean Pelletier believed that the outcome would be much like the 60–40 spread of 1980. In Cabinet, the lead minister for Quebec, Public Works Minister Alfonso Gagliano, presented an unfailingly rosy picture to the others around the table. Since the referendum was a Quebec show, Anglo ministers were expected not to protest. "What would happen," recalled the Treasury Board president, Art Eggleton, "was that

Gagliano would give us a report and the prime minister would make comments on it. Then he might let another one or two Quebec ministers comment on it, and the non-Quebecers would just sit back and listen." There was only one minister, recalled Eggleton, who would challenge what they were saying. "Brian Tobin."

On September 7, Parizeau tabled the referendum question: "Do you agree that Quebec should become sovereign, after having made a formal offer to Canada for a new economic and political partnership, within the scope of the bill respecting the future of Quebec and of the agreement signed on June 12, 1995?" Chrétien was silent, refusing to comment on either the question or a bill that was introduced the same day in Quebec and laid out the framework for the province's independence. He had told reporters earlier, in a private moment, "You know, I would like to kill these guys, but I have to remain civilized."

According to Quebec legislation governing the referendum's proceedings, the Liberal Party of Quebec, headed by the dour Daniel Johnson, would have control of the campaign. Naturally this did not sit well with some in Ottawa, particularly since the provincial Liberals were making it clear that if Jean Chrétien went on vacation to Bolivia for the duration of the referendum, it would be fine with them. One of the co-chairs of the Quebec Liberals' campaign was Liza Frulla, a former minister in the Bourassa government. She and her team were still furious with Chrétien over Meech Lake. They felt that he would only throw oil on the referendum fire, resorting to scare tactics. Such tactics might have worked in 1980, Frulla said, but after Meech and Charlottetown, Quebecers were no longer naive. "We've had a crash course," she told Ottawa. "So don't give us that shit."

Sheila Copps got an early taste of who was in control. She went to Quebec City to campaign, but was booked to speak to a group of anglophones, who, of course, were already on board. "I said, 'Wait a minute. If I'm going to Quebec, I would actually like to be with people I can bring onside.'"

On September 18, Bouchard and Chrétien stood face to face in the House of Commons to open the debate. Before any words were spoken, they made eye contact, sharing faint smiles. The seats were full. Bouchard tried to get Chrétien to say he would not respect a Yes vote. He wanted to fan the flames, but Chrétien declined to give a specific answer. Preston Manning pursued the issue, asking if a vote of fifty plus one would be decisive. A clearly angered PM rose to his feet, charging that the separatists "have clouded the issue [by] talking about divorce and remarriage at the same time. And they want me on behalf of all Canadians to say that with a clouded question like that, that with one vote, I would help them destroy Canada. . . . You might. I will not, Mr. Manning."

Chrétien had support for his position from the Quebec courts. A ruling that same month said that the Quebec government's plan to declare independence after a Yes vote was illegal and unconstitutional, but that the vote could go ahead. The federal side was putting out contradictory messages, however. Chrétien's referendum minister, the meek but dignified Lucienne Robillard, said that Ottawa would honour the referendum result—no matter what it was.

For his first of three speeches in Quebec, Chrétien travelled to his hometown on October 6. "They taught me to be proud of being a francophone, and I am," he said. "They taught me to be proud of being a Quebecer, and I am. And last, they taught me to be proud of my country, Canada, and I am." He went on to point out that Quebecers, with 25 percent of the population, had come to dominate the power structure in an Ottawa that was once an Anglo enclave. For almost three decades running, the prime minister had been a Quebecer. In this, the year of the referendum, the finance minister and the foreign affairs minister represented Quebec, the prime minister's chief of staff was francophone, as were the clerk of the Privy Council, the governor general, and the leader of the official Opposition. French power was there in spades, but this appeared to have little effect on the sovereignty debate. Parizeau had talked of it earlier. "One day we will have to understand this method of using Quebecers in Ottawa to carry out designs, to achieve things that anglophones would not dare to try [to] achieve on their own."

The referendum campaign wasn't going well for Parizeau. As the October 30 vote loomed, there was no sense of momentum in his camp. He wasn't touching the masses. He came across as smug and too well fed. Bouchard noticed the lethargy. "There is a kind of worrisome silence running through Quebec at this time, a sort of apathy," he remarked. How could it be, he wondered, that Chrétien was suggesting that he might not even recognize a sovereigntist victory, a democratic majority of fifty plus one—and yet no one was reacting? "Never have Quebecers accepted such a provocation."

With three weeks remaining in the campaign, the big shakeup came. Bouchard was named negotiator-in-chief for the sovereigntists. If Quebec won the referendum, he, not Parizeau, would do the bargaining with the federal government. Though it wasn't fully realized on that day, the anouncement meant that Bouchard was now the de facto head of the campaign.

To Ottawa, this was the surest of signals—"I think our initial reaction was to laugh," recalled one PMO insider—that the separatist cause was foundering. They were dumping their leader in mid-campaign. It was a clear admission of defeat. What would follow, Chrétien's people believed, would be days of headlines saying the movement was in disarray.

But those days didn't come. The secessionists had played this one smartly. By naming Bouchard negotiator-in-chief, they could say that Parizeau was still the leader and avoid those headlines. While not alarmed, Goldenberg thought it was a clever move. "Quebecers like negotiation. What happens at the end of negotiation is usually agreement, and agreement that is not a radical agreement. So there was a comfort level."

Bouchard had expected to spend much of the campaign squaring off with Chrétien in the Commons. Now he was on home soil, and his people, touched by his near-death experience a year earlier, responded to him in cult-like fashion. In Compton Station, in the Eastern Townships, an older woman talked to him of the great men of history. "For me, you are Quebec's Gandhi, Mr. Bouchard." It was as if his suffering had granted him immunity from criticism. The Quebec government, under its minister of restructuring, Richard Le Hir, had conducted a series of studies on the economic impact of sovereignty. The studies had confirmed there would be major job losses in Quebec. With a dismissive wave of the hand, Bouchard promptly did away with them. "I don't want to hear anything about the Le Hir studies. These are not my studies." As he was approaching a podium later that day, an onlooker shouted, *"Viva, el Presidente!"*

His rhetoric took flight. On the podium, his limp pronounced, his cane a religious symbol, he bore the grievances of his people. He would start his speeches slowly and then, his eyes burning with the fury of a Rocket Richard, escalate into great, sonorous symphonies of hurt and of hope. A good part of him had never been able to shed the distress of his past: the onerous weight of the Anglo overlords on his culture; how his father, gigantic in his mind, had been deprived of the life of fulfillment he deserved. Bouchard could alternate rapidly between the rational and the emotional, and now he was in the emotional red zone, caught up in the role, seizing the moment. Old scores had to be settled, and they would be settled now. No one had so captivated the public imagination since Trudeau in 1968 and John Diefenbaker a decade before that.

The negotiator-in-chief painted a glowing portrait of a sovereign Quebec. "A Yes has magical meaning because with a wave of a wand, it will change the whole situation," he said. "The day after sovereignty, there will be no more federalists, no more sovereigntists. There will only be Quebecers." While he demonized Jean Chrétien to great effect, the PM, though mockingly pointing out that no one should believe in magicians, did not respond in kind. Debates raged in the PMO about how to answer Bouchard. Most were of the view that he was too popular to criticize. The effect was to give him a free ride, to let his calumnies stand.

"We were fifteen to twenty points ahead in the polls up to two or three weeks before the referendum," recalled Goldenberg. "You can't forget that." When they looked at the polls a few days after Bouchard's ascendancy, there was a jump of only a couple of points. Not to worry.

After spending more time in Quebec, Sheila Copps sensed trouble. She returned, went to a Cabinet meeting, and heard the same lame reports from Gagliano and company that she had been hearing all along—that "everything was going along just tickety-boo." Copps, who normally had deep faith in the instincts of Jean Chrétien, couldn't believe the attitude. Wait till thirty years from now, when the Cabinet notes are allowed to become public, she recalled thinking at the time. What a shocker it would be for Canadians to read the remarks of their Cabinet ministers and know how wrong they were.

Copps and many of her colleagues were appalled by the arrogance of the provincial Liberals. She claimed that one of them told her that they didn't even want a big victory. "What's most important," she quoted him as saying, "is that, win or lose, the margin not be too wide." Well, Copps said she thought, almost falling out of her chair, now the cards are on the table. No wonder their campaign was so anemic! There was a suspicion in federalist circles that the provincial Liberals did not want a big referendum triumph because then Ottawa would be able to lord it over the provincial wing—just as Trudeau had done following the decisive victory in 1980. The provincial Liberals would never get Ottawa to agree to the concessions they wanted. And here, Copps noted, they were as much as admitting it.

As the campaign had progressed, the divisions between the two jurisdictions in the federalist camp had widened. When Bouchard took over and the federalist lead began to disappear, the blame game started and the rift became severe. The future of the country was at stake, and the forces fighting separation couldn't stop fighting among themselves.

The focus of much of the year had been on divisions in the separatist camp, divisions between Parizeau and Bouchard. But now the most crippling division was on the Save Canada team. The phone lines between the two factions were barely open. Chrétien and Daniel Johnson were hardly talking. "It was war," recalled Liza Frulla. "It was war between us and Mr. Chrétien."

The provincial wing wanted constitutional concessions, some devolution of powers, something they could sell to the fence-sitters in Quebec who could well cast the deciding votes on referendum day. It got so that the normally calm John Parisella, a provincial Liberal with strong ties to Ottawa, pounded the table in a meeting with the federalists and shouted, "For God's sake, you've got to give us something."

Some PMO staffers moved to Montreal to work in the No headquarters for the final three or four weeks of the campaign. They included Dominic LeBlanc, the son of the governor general, and Chrétien's long-time aide, Jean Carle. They didn't feel welcome. It was as if they were from another team. "It was marked, the division," recalled LeBlanc. When the provincial staffers went out for a beer, LeBlanc and friends were left behind. They were Chrétienites. They weren't wanted.

"The relations were not good," recalled Jean Pelletier. "We were frustrated, you know. It's difficult for a Quebecer who is at the federal level to be seen as a stranger in his own province. . . . And even the federal Liberals from Quebec were not welcome by other provincial Liberals, which I think is nuts. Because as a citizen of Quebec, you have the right, even if you work in Ottawa, to show your opinion. So this was disturbing and certainly unpleasant."

The situation grew so difficult, recalled Pelletier, that "we suddenly had to impose a few things. The leader of the No camp, Daniel Johnson, he didn't want to see André Ouellet or Madame Robillard. He didn't want to see Chrétien. He didn't want to see anybody. But, you know, it was then the future of the country."

Chrétien's close friends, like Ross Fitzpatrick from Vancouver, were telling him that he had to get more involved, that he couldn't be kept in shackles and hope to win, that he had to start counterpunching. "I was there in 1980," the seemingly unworried Chrétien told the media. "You remember the polls. So check them out and look at the results, and you will feel confident. Because last time, it was much closer than this time and the result was 60–40." Lucien Bouchard was dismissive. "He's betting on 60–40?" he asked. "For whom?"

For his second of the three planned appearances, Chrétien went to Quebec City, where he tried to cast doubt on Bouchard's idea of a partnership with the rest of Canada in the event of a Yes vote. He referred to him as Lucien in Wonderland. "The truth must be told: In the real world, there are no magic wands."

Paul Martin, meanwhile, had journeyed to Bouchard's home territory of Chicoutimi and found out what a little magic could do. On a hotline show, he was "absolutely hammered" by callers who alleged that Quebec was getting a bad deal from Ottawa's equalization-payment formula with the provinces. The truth, the finance minister tried to tell them, was exactly the opposite. But he got nowhere. "I remember being absolutely stunned, and then I found out it was a common view." At that point, he realized "what a job" Bouchard and Parizeau had done on Quebecers.

In Quebec City, Martin warned that a sovereign Quebec would not have membership in NAFTA, which could well mean "the economic isolation of Quebec." This would jeopardize "90 percent of exports; close to one million Quebec jobs." Parizeau took out Martin's qualifiers and told reporters that Quebec had only 3.2 million people working to begin with, and that Martin's remarks were outrageous scare-mongering. The Quebec media beat up on Martin. He hadn't made many mistakes since becoming minister of finance. This was one of them—and it hurt. "What happened was I didn't say that," he explained. "Parizeau took it and distorted it."

In another outbreak of fear-mongering, Claude Garcia, the president of the Standard Life insurance company, told a meeting that separatists must not only be defeated, "We must crush them." When Liza Frulla, the Quebec co-chair for the No side, heard this, she could feel the chills. "I was sitting there, and shivers ran up my spine. I said, 'Oh my God, we're in deep shit. It started there. . . . You can't put people down like that."

With a week and a half remaining and Bouchard in full fury, the momentum had swung dramatically to the Yes side. Chrétien was now being told straight out that he had to forget about Daniel Johnson and do something. Tobin, Collenette, and Copps were coming at him hard. They were telling him to "get off your ass or we're going to lose the country."

Sheila Copps organized a trip to Sept-Îles, in northern Quebec, but Johnson's provincial wing wanted it cancelled. The deputy prime minister of Canada, a bilingual patriot of deep passion, wasn't being allowed in. Johnson's troops were trying to pull the plug on her appearances. "This was the last week. This was after we knew that it was an absolute panic situation," Copps remembered. She ignored the orders and went anyway. "There were three hundred people there, and they said, 'Where have you been? We didn't think Canada cared.' Do you know how painful it was to be told that?"

Daniel Johnson told reporters that it would be nice to have Chrétien commit to a constitutional amendment recognizing Quebec as a distinct society. The PM was in New York for ceremonies marking the fiftieth anniversary of the United Nations. He was caught off guard and gave a response that sounded like a No to what Johnson was asking. Now the split was public. The Quebec newspaper headlines were scathing; there was a week to go, and federalist support was falling further behind. The No campaign was down six or seven points, and all the momentum was with the other side.

Fear was taking over. Peter Donolo found the atmosphere surreal. "When I think back to that period, I think of a two-week stretch of nausea so strong that I was almost physically ill." The mistake, he said, was "to play second fiddle to the other guys." Unlike other Chrétien loyalists, who later sought to play down the extent of the crisis, Donolo was forthright. "We were panicking left and right."

Captain Canada came forward. Throughout the campaign, Brian Tobin had chafed at being told to stay at home and not get involved. "I refused to acknowledge that a sovereigntist government should frame the question, shape the debate, and tell the rest of Canada it was none of our business." With exactly one week to go before the vote, he sat looking at dismal polling results and told his staff that this was "surreal," that the country could be gone in a week and everybody was just sitting around. Someone asked him what he could do that might have an impact. Tobin put that question to his policy director, Françoise Ducros, who checked out possibilities and reported back that some businesspeople in Montreal were planning a rally at Place du Canada. The event was only four days away, but Tobin seized on it. Why not turn this into a giant pro-Canada, pro-unity rally? He hit the phones. He called premiers. He got Peter Donolo with the PM in New York. He asked the head of Air Canada for free planes.

He still needed final clearance from the PMO, however. Goldenberg—rarely keen on Tobin ideas—wasn't enthusiastic, but Copps was pushing hard to do it. The PM canvassed other Cabinet members and found some reticence, but the majority seemed to think the Hail Mary pass was worth a try. Finally, Chrétien looked across the table and said, "Brian—Go!" The Tobinator put the word out to everyone—everyone except provincial organizers for Daniel Johnson. The feds were going in, and Johnson and his team could take it or leave it.

"We muscled in," recalled Jean Pelletier, Chrétien's chief of staff. He felt that's what should have been done earlier. "We were told that we should play by the rules of the day. In retrospect we should not have played by the rules of the day."

Pelletier had been studying the falling numbers like everyone else. The feeling, he said, was "that if we plan a good week and get a good week, we'll reverse the trend." They knew that in other referendums and in Quebec elections, the sovereigntists had often scored higher in polls before voting day. In the booth a chill set in for some voters, and they took the safer option.

President Jacques Chirac of France disappointed Ottawa when he appeared on CNN's *Larry King Live* to say he would recognize a sovereign Quebec in the event of a Yes vote. The French president's comments, however, were more than offset by Bill Clinton's pitch for a unified Canada. The U.S. ambassador in Ottawa, James Blanchard, lobbied hard for the White House statement. Because Quebecers often paid close attention to the president's words, many provincial Liberals, including John Parisella, thought it might have made the difference.

Chrétien had his last big speech scheduled for Tuesday night in Verdun, on the island of Montreal. New polls came out, but they were so grim that Chrétien's advisers wanted to hide them from him. The PM, however, asked Goldenberg about them over the phone, and his adviser decided to be frank. The numbers convinced Chrétien that he had no choice but to convey a message of change. As in the deficit crisis, the moment when his hand was forced had come. He was given a speech that said nothing was off the table with regard to the Constitution—that he was in support of recognizing Quebec as a distinct society, and that Quebecers could have their constitutional veto, as well as control over labour market training.

A massive crowd looked on in Verdun. Chrétien did not perform with the conviction he was capable of, but he got out the message that he was prepared to move from the status quo. During the Meech Lake drama, he had procrastinated, straddling the fence right into the weekend when the accord collapsed and he was elected leader. With the referendum, he waited until the very last week as well.

At a suite at the Delta Hotel in Montreal, he met with federalist campaign workers who were having beer and pizza. "He was acutely aware it was not going well," recalled Dominic LeBlanc. "You could see that the pressure of this was weighing on him." That pressure became amply evident to everyone in the hotel room when Chrétien looked coldly at them and said, "I don't want to be the last prime minister of Canada."

The next morning, he met with his caucus in Ottawa. It was October 25, exactly two years to the day that he was elected prime minister, and the polls were still frightening. He knew that if the vote was lost, he would be so discredited that the party might soon be demanding a new leader. He would be out. He would go down as one of the weakest leaders in the country's history. He would be the leader who lost the country.

As he stood before 170 or so Liberal MPs, the burden of power was too enormous for him to bear. His troops had never seen him so weakened. He had shed tears in the days following his defeat to John Turner, but only privately. He had been shattered by the criminal charges against his son Michel. He had thought about quitting when Trudeau humiliated him as finance minister in 1978. But no one in the party had seen the tough guy like this. He spoke of the crisis that was unfolding, and of how absurd it was that the separatists were getting away with lies, lies, and more lies. He accused the media of succumbing and putting "the big pile of shit" in the newspapers. He described the weekend he had just spent at the United Nations, with leader after leader telling him that they couldn't understand what Quebec was doing, that Quebecers had the run of the country and yet they still wanted to break away. He talked of how Islamic leaders had come to him to say that they were praying for Canada, and he talked of how everyone had to fight back in the final week.

His voice broke and he turned his head away. His eyes welled up with tears. The country was on the brink, and its leader was breaking down. Caucus members watched in stony silence as their tough guy melted before them.

Jane Stewart, the caucus chair, held the prime minister to try to compose him. A moment later, he was able to address them again. There was still time to turn back the enemy, Chrétien said, just as they had been turned back before. The separatists, he reminded them, thought they had him beat in his own riding in 1993, but he had fought back to win. Parizeau, he said, had come to his hometown to call him "a cretin," and still he had won.

Bonnie Brown, the MP from Oakville, Ontario, looked on. She thought he was so hurt because he believed he'd let the country down by misreading the situation. But his emotion was prompted all the more, she felt, by his sense that his own Quebec people were doing this to him. "How can a person from a small town in Quebec give his whole life to public service in their cause and this many years later have his own people turn on him?"

That afternoon, he taped two television addresses, one in English, one in French, to the nation. The strain showed. In English he spoke slowly, like someone who was still taking language lessons. He came across as tentative and scared, as if staring into the abyss. But it was the address in French that counted, and in his native language, he was more effective. He wanted to dispel some of the myths that Bouchard had been promoting. He wanted to cast doubt on the idea of a partnership or an association. He wanted Quebecers to know how vital their decision would be.

Goldenberg viewed this five-minute speech as more important than the one in Verdun. It was direct, concentrated. His appeal for TV time made everyone take note. The fact that he hadn't made many appearances in the campaign made the moment more impactful, Goldenberg thought. Had the PM been going in every day, the currency would have been devalued. Others contested that notion, believing that given his standing in Quebec, there simply wasn't much currency to devalue.

Bouchard followed Chrétien with a five-minute telecast of his own, and the contrast was stark. He was confident—in a cold-blooded way—and he was equipped with a prop. During his address, he dramatically unveiled an oversized copy of *Le Journal de Québec* from November 6, 1981. The tabloid headline read, "Lévesque Betrayed by His Allies," a reference to the so-called Night of the Long Knives. The photo showed Chrétien and Trudeau laughing it up—the suggestion being that they were laughing at the expense of fellow Quebecers. "Mr. Chrétien," intoned Bouchard on the TV screen, "you won't pull the same trick on us twice."

Chrétien fumed when he saw this. The picture was not even from that night, and moreover, this story was fourteen years old. The case for betrayal was dubious, to say the least. Earlier in the day, Bouchard had accused Chrétien, who had not personally attacked the Bloc leader with any low language, of "having brutally stuffed an entire constitution down Quebec's throat." Even Bouchard's close friends thought he was taking his insults too far. "I hated that," Senator Jean-Claude Rivest said of his brandishing of the newspaper. "There is a bitterness there that I never heard from anyone on the federalist side. It was so heavy and so harsh, and Lucien Bouchard made a demagogic speech at that time."

Soon, federalists were receiving polling results that took into account the Verdun speech and the TV address. Chrétien's appearances had not only stopped the bleeding but pulled the No side into a tie or a slight lead. No one could forecast the outcome with any certainty.

The federalist side had its big rally planned for Friday, October 27. The preparation for it—the buzz, the signal that the rest of the country was coming together in a show of goodwill—was a momentum builder. The secessionists had had all the momentum before, but now they miscalculated. For the final days, they had no end-game strategy, no final push, no climactic set piece. They had planned no follow-up of their own to the pro-Canada rally scheduled for Friday in Montreal. Had they done so, they could very well have regained the edge by voting day. It was perhaps—given the narrowness of the victory—the biggest mistake they ever made. Jean Chrétien was of that view. Looking back, he recalled, "I knew that the last week we had gained, and I knew that they were complacent. They stopped on Thursday!"

Brian Tobin had taken a room near the top of the towering Château Champlain, and he stood there the morning of the planned rally, looking out over Place du Canada. It was getting close to noon, and a nervous feeling crept into his stomach. Hardly anyone was there. For a moment, he thought that his appeal to the rest of Canada was going unanswered and that he would be embarrassed forever. But then they came in waves—from the buses and the trains and the malls and the hotels—to fill the square. Tobin was thrilled. Sheila Copps had been fighting the Quebec Liberals almost as much as she had the separatists in the previous few weeks. She was relieved, but the Daniel Johnson gang got in the last word. They didn't let her speak at the rally.

A bad sound system combined with whirling winds made it difficult for anyone to be heard anyway. Some Quebec media outlets took a cynical view of the proceedings. One radio station put the crowd, estimated at seventy-five thousand, at a mere thirty-five thousand. Bouchard characterized it as a disgraceful display, with corporate Canada trying to buy a victory. "Friday, two days before the vote, they have come to say they love us." Where were they, wondered the very same politician who had been so touched by the outpouring from across Canada during his illness, "the rest of the time?"

For much of the following two days, the prime minister tried to determine how the vote would go. He called pollsters and was greeted with cautious optimism. He told some colleagues that he thought the federal side would end up at 53 percent. He was already admitting privately that it had been a mistake to defer to the Quebec Liberals so much, and he was vowing never to let it happen again.

Liza Frulla went to bed the night before the vote and was awakened by a phone call from someone close to Bouchard and Parizeau. The caller said, "Liza, will you be with us tomorrow when the referendum passes? Will you be with us to calm everything down and build a new Quebec?" She warned the caller not to be so confident. But then she realized he probably had reason to be. "I went back to bed and said, 'Oh my God!'"

Her Quebec riding covered much of the same territory as Paul Martin's federal riding of LaSalle-Émard. It was heavily populated by Italian Canadians, and she discovered to her consternation that some duplex owners were receiving warnings from their secessionist tenants. "In a week, you better get out of here," they told the Italians. "You better go back to your own country." Frulla had even experienced some of this racism herself. "Someone came to me [at Montreal's Atwater Market] and said, 'I like you a lot. But you are an Italian, and in the referendum you're going to lose your cause.'" Then came the same message that the Italian landlords were receiving: "You're going to have to go back to your own country."

On the night of the vote, about a dozen of the prime minister's close friends and advisers gathered with him and Aline at 24 Sussex. When the first results came in from Les Îles de la Madeleine, Chrétien turned to his son-in-law and said, "We'll win by 1 percent." He knew the voting patterns on the sparsely populated island intimately, and to him, the narrow win for the sovereignty camp there meant it would be extremely close but a victory would come by night's end because of the more favourable federalist trends in the south of the province. Chrétien recalled having a "fatalistic" attitude that night. For the ultimate pragmatist, it was an unusual mindset to be in.

The separatists had an early lead, and the lead held well into the evening. The churning in the stomachs of the prime minister's people got so bad that they were almost buckling over. Needing to get away from the others, David Zussman moved downstairs, where he found an empty room and a television. A little while later, Chrétien walked in and found Zussman, whose first degree was in statistics, playing with numbers on an envelope. He shared some of his analysis with the prime minister. One of the things Zussman told him was that he should have a statement of concession at the ready. Chrétien in fact had a losing speech already prepared—but it wasn't what could be called a concession.

Throughout the campaign, there had been mixed signals on how Ottawa might react to a loss. Would Chrétien accept the verdict? Would he enter into negotiations for sovereignty-association with Quebec? Or would he come out and defy the separatists by declaring that he was not heeding the outcome? Would he say that a Yes vote was no, that he was demanding a majority larger than 50 percent plus one?

A negation of the verdict in front of tens of thousands of celebrating Quebecers would have risked a bloody backlash. But in fact, that is what Chrétien planned to do. Goldenberg recalled the speech he prepared for Chrétien that night. "He wasn't about to let the country break up," he said. Chrétien's speech would say "we are getting a message from the people. But this is not the breakup of the country. We have work to do, but this is not the breakup of the country. . . . We have problems to solve, and we are going to work together." Chrétien was to say, recalled Solicitor General Herb Gray, that "the referendum was a consultative exercise, and that nothing in our Constitution allows anything to be changed by a referendum." Gray and most Cabinet ministers agreed with the hardline approach. "The result wasn't going to be ignored," he said. "But it wasn't going to change anything."

Defence Minister Collenette was ready, in the event of a loss, to make the federal presence felt. For starters, the army was to protect federal property and federal assets from a sovereigntist takeover. "I was in a tough position," he recalled years later. "I was minister of defence. There were things that went on that we had to prepare for that I don't even want to talk about."

Separatists were telling their landlords they'd better be prepared to leave. Chrétien was saying he wouldn't accept the verdict. And as further testimony to the explosiveness of the situation, there were the words of Jacques Parizeau. As he would later make clear in his book, *Pour un Québec souverain,* he was well prepared to declare unilateral separation if it appeared the federal side was not going to go along with the verdict. Parizeau's erratic behaviour in the hours following the referendum result lent credibility to the notion that he was prepared to go the limit. Chrétien's reaction to the verdict could well have compelled him to do just that.

Few could imagine a civil war playing out in a country like Canada. But this alarming mix of circumstances suddenly made it seem possible. It was perhaps even likely. With troops on the streets, ethnics being threatened, emotions stretched to the limit, Quebecers' verdict being called into question, and Parizeau inciting them, who could imagine calm? "Tell me this," said a PMO official. "Do you think Chrétien's the type of guy who would turn the province over to the PQ, guys he hated all his life?"

"You know, at fifty plus one, I was not about to let go the country," Chrétien himself later reflected. "You don't break your country because one guy forgets his glasses at home." If Parizeau had tried a unilateral declaration of independence, it would have been a big problem for him, said Chrétien. "Who would have recognized him?" Chrétien would have rejected the verdict on the basis that the question was unfair. The majority of Quebecers who voted yes would not have accepted that line of reasoning.

At 24 Sussex on referendum night, Goldenberg had found a quiet room where it would be easier to bear up under the pressure, but others joined him. As the country hung by a thread, they paced back and forth. Though reports on television said that the late results would be coming in from Montreal, and that they could very well tilt the verdict in Ottawa's direction, the prime minister's people weren't at all certain. They could have been coming from a heavily separatist region, for all they knew. "Believe me," said Goldenberg, "nobody knew."

When it finally became clear that the federalist side had won by the thinnest of margins, there was no great elation at 24 Sussex. It was easier, so much easier, to find air to breathe, but the faces were still white. It was apparent that the prime minister and his team would be the subject of intense criticism for their campaign strategy. It seemed clear that the separatists would want another referendum to push them over the top.

There was little time to digest what had happened. Chrétien had to return to his office to address the country. Goldenberg put the final touches on the short speech, changing it to reflect the closeness of the result. Chrétien then climbed into his limousine, and it sped up to the Parliament Buildings. A few Canadians were waiting there. They gave the prime minister a cheer, and Chrétien smiled and said, "We won."

He delivered the speech, got back in the car, looked at Goldenberg, and told him what a relief it was not to have given the other speech he had prepared for him—the one negating a sovereigntist victory.

CHAPTER SEVEN

HITTING BACK HARD

T HE PRIME MINISTER WOKE UP the next morning to a fusillade
of abuse for what Preston Manning called his lame-brain referendum strategy. Jane Stewart found him not much improved from the
distraught state he had been in at the caucus meeting before the vote.
Every fibre of his body, he explained to one MP, had told him that he
should have been more involved, that he shouldn't have let the provincial Liberals dictate the campaign. But he had failed to trust the very
thing that had made him as a politician—his gut instincts.

He went to a Toronto fundraiser, where he could sense disappointment and disapproval. "A cold shower," as his chief of staff, Jean
Pelletier, put it. Never, Chrétien promised the gathering, would this be
allowed to happen again. No more free rides for the country-breakers.
Peter Donolo asked him backstage how he intended to back up such a
statement. "Don't worry," Chrétien told him. "I'll back it up."

Chrétien had survived the two crises of 1995—the deficit and the
referendum. The country had been taken to the brink on each, and
he was lucky on each. Paul Martin's sustained pressure had convinced
a reluctant Chrétien to launch an unprecedented attack on public
spending. In the Quebec referendum, he was saved by less than 1 percent
of the vote.

Each crisis had proved that passivity was his Achilles' heel. On the
economy, he had followed his cautious first budget with the remarkably wrong-headed assertion that no more cutting would be necessary,
that the status quo was fine. On the unity crisis, he had similarly
under-reacted. As Jean Pelletier later remarked, it was unimaginable

that the separatists could change leaders midway through a campaign and get away with it. But Chrétien had still waited until the very last week to wake up.

His favourite hockey player was the old Montreal netminder Jacques Plante, whose secret, Chrétien analyzed, was to let the other guy make the first move. The secret of Plante was that very thing. In the boxing ring, Jersey Joe Walcott, the counterpuncher, did the same. But these sporting models were useful only in the right circumstances. Chrétien had learned in 1995 that his modus operandi would have to change.

He had other weapons in his arsenal, personality traits ingrained at a young age that could be brought to bear. There was a thick layer of aggression in Chrétien and, lurking below that, a bully streak. There was a part of Jean Chrétien that was quite capable of going to any extreme—as his missing appendix testified—to get his way. This was the part to which, after what could well be called another life-threatening experience, he would soon turn.

ON THE WEEKEND following the referendum, he prepared for a long trip to a Commonwealth conference in New Zealand, which was to be followed by a meeting of the APEC group in Japan. His plans changed when, on the day before his scheduled departure, the Israeli leader, Yitzhak Rabin, was assassinated. The prime minister, shocked by this news, would now travel to Israel first to attend the funeral.

Having taken medication and gone to bed early to fight off a cold, Chrétien was in a deep slumber when, at about 3 a.m., his wife, Aline, heard footsteps downstairs and, moments later, noise in the hallway right outside the bedroom door. She first thought it might be their staff preparing her husband's luggage for the morning flight, but she was soon disabused of that notion. She went to the door, which was only a few feet from the bed, and saw a man with a knife in his hand. She locked the door, ran to another, locked it, and woke up the prime minister. She assured her startled husband that she was not dreaming, that there was an armed man in the house.

Chrétien called the RCMP, then took an Inuit carving of heavy stone as a weapon and waited interminably for the Mounties to arrive. The first officers who came scurrying up to the house couldn't get in—they had forgotten the keys. When at last they were able to enter, they apprehended a man named André Dallaire.

Dallaire, a former convenience store worker and hard-line separatist, had been embittered by the referendum result. He believed that killing the prime minister—his plan was to slit his throat—would have made him a hero in Quebec. He bore no ill will towards Aline Chrétien, who, in waking up in time, might very well have saved her husband's life.

The Mounties had failed to respond to an alarm that went off when Dallaire entered the prime minister's compound. He then wandered the grounds for several minutes before smashing a window and breaking through a door to get in. After Dallaire was apprehended, Chrétien telephoned aides. He angrily told them that there had been a complete breakdown in security. "My friend," the prime minister told Peter Donolo, "I was almost killed."

He decided to proceed with the trip abroad and leave as scheduled to attend the Rabin funeral. At the Ottawa airport, he stepped out of his limousine and came face to face with his RCMP guards. With barely concealed hostility, Chrétien told them, "You could be wearing your red serge today, carrying my coffin."

It was the most serious attempt on a prime minister's life in the history of the country. Somehow, however, its gravity did not register with the public. Canadians woke up on the Sunday morning to news reports that made it sound as if some prankster or drunk had broken into the residence on a lark. There was no mention of an assassination attempt. Not wishing to publicize its own folly, the RCMP had downplayed the threat posed by the break-in.

When Donolo phoned the Mounties to find out how they intended to handle the story, he was told the line would be that the PM's residence was vandalized and he was never in any serious danger. Donolo didn't think that was right, but he was hesitant to dictate what the police should tell the media. The Mounties put out their tame version of events, and Canadians chuckled as they heard the morning news.

At the airport, Chrétien, informed of the Mounties' position, asked Donolo what to say about it. "Say exactly what happened," Donolo offered. Chrétien gave a sombre scrum, credited Aline with saving his life, and boarded the plane for a ten-hour flight. On the way, he told reporters it was a good thing that the man had had only a knife and not a gun. The door was so close to the bed that "if the intruder came through, I probably would not have survived to wake up." He had reason to stew, as the media continued to treat the incident without the gravitas it deserved. And he had reason, on learning of Dallaire's political bent, to regard the separatist threat with even more alarm.

Aline Chrétien spent many subsequent nights in fear. "I would wake up at three o'clock in the morning," she recalled. "It was like an alarm clock." It got so distressing that she left 24 Sussex for a period to stay at her daughter's home or sometimes a private retreat. She credited reflex action as saving her and her husband. There was an automatic reaction, she explained, like she felt when driving in snowstorms. Running to slam the doors was "like driving a car and having good reflexes."

Dallaire was charged with attempted murder. He underwent a psychiatric assessment—"I am a gentle man, and I am a good man," he testified—but was soon released to live in a group home near Ottawa.

BACK HOME AGAIN, Chrétien stumbled badly on the question of extending a constitutional veto to Quebec. Having made promises to the province in the final week of the referendum campaign, the PM wanted to bring in a constitutional amendment to fulfill them. But it was soon clear that English Canada still could not speak with one voice on the Quebec issue. Amendments required the support of seven provinces making up 50 percent of the population. The prime minister was hoping he could get six, then go to the Quebec leaders and say he was prepared to make a deal if they would sign on as the seventh. Bouchard would be trapped. But the PM's hopes were toppled when Ontario's Mike Harris, tired of the appeasement game, gave him a flat no. Chrétien now had to go the lesser route of fulfilling his referendum pledges by way of parliamentary resolutions, something he knew Quebec would scoff at.

He planned to extend the veto to all regions, not just Quebec. Ontario, Quebec, the West, and the Atlantic provinces would be the four recipients. But the Western provinces began to complain about having to exercise a veto as part of a group while the two central Canadian provinces had individual vetoes. Then a bigger problem emerged: British Columbia didn't consider itself a part of the Western group. It was the third-largest province in Canada. It wanted its own veto.

The ensuing uproar exposed Chrétien as a leader who was as numb to Western sensitivities as his Liberal predecessor. "For the first time in my life," said Roger Gibbins, a political scientist at the University of Calgary, "if there was some sort of Western separatist movement, I'd be interested in looking at it." Gibbins was considered a moderate. Others voiced similar sentiments, with the outcry becoming more fierce by the day. Brian Tobin and others, such as the B.C. MP Herb Dhaliwal, warned Chrétien that he would have to change his plan. But the stubborn prime minister dug in. Finally, the din of protest reached such a decibel level that he had no choice. Justice Minister Allan Rock announced the inclusion of a veto right for B.C. "In a word, the government has listened," he said. With that, with a resolution giving Quebec a limited form of distinct society status, and with changes to labour training brought in by Lloyd Axworthy, the pledges of the referendum, made at Verdun, had been fulfilled, however meekly.

But there was no relief from the scorn of opponents. Jean Charest had met with Chrétien earlier and warned against such cosmetics. The exchange was bitter. Charest had become totally disenchanted with Chrétien. "If it wasn't for that bastard," the Quebec journalist André Pratte quoted Charest as saying, "the national unity problem would have been settled a long time ago."

Preston Manning went further. He was incensed that Chrétien was offering a constitutional veto to a separatist government. He had heard reports about the PM almost breaking down in the caucus meeting the week before the referendum. Now, in a gambit that had the look of a man absolutely desperate for power, he issued the extraordinary statement that the governor general should be prepared to make a change at the top if it became evident that "there is a screw loose in the Prime Minister's Office."

"Suppose this government starts to come apart the way the Diefenbaker government came apart in the 1960s because the leader starts behaving in a pretty particular way," said Manning, referring to the collapse of that government over a controversy with Washington on stationing nuclear warheads in Canada. "Can you imagine what would happen if that occurred three months or four months before the next referendum?"

The Manning offensive was yet another attempt to portray Jean Chrétien as too inept to hold the office. Parizeau had come to Chrétien's own riding and insulted him, Alain Dubuc had said he did not have enough sophistication, the Tories had launched their infamous face ad, and now Reform was engaging in its own brand of personal slur. Yet again, it was clear to Chrétien that not much had changed since his days on the streets of Shawinigan. Even becoming prime minister couldn't stop the mockery. Other prime ministers were condemned for their actions. Jean Chrétien was condemned because of who he was.

ON THE NIGHT OF THE REFERENDUM, Jacques Parizeau had created a furor with his scathing declaration that the federalists had won as a result of "money and the ethnic vote." That, in combination with a pledge he made in pre-taped interviews to resign in the event of a loss, led him to vacate the premier's office in favour of Bouchard. This was hardly a welcome development for Chrétien. What if Bouchard chose to call a snap election to get his own mandate from the people and campaigned on the basis of wanting to take Quebec out of the country? With the momentum he possessed, he could very well succeed. Given such scenarios, Chrétien still had to worry about his job security. Faced with another showdown, Liberals might think of turning to someone who was more popular in Quebec.

Having dealt with the Verdun promises, Chrétien signalled a new strategy of counterattack early in the New Year with a statement in Vancouver. He declared that "if Canada is divisible, Quebec is divisible too." With that surprise assertion, he was giving tacit support to what was becoming known as the partition movement. In three areas of Quebec—the north, which was heavily populated by Native peoples; the Outaouais, a region along the Ottawa River valley, and the west island of Montreal, where anglophones formed the majority—organizations were being set up to secede from Quebec should Quebec secede from Canada. Chrétien, in effect, was telling Bouchard, "If you do it to us, we'll do it to you." The secessionists were outraged that they had no convincing comeback. They were unable to find an intellectually valid rebuttal of the partitionists' case.

The PMO felt it had scored a hit. Looking back, Peter Donolo and others regretted not pressing the partitionist case even harder. They were initially hesitant to use the word, fearing it was too inflammatory. Nonetheless, they were signalling a major shift. Chrétien was prepared to take Ottawa out of its traditional defensive posturing in the Quebec debate. The days of pussyfooting were over.

To spearhead the new strategy, Chrétien brought in a recruit from his home province, an arch-federalist with pale skin and a choirboy countenance who knew the word "backbone." Stéphane Dion had been brought to the PM's attention by Aline Chrétien. Her husband had watched the University of Montreal professor on television during the referendum campaign, and was impressed, as were many others, by the way Dion crystallized his thoughts. Chrétien talked to the young academic over Christmas. His government was in need of some wise men from Quebec, just as Lester Pearson's government had been when it brought in Pierre Trudeau, Jean Marchand, and Gérard Pelletier in 1965. Dion would fit the bill. The son of the visionary academic Léon Dion, he was completely lacking in Trudeau's charisma, but he had a comparable rapier-like intellect and his defence of the federalist position was trenchant.

Along with Dion, who made his way from Montreal to Ottawa by bus and called Goldenberg from the station, Chrétien recruited Pierre Pettigrew, a high-profile Montreal Liberal with a career in finance and a certain stylistic panache. The appointments coincided with the departure of Brian Tobin, who was returning to Newfoundland to take up the premier's job. With his work in the fish wars and the referendum rally in Montreal, the little guy from the Rock had stamped himself as a possible leadership contender in the years to come. His departure was a loss, but in bringing in Dion Chrétien had found some compensation.

Dion immediately put himself in the forefront of a growing chorus of MPs determined to set down rules that the sovereigntists would have to play by in future referendum campaigns. Preston Manning and his Quebec specialist, Stephen Harper, had been pressuring Chrétien for such changes, and now their voices were being heard.

Strategies referred to as Plan A and Plan B entered the political lexicon. Plan A was the traditional soft talk, while Plan B was the hard-edged strategy of outlining referendum rules, threatening partition, and countering any separatist charges with forceful rebuttals.

CHRÉTIEN'S NEW AGGRESSIVE TURN was on display in an astonishing unscripted act on February 15, 1996. The occasion was the inaugural Flag Day, and the prime minister was in Jacques Cartier Park in Hull, across the river from the Parliament Buildings. In a heavy black coat, dark sunglasses, and black gloves, he was moving through the crowds, taunted along the way by protesters. Not in the best of humours, he brushed past one microphone and moved a youngster out of his way with his arm. He saw a demonstrator in a woollen hat bearing down on him while shouting into a big bullhorn. Protesters were hollering, *"Chrétien, au chomage!"* ("Chrétien, you should be unemployed!"). While the PM's bodyguards looked on, the demonstrator moved boldly into Chrétien's path. The prime minister didn't wait for a security guard to act. His jaws tightening, he grabbed the demonstrator by the neck and, with the force of a thug, thrust him to the ground. Then he pushed ahead with a look that said "Who's next?"

The television cameras captured the image. In his dark shades and gloves, the prime minister could have been mistaken for a Mafia hit man. When Aline Chrétien saw the video clip, she was horrified—so much so that she told Peter Donolo she thought he would have to resign. No prime minister could get away with exercising so little self-restraint. Chrétien hadn't behaved like this—at least as far as anyone knew—since his late twenties, when he flattened a fellow lawyer in a bar in Trois-Rivières with a series of brutal punches that left him sprawled on the floor.

"He shouldn't have been there," Chrétien said of the protester. "What happened? I don't know. . . . Some people came in my way. I had to go, so if you're in my way, I'm walking." A little later, he was more blunt. The protester "was right in front of me, shouting and trying to block my way, so I took him out. He was a lightweight, probably. I just moved him out," he explained.

No one could remember a head of state from a civilized country handling a demonstrator in this way. It explained why some thought it might cost Chrétien dearly. But they miscalculated the public reaction. Canadians weren't outraged: in fact, a majority seemed to be cheering him on. For many, this was the Chrétien they hoped to see. This was Chrétien the tough guy, the scrapper who had gone missing in the referendum fight.

But having been admonished by his wife and others, Chrétien fretted about the potential reaction. He called friends, including Brian Tobin, to get their views, and when he called his communications director for his press briefing, Donolo noticed he was in a state of high anxiety.

"So what are they saying?" Chrétien asked him.

"Well, there's a poll in the *Toronto Star* this morning," replied Donolo.

"Yes, and what did it say?"

Donolo paused. "Well, " he responded, "I don't want to tell you, Prime Minister. Because if I do, you're going to want to go out and throttle somebody else."

Foreign leaders called with their congratulations. Admiring sentiments came from the prime minister of Japan, among others. Demonstrators had learned a lesson, joked President Bill Clinton. From now on, when they wished to protest Chrétien, they were going to have to take their own security teams with them. At the PMO, staffers asked Chrétien if he would give them his sunglasses so they could auction them off at a Young Liberals meeting. "I'll get a fortune for them," said Dominic LeBlanc.

In Quebec, the reaction wasn't so forgiving. The radio host Robert Gillet captured the mood, calling the PM "Mad Dog Chrétien." One headline said, "Chrétien Loses His Head"; another, "Chrétien Brutalizes a Protestor." Clément Godbout, the Quebec Federation of Labour president, described the PM's behaviour as "savagery." *Le Soleil*'s editor, Gilbert Lavoie, said he should leave office. "At a time when this country needs inspired leadership, a period of reconciliation and calming reassurance, the prime minister was knocking over protesters and talking about the partition of Quebec."

Though Bill Clennett, the protester, complained of having been attacked by Chrétien, he declined to have any charges brought forward. That was left to a penniless man from New Brunswick. Kenneth Russell, forty-four, an unemployed salesman, saw the scuffle on television, then spent hours in the University of Moncton's law library looking for a provision in the Criminal Code that allowed a private citizen with knowledge of an alleged crime to launch a prosecution. He went to Ottawa with seven dollars in his pocket and lived on the street until the district court in Hull took his case. The judge issued an order summoning the prime minister to court to face a charge of common assault. But Paul Bégin, the justice minister in Quebec, came to his defence. He ordered a stay of court proceedings, saying it was unlikely that Chrétien would ever repeat his actions.

As fortunate as he was with this case, Chrétien was not as lucky as he was when he beat up the lawyer in Trois-Rivières. For that incident, he could well have faced assault charges that would have hurt, if not crippled, his political hopes. The lawyer declined to press them.

CHARGES WERE AT THE CENTRE of a story involving another prime minister that became public at this same time. The mutual loathing society that Jean Chrétien and Brian Mulroney had formed over many years was well known, with the two clashing over the Meech Lake Accord, relations with the United States, the GST, and other issues. Most of their disputes were behind them, however, and since it was unseemly for prime ministers repeatedly to bait each other, there was little reason to suspect a heightening of the feud.

But shortly after the Quebec referendum, one of the sorriest chapters in the history of the federal justice system began to unfold. The drama would cast a pall over the prime minister and some of the top administrators in his government, raising legitimate suspicion about justice being overtaken by malice.

The Mulroney administration was in power in 1988 when Air Canada bought thirty-four Airbus A-320s for $1.8 billion. Rumours of favouritism towards the winning consortium surfaced at the time. The RCMP had a quick look but closed the file. When the Chrétien government had been in power barely a month, Justice Minister Allan Rock told Solicitor General Herb Gray about information he had received in connection with possible irregularities in the purchase of the aircraft. The CBC's *Fifth Estate* then displayed documents that fuelled suspicions and prompted the Mounties to reopen the file. Rumours of kickbacks to a long-time Mulroney associate, Frank Moores, surfaced. Then, in the summer of 1995, the RCMP informed the Department of Justice that Mulroney himself was under investigation.

The justice department decided that it needed help from the Swiss, since the case involved secret Swiss bank accounts. In late September, while the referendum campaign was underway, Kimberley Prost, a justice department lawyer, sent a letter to the Swiss government implicating Mulroney in the alleged kickback scheme. With reference to Karl-Heinz Schreiber, a German-Canadian businessman, Prost wrote that "the RCMP has reliable information that Mr. Schreiber was given these commissions in order to pay Mr. Mulroney and Mr. Moores to ensure that Airbus Industrie obtained a major contract with Air Canada for the planned upgrade of their aircraft fleet." Prost wrote that Moores had opened two bank accounts that were to accept the payments. One of the numbered accounts was allegedly for Mulroney, and was code-named Devon, after the street Mulroney had lived on in Westmount in Montreal. Mulroney, the communication said, had benefited not only from the Airbus deal but from two other transactions in which payoffs were made. All three cases, Prost told the Swiss, "demonstrate an ongoing scheme by Mr. Mulroney, Mr. Moores, and Mr. Schreiber to defraud the Canadian government of millions of dollars of public funds from the time Mr. Mulroney took office in September 1984 until he resigned in June 1993."

The justice department was operating on the assumption that the letter would not be made public. But that didn't excuse the heinous wording of the document. Neither the RCMP nor the government, as would be made clear in the settlement of a future lawsuit, had any basis for implying there was proof of illegalities.

Two days after the October 30 referendum, Schreiber, the business-man who was the go-between on the sale of the aircraft, informed Mulroney of the existence of the letter. The former prime minister hired top legal help to try to get the letter withdrawn, but he made little progress. Mulroney was worried that it would leak to the media and prepared to file suit. The leak came first on Swiss television, in a general report about Canadian politicians being paid off, and later in the November 18 edition of the *Financial Post,* which carried a story based on the letter to the Swiss and named Mulroney. Five days later, Mulroney announced his intention to file a $50-million libel suit against the government.

The Airbus story dominated the media for weeks. It served the Liberals well in that it deflected attention from their weak referendum performance, and because of this, suspicions arose that the PMO might have been behind the leak. That was clearly Mulroney's belief. In private conversations, wrote William Kaplan, the author of *Presumed Guilty,* a book about the case, Mulroney made clear his belief that it was Chrétien's office that put out the story.

The prime minister denied having any prior knowledge of the investigation or the letter to the Swiss government. As he told golfing companions, the Tories had been reduced to two seats, and Mulroney's reputation had been damaged badly, and he was a spent political force. Why would Chrétien want to rub it in by urging the police to go after him?

Solicitor General Gray oversaw the activities of the RCMP. Normally, it would have been Gray's responsibility to notify the prime minister of the investigation. But while he was aware that the Mounties were investigating Mulroney, Gray said he never told the prime minister of the matter. Was it not his duty to inform him? "No, I didn't see it that way," Gray said in an interview some years after the case was settled. "In fact, I thought I should be extra careful in terms of the convention. I didn't get involved in operational matters. You could argue that maybe I should have done that, but I didn't." In defence of his actions on the file, Gray added, "By the way, Mulroney didn't sue me. . . . That may be a point of interest."

In the same interview, over lunch in late 2002, Gray defended the PM. "As far as I know, he had nothing to do with it," he asserted. "The idea that he directed the investigation, or called for it, I can say that as solicitor general I have no indication of that." Gray noted as well that letters are sometimes sloppily written. "It wasn't the Mounties or me who sent the letter to the Swiss. It was the Department of Justice. You can say the wording should have been done more carefully, but apparently they've sent other letters like that."

The latter was a remarkable admission. Gray was saying that this kind of thing was done often by the government; that on the basis of speculation only, letters were sent alleging crimes by Canadians all the way up to the highest office holders in the land. Anyone could be the subject of a wild goose chase, he implied. He even went further, alleging that this was done during Mulroney's period in office. In defending Kimberley Prost, he said she was following tradition. "I think she may have felt she was acting on good faith and following a model for letters that had been sent in other cases by her predecessors. I think letters like that were sent out during the Mulroney regime."

Mulroney's work with his Montreal law firm depended on his international reputation. That reputation was blackened, and for weeks the former prime minister, barely able to sleep, paced the floors of his home in Montreal, hoping to get the lawsuit underway and clear his name. When he got his chance during discovery examinations before a media circus in Montreal, he took full advantage. He held in the air the letter Kimberley Prost had written to Swiss authorities. "When the document said that I had a bank account in Switzerland: False. When the document said that I received 25 percent of twenty million dollars: False. When the document said that I received money from Frank Moores: False. When the document said that I had an account elsewhere: False."

The RCMP wasn't backing down. "We've been confident from day one that all of our actions have been completely justified," Commissioner Philip Murray told the *Ottawa Citizen* editorial board. Schreiber, the so-called go-between, countered that the whole thing was the biggest hoax since the faked Hitler diaries.

In fighting Mulroney's lawsuit, Justice Minister Rock hoped he could win the case by showing that the leak of the letter to the Swiss likely came from someone in the former prime minister's camp. The theory was that Mulroney had wanted the letter leaked so as to ward off the investigation. But that angle didn't stand up to scrutiny. Eventually, the justice department, conceding defeat, decided it had better seek an out-of-court settlement with Mulroney. The settlement awarded him more than $2 million in legal costs shortly before the start of what would have been a sensational $50-million libel suit against the government and the RCMP.

With the settlement agreed upon, the Chrétien government could have cut its losses by making a sincere apology to Mulroney. But the decision was made—and here Prime Minister Chrétien was certainly involved—to do the opposite. The Jean Chrétien who would go to any extreme to avoid conceding defeat was alive and well.

Allan Rock announced the settlement to the media. He began his press conference by saying that there had been much speculation about it. "Let me start by telling Canadians what is not in the settlement agreement. There is no $50-million damages payment to Mr. Mulroney, as he has been demanding for more than a year in his lawsuit. In fact, Mr. Mulroney has now dropped any claim to compensation by way of damages. Second, this agreement does not stop the RCMP's ongoing criminal investigation into Airbus, or give anyone, including Mr. Mulroney, effective immunity from such an investigation."

A CBC reporter thought it curious that the government was both apologizing and continuing the investigation. How could that be? "Let's make it clear what we're apologizing for," Rock said. "We're apologizing for some language used in the letter of request, which, read on its own, leads some to conclude that there has been a conclusion of wrongdoing."

If it was an apology, it was a grudging, mean-spirited one. Rock's tone was not the least bit regretful. It was almost aggressive. It was as if he were saying that they would still get Mulroney, given time. The result only heightened suspicions that the government really had been out to impugn the former prime minister.

The RCMP, it seemed, didn't want to appear to have been on a witch hunt, and so would continue its investigation. It seemed as well that the Liberals didn't want to appear to have been part of such an endeavour, and so they, too, were pleased to have the investigation continue.

After the announcement of the settlement, Mulroney received calls from George Bush, Sr., Margaret Thatcher, Prime Minister Laurent Fabius of France, and others. A call also came in from Chrétien's office. "When would it be convenient for Mr. Mulroney to receive a call from the prime minister?" Mulroney's assistant was asked. The assistant, as instructed, said that there would be no such time. "Mr. Mulroney is otherwise engaged."

Though the call made it seem as if Chrétien wished to apologize, he had not been prepared to do that publicly. Rock's office later put out the word that the justice minister had wanted to deliver a more sincere apology at the press conference, but that, at the last minute, the Prime Minister's Office ordered a change in the statement, a hardening of it. That was news to Herb Gray. According to him, they all wanted the tough statement, Rock included. "I was involved in the drafting of the statement by Rock," Gray revealed in an interview years after the event. "The statement had to be signed off by me. There were discussions back and forth. But I didn't go to the press conference saying, 'Oh my God, there's something different here.'"

Neither Chrétien nor Gray was in favour of a gracious apology. Prost was not disciplined. Nor was anyone in the RCMP. Having bungled the break-in at 24 Sussex, failed to keep protesters out of Chrétien's way on Flag Day, and now participated in an apparent travesty of justice, the Mounties received a vote of confidence from the prime minister. In defending his own office, Chrétien declared that "an inquiry is an inquiry, and there is no political interference with that." This would soon be viewed as a curious statement in the wake of his shutdown of an inquiry into the behaviour of Canadian soldiers in Somalia.

After the settlement was finalized, the investigation into Airbus continued for another six years. It wasn't until April 2003 that the RCMP finally closed the case, and Mulroney received total clearance and vindication. One headline labelled the whole affair a comedy of errors. More precisely, it was a tragedy of errors, and one for which none of those responsible paid a price. In the end, there was no statement of regret from the prime minister.

Looking back, Eddie Goldenberg said that he had a lot of sympathy for Mulroney, but that the PMO had not been in a position to intervene. "I found out about it in the *Financial Post*. We had no idea, and we couldn't do anything about it. We couldn't call the RCMP and say, 'What are you guys up to? . . . Either you guys got the goods or you don't.'" To do that, Goldenberg maintained, would have been to leave the PMO open to charges of interfering with a police inquiry.

He said that the clerk of the Privy Council, Jocelyne Bourgon, was one of the first told of the investigation by the RCMP. "But the clerk has certain responsibilities where [she] report[s] to the PM and certain where she doesn't, and in this case she didn't." Since the letter sent to the Swiss by the justice department clearly suggested that Mulroney was guilty without providing proof, why wasn't the letter withdrawn? Goldenberg admitted talking to Bourgon about that, but in the end he felt there should be no involvement from the PMO in a police case. "So I understand Mulroney's frustration. I would feel the same way, but I don't think the PM's office could do anything about it." The Mounties were the problem. "I blame the RCMP. When you're going after a former prime minister," said Goldenberg, "you should know what you're doing."

Politically, the Liberals were again fortunate. Canadians had a deep loathing of Mulroney and were perfectly prepared to believe he was a crook. Had it been another prime minister, there might have been a sustained public outcry about the deplorable handling of the case. But since it was Mulroney, there was none. Kaplan discovered this when he did a cross-country tour to promote *Presumed Guilty*. He found the talk shows full of respondents unloading on the man who had been unjustly accused.

Chrétien didn't suffer in the polls. It was beginning to look like very little could hurt him or his party. Many believed the Liberals would tumble in popularity after their halting performance in the referendum. They didn't. The party's leader appeared to be benefiting from permanently low expectations. It was as if, because of his ordinary style, he was expected to make the mistakes of an ordinary man. His government continued to make them. Airbus coincided with not only the Somalia affair but the GST follies and the Pearson airport controversy. There was enough blundering, or so it seemed, to undermine the credibility of any government.

OF MORE DIFFICULTY FOR CHRÉTIEN—and something Mulroney could take some pleasure in during his ordeal—was the Liberals' performance on the GST. The Mulroney team had shown far-sighted economic sense—if no political sense—in bringing in the big tax. It was hated because every time Canadians made a purchase, the 7-percent add-on smacked them right between the eyes. As Opposition leader, Chrétien was pressured by his caucus to come out against the GST. But given the enormous deficit, there had to be an equivalent revenue-producer, and the Liberals therefore vowed in their Red Book to replace the tax with another tax. On the hustings, however, they overplayed their hand. In the enthusiasm of trying to reach out to voters, they made it sound like they were burying the GST, not replacing it.

One of those who got caught truth shaving was Sheila Copps. "If the GST is not abolished under a Liberal government," she declared during the 1993 campaign, "I will resign." Once the Liberals were in power, Paul Martin began his search for a replacement tax. His intention was to harmonize the GST with the provinces' sales taxes, creating one overall tax that would go under a different name. Martin made progress on the plan with provincial governments in the Maritimes but then felt he was undercut by Ontario's Mike Harris. "Harris had been publicly in favour of harmonization," Martin explained in an interview. "He had come out and said, 'We should harmonize.' So I took Mike Harris at his word, and I knew that if Quebec, Ontario, and Atlantic Canada harmonized, then the rest of Canada would too. But Ontario wouldn't, and therefore the rest of Canada wouldn't."

Unable to kill the tax, the Liberals found they weren't able to replace it either. By the spring of 1996, the Opposition was in full fury, with the Reform Party house leader, Deborah Grey, hurling her copy of the Red Book across the Commons floor. "I've been sitting with this Liberal bunch since 1989, and I believed them and I trusted them and I am ashamed of myself," she frothed. "And that Red Book stinks, and that's where it belongs—on the floor."

Chrétien tried to hold his ground, reciting the Red Book promise that the tax would be replaced by the harmonization formula and stating that "this is exactly what we have started to do. We have succeeded in doing it with three Atlantic provinces, and we are negotiating with others." But he and his finance minister, much to Chrétien's annoyance, were not on the same page. As the PM was talking up harmonization, Paul Martin, aware the controversy was deepening, decided it was time to come clean. Martin told the media that the Liberals had "made a mistake" with their election promise.

Years later, he would explain. "I was the minister stuck with this, and my own view was that it was going to be an anvil around our necks forever unless we basically exorcised it. And I thought the only way to exorcise it would be to stand up and say, 'I apologize for any misunderstanding.'"

John Nunziata, the high-octane Toronto MP with maverick tendencies, took a different tack. He protested his party's lack of action on the GST by standing against one of the government's budget motions. Chrétien expelled him from caucus, saying he would sit as an independent MP. "I wish him good luck to be elected as an independent candidate," said Chrétien with barely concealed sarcasm.

The PM could get by without Nunziata. But losing Sheila Copps, the deputy prime minister, would be harder to take. Copps was one of the most partisan creatures the party had ever produced. In her days as a member of the Rat Pack, attacking the Mulroney government, she had once leaped over chairs to block Sinclair Stevens, who was facing accusations of conflict of interest, from making his way to the door. In need of a photo-op, she once climbed into a wetsuit to test the allegedly sewage-filled waters of Hamilton Harbour. Her Commons scraps with the acerbic John Crosbie, who labelled her a "dough-head," were legendary.

Now she was ambushed. The finance minister was saying that the tax wouldn't be replaced, and she was on videotape saying she would resign if it wasn't. The television clip was found, and it was rerun over and over, until the pressure built to breaking point.

Chrétien didn't want to accept her resignation. He was still claiming he was being true to his Red Book promise. One of the only times he chastised Peter Donolo was on this file. He blasted Goldenberg too. They were both on the line when Chrétien phoned and reamed them out for failing to convey the message that the party was sticking to its promise.

Copps offered to resign, but Chrétien refused. A temporary diversion came with the revelation that Bob Ringma, the Reform Party whip, had beaten a path to racism's door with the observation that he would have no problem firing a gay or black person, or ordering him to work at the back of the shop, if his presence offended other customers. When Deborah Grey lashed out at Chrétien for not demanding Copps's resignation, the PM said she might consider asking someone in her own party to step down. What hypocrisy, shouted Chrétien, to have these people trying to teach the government a lesson on ethics. "I will not be put in the corner by the bully from Alberta." But the prime minister could not stem the furor against Copps, whose fighting spirit he admired so much. A day later, the deputy prime minister, teary-eyed and shaken, resigned her Commons seat.

In keeping with his post-referendum style, Chrétien had been prepared to tough it out. On Airbus, he refused to issue an apology. With the Flag Day protester, he was the ruffian. On separatism, he was taking a hard line. On the GST, he didn't want to give an inch.

William Thorsell, the editor of *The Globe and Mail*, described Chrétien as someone "who is very wary indeed of losing what he so unexpectedly accomplished in the world." Oftentimes, Thorsell observed, he "tends to assume the defensive stance of a bully. He digs himself into a fixed position and equates immobility with strength." By "the simple act of denial, he believes he can unilaterally define the landscape." "Chrétien loves his job," observed Carolyn Bennett, the Toronto doctor turned MP. "I don't think when he was a little boy he could ever have believed he could get there—and I think it's almost like an insecurity or lack of real confidence that explains some of his behaviour."

THE SOMALIA FILE, among the many controversial dossiers left over from the Conservative government, offered another example. The impoverished country in northeast Africa, divvied up among tribal warlords vying for power, had fallen into chaos three years earlier, in 1992. Drought and civil war had left hundreds of thousands on the brink of starvation. The United Nations, led by the United States, sent in forces to restore order and get the relief food lines moving. In early 1993, Mulroney contributed nine hundred members of the Canadian Airborne Regiment Battle Group. The regiment was soon caught up in scandal when a sixteen-year-old captive named Shidane Abukar Arone was tortured and beaten to death. Ottawa ordered a military police investigation in March, after a member of the regiment attempted suicide while being held in connection with Arone's death. Court-martial proceedings against soldiers and officers eventually resulted in four convictions.

In May 1994, some months after Chrétien came to power, a CBC reporter, Michael McAuliffe, received several Somalia-related documents through the government's Access to Information Act. They were found to have been altered. Then, in January 1995, the CBC aired disturbing videos of extreme hazing rituals at the Airborne base in Petawawa, Ontario. Defence Minister David Collenette announced the disbanding of the regiment, and two months later, he established a three-person commission of inquiry into the deployment of Canadian forces in Somalia.

The inquiry revealed more cases of alleged tampering with documents and document destruction, and it was clear it was causing annoyance at the highest levels. Signalling his displeasure, Chrétien complained that during interrogations at the inquiry, public servants were being treated "as if they were almost criminals." Moreover, the commission was expensive and was going on too long. "Even the Watergate," said Chrétien, "was settled in six or seven weeks in the United States." His memory was deficient here. The special Watergate senate committee ran for twenty months.

Meanwhile, the Opposition was claiming that the full story wasn't coming out. "The prime minister is getting pretty close to participating in the cover-up by the military," said Preston Manning, who was demanding the resignations of Collenette and General Jean Boyle, the chief of the defence staff. Deborah Grey labelled the two men the Laurel and Hardy of the Canadian military.

The highly combative Collenette was under the gun for not dumping Boyle, whose testimony before the inquiry suggested that he had tried to thwart the Access to Information Act. Collenette was angered that the three commissioners, one of whom was the former journalist Peter Desbarats, gave so much credibility to media reports. Journalists like McAuliffe, he claimed, were convinced there was a conspiracy, and the commission too often looked like it was on a polit- ical witch hunt. A big deal was being made over alleged document shredding, but Collenette tried to explain at least some of it away by saying that many of the documents contained responses to questions that might be put in Parliament. These responses often changed from week to week, the minister explained, and his department simply wanted to "get rid of the old stuff." The mistake the government made, Collenette felt, was having three commissioners instead of only one.

Collenette was soon sidelined, not by defence-related issues but by a minor violation of the government's ministerial code of ethics. He had written a letter to the refugee board in support of one of his constituents. Because of his close relationship with the prime minister, he said he thought it was the right thing to resign, at least temporarily.

Succeeding Collenette in the defence portfolio was Doug Young. But if the Somalia commissioners hoped they might now be left alone to do their work, they didn't know Young. In a striking moment of candour, Collenette compared his own style with that of his successor. "We both play hardball," he offered. "The difference is that I am a bit more clinical in the way I disembowel people."

General Boyle's resignation followed. Though it had never been proven that he had knowledge of any document tampering, his dodgy performance at the inquiry sealed his fate. After more criticisms of the commission by Chrétien, Young made it clear that he didn't want the inquiry to continue much longer. If necessary, he would disembowel it. Then, in a remark that tested the limits of political cynicism and shocked the Somalia commissioners, Young told the CBC that he "certainly wouldn't want to be in an election campaign with the inquiry still going on."

During the Airbus affair, the Chrétien PMO had let Mulroney twist in the wind for years because, it claimed, it didn't wish to influence a police investigation. While a semi-judicial inquiry like the one into Somalia wasn't quite the same, a senior Chrétien Cabinet minister was flatly declaring that it could well be subjected to political priorities. "Young's linking of the effects of our work to the coming election campaign," Desbarats wrote later "brings political considerations across the barrier that separates and insulates us from government interference."

Despite any coming election, despite warnings from the prime minister that the inquiry was going on too long and was hurting morale in the military, few thought the government could be so imperious as to arbitrarily shut it down. As far as Desbarats could determine, such an act had no precedent in British parliamentary history.

But that didn't stop the increasingly defiant prime minister. Doug Young took the knife to the Somalia inquiry, announcing at the start of 1997 that the commission had to complete its hearings within three months. That did not leave the commissioners time to finish investigating the murder of Arone or the allegations of a subsequent cover-up in Ottawa. But if the early election call came, the Liberals wouldn't have to worry about Somalia revelations coming at them in the middle of a campaign. And they wouldn't have to worry about future whistle-blowers coming forward to tell stories, because many of the officials implicated in the Somalia affair—just like the Airbus principals—fared well in the aftermath or even got promotions.

The commissioners continued their work under protest. The political interference was deplored by the Opposition, but it was not an issue—and the PMO knew this from polling—that caught fire with Canadians. The public, like Chrétien, was tired of hearing about Somalia. He knew he could get away with shutting it down.

Years later, a top PMO official who was close to the file would say that the closure was unnecessary and inexcusably authoritarian. Years later, Peter Desbarats would still be wondering what was behind the decision. "The fact," he said, "that Chrétien was willing to tamper with something like an independent inquiry for the sake of what appeared to be minuscule political advantage, I just thought, Wow, if he'll do that, he'll do anything." As a journalist, Desbarats had once accompanied Chrétien on a trip through the Arctic, and he had been impressed by his straightforwardness and integrity. But Chrétien's interference in the Somalia inquiry "changed the way I look at him totally."

PMO officials said it was pressure from Young that made him do it. Young hit the PM hard with the argument that the military could not be humiliated and demoralized any longer. But, as the Opposition argued, inquiries were supposed to do their work, no matter how demoralizing. If all inquiries were shut down once they became demoralizing, what was the good, critics asked, of even having them?

THE SQUABBLE OVER yet another venture of the Mulroney Tories, the privatization of Toronto's Pearson International Airport, took place in the same time period. Though not as controversial as Airbus, Somalia, or the GST squabble, this issue, with its soaring settlement costs, was dismaying to taxpayers.

The airport deal was done in the dying days—there were hardly any other kind of days—of the Campbell government. It was a $700-million contract awarded to a consortium of businesspeople, including several high-profile Tories, to redevelop and operate the two old terminals at Pearson. Decrying the deal as a cozy arrangement among Tory friends to enrich themselves, Chrétien promised during the 1993 campaign to kill it. At his very first Cabinet meeting, he ordered a quick study by his good friend Bob Nixon, the former Ontario treasurer. When Nixon recommended rejecting the deal, a bill was brought forth cancelling the contract and denying the consortium members any compensation for losses. Doug Young, then transport minister, once again didn't mince his words. He described the Pearson deal as "the biggest rip-off in Canadian history."

The complication in killing it came from the Senate, which housed a Tory majority and was only too happy to delay passage of the bill long enough for the rejected consortium to launch a lawsuit demanding compensation. The courts ruled that the Liberals had breached the contracts and were liable for damages. The Tories also conducted a Senate inquiry, which raised questions about the validity of the Nixon report, arguing that the airport deal had built-in safeguards to protect taxpayers and had set a competitive rate of return for the developers.

The Liberals countered that the arrangement had sweetheart deal written all over it. For one thing, it was for an astonishing fifty-seven-year term. The consortium was to make $700 million in improvements during that time, but there were no guarantees that it would spend more than the $96 million designated for the first few years. Charges of cronyism were rampant. It was revealed that an employee of Mulroney's office, who later became a consultant, would get a tidy $2 million for work on the Pearson deal. At the Department of Transport, the bureaucrat responsible for the file was replaced because promoters of the deal thought he was proceeding too slowly with the negotiations. Mulroney seemed to take a healthy degree of interest in the project. From late 1992 until June 1993, when he stepped down, he received ten memos from the clerk of the Privy Council on the subject; the last came just four days before he left office.

The Senate killed the Pearson legislation in June 1996. Chrétien came under increasing pressure to agree to a settlement so that the Pearson Development Corporation would drop its $662-million lawsuit. His other option was to present a new bill to cancel the deal. He appeared to be leaning towards that. "There will be a bill, I'm telling you. I've not changed my mind about it," he asserted.

But by April 1997, he was in the course of planning an early election, and a settlement took on more importance. In the end, the government agreed to a compensation package for the Pearson Development Corporation. The taxpayers' tab? Sixty million dollars.

CHAPTER EIGHT

THE SECOND MAJORITY

C ABINET MEETINGS BEGAN at ten on Tuesdays. They had to end by noon, a rule laid down by the punctual Chrétien, who never forgot those interminable hours he spent shuffling his feet at the Trudeau Cabinet table, when meetings were run like university seminars.

Occasionally, Chrétien ripped through the agenda so quickly that the meeting was over before the appointed hour and he would have to instruct his members to think of something to fill in the gap. If they all left early, it would look as if they didn't have enough to do. On the other hand, if noon arrived and there were items that hadn't been covered, the PM would move them to the next meeting.

"The first thing everybody wanted to know when Chrétien entered," recalled Art Eggleton, "was, 'Okay, what kind of a mood is he in?' Sometimes he would start off by saying, 'Goddamn it, we made this decision in here and the next thing I know, it's in the newspapers.'" One time, he threatened to find and fire the source of a leak. If he wasn't able to find the offender, there was another threat. "You know what I might do?" he asked the anxious group assembled around the table. "I might pick some name out of a hat."

The leakers were at the top of Chrétien's hit list. Gasbags weren't far behind. He respected ministers who made a concise contribution but was impatient with those who rambled on. He wasn't rude to them, but he took notice, and come shuffle time, the motormouths were invariably dropped or demoted.

In his own remarks at Cabinet, the PM could normally be counted on to linger over one subject. "In every Cabinet meeting I was in," noted

Eggleton, who sat through eight years of them, "there was nothing more important than the political situation in Quebec. Nothing close." Chrétien often issued reminders of how, throughout his political career, he had stood up for Canada. He talked of his pride in the country, of the sacrifices he had made, of the scars on his back, of being beaten up in his own backyard. And he would talk of how important it was for him to leave office with the situation calm in Quebec. Chrétien's biggest theme, recalled Herb Gray, was a united country.

With that and the last referendum in mind, the prime minister began in late 1996 to formulate what would eventually become known as the clarity legislation. In August of that year, the Quebec Superior Court, proceeding on an action initiated by the lawyer Guy Bertrand, had ruled that the courts did in fact have jurisdiction over the secession issue. That gave the Chrétien government its opening.

Prior to this, Ottawa had treated sovereignty as more of a political question than a legal one, and had therefore failed to take advantage of a good opportunity to throw up a roadblock against the secessionists. Pearson, Trudeau, and Mulroney had all missed the chance. Chrétien, who had seen those prime ministers come and go, didn't hit upon the idea himself. It took Bertrand, a former separatist who had done a *volte-face,* to come forward to make the legal challenge. When he did, the federal Liberals were nowhere to be seen—until the judgment was proclaimed in his favour.

A month after the Quebec Superior Court's decision, Chrétien took the matter to a higher authority, referring the issue to the Supreme Court of Canada. Justice Minister Allan Rock submitted three questions, the basic thrust of which was whether law—be it international or Canadian—gave Quebec the right to secede without the approval of the rest of the country. While acknowledging that a referendum could be legitimate, Rock contended that "the result of a referendum does not, in and of itself, effect legal change."

Separatists leaped at the opportunity to portray the federal government as once again trying to belittle the rights of Quebecers. "Our reaction is quite clear," said Lucien Bouchard. "There is only one tribunal to settle Quebec's future, and that's the Quebec people."

Stéphane Dion, who had pressed Chrétien to make the reference, made it clear that Ottawa would proceed from the Supreme Court ruling to then negotiate rules acceptable to both sides for a future referendum. With a notable degree of foresight, Dion predicted that support for sovereignty in Quebec would decline when Quebecers realized the overbearing difficulties involved in unilateral action. The partition debate, now being pushed by Anglo-rights groups in Quebec, was sending cold winds through the province, raising questions that Quebecers hadn't considered. Chrétien and Dion fervently hoped that the Supreme Court would place before the people of the province an even larger deterrent.

To no one's surprise, the provincial Liberals opposed Chrétien's initiative. Going the legal route could lend credibility to the whole separatist enterprise, Daniel Johnson's Liberals argued. The Supreme Court could give secession a legal imprimatur, thus emboldening the Quebec population. Moreover, they predicted that the very act of making the legal challenge would inflame passions in the sovereigntist movement.

Johnson preferred the old method of trying to renew federalism by making concessions to appease the Péquistes. Chrétien no longer wanted to use that option. He had seen it tried for decades. At Laval law school in the early 1960s—while Chrétien was being elected to Parliament for the first time—Lucien Bouchard was writing in the student paper that the best way to get power from Ottawa was via the blackmail route. "Fearing that French Canadians will create a separate state," Bouchard wrote, "there is no doubt that Canadians at large will give them what they've demanded for so long: the respect of their provincial autonomy." Thirty-five years later, he was still adhering to the strategy.

In Ottawa, the Tories of Jean Charest opposed Chrétien's legal gambit, while Manning's Reform Party, as expected, was supportive.

Manning had helped set the agenda not only on this issue but on deficits and the debt and high taxes as well. Early in his stewardship, Chrétien had been criticized for borrowing from Mulroney's Tory agenda. Now Reform was leading the way for the governing party. Stealing the good ideas from rival parties was the traditional Liberal method of clinging to power, and Chrétien had learned it well.

On most big issues, observed his top aide, Jean Pelletier, Chrétien was methodical. He would display quick-tempered reactions behind the scenes, but then he would go away and contemplate the longer-term effects of an issue before rendering a final judgment. Pelletier admired that patience. It's what set him apart from Bouchard. "Mr. Bouchard could make a sharp turn in an instant. Chrétien always planned." It helped explain why the mercurial Bouchard drifted through five different political parties, while Chrétien, wearing the same old uniform, lasted longer than anyone.

Chrétien had experience dealing with the Supreme Court on constitutional matters, having served as Trudeau's justice minister during the 1981 reference seeking a legal basis for the unilateral patri-ation of the Constitution from Great Britain. As prime minister, however, he had neither the time nor the intellectual credibility to engage his sovereigntist opponents on the legalisms of the Constitution. But now, with Dion as intergovernmental affairs and unity minister, he had the rapier at his side. Dion used the tactic of sending open letters to the Quebec premier to rebut the secessionist logic. In crafting them, he called on the sharp legalistic mind and writing punch of his top aide, Francie Ducros, who had moved over to Dion when Tobin left for Newfoundland. The letter-writing campaign was a much smarter way of dealing with complex matters than in a media scrum. And it worked. In the intellectual arena, the Péquistes no longer had a free ride.

"Stéphane is brilliant," said Liza Frulla, a Quebec Liberal who seldom agreed with his hard line but came to appreciate his mind. "He is a very sensitive person, but when he thinks, he thinks as a computer." With Dion, she said, it was like Trudeau. It was all about the conquest of emotion by logic. Frulla and her provincial Liberal flock were of the view that politics in Quebec was more emotional than logical. Chrétien, however, was more like Dion. He told caucus members when talking of the Supreme Court reference that they should not worry. "Quebecers will obey the word of law."

HE WAS PLANNING AN ELECTION for 1997, perhaps early in 1997, and to close off 1996 he appeared on one of the CBC's televised town halls. The CBC had been ravaged by Ottawa's budget cuts of two years earlier, and Doug Young, the hardline Liberal who had a penchant for shutting down public enterprises, had even suggested it should be privatized.

Though town halls were supposed to be freewheeling sessions with the public, open bear-pit sessions for a PM's supporters as well as his critics, they were in fact orchestrated events, with the questioners—in this case, thirteen from an audience of two hundred—pre-selected and even given a little coaching on how to put their queries.

For this town hall, questioners were in a confrontational frame of mind, the mood evident when a woman with three university degrees, Lori Foster of Saskatchewan, got up and told the PM that her credentials had resulted in nothing at the job counter. Chrétien showed little sympathy. "Some are lucky, some are unlucky," he replied. That's life. I think you have to keep trying." If she couldn't get work in Saskatchewan, he suggested she try moving somewhere else.

To another unemployed woman, a fisheries worker from Cape Breton, he was just as callous. Interest rates are low, he offered. Maybe you should start your own business. "Excuse me," the woman ripped back, "but wouldn't you have to have money to start a business? If you don't have a job, you pay your rent, you buy your groceries, you pay your power bill. You don't go out and start a business."

The host, Peter Mansbridge, adroitly recalled that this was the same Chrétien who had blasted Kim Campbell during the last election campaign for saying the government couldn't do much about unemployment until the turn of the century. Now he seemed to be suggesting the same thing. Chrétien slid under the volley, pointing out that his government had created more work than Campbell had anticipated.

On the question of the GST, a feisty Montreal waitress, Johanne Savoie, confronted Chrétien on his promise to get rid of the tax. "I didn't hear tinker," Ms. Savoie declared. "I heard scrap!" No, no, the prime minister countered, it's right in the Red Book—the promise to replace the GST with another revenue-gathering measure.

Baloney, responded Savoie. That wasn't what was stated in the campaign. The Tories were thrown out, she added, because they were "duplicitous in kind of saying one thing and doing another."

With an audience that wanted empathy, Chrétien remained aggressive throughout the show, ceding no ground and behaving like he was in Question Period in the Commons. That he didn't realize he had miscued became evident backstage, when he told Mansbridge that he thought the show had gone well. Mansbridge was glancing over at Donolo and could see a different reaction. The rolled-eyeball look.

Donolo was thinking, as he later recalled, "We made a mistake. We shouldn't have scheduled the town hall so soon. He and Chrétien had just returned from a long international trip and hadn't had time to acclimatize. Chrétien had always appeared to be on the side of the people, but this time he had come across as being on the other side. He and Donolo were barely out the door of CBC headquarters when the complaints began flooding in.

To Chrétien's distress, the show had opened the GST hornet's nest again, with Manning up in the Commons the very next day alleging that the prime minister had lied about his promise to scrap the tax. Chrétien again tried to explain that he was working on bringing in a replacement tax, but he was fed up. He had lost Sheila Copps over this (though she had since won her seat back in a by-election). He had lost John Nunziata. He'd had a quarrel with Paul Martin. He had chewed out his own staff. Now it was coming down on him like a five-hundred-pound hammer again. He hesitated to issue a formal apology, but on a trip to Newfoundland finally relented. "If I and others left the impression with anyone that we would be able to do away with the tax without a replacement, I want to tell them I am sorry."

He was more sorry that he hadn't followed his own gut instincts. When he was Opposition leader, he warned his Liberal caucus members against promising to eliminate the tax, arguing that it would come back to haunt them. But he gave in to the majority, and more than a decade later the members of Chrétien's high command would still be lamenting that decision. They felt the same about the decision to stay out of the 1995 referendum until the last week. Few politicians had the gut instincts of Chrétien. In these two instances, he and the party paid a heavy price when those instincts were not followed.

It had not been a good season for him. But for those keeping track of the big picture, the portents were fair enough. The trend-line showed that the deficit was disappearing at a rate far quicker than anticipated, and even more encouraging was the apparent cooling of sovereigntist fever in Quebec. Since the referendum, the pro-sovereignty numbers had levelled off. This was of particular importance to Chrétien because in his own riding of St-Maurice, he would be confronting a popular separatist in the coming election. He desperately needed a change of momentum—and it appeared to be coming.

As a prelude to the election campaign, he went to Washington to visit President Bill Clinton. Chrétien had met him at many multilateral meetings, but this was his first official visit to D.C. Usually, Washington was the first stop on a new prime minister's itinerary, but Chrétien had already been to thirty-four other capitals. In order to set himself apart from Mulroney, he had been anxious to demonstrate, as his Red Book stated, "an independent foreign policy for Canada."

Appearances had to be kept up—even if it meant doing some strange spinning. At one point, Clinton's press office was sounding so enthusiastic about the relationship with Chrétien that Peter Donolo put in a call to Mike McCurry, the president's press secretary, to tell him to tone it down. The gambit—"Please say the Canadian relationship is not so good"—may have been a first in bilateral history. Normally, of course, press secretaries rushed forward to overstate the harmony. The most famous such example came after the notorious Camp David meeting in 1965, when Lyndon Johnson berated Lester Pearson for having criticized his bombing campaign in Vietnam. Lecturing Pearson on the porch, Johnson took him by the shirt collar and let him have it. "You pissed on my rug!" he thundered. Turning that meeting into an example of bilateral bliss was quite the challenge. But the government PR men went to work. Following the summit, the headline for a report in *The Globe and Mail* blared, "Lester and Lyndon: A Unique Friendship." The subtitle read "Nowhere Else Are There Two Leaders Who Enjoy Such an Easy Relationship." The *Globe* correspondent waxed on about a "complete absence of rancour," quoting Canadian authorities as saying that the latest round of talks was "the most effective and rewarding they have undertaken."

In Clinton's Washington, Chrétien attended a National Press Club luncheon where the host referred to the criticisms levelled at Mulroney for being too cozy with presidents. Asked to characterize his own relationship, Chrétien said, "Good—and not too cozy." He had once mocked Mulroney for going fishing with Bush and ending up looking like the fish, but he now enjoyed the occasional golfing outing with Clinton without being accused of looking like the caddie. In a game in Halifax, Clinton had beaten Chrétien on the first nine holes. The president kept pointing out how Chrétien should stand, how he should grip the club, and Chrétien was becoming quite distracted. For the back nine, Chrétien asked that they play a straight game—no extra shots, no tips. "You're the big guy from Little Rock. I'm the little guy from Shawinigan. Let's go!" The PM won the back nine.

During his U.S. trip, Chrétien was quick to point out the differences between the two countries. He boasted of Canada's superior health insurance system, though this was in jeopardy because of his budgetary cutbacks, and needled the neighbour about its uncivilized gun laws. "We have recently enacted one of the toughest gun-control laws in the Western world," he told reporters, "and I must say that we are very pleased that—even with open trade between our countries— the National Rifle Association was unsuccessful in its attempt to export some of its expertise to Canada."

Then it was home to launch his bid for re-election.

SINCE AN ELECTION DIDN'T HAVE TO TAKE PLACE for another year or year and a half, the timing put Chrétien immediately on the defensive. Reminders quickly popped up about how Premier David Peterson of Ontario had, a few years earlier, smugly gone to the polls well in advance of the necessary date and suffered an embarrassing defeat.

Chrétien's call, only forty-three months into his mandate, marked the earliest a government with a majority had called an election in Canada since 1911, when Wilfrid Laurier, one of Chrétien's heroes, faced the voters less than three years into his term and was defeated. Chrétien had witnessed the dangers of early election calls first-hand. In 1965, he had advised Lester Pearson, who had a minority government, against an early campaign. Pearson declined his advice, jumped into the ring with Diefenbaker, and was returned with only another minority. In 1984, after Turner defeated him for the leadership, Chrétien advised him to wait until the New Year before going to the polls. His advice was rejected. Turner was swamped.

One reason Chrétien wanted a quick call was Ontario. In the province that mattered, he had an enormous lead. He had won ninety-eight of ninety-nine seats there in 1993, and David Smith, his Ontario manager, was telling him he could do it again. Chrétien had introduced Smith to President Clinton and told him of the last Ontario result, lightheartedly scolding Smith for losing the one seat. "Well, ninety-eight of ninety-nine isn't bad," said Clinton, cigar shooting out from his mouth. "Would you like to move to Washington?" he asked Smith. "I've got a job for you."

David Smith saw no problem in Chrétien going early. "The sun, the moon, and the stars were all sort of coming into an alignment where the essential ingredients of a win were there." But Chrétien knew, or should have known, that the media would be all over him, demanding a more profound rationale for an early call than just political opportunism. Everyone expected that when he emerged from the governor general's residence to sound the starting gun, he would have his lines prepared. But as was often the case with this politician of instinct, he stumbled, words failing him.

"It is because it is the fourth year of the mandate," he explained, offering up the most lame of rationales. "We had four budgets. Because of the success of our fight against the deficit, Canadians have to make a choice: to finish the job and invest in health care, children, jobs for tomorrow. Because for me, it is very important that we go to the people." And on and on he rambled, one puff of persiflage following another. No use delaying until the fall, he said, because the anticipation was now in the air. "We don't want to have an election that will last like the Americans—six months."

In Manitoba, meanwhile, flooding from the Red River was the worst in a century. Painting a scenario in which the government would be forcing Manitobans to go to the polls in canoes, Lloyd Axworthy had tried unsuccessfully to convince Chrétien to postpone the campaign. The PM visited the stricken area, where dam building was in progress, and was handed a sandbag. With the cameras rolling, he was heard saying, "What do you want me to do with it?" Sharon Carstairs, his Manitoba friend, was looking on. "Some birdbrain," she recalled, "told him to 'throw the bag on the pile.'" Following the birdbrain's instruction to the letter, Chrétien threw just the one bag and then left the scene for the next event on his schedule. The TV clip of the token toss was replayed time after time, becoming a fixed image of the early campaign: Chrétien was the great dam-builder—the one-bag man. It was doubly unfortunate, Donolo recalled, because "the Manitoba flood just became a symbol of an unnecessary election."

At dissolution, the Liberals held 174 seats, the Bloc Québécois and the Reform Party each had 50, the New Democrats had 9, and the Tories 2. Manning was planning to campaign on jobs and lower taxes, the NDP would fight the Liberals on their cuts to social programs, and Jean Charest's two-seat Tories were veering right to borrow from Mike Harris's Common Sense Revolution, thus battling Reform for hard-rock conservative turf.

In the campaign, several important questions had to be answered. Chief among them was whether the country would return to its traditional two-party-plus system by awarding one of the opposition parties enough seats to really distance it from the other small regional formations. If not, if the breakdown remained much the same as in the previous election, if the pizza parliament was entrenched, there could well be a continuance of one-party domination. Liberals forever!

The Grits had held an impressive twenty- to thirty-point lead in the polls since the last election. None of the other parties had captured the attention of the voters. Chrétien was in a position much like the one he had been in when he became Opposition leader in 1990. All he had to do to win was keep breathing. Once again, that would provide a challenge for him as he turned in a desultory campaign that asked voters to go with the status quo and nothing more.

The status quo wasn't wonderful, but it wasn't lamentable either. The federal deficit had been cut by two-thirds, inflation was at only 2 percent, and interest rates had fallen to a thirty-year low. At the same time, however, unemployment was still at 9.5 percent, the incomes of average Canadians were still falling, especially in comparison with those in the United States, and the GST was still in place. The latter was the issue that grated on Canadians the most. As for Airbus, Somalia, Pearson airport, taking protesters by the neck, the weak performance in the referendum—these hardly registered. But the

GST was the pocketbook issue, and the Grits had handled it like the Keystone Kops. It was an issue that embarrassed the governing party every time it was mentioned. It was an issue that was there for the taking, a diamond as big as the Ritz. But remarkably—and here the prime minister fell on good fortune once again—none of the opposition parties picked up on it. None came forward with a pledge to reduce the tax by 2 or 3 percent at this time and more in the future. Economists argued, with good logic, that cutting the GST wasn't good fiscal policy. But that had never stopped vote-hungry opposition leaders before. Reform, the party of tax cuts, looked at the idea, its campaign director, Rick Anderson, recalled, but took a pass. In the case of the NDP, Alexa McDonough could well have argued that the GST was a regressive tax. She could have targeted the rich to make up for the revenue shortage that would have come with reducing the GST. But the Dippers took a pass as well, and the Grits—even though they kept stumbling—could breathe easy.

They suffered another embarrassment while preparing to roll out Red Book Two, the new policy bible. It wasn't Chrétien who released it. Preston Manning did the deed for him. A copy had been faxed anonymously to Reform's campaign war room, and the Reform team gladly handed out copies to startled reporters who were trailing Manning in Quebec City. Manning put on a show, chucking the book to the floor while explaining that since there was nothing in it, he would gladly promote it.

Team Chrétien had wanted its release to be a significant campaign event even though the document was a collection of bromides. One big Red Book promise, restoring a chunk of the transfer payment cuts announced in 1995, had already been made public. Another was to double the $850 million in spending on the child tax benefit that had been announced in Martin's February budget. The rest of the platform was marked by caution. The problem, as Eddie Goldenberg and Jean Pelletier would make clear, was that many of the promises from the first Red Book were still being implemented. Moreover, with the deficit question unsettled, it was unclear how much money would be available for new spending.

Some Liberals had advocated bringing in a national projects agenda to give the country a sense of ambition and to have a big-bang item to take into the campaign. MP John Godfrey and the pollster Frank Graves, for example, were pushing for a plan to eradicate urban poverty. Chaviva Hosek, a key policy strategist for Chrétien, supported the plan, but the idea didn't get past the desks of Goldenberg and John Rae, who thought it was pie in the sky. Their incrementalist, or, as critics would say, "pedestrian" approach to governance was less risky. Small expectations could be realized. Big ones usually went unfulfilled, leaving the public disappointed. "We are led by a prime minister," explained Anne McLellan, the Cabinet member from Alberta, "who has a very profound belief that grand strategies and grand gestures are sometimes empty strategies and empty gestures."

Jean Charest came forward to take his blast. The Red Book was entitled "Securing Our Future Together." The initials, Charest pointed out, spelled SOFT. "Soft on tax cuts, soft on jobs, and soft on leadership."

The New Democrats, off the political map ever since Ed Broadbent left as leader, were trying to re-establish a base under Nova Scotia's Alexa McDonough, and with his cutbacks on unemployment insurance payouts Chrétien had handed her a nice opportunity, especially in the East, where joblessness was highest. Liberals like New Brunswick's Andy Scott threw up red flags about Axworthy's changes and how many Maritime seats they might cost the party. For his little piece of dissent, Scott discovered one day that he had been quietly removed from the Human Resources Committee, which had jurisdiction in the area. He was learning, as other MPs would also learn, that with Jean Chrétien at the helm, the centre was not to be challenged. As a backbencher, Scott couldn't get much media attention either. Julie Van Dusen, the perky CBC reporter, told Scott, "I'd like to get you on TV, but you ramble too much."

The Bloc Québécois had a new and sometimes capable leader in Gilles Duceppe, but he made the neophyte's classic political mistake of agreeing, while doing a factory tour, to don the suggested headgear. In this case, the Bloc leader was touring a cheese factory and slipped on a hairnet that made him look like an alien in a dunce cap. He became the butt of jokes for the rest of the campaign. With the media always on the lookout for something unusual to enliven dull campaigns, small mishaps could capture big air time. Poor Duceppe also had the misfortune of employing a campaign bus driver who was directionally challenged. The driver made it, unfortunately, to the cheese factory, but he lost his way on too many other occasions. The media used him—until he was dumped—as a metaphor for the Bloc campaign.

Chrétien was keeping a close watch on Duceppe and the separatists because of the challenge they posed in his riding of St-Maurice. In the 1993 campaign, he had faced a low-profile Bloc opponent, but Chrétien was now up against his longtime local arch-enemy, Yves Duhaime. Chrétien regarded Duhaime as a pompous ass, and Duhaime regarded Chrétien as a lowbrow thing. Their mutual loathing was legendary. Chrétien had warred with Duhaime intermittently for almost thirty years. They sneered at each other whenever they came in contact, and had almost come to blows on a number of occasions. One came during a quarrel over a piece of land Chrétien wanted to expropriate and turn into a federal government taxation centre. Duhaime, whose mother-in-law owned a piece of the land, was trying to block it. They met up at a bar association meeting at the Shawinigan Golf Club, where Chrétien, with the town's legal establishment looking on, threatened to beat Duhaime to a pulp. Before the donnybrook could ensue, other lawyers rushed in to separate them.

Duhaime was a popular figure in the Shawinigan area, which in the 1995 referendum had voted 56 percent in favour of sovereignty. Unemployment was high in the riding, and support for the federal Liberals across Quebec had fallen to 32 percent. For Chrétien to lose his own riding as prime minister would be humiliating, but losing it to a separatist would make it far worse, and losing it to Duhaime would be torture.

The prime minister went to his riding for his first rally of the campaign, and set the crowd rocking as he banged up Lucien Bouchard over his constant whining about never being satisfied with Ottawa. "How tiring it must be to get up every morning and feel humiliated," shouted Chrétien. "Me, I don't feel humiliated. . . . Look at this team of Quebecers I have with me in Ottawa. . . . We don't feel humiliated when we know for the last thirty years—twenty-eight years, I think—that the prime minister of Canada has come from Quebec. Where does this idea of humiliation come from?"

But his overall strategy was to stay away from the local riding fight, to be prime ministerial and above the fray. If he got down in the dirt with Duhaime, he knew any number of things could happen, including some behaviour highly unbecoming of a prime minister. So while the area residents and the media were expecting a titanic clash, they never got one. Chrétien never showed up, leaving Duhaime to pound away at an absent target.

Chrétien, however, wasn't helping his cause in his own riding with his nationwide campaign. There was no energy. Too much was wrong, beginning with the early election call. "In hindsight, it was a mistake," he later admitted. "It was clear it was a mistake within weeks. It wasn't a disastrous campaign, but it wasn't an inspired campaign."

The televised debates came early, an insurance policy for leaders who didn't want them to be too determinant. Often derided as one of the most inarticulate of prime ministers, Chrétien faced the smooth and telegenic Charest and the clear-spoken, if grating, Manning. Just as in the 1993 campaign debate, the Liberal leader had the ideal combination of low expectations and a big lead in the polls. All he had to do was show up and duck. Despite all the problems of his campaign, no other party was catching on. In the debates, none did either. The highlight of the two evenings came late in the second round, the French-language debate, when the moderator, Claire Lamarche, was just about to open a crucial segment on the percentage of the vote that would constitute a referendum victory. As the contestants eyed one another warily, she fainted, collapsing to the floor like a sack of potatoes. It brought a quick end to the evening's events and let Chrétien off the hook.

Charest was the best debater. He was cocky and quick and came across with the only big applause-winning line of the English-language contest. "If there is one commitment I have made to my children," he declared, looking directly at the cameras, "it is that I'm going to pass on to them the country I received from my parents. I'm determined to make that happen." Though a banal piece of patriotic slop, it struck a chord with the audience. Having tested the line before the debates, Charest knew it was a good one. While the cameras were on others, Manning had caught sight of the Tory leader mouthing the words in preparation for the delivery. Manning lamented his own inability to engage people's emotions. His skill, considerable enough, lay in his ability to clinically dissect the issues. It was only after the debate, he recalled, that he thought of what would have been the ideal response to Charest's line. The one commitment Manning would make would be to pass on a "better" country to his children.

Chrétien, meanwhile, had fun with Duceppe. When the Bloc Québécois leader started listing the government's faults, the PM replied that if he was going that far, why not blame the government for his bus driver losing his way as well? "That was the only time it wasn't the federal government's fault." He went after Charest too. When the Tory leader made reference to fighting between Chrétien and the Bloc on the Commons floor, the PM interjected, "You were never in the House." But Charest was quick on the uptake. "I don't have the impression I missed much."

Chrétien survived, but the critics had at him. "In the English-language leaders' debate," wrote the right-leaning former Liberal Gordon Gibson, "we saw a face without confidence, eyes without vision, heard words with no greater purpose than to get through the ordeal." Robert Fulford, the former long-time editor of *Saturday Night* magazine, found it extraordinary that "this is the first election ever in which only one party claims to be running for first place." Chrétien, he observed, "has adopted the policies of the most unpopular prime minister in history, he has made about 40 percent of us like these policies and he has persuaded the rest of us that he is at worst an honest fellow, though not too bright." In a withering cultural broadside, Fulford added that Chrétien understood something that Mulroney did not: "Deep within the Canadian spirit lies the idea that there is something honest about ignorance and something slick about knowledge."

With that pitiless put-down, Fulford was dipping into the Quebec intellectuals' school of calumny. Chrétien was popular because Canadians were sympathetic to such a doltish fellow, he was saying. How else could you explain it?

It was a sign of things to come. Chrétien was getting under the skin of the establishment class. He always had, but the elites hadn't minded it so much when he was a warrior in the Trudeau Cabinets. As prime minister, though, Chrétien was harder for the blue bloods to stomach. They feared he was making it politically correct for a hick to be a leader of the country. What next? A truck driver as prime minister?

CHRÉTIEN COULD ROLL OUT some remarkable observations in some remarkable ways and, like the broken-down Chevy he was sometimes compared to, elicit more amusement than ire. In a rally in Edmonton, he was trying to defend Quebec and its importance to the country. Quebecers, he tried to explain, had saved Canada by not joining the American Revolution. "People have to read the history a little bit too before they open their mouths. We should talk about too, that if there is a Canada today, it is because we, the Francos from Quebec, refused to join the American Revolution. Only they decided to stay in Canada, and that gave the land to the Loyalists to come from the United States to keep, to stay, to keep staying into, you know, the British, the empire of the day."

Hearing such outpourings, Preston Manning would shake his head. "I think Preston tended to be one of those people who underestimated

Chrétien," recalled Reform's Rick Anderson. "He didn't understand what it was about Chrétien that a certain kind of middle-of-the-road voter would find reassuring. Preston would take the intellectual approach to everything, and Chrétien would reduce it to two paragraphs and make the political choice."

Because Chrétien's image was already that of the battered man, throwing more dirt at him usually didn't work. Picking up strength in Quebec, Jean Charest tried to exploit Chrétien's dubious image in the province by accusing him of being a foreigner in his own land. "Mr. Chrétien doesn't seem to come from Quebec," Charest told the *Journal de Montréal*. He "is a guy from Ottawa, and that shows in his choices." Chrétien took advantage, labelling the attack as below the belt. "I don't especially share Mr. Charest's opinions, but I don't question his Quebec origins."

Quebec origins became the focus of the campaign when Manning, with ten days left until voting day, chose to unleash an attack ad on French-Canadian leaders. Three of the parties in the race were led by francophones. The ad showed pictures of Chrétien, Charest, Duceppe, as well as Bouchard, and advised that enough was enough. There should be "a voice for all Canadians, not just Quebec politicians," the voice-over asserted. To emphasize the point, the ad featured a large circle with a slash running through it, the suggestion being that the Franco leaders be wiped away. This was a last-minute addition to the advertisement—and one the Reformers would regret. It allowed opponents to slam Manning as intolerant. Charest called him a "bigot" who was appealing to "the worst in human nature." Chrétien didn't mince his words either, alleging that Manning was running "the most divisive campaign in Canadian history."

The Reform ad had been prompted by Manning's suspicion that there was much bitterness left over from the 1995 referendum campaign, when English Canada was virtually shut out of the debate. He was losing ground to the Tories and needed to do something dramatic. His ad was not an attack tactic of the type the Tories had

used in 1993, when they portrayed Chrétien as an embarrassment. But
it played to the party's stereotype redneck image and, while helping
Reform in its core support areas, prompted a backlash in the East,
where Manning had hoped to make inroads.

The campaign had become a fight for second place, but for the
Liberals the danger as the final week approached was that the regional
splinter parties would accumulate enough seats in their respective areas
to deny Chrétien a majority. Polling suggested that could well be the
result. The Liberal campaign had simply sputtered along, giving off
the impression that the election was about nothing except maintaining a grip on power.

In the final week before voting day, three Western premiers came
together to attack the government on medicare. Ralph Klein of
Alberta noted that Ottawa paid only 11 percent of his province's
health care bill. "If you owned a business and you were an 11-percent
partner and you called the shots, I don't think the people who pay
89 percent would appreciate it." In the Atlantic provinces, where
Chrétien was suffering heavily from the effects of unemployment
insurance cuts, three Liberal premiers came together to attack the
platform of Jean Charest, saying he would gut health, education, and
social services.

The Bloc, after its embarrassing start, had recovered some ground
in Quebec, and Chrétien continued to be uncertain about the
outcome in his own riding. Surveys showed that he held a big
advantage as a sitting prime minister because he was perceived as
being able to do more for the riding. Yves Duhaime tried to counter
that impression, painting Chrétien as an autocrat who had done
nothing for the constituency.

Reminding voters of Chrétien's vow not to recognize a simple
majority in a referendum campaign, Duhaime compared him to an
African dictator. "Mr. Chrétien has a little bit of an African side
which we don't know," he said. The Bloc candidate ran a bitter
campaign that reflected the poor relations between the two men.

Though Chrétien hardly showed up, residents said they were used to it. Alain Lord, owner of the Taverne Moderne, could name the exact date, April 5, 1994, when the PM last came to visit his bar. He came in, recalled the owner, said hello, ordered a beer, "made, like, one gulp," and left.

Four days before the vote, Chrétien's campaign announced a loan of $615,000 to the Auberge Grand-Mère. The loan came from the Business Development Bank of Canada, a Crown corporation. Duhaime fumed. He knew this was a good answer to his allegation that Chrétien did nothing for the riding—and he suspected that all was not above-board with the loan. Chrétien and several friends had once owned part of the hotel and the Grand-Mère Golf Club, which sat close by. They'd made the purchase in 1988, but neither the club nor the hotel business did well, and Chrétien sold his interests in both in 1993. As the 1997 campaign rolled on, he was still owed approximately $300,000 on his sale of the golf course. The recipient of the hotel loan, as Duhaime sourly pointed out, was a different Duhaime, Yvon Duhaime, the businessman who had bought the hotel from Chrétien in 1993, taking a money-losing proposition off his hands. Now he was receiving government largesse. It was a bit strange, Yves Duhaime thought. It was not known at the time the announcement was made, but Chrétien worked hard to get the loan for the Auberge Grand-Mère. That he personally lobbied the head of the Business Development Bank for it was to become a matter of high controversy.

Election night started dismally for the prime minister. The people of Atlantic Canada sent him a chilling message. Although he had practically swept the Maritimes in 1993, now he was being beaten up by Alexa McDonough's NDP, with help from Charest's Tories. The Grits lost twenty seats in the four provinces, and their share of the popular vote dropped by 40 percent. Nova Scotia and New Brunswick turfed out two strong Cabinet members, David Dingwall and Doug Young. The Liberals had won all eleven seats in Nova Scotia in 1993. This time they lost them all.

In St-Maurice, the results were close. At 11:30, with eighteen thousand votes counted, Chrétien was leading Duhaime by only six hundred votes. But soon the spread was more than a thousand, and he was safe. Across the rest of Quebec, however, the news wasn't terribly encouraging. The Liberals had survived the threat from Charest, but not the Bloc. Charest had taken a hit late in the campaign when Lysiane Gagnon of *La Presse* painted him as a son figure to Brian Mulroney. The Liberal communications team sent her column out to all media, making sure it was well noted, and Charest's support dropped badly. He won only 5 Quebec seats, while Chrétien's Liberals took 26 and the Bloc, forty-four.

The key for the Grits again was Ontario. This time, the province offered 103 seats. The Liberals won an astonishing 101 of them, taking the province by the throat just as they had done in 1993. It was all that the Ontario Party, as it could well have been called, needed. The seats they won in all other areas of the country equalled only half the number from Ontario, but there was enough to form, by a bare margin, another majority government. It was not confirmed until late in the evening, when British Columbia reported that the tidal wave for Reform had stopped in the heart of Vancouver. The five seats won in those urban ridings, rich in Asian immigrants who customarily voted Liberal, put Chrétien over the top.

The Liberals won 155 of the 301 seats available. The Reform Party became the official opposition with its 60 seats. The Bloc held 44, the NDP 21, and the Tories 20. The results were not much different from those of the 1993 campaign. The opposition couldn't sort itself out, and there was only one team vying for the championship. All the other contenders were still in division two.

"I won a second majority, so the Liberal Party knows it's quite a performance," Chrétien told reporters outside his office in Shawinigan. Oddly, the party had not won back-to-back majorities since 1953. Chrétien had achieved the feat, but it was hardly a triumph—and arguably not even "quite a performance." He won only one of the country's five regions. He ran on no big agenda, received no big mandate, had no big plans.

But more important, he still had no big opposition. He was the only game in town. In the kingdom of the blind, as the old expression had it, the one-eyed man ruled.

CHAPTER NINE

SOFT POWER, HARD POWER

Having called the 1997 election for no big reason, having made no big promises in the campaign, Jean Chrétien ambled into his second mandate not even bothering to change the team he'd had in the first. His majority had been substantially reduced. The people seemed to be sending a message. But if that was the case, the prime minister wasn't paying much heed.

He liked his Cabinet team and he liked his office team. Some of those already in Cabinet had to be shuffled because he had lost two of his pugilists from down East, Doug Young and David Dingwall. But no backbencher or newly elected MP received a battlefield promotion. The more ambitious members of the Ontario Party, as some now referred to the Liberals, would have to wait—and probably wait a long time. It raised the possibility that they would start looking to curry favour with someone more likely to satisfy their ambitions. "In 1997 we were regaining control of public finance," recalled Jean Pelletier. "We were still on the program of what had been launched in 1995." An election didn't necessarily mean a major turn. It wasn't a case, he observed, of "reinventing the wheel every four years. It's not possible. We had to finish what had been proposed to Canadians."

Pelletier, the self-described man of the centre, fit well with the prime minister's other closest confidants, Eddie Goldenberg, John Rae, and Mitchell Sharp. He was prudent, not given to big plans or wild scheming. The young guys around the PMO, Dominic LeBlanc and the Westerner Raj Chahal and Jean Carle, the gatekeeper, saw him as a father figure, and they admired how utterly calm and unflappable he was in handling the affairs of state. "We used to watch him in the summer, going down Sparks Street for a walk or for lunch," recalled LeBlanc. "It would be thirty-two degrees and he'd have this heavy blue suit on, all done up, and there wouldn't be a bead of sweat on him."

Cabinet ministers like Anne McLellan judged Pelletier too senior to use his first name. In her case, she chose to call him Mr. P. The other common name for him was the Velvet Executioner. He could plunge in the knife in the gentlest but deepest of ways, without changing the expression on his face. It was a style of diplomacy that probably came from his having been an elected official himself, a mayor. "I had my experience and my white hair," he said. "I could do it in a way that would not hurt as much. It's probably what gave me the name."

The considerably younger Peter Donolo found himself surrounded by these managerial, regimented types, and while it was a bit staid, he came to admire the professionalism of the operation. "One thing that was good about the office, we weren't a gang. We weren't a clique. We didn't go out and carouse together on the weekend. We all had our separate lives. . . . We were very different from Paul Martin in that regard. Paul is an emotional yo-yo who gets very personal with his entourage and takes an interest in their private lives. Chrétien is not like that at all."

Chrétien told old political stories but seldom got personal with his staff. His view of the business of politics was well illustrated one time when a reporter was in his presence as he sat with Donolo and Jean Carle. "You see these two guys here?" Chrétien said to the journalist. "If you asked them, they would probably tell you they are my friends. But they are not. In politics, there is no room for friendship." This would become all the more clear to Donolo as time moved on. "He asked me about my personal life once," he recalled. "It was after I had left."

Though he had a somewhat folksy public image, Chrétien was as Prussian as any of them. "He has a routine," said Bruce Hartley, his closest personal aide, "and he never breaks the routine." He went home for lunch with his wife at 24 Sussex almost every day. In the evenings, he was loaded down with homework to take back to his study. On the road, it was dinner, then right up to his room. He read a lot, didn't watch much TV, and was rarely away from work, except, said Hartley, when he was at the golf course. Chrétien met with Pelletier and the clerk of the Privy Council every morning at 9:30. Pelletier would come directly from a meeting of the PMO's senior staff on the second floor of the Langevin Block. If you were late for that meeting, you didn't enter. Pelletier did a *tour de table,* with each person reporting on his or her area of responsibility. He showed a sense of humour, but he didn't like gossip. He told the staffers to remember something: "The only thing you can control is what you don't say." He realized, said one member of the team, that "telling people everything doesn't get you where you want to go."

The PMO meetings were dominated by central Canadians, which, as a Westerner put it, led to predictable results. "There weren't enough Westerners here, [and] Western issues that could easily have been resolved weren't resolved because of that."

The question of who was more powerful, Pelletier or Goldenberg, was a subject of some debate. Because Pelletier had to spend a lot of time on administration while Goldenberg stuck largely to issues, Goldenberg appeared to have more influence on the policy direction of the government. Goldfinger, as some MPs called him, ran the senior staff meetings when Pelletier wasn't there. He knew that he didn't have to impress anybody with his position. If anyone tried to go around him, they would soon realize they had committed a grave error. He lacked Pelletier's smooth way with people, and in those times, when relations with caucus members were becoming difficult, when a lot of egos had to be soothed, his edginess—the sometimes blunt way with which he dispensed power—did not play to his advantage.

He and Pelletier and the prime minister usually agreed on the general approach the government should be taking. "The PM's approach is a material approach, and a very safe political approach," said another staffer. "You don't fix problems that you don't have to. You don't make a decision you don't have to—until it has to be made. Nobody was sitting around saying, 'Christ, we're just maintaining the status quo—and why don't we do something exciting?' Good government is boring government." It was perhaps this attitude that gave rise to a sporting analogy Joe Clark used to describe Chrétien's performance as prime minister: "A very serviceable utility infielder."

In replacing Doug Young at defence, Chrétien was in need of someone who could handle the Somalia fallout, keep the decibel level low, defuse difficult situations. Who better than the man who had been mayor of Toronto for eleven years without anyone knowing it? Art Eggleton would do fine.

Chrétien called him over to Sussex Drive, sat him on the couch, and asked Eggleton, who had moved to trade after the Treasury Board, what he would like to do next.

"Well, Prime Minister, I'd like to stay in trade. I've been there only a year and a half, and I helped with the Red Book policy on it and—"

"Have you thought about defence?" the PM interrupted.

"No, but let me tell you what I'd like to do in trade."

When he was finished, the PM said, "You sure you don't want to talk about defence?"

"Well, Mr. Prime Minister, I'm a team player and . . ."

Chrétien smiled and said, "I'll call you."

A couple of nights later, Eggleton was dozing during the national news when the telephone rang. Chrétien came on the line and said, "Hello, Minister of Defence."

Eggleton sighed. "Okay, Prime Minister, I'll do my best."

Chrétien said, "I know you will," and hung up.

To fill the vacancy in health, the PM turned to the unlikely person of Allan Rock. The justice minister had no experience in the field, and with his legal background and his pinstriped precision, he was hardly an ideal fit. He was a man for the boardrooms, not the emergency wards. But experience in the area of responsibility was never a major prerequisite for a Cabinet minister. When Trudeau wanted to make Chrétien Indian affairs minister, Chrétien objected, saying he knew absolutely nothing about the Native peoples file. That's why, Trudeau told him, he wanted him for the job. Fresh perspective.

As well as making her deputy prime minister, Chrétien had saddled Sheila Copps with the environment portfolio. It was too much. Never known to be contrite, Copps conceded as much when she looked back on her early years under Chrétien. "There's a fairly steep learning curve when you get into government, and there's nobody who hands you a road map and says, this is how you do it." As deputy prime minister, "you literally had to be up to speed on every issue of every portfolio. You had to be ready to speak on all issues." She found environment complicated enough without every other issue of government on her plate. Copps said she was often acting from the political perspective. "I'm not sure that is what was wanted," she said. "I would do it differently now. I'd understand the process better."

Chrétien decided to replace her as deputy prime minister, and he looked to a senior statesman to take over the job. Herb Gray, at sixty-six, had served in Parliament for thirty-two years. His storehouse of knowledge was vast, he was studied and pensive, and he had the respect of his colleagues. And, of course, there was another aspect of Herb Gray which garnered much comment. He could render throngs of listeners comatose in a matter of minutes. He had the capacity to take a controversial subject of an utterly compelling nature and suck the blood right out of it. It was a strange phenomenon. Gray spoke with clear logic and sound syntax, but the sum total was a pile of rubble, every sharp edge dulled to the point that people just said, "Oh, forget it," and moved on. But for defusing controversy, there was no one like Herb Gray.

Chrétien's Cabinet was hardly stellar. Besides Paul Martin, who remained in finance, there was no one who commanded much authority. Industry Minister John Manley was competent and a man of good judgment, but he was frighteningly stolid. "Manley is so dull," cracked one wag, "that in the moment before his death, images of someone else's life will pass before his eyes." Unity Minister Stéphane Dion had shown intellectual vigour in his short time in town, but with his withdrawn countenance, he seemed more like an undertaker than a star of the future. Lloyd Axworthy had replaced André Ouellet in foreign affairs and was finding it a much more welcome venue. Though he had a jumbled way of speaking, he never lacked in smarts or high ideals.

With Herb Gray and Mitchell Sharp still around, Chrétien could find the odd holdover from the 1960s, but many of his original colleagues had passed on. Pierre Trudeau had suddenly become old and frail. Jean Marchand had passed away, and now, a couple of months after the election victory, Chrétien heard of the death of the third wise man, Gérard Pelletier. His honourable approach to political life was summed up well at his funeral by Claude Ryan. Pelletier, said the one-time leader of the Quebec Liberals, "believed in the dignity of the human person. He did not seek his own aggrandizement. He sought the common good in the noblest sense of the term."

The starlit trio were left-leaning Liberals and Chrétien couldn't help being discomfited by his government's dismantling of some of the work these men had done. He knew there had been little choice in the matter, given the deplorable fiscal situation. That condition was now close to being corrected, but he still suffered the comparisons of looking like a Tory. The Mulroney government hadn't had to cut as much from health or education as he had. It hadn't made the big cuts in unemployment insurance. It had a more progressive record on the protection of land, air, and water.

As an outdoorsman and as the politician who had created so many new federal parks under Trudeau, Chrétien was most bothered by the latter comparison. Mulroney had been able to sign a far-reaching acid rain treaty with the United States. It was quite a feat, even Chrétien would acknowledge, given Ronald Reagan's dismissive attitudes on the subject. The Gipper was the one who declared, "A tree's a tree. How many do you need to look at?" On another occasion, he argued that trees polluted the atmosphere more than automobiles. Students thought he was a little excessive with that claim. While touring California, Reagan was greeted at a college campus by a sign strung across a big oak. It read, "CHOP ME DOWN, BEFORE I KILL AGAIN!"

In 1991 in Rio de Janeiro, the Tories signed a global accord with 154 countries to stabilize carbon dioxide emissions at 1990 levels by the year 2000. The Liberals' Red Book of 1993 promised more. Paul Martin had once been the Liberal environment critic—a task he took most seriously, even resisting pressures to change to a more high-profile position. Like other Liberals, he backed a pledge to cut emissions by 20 percent by the year 2005. But in the Liberals' first four years in power, emissions increased. Chrétien conceded Canada's failure at the United Nations, where Britain's Tony Blair, sporting a better record, condemned the laggards.

Chrétien was still very much the learner on the world stage. He had never taken a particular interest in diplomacy and global affairs, fields he felt were more suited to academics and intellectuals than a small-town man. He had served under John Turner as Opposition critic to Foreign Affairs Minister Joe Clark, but he had failed to make an impression. Looking back, Clark asked, "Chrétien was foreign affairs critic under Turner? Frankly—and this is an awful thing to say—I can't remember if he was the critic."

But now, after four years in the prime minister's chair, he was beginning to gain some confidence, so much so that he didn't mind letting the leaders of nations know what he really felt. While attending a NATO conference in Madrid in the summer of 1997, he fell into conversation with Jean-Luc Dehaene, the prime minister of Belgium, about the deficiencies of the American political process. A nearby microphone had accidentally been left on, and Chrétien, unaware he was being recorded, expressed amazement at the cheap horse-trading that drove the U.S. system. "In your country or my country, all the politicians would be in prison if they sold their votes the way American politicians do," Chrétien asserted. If the president wanted a congressman's vote, the congressman would tell him, "You have to build a bridge for me in my electoral district."

The Belgian prime minister chuckled in agreement as Chrétien continued, tooting his own horn when he got the chance. Once, he said, he had brokered discussions between Clinton and President Jacques Chirac of France, and the president reported back, "Jean, you saved my bacon."

The Canadian prime minister, as the conversation made clear, was also not above a little horse-trading himself. Clinton had asked him for help in easing a crisis in Haiti, where the president had recently sent troops. So what did Chrétien do? "Okay, I send my soldiers. And then afterwards, I ask for something in return."

From his comments, it was easy to discern elements of his policy towards the only superpower. "I like to stand up to the Americans," he told Dehaene. "It's popular. . . . People like it." Fortunately for Chrétien, Bill Clinton had a sense of humour and took his remarks in stride. The candid conversation prompted far more of a flurry in Canadian political circles than anywhere else.

In replacing André Ouellet with Lloyd Axworthy as foreign affairs minister, Chrétien knew which way he was turning. Since his years as a student at the bucolic Princeton of the early 1960s, where he had studied the role of middle powers, Axworthy had been a proponent of an independent foreign policy for Canada. At that time he, like Trudeau, opposed Lester Pearson's policy of allowing American nuclear warheads to be stationed on Canadian soil. Axworthy even had the gumption to write Pearson and offer some gratuitous advice on how to operate in the world. He suggested that the solution to the Cold War was not military buildup but diplomacy.

Throughout his career, and into his tenure at foreign affairs, he sought to occupy the moral high ground. Canada, Axworthy pointed out, had "never claimed to be the world's conscience. But we have come to be regarded internationally, on the basis of our record, as motivated by conscience as well as by interest." But that type of motivation was not readily evident in the Chrétien government's early record. Martin's 1995 budget took the meat cleaver to foreign aid, slashing it by 20.5 percent. The Canadian military had also taken a crippling hit. The dollar diplomacy, with it's emphasis on trade missions, favoured by Chrétien was hardly in keeping with humanitarian goals. Nor, for that matter, was his reluctance to criticize China's human rights violations or the record of his armed forces in Somalia.

While the Somalia affair occupied the headlines, Chrétien tried acting in another area of Africa to bring some honour to the military, the government, and himself. In the fall of 1996, the fallout from the two-year-old Rwandan catastrophe set off a mass exodus of over a million Hutu refugees to eastern Zaire. The refugee camps fell under the control of factions of the Rwandan army, and the refugees were not getting needed relief supplies. To try to ward off another humanitarian disaster, Chrétien came up with a plan for Canada to lead a multinational military force in the region. His nephew, Raymond Chrétien, was both an ambassador and the United Nations special envoy to the area. The prime minister, his wife, and Raymond worked the phones to get the plan off the ground, calling a dozen foreign leaders in one weekend.

Lloyd Axworthy sensed that the PM was genuinely moved by the suffering and thus was prepared to go into overdrive. "It was just the image of these million people starving and in chaos, and he called me and Doug Young up and we sat down and he said, 'We want to do an international mission.'"

But the refugee crisis started to ease, and it was becoming clear that Ottawa didn't have the clout to make the mission work in the first place. "We had the opportunity to establish a really effective UN presence there," said Axworthy. "We were hamstrung by the fact that we didn't get the right kind of backing from our friends. We weren't getting the right kind of intelligence, and our own military was very unhappy to go there."

Short on resources, Axworthy was trying to find a way to make Canada's presence felt through other means: soft power as opposed to hard power. The foremost manifestation of this was in Ottawa's push for a global treaty banning the use of anti-personnel land mines. Such mines were responsible for killing or maiming an estimated twenty-six thousand people a year, the great majority of them civilians. Canada had joined a global coalition against landmines in 1996, with some of the groundwork laid by Axworthy's predecessor, Ouellet. But major powers such as China, Russia, and the United States had balked at signing the treaty. In Oslo in September 1997, Axworthy proposed a new set of fast-track negotiations, dubbed the Ottawa Process. The death of Diana, the Princess of Wales, in August had spurred the global campaign because it had been one of her leading causes.

Chrétien began a strong personal lobbying effort that took him to Moscow to meet with President Boris Yeltsin. The prime minister had taken a shine to the big boozy Russian when he saw footage of him standing atop a tank in downtown Moscow to signal his resistance to a coup attempt against Mikhail Gorbachev, whose opening up of the Soviet bloc with democratic reforms had helped trigger the end of the Cold War. Yeltsin took Chrétien out to his country dacha, where they feasted for three and a half hours on fish soup, wild game, and mushroom salad. The dacha had gained some renown in 1993, when Mulroney, in his twilight months in power, joined Yeltsin there on a wild boar hunt. A photograph showed the two men hoisting high-powered rifles and sporting wide grins as they stood over two dead boars. Chrétien got a big bear hug from Yeltsin but hunted no boars. He received instead a written commitment from Yeltsin to bring a permanent halt to Russia's export of land mines. During a subsequent meeting of Commonwealth leaders in Edinburgh, he persuaded the heads of six smaller states to sign on to the accord. In December, the treaty was formally ratified in Ottawa. Though the U.S. and some other major players did not sign, it was a good moment for Canada—and for Lloyd Axworthy.

The foreign affairs minister and Chrétien had also begun lobbying world leaders for the creation of an international court to bring to justice war criminals such as Cambodia's Pol Pot or terrorists such as the Libyans suspected of the Lockerbie air disaster in December 1988. Moving far and wide, Axworthy took on an array of other soft-power causes, including campaigns against child labour, child soldiers, and the spread of small arms. He partnered himself with the Norwegian government to build a coalition with countries like Austria, Ireland, and South Africa to act together on nine different humanitarian issues. Though Clinton was personally in favour, Washington continued to balk at the land mines initiative and opposed the International Criminal Court as well.

Axworthy was given a lot of scope on foreign affairs, which stood in direct contrast to the opposition he met at head office over his proposed social reforms. In the area of foreign policy, his soft-power approach, while much derided by conservatives, put the government on the map. Chrétien knew it wouldn't hurt him politically because, as he told the Belgian leader, it's popular for Canadian politicians to tear a strip off the Yanks. Chrétien took personal pride in some of the Axworthy initiatives, telling the journalist Don Martin that perhaps he deserved a bit of credit. "Oh, everybody takes too much credit all the time," he explained. "In a way, take land mines, our international agenda. Lloyd got all the credit. But I started that in 1994. You know, good for him." Axworthy recalled in a later interview that it was in fact Chrétien who insisted—while most every other government program was being downsized by Martin's attack on spending—that an exception be made for the land mines initiative.

Of Martin's budgetary reforms Chrétien said, "I don't mind if ministers take credit. It's good for me. I'm not jealous to the point that I want to take all the credit for it. He was a good minister of finance, and I back him up all the time. But who was having the flak?" And what about the deputy ministers who had to implement the unsparing cutbacks? he asked. "It was a collective activity."

Putting his raw pragmatism on display, he claimed that he didn't care much about how he was perceived over time. "Legacy?" he said. "I don't give a damn about legacy. You know, you die and you cannot read it any more. The last thing you should do is be preoccupied with what they say about you when you're not there." These were typically charming Chrétienisms, but few believed that having fought all his life for power, he didn't want to leave something memorable behind. Though not as fixated as Mulroney, he was a close observer of what the media said about him. He would not have published a memoir when he first left politics if he didn't care about what the public thought.

Through this period, he was reading David McCullough's large and loving portrait of Harry Truman, and he liked to point out that when Truman left office in 1952—Chrétien was eighteen at the time—he was viewed as a mediocre, if not lousy, president. Much, much later, the spin became more favourable, but it was too late for Truman to know about it. He died in 1972.

Chrétien's style, bare and basic, was often compared to that of the president from Missouri. What Chrétien admired most about Truman was his backbone. Both men had a lot of internal strength. Those who worked with Chrétien saw this quality in him. The Oakville, Ontario MP Bonnie Brown, a gutsy woman in her own right, described this as a crucial difference between him and Turner, and possibly Paul Martin as well. "I always thought Turner was a very nice man who wanted to make everybody happy, but he didn't really know who he was. I always think inside of you is an imaginary part, like a rod that comes up the middle of your trunk. You build that rod into steel by being who you are, by being your authentic self as frequently as possible." Chrétien had done that, she felt, but Turner was wobbly. The people detected his lack of inner confidence and didn't elect him. Brown worried that Paul Martin had the same shortcoming. Though he was a fierce competitor, she sensed that he was overly sensitive, too anxious to please.

Patrick Lavelle, Chrétien's long-time campaign organizer, said of his boss what some said of Truman. "I feel very strongly that Chrétien has a core, when so many other politicians in public life have absolutely none. It will sustain him."

"Balls of steel" was the descriptor that Duncan Fulton, who worked on Chrétien's communications team, favoured for his boss. But while his supporters admired his toughness and found it Trumanesque, others worried about the potential downside. Examples of him crossing the line into authoritarianism were accumulating, a prime example being the summit for Asia-Pacific Economic Cooperation (APEC) in Vancouver in November 1997. Planning for this major international gathering was difficult because of the expected appearance of President Raden Suharto, the Indonesian strongman. With his dismal human rights record, he feared for his safety in Vancouver and made repeated security demands of the Canadian government. Assurances were given that demonstrators would not be permitted to get close. The RCMP was told in early August that it was the prime minister's wish that there be no distractions at the conference. The choice of location was making that difficult. It was a big mistake, Goldenberg would later say, to hold it at the University of British Columbia. Having a summit of this nature on a university campus was only asking for disorder.

Even before the parley was underway, the crackdown began. A graduate law student holding a sign was threatened with arrest as she stood outside a residence near an area the motorcade would pass. Later, students were arrested for the simple act of protesting. Before being released, they were required to sign pledges saying they would not participate again in APEC protests. Those who refused to sign had to remain in custody until the conference was over. Two journalists who had been invited as observers had their credentials stripped because they were deemed to be overtly sympathetic to the protesters. On the opening day of the conference, one law student, Craig Jones, was arrested and held for fourteen hours for displaying small signs calling for freedom of speech and human rights. In the most controversial development, police used pepper spray on students—in full view of the television cameras. Chrétien made light of it, telling reporters, "Pepper? That's something I put on my plate." He hadn't realized, or so his office explained, that students had just been doused in it. "I could have killed him," said Donolo. Chrétien's insensitive remark made the story bigger than it might otherwise have been.

Behind much of the activity was the heavy hand of Jean Carle. He was the prime minister's chief of operations, which sometimes translated to henchman or bouncer. "I don't know why Chrétien kept a guy like him around," said a friend of Chrétien's who had seen Carle in action. "He was always getting him in trouble."

A graduate of the University of Montreal, Carle served as John Turner's youth director in Quebec in the 1984 leadership campaign against Chrétien. Later, he sought out Chrétien for a speaking engagement. When he went to his office, Chrétien coldly asked him why he had supported Turner instead of a fellow Quebecer. Carle felt badly about it and switched allegiance there and then. Chrétien soon hired him as his aide, and took such a liking to him that when he saw Carle was short on money, he let him board in the basement of his home. In 1986, when Chrétien decided he could no longer work with Turner as leader and left politics, Carle cried like a baby.

They remained close, and when Chrétien at last came to power, some of that power was turned over to Jean Carle. Carle moved into the PMO, and moved some of Pierre Trudeau's suede furniture into his own office. He was efficient as director of operations—so efficient, said a colleague, that he gave the impression of working in a Latin American dictatorship. At the University of British Columbia, what Axworthy called the "country with a conscience" was turned—with Carle's help—into an armed camp with concrete barricades, legions of stone-faced police, the stench of gas, protesters being piled into vans.

In the late 1950s, while he was in law school at Laval in Quebec City, Jean Chrétien had led demonstrations against the Duplessis government. At one such protest, the police manned the legislature, dispersing him and the rest of the rebels. But at APEC, his government was making Duplessis's handiwork look like soft power. In its defence, the government was under heavy pressure to protect heads of state like Suharto and Clinton. Had an incident occurred, Chrétien would have been pilloried for the lax security. Also, what went on at UBC, though undoubtedly heavy-handed, was child's play compared with the police brutality that rocked university campuses throughout the 1960s and early 1970s.

It was a bad week. It even rained on Clinton and Chrétien's golf game. But the prime minister had only begun to hear the worst of it. The protesters were not going to let this pass. In the New Year, allegations surfaced that the PMO was directly involved in giving orders to police to suppress dissent. A Native leader said she saw the prime minister barking orders at the Mounties to prevent the protest signs from being seen by the world leaders. Documents that later became public revealed the extent to which the government had gone to ease Suharto's concerns about security. Others appeared to confirm the charge that the PMO had endorsed the decision to keep protesters out of sight. Hounded in Parliament, Chrétien issued an apology. "I am sorry that some people had a problem with the police there," he said. "No one wished for that to happen and that is why there is an inquiry." He also expressed regret for the pepper joke, a comment that was replayed time after time.

Just as the Commons cacophony was diminishing, Solicitor General Andy Scott was overheard on an airplane talking about how the RCMP would be made to take the fall on what went wrong at APEC. Dick Proctor, an NDP MP, overheard the remarks and reported them to the House. He took nine pages of notes on what was discussed on the plane, including material related to the Airbus controversy. Scrambling to recall who he had talked to on recent flights, Scott faced reporters in a scrum after Question Period and dug himself in deeper. As he evaded the questions, the reporters grew more and more testy about his seeming lack of memory. One asked if he had recently been hit by a rock.

His companion on the flight was Fred Toole, a lawyer from Saint John, New Brunswick. Toole's memory of the conversation, while not terribly damning, did provide enough support for Proctor's story to increase the pressure on Scott to resign. Not wishing to yield to the critics, Chrétien put up a fight, just as he had with Sheila Copps. First, the PM had intermediaries talk to Scott. Then one Sunday, shortly after returning from a trip to China, Chrétien called him over to 24 Sussex. For two hours, with just the two of them in the room, the PM pressed him. "I felt completely supported," Scott recalled of the conversation. "He wanted me to stay." It was typical of Chrétien's style. Don't cave to the critics. Beat them down. Fight your way through it. He was worried, Scott recalled, about setting a precedent that would allow someone to overhear a conversation and force a Cabinet resignation. "He felt that I was simply overreacting to a moment in time that would go away."

It didn't go away, however, and ultimately, the PM replaced Scott with Lawrence MacAuley. Still, the heat didn't let up. Chrétien, often good at defusing controversy with his offhanded style, seemed to keep inviting it with APEC. He looked unsure of himself in the Commons. His ill-timed remark about pepper on the plate was followed by another flippant observation about pepper spray being less lethal than baseball bats. Peter Donolo was not exercising his usual skills. The protesters had hardly been unprovocative. They swarmed a police line, tried to set up human roadblocks, and tore down a security fence. But their actions never became a focus of the story, as they might have. Donolo challenged the CBC, alleging that the network was excessive in its coverage. Indeed, the CBC ran the same footage of the students being pepper-sprayed ad nauseam. But when it came to factual errors in the reporting, the PMO had little to stand on.

THE NEW YEAR, 1998, opened with a crippling ice storm that paralyzed regions of eastern Ontario and Quebec, leaving them without power for several days. Chrétien spent the better part of a week touring the afflicted areas and trying, like other politicians, to be seen to be doing the right thing. He had to delay his participation in his latest trade mission, this one to Latin America.

These missions, which included the premiers and scores of businesspeople, had become popular annual events since he took power. The premiers got to know one another better, and they enhanced their rapport with the prime minister. The missions helped dilute the perception that Canada was entirely dependent on the American market. With every foray came a flurry of announcements suggesting that billions of dollars in new agreements had been sealed. The result was usually much more modest, but the sums were still substantial and contacts had been made for possible future transactions.

In South and Central America, the government was broadening its interests. Chrétien was keen on developing a free trade zone of the Americas as an extension of NAFTA. He also took up where Trudeau had left off in cultivating relations with Fidel Castro's Cuba. Though he didn't become close friends with Castro, as Trudeau did, he was the first prime minister to visit the island in twenty-two years. He didn't get far on the touchy issues of political prisoners and free elections, but the open dialogue with the dictator was a sign back home of Chrétien's willingness to take a more progressive stance than Washington. In the pre-Castro period, the U.S. had been quite happy to do business with the corrupt regime of Fulgencio Batista, turning a blind eye to the death squads and the torture of political opponents.

Chrétien preceded his Cuba visit with an appearance before the well-heeled Economic Club of New York. Rather than play to the big commercial interests, he pulled no punches. For openers, he told the New Yorkers that the Canadian medical system was far superior to theirs because it protected everyone, whereas "you have forty million people who are not covered in the United States." He spoke of his pride in the fact that Canada had fewer poor people than the United States. There were "less rich people" in Canada, he said, but that didn't bother him, because "I never met a millionaire who was rich enough."

The assertion said a lot about him. There was nothing wrong with having money, he acknowledged, but he didn't enjoy the company of multi-millionaires, the high rollers. "They just talk money," he said on another occasion. "To have discussions about how much you paid for a dress for your wife in New York? Bahh!" It was an attitude that coloured his perception of the United States. But his slam on excessive wealth, as one American commentator wrote, was hardly appreciated. "I suspect what I heard was the simultaneous grinding of a thousand sets of privately insured teeth. We don't make fun of the rich down here nowadays. It simply isn't done."

Chrétien was perhaps entitled to sound off. This was a *Wall Street Journal* type of crowd, and only three years earlier, the *Journal* had named Canada an honorary member of the Third World. But now the $40-billion deficit, the prime minister informed those gathered, was gone, erased entirely. No one, certainly not Paul Martin, had suspected that it could be done so quickly. The budget cuts had wiped out a lot of the deficit, but rapid economic growth was the key. The massive national debt remained—more than half a trillion dollars of it—but the government was now in a position to start hacking away at that too. No one was insulting Canada any more.

If Paul Martin's February 1995 budget had marked one signature moment, the one in February 1998 marked another. Remarkably, it was the first time since 1969 that Canada had brought in a balanced budget. When the Chrétien crowd started in 1993, with the deficit at $42 billion, no one had thought this day would ever come—certainly not within just a few years. The day after the big announcement, Bruce Hartley and Donolo were driving to work in the morning and they were delighted to hear the disc jockey make special mention of it. The DJ spun a song from three decades earlier. It was "Here Comes the Sun."

With the deficit books clean, the government could start looking Liberal again. Shortly after the budget, Ottawa, in cooperation with the provincial and territorial governments, brought in the National Child Benefit program, which provided subsidies to all low-income parents. It didn't matter whether recipients were working poor or non-working poor because one of the ideas of the program, whose payouts would increase in the years to come, was to get Canadians off welfare.

It was another instance where Chrétien and Martin, while clearly not enjoying each other's company, had got the job done. Working through intermediaries like Martin's highly skilled assistant, Terrie O'Leary, and Eddie Goldenberg, they had agreed on moving out John Crow, on cutting drastically in the 1995 budget, on introducing the child benefit, and to begin 1998, on turning thumbs down to bank mergers. The Royal Bank and the Bank of Montreal wanted to merge, and Bay Streeters were arguing that a bigger conglomerate would enable them to better compete globally. Martin and Chrétien weren't convinced of that and looked instead at the thousands of jobs that might be lost as a result of the amalgamation. Reducing the issue to the most basic, pragmatic terms imaginable, Chrétien wondered why bigger was better. "Better to be big?" he asked. "You know, for me, even if I were 350 pounds, it will not make a better prime minister." It was classic Chrétien, the type of language everyone understood. The politician who had scolded the rich in New York for never having enough was unlikely to let them have more.

But if Jean Chrétien was the leader who stood up for small people and their values on some issues, he could dumbfound them with his insensitive or heartless behaviour on others.

Again, an issue from the previous decade reappeared to corner him. Between 1986 and 1990, an estimated twenty thousand Canadians were infected with the hepatitis C virus through the reckless adminis-tration of blood products. Governments were liable because of their failure to take a simple precaution—a test that could have prevented the vast majority of infections. Ottawa and the provincial governments offered up $1.1 billion in compensation, but the package left out those contaminated before 1986 or after 1990—perhaps as many as twenty thousand more. An inquiry by Justice Horace Krever had recommended compensation for all.

Ottawa adopted a hard line. Its principle was that the government should not be compensating people for something that happened outside its jurisdiction. For the four years in question, 1986 to 1990, there was culpability. Outside those years, the government determined, there was not.

The issue stretched emotions. People who had contracted the potentially debilitating liver disease and their supporters portrayed Ottawa as uncaring and cruel. Their protests took them to Parliament Hill, where they staged a long procession remembering the dead and asking for justice for the living. In the Commons, the opposition came at Allan Rock for seven weeks. In one four-day stretch, he was on his feet forty-nine times to field questions related to hepatitis C.

The issue divided the Liberals, who held only a slim majority in the Commons. When the Reform Party presented a motion demanding compensation for all, the prime minister would not risk allowing his troops to vote with their conscience. There would be no free vote. It was trained-seal time. As an M.D., Carolyn Bennett was especially affected by the drama. Favouring more compensation, she tried to lobby Rock and Goldenberg, but she found their attitude cold and lawyerly. Chrétien was no different. He was taking a clinical, hard, and legalistic position on an issue that called for compassion. As a PMO official later put it, he got boxed in on the issue early and then—classic Chrétien, too—did not want to be seen as caving to his critics.

When the vote on the Reform motion came up, Bennett stood with her Liberal colleagues to defeat it. Deborah Grey was shouting from across the floor, "You should be ashamed! You should be ashamed! You're letting them die! You're letting them die!" The public galleries were filled with victims, and Bennett dissolved into tears. She preferred a different form of support than what Reform was proposing, and so didn't feel hypocritical in voting against the motion, but she was dismayed, as were many in the party, that Chrétien had not shown a more compassionate side on the issue. It was left to Mike Harris, the hard-edged Ontario Tory, to come up with a better package. "A lot of the activists on this file ended up loving Harris," Bennett said. "The Tories used hep C to fix their image." Something else bothered her as well. "When you see $57 million going to lawyers on this file, it just breaks your heart."

Rock, meanwhile, chafed behind the scenes. In the early days of the controversy, he had sounded full of sympathy for the victims. With Chrétien's decision, which he later signalled he hadn't supported, he looked mean-spirited. Rock had been the one to deliver the harsh words at the press conference on the Mulroney Airbus settlement. He had faced strident opposition on his gun-control legislation. And now he was being pounded so hard on the hepatitis C controversy that he was considering resigning. But Chrétien called him over for a pep talk, and Rock, who had considerable admiration for the PM's experience and political knowledge, went away feeling better.

Polls registered voter disapproval of Chrétien's handling of the blood issue. He told reporters how difficult it was for him. The government could not have compensated everyone, he offered. "That would have been irresponsible. It's not that I don't bleed for the people who have problems. It's why we have medicare in Canada."

His attitude on contaminated blood was lumped in by critics with his other callous acts. If anyone wanted to portray him as a bully, there was no shortage of evidence to draw on. There were the Somalia shutdown and the Shawinigan chokehold, the CBC town hall and the Airbus affair, APEC and hepatitis C. It was a long list. But the street-fighter was only getting started.

CHAPTER TEN

SIGNS OF TROUBLE

QUEBEC WAS QUIET, and Jean Chrétien wanted to keep it that way. In 1996, his government had asked the Supreme Court to rule on whether Quebec had the right to secede. Now, two years later, the nine judges gave their response. The court—as it had in its ruling on the patriation of the Constitution—took a decidedly middle-of-the-road position. No, Quebec could not unilaterally secede under either Canadian or international law. But if a clear majority of Quebecers voted for secession on a clear referendum question, the rest of Canada would be obliged to negotiate separation. The decision allowed each side to claim victory. Premier Lucien Bouchard contended that the verdict had legitimized the sovereignty project. But Chrétien could—and did—read into the verdict that a clear question and a clear majority were now required, and that no unilateral declaration of independence was possible.

His retinue viewed the decision as a victory, so much so that tears were flowing in Stéphane Dion's office when it was announced. Chrétien made clear that in the future, no obfuscation on referendum ballots would be tolerated. The question would have to be: Do you want to separate from Canada or not? "The words are well known to everyone," he said. "No need of dictionaries."And if the Quebec sovereigntists didn't believe he would hold to his pledge, he had something in mind—though he wasn't announcing it yet—that would clarify matters for them.

In light of the court's decision, federalists could only wish that they had gone that route earlier, that they hadn't waited for Guy Bertrand, a lawyer from the private sector to whom they never gave proper credit, to show them the way.

A Quebec election approached. Jean Charest had answered the call in the spring and departed the federal Tories for the leadership of the provincial Liberals. A boomlet in the polls suggesting he was the only one who could counter Bouchard, and the secessionists forced the decision on him. But the bloom on the rose quickly faded, and as the campaign began, Bouchard appeared to have recaptured the momentum.

Chrétien then stumbled badly. He felt that in the three years since the referendum, his government had made concessions to Quebec— on a constitutional veto, on distinct society status, and in areas of jurisdiction such as mining, forestry, tourism, social housing, and labour training. Speaking to the newspaper *La Presse,* he suggested therefore that Quebec had already achieved most of its traditional demands. Then, seeking to make the point that no one gets everything he wants, he added that "the Constitution is not a general store."

The remark sparked outrage in Quebec. With this statement, Chrétien was deemed to be shutting down all hopes for constitutional change. In uttering it, he had hurt the hopes of Charest, who had wanted to dangle some carrots before the voters. Bouchard celebrated. "A door has been brutally slammed on him," he said in reference to Charest. The Quebec media stomped all over Chrétien, who was headed for the Commonwealth conference in Kuala Lumpur at the time. A nice place, one commentator suggested. He might consider staying there for the duration of the Quebec election.

The antagonism was now so deep that the provincial Liberals wouldn't even let Jean Chrétien's brother work the hustings. The octogenarian Gabriel, the second oldest of Chrétien's brothers, was a staunch defender of Canadian federalism, like every Chrétien, and, also like every Chrétien, he was a proud man. It hurt him when he was told that he was not wanted. "On account of my name," he explained, "they would not accept me in the front lines."

But the campaign turned out well enough for Gabriel's younger brother. The Charest Liberals won the popular vote, but owing to vagaries of the electoral system, Bouchard came away with the majority of the seats. The result effectively neutralized him, however. Having hoped for a big mandate to push forward the sovereignty option, he was instead the emperor with no clothes, the leader without the votes. There could be no prospect of a referendum in the near future. Only three years earlier, Quebecers had moved to the brink. Now they were stepping back.

Chrétien was much relieved. A sizable Bouchard triumph would have put more pressure on him to vacate the prime ministership without a chance at a third term. But this was another instance where luck struck. With no imminent threat from Quebec or the economy, which was humming along, he could put up his feet and watch the games on the other side of the Commons chamber.

Preston Manning was rolling the dice. His Reform Party had stalled after the 1997 election and was now languishing badly in the polls. It was still dividing up support with the Conservative Party, so Manning proposed the creation of "a united alternative" that could compete with the Liberals.

No one could dispute the logic of the proposal. One big party was clearly a more credible threat to the Grits than two smaller ones. But it was Manning's Reformers who had split the political right in the first place. Now they wanted to put it back together again—on their terms. The gall of it outraged many Tories, who, in the fall of 1998, were in the process of choosing a new leader to replace Charest. The grand old party, lacking fresh talent, turned back the clock to a Chrétien-era man: Joe Clark, who had led the party from 1976 to 1983, was put back at the helm to fight the Liberals. Canadians seemed to like Clark more the second time around than they did in times past, when he was famous for his ungainly style and geekish observations. "What is the totality of your land?" he once asked a farmer while touring the Middle East. As a follow-up, he demanded, "How old are the chickens?"

Now he was an elder statesman. "Two things happened to me," recalled Clark, in a reflective mood one day. "One, I had to get beaten up pretty publicly and pretty decisively. Second, I had to hang in. And that combination of being beaten up and hanging in very much changed the perception of me."

Having settled in for his second go-round—this time with his party a hugely diminished force—he gave a flat no to the Manning unification proposal. It was fraught with too many difficult questions. Which party would provide the leader? Which party would sacrifice which policies? What banner would members run under in their individual ridings? Manning was not about to relinquish the bid, however, and the protracted war on the right began. Chrétien watched as his opposition parties took runs at each other instead of concentrating their forces on him. It was a good way to spend his sixty-fifth birthday.

On that day, January 11, 1999, Chrétien looked almost as fit and energetic as he had ten years earlier. The office hadn't dragged him down. "I know what keeps a man young," Churchill once told Nixon. "It's power."

Having reached the magic age, Chrétien began hearing speculation—certainly from the Paul Martin camp—that within a couple of years, he would be ready for a graceful exit. "You don't want to be another Louis St. Laurent," he was told. Uncle Louis was like Chrétien, in that he served in economic good times, had little in the way of opposition, governed in a low-key managerial style, and won two majority election victories. But when Uncle Louis, in his late seventies, tried for a third term, he was defeated by John Diefenbaker and ended up leaving on a sad note.

Observers like Michael Bliss of the University of Toronto warned that Chrétien was in danger of making the same mistake. "The country is on the verge of losing patience with the Liberals," he wrote. For Chrétien to stay on would be a disservice. "It will be a surrender to ego, and it will be damaging to him, the Liberal party, and the country."

One day, while Chrétien was golfing, the Uncle Louis comparison was put to him by a journalist. He clearly had done some thinking about it, because he had an answer at the ready. A three-point rebuttal. The Liberals of St. Laurent's time had been in power twenty years, he noted, three times as long as the current tribe. The Grits of the period also faced a debilitating controversy, the pipeline debate, and St. Laurent was considerably older than he was. As the humorist Allan Fotheringham cracked, Chrétien hadn't reached the stage where, like Uncle Louis, "he got winded playing chess."

At the time of the PM's birthday, the reporter Sean Durkan, a chubby fellow more than a generation Chrétien's junior, asked him about retirement. The prime minister responded that he would step down when the reporter could beat him in a race up the stairs. No one was willing to bet on Durkan. Raymond Chrétien, the ambassador to Washington, admired his uncle's stamina. "Physically, if you take away the inevitable wrinkles, he has almost the same silhouette that he did thirty years ago. . . . He is the only leader in the G7 who can still slalom on water skis, with one of his grandchildren on his shoulders."

Mentally he was just as sharp, or—as his critics would have it—just as dull, as he ever was. Linguistic problems still plagued him, feeding the stumblebum stereotype his detractors liked to pin on him. In New York, while talking about the secretary general of the United Nations, whose first name was Kofi, Chrétien waxed on about his dealings with "Goofy" Annan.

Chrétien was never good with names, sometimes forgetting even those of prominent members of his caucus. At a loss, he would reach for an identifier of some kind. For George Baker, the Newfoundland MP, Chrétien would just use the French word *boulanger,* leaving Baker to protest that his life's vocation was never that of pastry maker. The name of Andy Scott, who worked on the handicapped people's file, was a tough one for the PM to remember, so he would just refer to him as "the disability guy." Sometimes Chrétien would draw a complete blank—as he did once when trying to introduce caucus members to Italian dignitaries—and would glance around for someone to bail him out.

Occasionally, he got caught not knowing a particular file, but it was not often. He deeply objected to any suggestion that he didn't read much or was a lightweight of the Ronald Reagan school of leadership. A congressman had once said of the Gipper that "if you walked through his deepest thoughts, you wouldn't get your feet wet." Once, when it was suggested to Chrétien that he was a one-memo guy, he got visibly testy. "That is nonsense. Nobody knows what I read, sir!" Officials came to him "with a brief every night, and they have their answer in the morning and they can question me on all these documents. Of course, when you have been in government so long, you read sometimes one page and you under-stand the problem. I don't have to carry on. . . . [But] you cannot be minister of finance and president of the Treasury Board and minister of trade—all the success I had as a politician—and not reading anything. That's stupid, those who write that."

At sixty-five, he could not be accused of slowing down. Joe Fontana, who was caucus chair for the Liberals in the late 1990s, got Chrétien to join the backbenchers' brass band. The PM's tastes weren't exactly modern; his favourite songs were "Love Me Tender" and "Blue Moon." But he could get by on a few bars with the trombone, and one night, Fontana got him to put on shades and a sequined jacket and do a few numbers with the backbench boys at Barrymore's, a local Ottawa club. The PM blew some bad notes and bought a few beers.

To keep the physical motor fine-tuned, he went off after his birth-day to do some skiing in Whistler, British Columbia. It was a badly timed getaway. While he was there, the popular King Hussein of Jordan passed away. The cancer-ridden leader, eyes still sparkling, had been transported around the world in search of a life-saving operation, and the image, shown repeatedly on television screens, elicited great waves of sympathy. He had been a beacon of stability and hope in an unstable and seemingly hopeless region, and his funeral attracted heads of state from everywhere. Bill Clinton and three former American presidents attended. Russia's Boris Yeltsin left his sick bed to be there. Prince Charles went, as did Prime Minister Tony Blair. One of the only no-shows was Jean Chrétien. The planes couldn't get there in time, his office said.

Outrage followed, with opposition politicians and Canadian Arab leaders suggesting that the prime minister couldn't be bothered making the long trip. Forensic examinations of flight logs were undertaken to establish whether in fact it had been possible: Chrétien was no habitual shirker of death duty. He had gone to Yitzhak Rabin's funeral the very morning after the attempt on his own life at 24 Sussex. With his wife still in a state of shock, he certainly had had reason to stay home that day.

In the House of Commons, the opposition leaders were in high dudgeon, demanding the PM apologize. When General Maurice Baril, the chief of the defence staff, issued a statement saying, essentially, that the military was at fault for not having an aircraft on standby, critics charged that Baril was ordered to take the fall. Indignant Liberals said that the opposition members obviously knew a lot about funerals, having presided over their own for the past few years. But Chrétien eventually met his opponents' demands for an apology, even holding up a piece of paper on which he had scrawled "Sorry."

Years later, PMO insiders explained that Governor General Roméo LeBlanc was at fault. He was supposed to go to the funeral if Hussein died earlier than expected. But the GG wasn't available when the time came. Relations chilled between Chrétien and LeBlanc for months afterwards.

A more significant development, but one that garnered less attention, was Chrétien's crafting of a social union accord with the provinces. The pact was aimed at securing peace on the question of the delivery of social programs. Because of shared federal–provincial jurisdiction, endless squabbling had been the norm. But Ottawa was now vowing to refrain from undertaking any shared-cost or block-funded program without the prior agreement of at least six provinces. Provinces that had similar pre-existing programs could still get funding and use it in related areas. In return, the provinces agreed to justify their use of federal funds and give Ottawa credit for joint programs. In this way, the federal government was able to maintain a strong presence in areas of provincial responsibility. No surprise there, observed Joe Clark. "There is an instinct in the Liberal Party towards central control rather than towards the federation. The instincts are centralizing," he said.

Chrétien got his way on some points in the social union accord because he had a big carrot in the form of health care funding. He pledged $5 billion in added health spending for the next three years. Since his government had taken away so much of the funding in the first place, the idea that he could now use it as a bargaining chip struck many as odd. But he got away with it. For premiers like Brian Tobin of Newfoundland, who was in the middle of a re-election campaign, health care spending had become the dominant issue. He wanted the money.

The social union accord was a way of renewing and renovating federal–provincial relations without restarting the constitutional debate. But it had a major flaw: Quebec didn't sign on. Its absence left Ottawa in a situation where the introduction of a new social program could lead to confrontation with the province. But the debate didn't capture the usual intense degree of attention in *la belle province*. The provincial election result had been dispiriting for Club Sovereignty. As the century was closing, so was the passion for the secessionist enterprise. Parizeau and Bouchard, like dinosaurs, were lurching to oblivion, spent forces with spent messages. Their 1940s-style nation-alism seemed quainter by the day. They might well have been hearing a message from their people: "We are no longer victims. Get over it." Bouchard's big V-8, grievance-bearing engine had begun to look like a sputtering four-cylinder. He walked away from the social union talks—and everyone yawned.

The prime minister viewed the social union accord, which would quickly be forgotten, as a victory. He was little more than two years into his second mandate, but he was under increasing pressure to state his future intentions. Paul Martin, Allan Rock, and Brian Tobin were already revving up their pre-campaigns. The activities of the little guy from Newfoundland had reached the point that, on a trip to the Rock, Chrétien thought he'd better caution him against overzealousness. The headlines—"Tobin Taken to the Woodshed"—incensed the premier. It hadn't, in his opinion, been a lecture from the boss, just a chat. Someone in the PMO was undermining him, and he suspected his long-time adversary, Goldenberg. The Tobinator was so steamed that he got Chrétien on the line. "Get that statement corrected," he claimed he told the PM, "or you've lost yourself the support of one premier." Chrétien said he didn't know anything about it, but his office issued a statement saying there had been no lecturing of Tobin in Newfoundland.

The prime minister was making a strategic error at this time. By refusing to lay out his future political plans, he was creating a climate in which underground campaigns were launched, rumour mills stoked, internal rivalries hardened, and the flow of governance disrupted. After winning his second election, he might better have declared his firm intent to seek a third term, even if he changed his mind at the end of the second. This wouldn't have stopped all the speculation and jockeying, but it would have reduced it. Instead, in the uncertain climate he fostered, his each and every move, as well as those of his rivals, was analyzed within the context of the leadership question. Horse-race politics being the easiest story to cover, the media loved it.

WHILE CHRÉTIEN EYED THE WOULD-BE CONTENDERS for his job, his friend Bill Clinton was entrapped in the seamy Lewinsky scandal. Though that affair—"Bill Clinton and the zipper problem" the PM quaintly called it—tended to make Chrétien, and all other leaders, look good by comparison, it made dealing with the White House far more unpredictable. On matters of war and peace, questions surfaced about whether the American president was deliberately dramatizing foreign conflicts to distract from his domestic embarrassments. The impeachment proceedings in the fall of 1998 gave rise to accusations of wag-the-dog bombing campaigns against Iraq. The night before the impeachment vote, Clinton decided that it was imperative that he bomb Baghdad immediately. Many questioned the motives of the attacks, but Chrétien and his foreign minister, Lloyd Axworthy, not wishing to give Bill Clinton more trouble than he already had, remained on board. Chrétien was far more willing to support a friendly Democrat in his bombing campaigns against Saddam Hussein than he later would a Republican president.

Throughout 1998, Chrétien was hawkish—as Clinton surely wished him to be—on the subject of Hussein and weapons of mass destruction. In February, when the U.S. raided several Iraqi installations, Chrétien told the House of Commons, "If there is one thing Canadians cannot abide, that is any flaunting of the clearly expressed wish of the United Nations Security Council. And if there is one question on which the Security Council has spoken out clearly, it is the threat Saddam Hussein represents to his neighbours, and the entire world, with his weapons of mass destruction—his nuclear, chemical, and biological weapons." He said also, "We have proof that they were producing and are still producing them, and we want to terminate this production."

But Iraq became a sideshow when the focus turned to the former Yugoslav province of Kosovo. With the end of the Cold War in 1989, it was soon apparent that Yugoslavia could not hold together. In Slovenia, Croatia, Bosnia, Kosovo, freedom from Communism had been achieved, but another freedom remained elusive—freedom from the threat of Serb nationalism under Slobodan Milosevic. Milosevic had set himself up as the virtual dictator of Yugoslavia, which his Serb population dominated. To stop several non-Serb provinces from gaining independence, Milosevic turned bloody. He went to war against Croatia and Bosnia. In Bosnia, his forces exterminated tens of thousands of Muslims, including six thousand at the massacre in Srebrenica in 1995.

In Kosovo, the Albanians were the dominant ethnic group; they made up 90 percent of the population, while the rest were Serbs. Hostilities had been long in the making. Since 1993, Kosovo had been a civil war zone, with an estimated two thousand casualties. During that period, about two hundred thousand Albanians had been displaced. The international debate pivoted on how much repression Milosevic was directing from Belgrade and how much was being whipped up by the Kosovo Liberation Army (KLA).

The civil war raised difficult questions. "There are no innocents in this conflict," said the Liberal MP John McKay. "The Serbs have blood on their hands, [and] Kosovars have current and historical blood on their hands." Critics argued that Canada was getting involved in an ancient conflict and going against its commitment to international law. The case against the Serbs in Kosovo, many experts agreed, was not nearly as clear-cut as in the earlier Milosevic-directed conflicts of the decade.

While not disputing this possibility, Lloyd Axworthy later explained that he saw Canada's involvement in the Kosovo conflict as being consistent with the human security principles he set out in his soft-power campaign, which included the land mines initiative. "The whole thing was that we have to be concerned with the security of individuals, not just the security of the state. And what we were looking at in Kosovo was that there are people out there like Milosevic and others who will simply continue to break the rules until you're prepared to make some enforcement. The Kosovo case was pretty carefully tailored. There was no regime change. We tried to design the means that were appropriate to the ends."

Chrétien held fast to the NATO hard line as directed by Washington and its hawkish ally, Tony Blair. Because the consensus among the allies was so strong, he was in no position to buck the war effort, even if he felt it was unjustified.

Like most wars, this one was full of hypocrisies. Not long before the conflict began, the KLA was classified by U.S. intelligence as a terrorist organization. Almost overnight, its recruits became freedom fighters.

In putting down a rebellion in the breakaway Russian province of Chechnya, Boris Yeltsin's army massacred untold thousands more than had been killed in Kosovo. But Moscow was moving into the Western orbit at the time, and the eyes of the allies could readily turn away from that slaughter. In a shapely piece of irony, Yeltsin was toasted at a G-8 summit in Cologne, Germany, while leaders fulminated over developments in Kosovo.

Chrétien was asked in an interview if he didn't feel a little strange supporting separatists. "No, that has nothing to do with it," he replied. "It's the cleansing. Why we are there is because of the cleansing." He'd talked to the Albanians about what the Serbs had inflicted on them, he explained, though not to the Serbs about what the KLA had done. Hadn't the KLA committed acts far worse than those of the FLQ terrorists in Quebec in 1970, when his own government had sent in the army? "The problem," he interrupted, "is there was cleansing by Milosevic, and we want peace in this part of the world."

His government supplied air support in the conflict for a NATO bombing campaign that was sufficient to win the war. The question of sending Canadian ground forces as part of the NATO mission was a hotly debated one, but because no ground campaign was necessary in the end, the PM was spared having to make the tough call.

After the war, questions were raised about whether the Serb repressions in Kosovo had really been severe enough to justify the massive bombing attacks, with the attendant collateral carnage inflicted on civilians. James Bissett, Canada's former ambassador to Yugoslavia, led the critics and was backed to some degree by Lewis Mackenzie, the former major general who was experienced in the Yugoslav theatre. Bissett pointed out that the NATO bombing campaign resulted in far more civilian casualties than the two thousand lost in the civil war in that province before the campaign began. "After the NATO bombs began to fall, more than eight hundred thousand Kosovars were forced to flee from Serbian retaliation and NATO bombs," Bissett said. This was far worse than the two hundred thousand ethnic Albanians displaced by the civil war.

Evidence uncovered when inspectors went into the province following the war lent some credence to the charges of Bissett and other critics. The atrocities alleged by Britain's Tony Blair and Washington proved to be highly exaggerated. William Cohen, the U.S. defence secretary, had suggested that as many as one hundred thousand ethnic Albanians had been killed by the Serbs. The real number was only a tiny fraction of that. A NATO publicity blitz had talked about how the Serbs had buried their Kosovar victims in mass graves. The mass graves turned out to be a myth.

Years later, Art Eggleton, no longer defence minister as he was during the Kosovo war, was asked about some of the numbers NATO had used to justify the campaign. Eggleton acknowledged that there was a lot of wrong information. Speaking of the Americans, he said that "the propaganda was unbelievable." Lloyd Axworthy didn't contest the notion that there had been much exaggeration. But he said NATO could not take the risk of letting Kosovo escalate into another Srebrenica.

The prime minister appeared to have few second thoughts about the whole enterprise. Despite the civilian deaths and the refugee crisis that came with the bombings, it was worthwhile, he said. Milosevic, after all, had been brought to justice and the region would be spared more carnage that he certainly would have inflicted. Yes, NATO bombs had inflicted a lot of death or damage on innocents. "But the problem is that when you use bombs, you kill people. It's inevitable. It's not designed to kill civilians, but it's happening."

As the prime minister and Axworthy were scoring points with the Clinton White House for their support throughout the conflict, the broad subject of American relations was taking on a heightened

profile in Canada, owing to the birth of a new newspaper, the
National Post, which stood for all things American.

The paper was the creation of Conrad Black, who also bought up
the giant Southam newspaper chain and expected its member papers,
formerly centrist, to reflect the new pro-American ethos. This was
enough of a problem for the prime minister. But of immediate
concern were the stories the Black newspapers began publishing on
Chrétien's business dealings in his Shawinigan riding. The stories
would dog him for years to come, tarnishing his image as an ethical
man.

In his hometown, Chrétien had a long and colourful history as a
school rebel, a pugilist, a lawyer, a golfer, a golf club owner, and a Cabinet
minister who ran the constituency in the tradition of many old-style
Quebec politicians—like a fiefdom. The national media had never
paid much attention. It wasn't the custom to delve into the nitty-gritty
of riding affairs, since there were far too many matters of broader
consequence to examine. The local media didn't do much digging
either. Shawinigan didn't have a daily paper, only a weekly, so Chrétien
could operate free of any intense scrutiny. It wasn't until the 1990s, for
instance, that it became public knowledge that he had resorted to
some peculiar behaviour in elections in his riding in the late 1960s and
early 1970s. He had lined up a friend to run as an opposing candidate
to split the vote on the right, making it easier for him to win.

One of the few ethical controversies that did come to light was the
so-called Judges' Affair in the mid-1970s. Chrétien was one of several
Cabinet members who were revealed to have telephoned judges to
allegedly influence decisions in some way. But he was able to establish
that his call was innocent enough in nature to escape harsh criticism.

His image as a Mr. Clean of politics remained intact. The book
Chrétien wrote, the one that sold more than one hundred thousand
copies in the late 1980s, was called *Straight from the Heart*. The Stevie
Cameron book on Mulroney, which also sold more than one hundred
thousand copies, was called *On the Take*. So when Chrétien came to

power promising a new era of ethics and integrity, Canadians tended to believe him. That was one of the reasons, recalled Joe Fontana, the caucus chairman, why the stuff that Black's papers started printing drove him crazy. "Oh Christ, he'd just go nuts."

Until the close of his first term in office, all was quiet on the ethics front. There was only one story, which appeared shortly before the 1997 election campaign, that caused some suspicion. An investigation by the RCMP into the activities of a Liberal fundraiser, Pierre Corbeil, led to allegations of influence-peddling and eventually four charges of fraud. The case involved Corbeil approaching Quebec companies that had applied for federal job-training grants and asking them to make payments to the Liberal Party. He received the names of the companies seeking grants from the office of Marcel Massé, the senior minister for Quebec at the time.

The story caught the eye of the Conservative backbench MP André Bachand, who first brought the issue to the House of Commons. Bachand and others found it interesting that although the allegations came to light in March 1997, Liberal offices were not raided and charges not laid until after the June 2 elections. The RCMP said the investigation was done at a normal pace.

It became clear that Corbeil, an employee of the party, was in charge of fundraising for sixteen Quebec ridings, including Chrétien's. He pleaded guilty to the charges, was fined and ordered to do community work. The party was presumably thankful that the case did not go to trial, where more damaging details about the operation might have been revealed. When the Corbeil case was first aired, the Mounties said it appeared to be isolated, but it later became clear that it was part of a broader operation.

The case, though it seemed serious, did not receive broad media attention. The first case to attract that kind of attention involved the prime minister himself and his connection with golf course properties in Grand-Mère, a town neighbouring Shawinigan. Chrétien had been a golfer all his life, and he played a reasonably good game, shooting in the mid-eighties, a score that made him a good match for Bill Clinton. His wife, Aline, had taken up the game in recent years, and she called her husband in the summer of 1999, getting him out of an important meeting, with special news: she had shot a hole-in-one at the Royal Ottawa Golf Club. The prime minister congratulated her and announced that he was quite jealous.

As a young French Canadian in Shawinigan, he was not made to feel welcome at the establishment golf club in the area. The Anglos who ran the club wouldn't let him play there. The young Chrétien swore to friends that he would get his revenge. One day, the counter-punch would come and the score would be settled.

Indeed the day arrived. Not only did Jean Chrétien end up playing at the Grand-Mère course—he became its owner! He purchased the club, with two associates, in 1988. It was a moment to be savoured, one of great pride. His earnings in the private sector had enabled him, with his friends, to buy both the golf course and a part ownership—the furnishings—in the Auberge Grand-Mère, which sat close to the course and offered stay-and-play packages for golfers.

Neither venture was profitable. The anticipated joys of becoming a golf club owner turned sour. The course and the hotel were drains on the pocketbook, and by 1993, the year he became prime minister, Chrétien wanted to cut his losses on the properties. He and his part-ners sold both, with their part of the hotel going to the colourful and controversial Yvon Duhaime. He had had some run-ins with the law and had owned another hotel, the Hôtel des Chutes, an unsavoury place that was badly in debt and eventually burned down. Suspicions were that the fire was deliberately set so the owner could collect on insurance. But no charges were laid.

In early 1999, the Reform Party and the *National Post* began exam-ining government subsidies that had poured into the Auberge Grand-Mère in the period prior to the 1997 election. One was a $164,000 grant from Ottawa's Transitional Jobs Fund (TTF) program for an expansion to the hotel. Opposition critics zeroed in on two aspects of this grant. They argued that the Auberge was ineligible because it had large mortgage debts and other unpaid bills, and because its owner had not disclosed his past criminal record, as required by grant applicants. More significantly, they pointed to the fact that the grant, which was arranged through the Prime Minister's Office, was to help someone who had helped Chrétien. Wasn't this, asked the Reform MP Chuck Strahl, a conflict of interest? "A friend of the prime minister took a money-losing hotel off his hands at a very convenient time for the prime minister. Then that same fellow . . . received a grant following a meeting where the prime minister's personal assistant sat in."

Indeed, the prime minister's representatives were involved in arranging the grant, but that aspect of the case was not unusual. Under the $300-million TJF, run by the human resources department, cash grants were awarded to businesses and social groups in areas where unemployment was 12 percent or more. The review of grant requests was done in collaboration with the MPs in each riding, and Chrétien's office had the right to be involved. The idea was that the local MP knew more than bureaucrats in Ottawa about who needed grant monies in the riding. The weakness, however, was that this system left itself open to abuse. MPs could readily be accused of arranging grants for close friends and political supporters.

But the fact that Chrétien's office had the right to be involved didn't necessarily negate Strahl's charge of conflict of interest. Trying to knock down that allegation, Chrétien explained that he had left the dealings on the sale of the hotel to his two partners. "I was never involved in the management. I had put money in this adventure with my golf partners. I delegated the authority all along to my two friends."

The sale of the hotel furnishings fetched $200,000, which, Chrétien said, was paid up front to him and his partners. Not only was he not involved in the sale, he claimed in an interview in 2003, he didn't even know it had happened! "That was all run by my friend. I was busy in the [Liberal] leadership and so on. I never had a minute of discussion. I didn't even know that they had sold the furnishings. I did not know that."

A business deal involving tens of thousands of dollars—and he didn't know about it? "No. Come on. You know I bought this golf course because I love golfing. And it's a beautiful golf course. That's it. I did not intend to make any money on that. I said that to my partners. Three crazy guys like us will buy it someday."

He was angered by any suggestion that he was trying, through loans to his riding, to improve his financial position. "I don't need a goddamn cent, you know that. . . . You think after thirty-five years [in politics], I will want a guy to give me ten thousand bucks? It's all bullshit."

He knew countless people in Shawinigan, he went on to say, which made it all too easy for critics to say he was doing favours for friends. "You know everybody in Shawinigan. You see somebody on the street. 'How are you doing? How is your project? Is my staff helping you? Yes, thank you very much.' And so on. This is my job."

The case of the $164,000 grant was referred to the prime minister's ethics counsellor, Howard Wilson. "I have concluded that neither the prime minister nor his constituency office [was] in violation of any provision of the Conflict of Interest Code," Wilson ruled. "The important point from the perspective of the code is whether Mr. Duhaime continued to have a financial obligation to the prime minister. This is not the case."

The matter didn't end there, however. The TJF grant, as it turned out, was only a small percentage of the money the government poured into the hotel. It was revealed that there was also a federal loan of $615,000 from the Business Development Bank of Canada, a Crown corporation. This was the loan that Chrétien had announced in the waning days of his closely fought 1997 election battle against a different Duhaime, the separatist Yves Duhaime. The loan, the Bloc candidate had argued, gave Chrétien's campaign a critical boost in the final days. Duhaime had been hitting Chrétien hard for not doing enough for his riding, and he didn't like the look of this loan, even though the provincial government of Quebec, his own Péquiste government, was supporting the inn with subsidies as well.

Once again, there were questions about the inn's eligibility for the bank loan, and about the role political considerations may have played in the decision to grant it. But at this time, early 1999, the most controversial element—the fact that the prime minister had personally lobbied the bank president for it—was yet to be revealed.

The more the opposition parties looked at the Grand-Mère controversy, the more suspicious they became. The loans were one line of inquiry. Now they opened up another: the sale of the golf course itself. When Chrétien and his partners sold the club in 1993 to the Toronto realtor Jonas Prince, the PM did not receive payment for his portion. It was believed he was still owed in the neighbourhood of $300,000, which led to claims that he had an ongoing financial interest in the health of the golf club, and also perhaps the nearby hotel. Opposition MPs argued that any government subsidies or dealings enhancing the value of the golf course were a plus for the prime minister because Jonas Prince would then be in a better position to pay off the debt to him. If, however, the financially troubled club went bankrupt, Chrétien would be less likely to get his money back. Similarly, if the hotel went bankrupt, the value of the golf course might also fall.

The PMO made the case that Chrétien would have had the option of suing the buyer, Jonas Prince, for the money owed him, regardless of what happened to the golf course. Prince, however, was reported to believe that the nature of the sale didn't leave him easily open to a lawsuit. These were details that the average Canadian had neither the time nor the patience to follow. The complexity of the story—and it would only get more intricate—played heavily to Chrétien's advantage.

A central figure in the drama was Claude Gauthier, a highly successful and well-respected businessman from Shawinigan who was a good friend and major supporter of Jean Chrétien. Gauthier had given the prime minister $5,000 for his 1993 campaign, and in 1997 he upped that to $10,000, which was reported to be the largest individual contribution to the PM's campaign that year. In the fall of 1996, Gauthier bought for $525,000 a parcel of undeveloped land from the company running the golf club. Several aspects of the sale of that land, which was located beside the golf course, caught Chrétien's opponents' eyes. They claimed, for example, that the price Gauthier paid was far above the market value of the property, thus enhancing the solvency of the golf club.

Reform's Jason Kenney attacked the PM in the Commons, accusing him of personally benefiting from his friend Gauthier's purchase of the land because the deal could potentially enhance Chrétien's chances of receiving payment on the debt owed him. But there was more to Kenney's case than that. At the time of Gauthier's purchase of the property, one of his companies, Transelec Inc., was awarded a $6.3-million contract from the Canadian International Development Agency (CIDA). The contract was to strengthen the electrical grid in the African country of Mali. The public announcement was to come a year later. Wasn't it interesting, Kenney noted, that Gauthier got a nice deal from the government just at the time the golf course was getting a nice deal from Gauthier?

What gave added grit to Kenney's point was that Auditor General Denis Desautels found many irregularities in the bidding process for the Mali contract. He ruled not only that the bid from Gauthier's company did not follow established procedures, but that it should have been disqualified.

Chrétien reminded his accusers that the Transelec bid was 30 percent below the next lowest bid. At one point, he looked across the Commons floor and mockingly said that the Reformers were so incompetent that they would probably have given the contract to the bidder charging the highest price. Gauthier, he pointed out, also had a good track record with CIDA.

Inside the House, where he enjoyed immunity from prosecution, Jason Kenney declared the prime minister in clear conflict. "He has received both personal financial benefit and political financial benefit from somebody who has benefited from government decisions, grants, and contracts," he declared. "I don't know how else you define a conflict of interest."

Chrétien threatened to sue. "If they have any decency, they will make a clear accusation that I have a conflict of interest and have the guts to make it outside [the House], and we will meet them in court after that," he said. But Jason Kenney didn't back down. He said outside the House that there is "a clear, definite conflict of interest, and he can sue me if he wants." Chrétien didn't pursue the matter, his officials saying a lawsuit would only give Kenney more of a podium to shout from.

On the sidelines, Brian Mulroney was enjoying the proceedings, but he was baffled by what he felt was the media's tendency to let the Liberals off the hook. Chrétien, he told the CBC, "runs a patronage machine probably without precedent in modern history, and nobody says a word."

As the spring session of the Commons—a session devoted almost entirely to questions of ethics and conflicts—came to a close, yet another angle blew open in the escalating drama. The Placeteco company was a plastics manufacturer in Shawinigan. It was near bankruptcy when the same Claude Gauthier purchased it in June 1998. A month after the purchase, it received a $1.19-million TJF grant. Six months later, the Placeteco company went bankrupt. A creditor for the company alleged in a Quebec court that the TJF grant had had nothing to do with jobs but was awarded to trim the company's bank debt.

The Reform Party obtained documents through the Access to Information Act that appeared to show Chrétien was willing to go a long way to help his friend Gauthier. One memo showed that the Prime Minister's Office had instructed public servants—public servants who appeared to doubt that the company met the requirements for the money—to "do everything that is legally possible" to ensure that the $1.19 million went to Placeteco. Chrétien held to the line that nothing untoward was done in the awarding of this grant. "No, no. Everything is done according to the rules, as usual," he said. "It is the work of the government in the area of 12-percent unemployment, and it applies to all the ridings in Canada."

The file was fraught with enough controversy. But then it was revealed by an audit that the $1.19 million was placed—against the rules set by human resources department bureaucrats—in two trust funds. Gilles Champagne, a Shawinigan lawyer with ties to the prime minister, was put in charge.

The funds held the cash through the end of the fiscal year, even though Treasury Board requirements spelled out that such funds must lapse at the end of the year. A senior human resources official who travelled to Shawinigan disclosed that the funds violated the Financial Administration Act. Jane Stewart, the minister in charge, closed them down. A police investigation was conducted, but no charges were laid. On the trust fund matter, the Quebec bar cleared Gilles Champagne, taking the sting out of the opposition parties' attacks on the Placeteco file. But there were still plenty of conflict-of-interest allegations for them to feed on.

Chrétien would tell Joe Fontana, and anyone else who was within earshot whenever the question of the grants came up, that he "was only trying to help my riding. They want to call me a criminal for that!" His high degree of sensitivity made interlocutors wonder whether he did have something to hide or whether he had been doing only the regular work of an MP in his own riding and was the subject of a witch hunt.

But if Chrétien was entirely innocent of wrongdoing, he had certainly been careless in his management of riding affairs. In contrast to Mulroney, he was supposed to be setting an ethical example. He occupied the highest office in the land, and yet these subsidies that he steered into his riding had so many suspicious tie-ins that he had left himself wide open to the conflict allegations. That, as prime minister, he was not more scrupulous was difficult to fathom. Much more was to come on the file, including the serious matter of his lobbying of the

Business Development Bank of Canada to get money for the Auberge Grand-Mère—and also his activities in regard to the Immigrant Investor Program, which resulted in even larger sums being poured into the golf course properties.

The Reform Party was not backing down from its attacks on the prime minister, nor was Conrad Black's Southam newspaper chain. Despite their ideological differences, Black and Chrétien had known each other for twenty years and their relationship had been cordial. Chrétien attended Black's annual corporate dinners, and occasionally they saw each other in London, where Black spent time as proprietor of *The Daily Telegraph*. Responding to some of the reportage in the *National Post*, Chrétien phoned Black every now and then to register his discontent. On the Grand-Mère issue he became so angry that he went to the rare extent of writing a letter to the *Post* under his own name to refute the charges.

But for Chrétien, there soon appeared a better way, a much better way, of getting back at the proprietor than that. A new application of the Shawinigan chokehold he once put on the protester would do just fine. The perfect opportunity presented itself when Black began pursuing an appointment to the House of Lords. The upper chamber in Britain was a perfect fit for the press magnate. He had a deep sense of British history and politics, and he revelled in the rituals and the prestige of the institution, as well as its rich debating traditions. He was nominated for the peerage by Britain's former Conservative leader, William Hague. The British government approved the nomination, then waited for consent from Canada. Black had been informed by Roy MacLaren, who had become Canada's high commissioner in London, that there appeared to be no legal obstacle to his receiving a peerage. Canadian officials had further advised the British government that the peerage could go ahead if Black got British citizenship and didn't use his title in Canada. He had applied for and quickly obtained dual citizenship from the Blair government.

But two days before the appointment was supposed to be made, Chrétien struck. Some eighty years earlier, during the time of the Robert

Borden government, the Commons had approved the Nickle Resolution, which prevented Canadian citizens from receiving peerages. Specifically, King George V was asked to refrain from giving titles to Canadians.

Over time, the Nickle Resolution had not always been applied. Twenty knighthoods and two peerages had been granted, though none in recent decades. Though Chrétien could have approved the Black bid without anyone making any fuss over the resolution, he chose to invoke it. His claim that he was only following Canadian tradition found few believers. Most everyone could see that he was blocking Black's ascension to the House of Lords in retaliation for the coverage in the *National Post*.

This tempest, featuring two of the most powerful men in the country, included a Chrétien call to Black in Salzburg, Austria, in the middle of the night, European time. During the discussion, Black, recalled Peter Donolo, practically begged the PM for the appointment—and expressed interest in a seat in the Canadian Senate as well.

Having given Black the bad news, Chrétien appointed a committee, headed by Deputy Prime Minister Herb Gray, to look into the peerage question and give his invocation of the Nickle Resolution a smattering of credibility. The resolution had never become law, but it was reaffirmed by other governments, including the Pearson government in 1968 and the Mulroney government in 1988. Much of it was subject to interpretation, however. The 1988 reaffirmation, for example, said that foreign honours could be conferred on Canadian citizens who have dual nationality.

As expected, Gray's committee reported that Prime Minister Chrétien's position was valid and correct. Since the King and St. Laurent periods, Gray asserted, the resolution had been consistently applied. Those who were residents of Canada or Canadian citizens could not get British honours.

In exonerating the PM, Gray put himself in the line of fire—even from his wife. Sharon Sholzberg-Gray told him the committee was just a put-up job to cover for Chrétien. Sholzberg-Gray, the president of the Canadian Healthcare Association, had known the PM for forty years. She liked aspects of his character but knew what this was all about. "I remember being really annoyed at Herb while he chaired that committee." It was obvious, she said, that "the prime minister had made the decision before the committee studied it anyway." He and her husband's committee were "wrong." Her view was backed by a British diplomat who had to deal with Eddie Goldenberg at the PMO on the file. It was like running into a brick wall, the diplomat said. While acknowledging the obvious ill feeling towards Black, Goldenberg maintained in an interview that the prime minister would have invoked the Nickle Resolution against anyone seeking a peerage.

Opposition parliamentarians rallied to Black's defence. The Reform MP Monte Solberg said the case reeked of "small-minded, petty politics from a prime minister because the newspaper coverage of him was not always favourable." In Black's *National Post,* the tantalizingly baroque wordsmith Mark Steyn wrote that he found the Chrétien approach "an exquisite embodiment of psychologically crippled small-mindedness."

Chrétien held firm on his shaky ground. "I want to make it clear [that] I was guided in this matter by long-standing Canadian policy and custom," he said. On the very day he issued that statement, August 6, 1999, he went out for a game of golf at the course that was the target of the Black newspaper reports, the Grand-Mère club.

Black filed suit, claiming that the prime minister had abused his office by blocking the peerage. In the meantime, his papers were continuing the pursuit of the Liberals, working in tandem with their ideologically compatible political arm, the Reform Party. They were interested in more than just stories on alleged abuse of power. The newspapers, in combination with the Opposition party, hammered away daily at how poorly Canada stacked up against the big neighbour. They detailed the widening gap between Canadian and American standards of living, as well as the big gap in tax rates, in the value of the dollar, in productivity, in the unemployment rate. All these differences, conservatives argued, were resulting in an increasing flow across the border of many of the best talents in Canada. The so-called brain drain.

The seriousness of the latter issue depended on whose statistics one believed. Chrétien argued that the brain drain was being exaggerated by the business community to press its agenda. In trying to sell the government on deep tax cuts, for example, business leaders found it useful to say that the high rates were driving Canadians south of the border. The reality, Chrétien claimed, was that there were fewer Canadians moving to the United States than had been the case twenty years earlier, and the ones leaving were compensated for by all the newcomers—the brain gain.

If people didn't like it in Canada, the PM said, they were free to leave. He was keen on increasing levels of research and development in the country and enhancing educational opportunity. He also was looking at a big reduction in the tax burden. But he saw no need to overhaul policy to be more in harmony with the American dynamic. His approach on American relations remained ad hoc and pragmatic. Neither increased integration with the United States nor an increased nationalization of Canada.

This view of things displeased both the nationalists on the left, like Mel Hurtig, who was publishing a book called *The Vanishing Country,* and the integrationists on the right, who still had Brian Mulroney as their champion.

In the 1980s, Mulroney had begun what White House officials, in memoranda, termed "a revolution in U.S.–Canadian affairs." The secretary of state of the day, George Schultz, called the Tory prime minister's changes a "potential watershed." Mulroney had succeeded Pierre Trudeau, whose attitude to the U.S. was prickly and was such a contrast that American officials worried that he was being seen in Canada as a lackey of Washington. They had to give him something in return, as National Security Adviser Robert McFarlane put it, so as "to permit Mulroney to claim that he can influence our actions."

Mulroney's integrationist efforts were being stalled by Chrétien. The prime minister was doing this not by policy design. In fact, he had turned his Liberals towards free trade and followed up on many other economic initiatives of the Tories. The change came more by way of his attitude than through concrete measures. His style, his blunt criticisms of the American way, and his rhetoric about Canada being the better country were enough to signal an attitudinal shift.

Though the myth was still around that Canada was a young country, it was in fact 132 years old and counting. In a world where borders had been redrawn so often through the great wars and periods of decolonization, Canada was not young at all. Its age was now its source of identity. Canadians had been around long enough to know who they were. Great writers, great entertainers, glorious or searing moments in time—the Soviet hockey series and Expo 67 and the Quebec referendums—had formed bonds. "Increasingly, we are cultural Canadians: Canadians by willpower rather than by policy," wrote Darrell Bricker and Edward Greenspon in their 2002 book, *Searching for Certainty: Inside the New Canadian Mindset.* "We feel attached to Canada because we like the smell of it. It is an affair of the heart."

CHAPTER ELEVEN

FROM THE HEAD DOWN

T HE CAUCUS HELD ITS ANNUAL MEETING in Halifax in August 1999. It was a happy time for the Liberal Party and its prime minister, one of its few remaining peaceful weeks. For all the talk from the right of the spectrum about a widening gap between Canada and the United States, for all the stories on conflict of interest, no opposition party had even half the ruling party's support. The Liberals' challenge, it seemed, was to try to find something to do with themselves. They were being described as the "couch potato party" in the media, and they weren't even complaining about it. So what if, as one wag put it, the highlight of the previous session of Parliament had been the passage of tax treaties with Algeria and Croatia?

Jean Drapeau, the legendary mayor of Montreal, the Cecil B. DeMille of his craft, was buried the week the Liberals met in Halifax, which was just four months before the turn of the millennium. Drapeau had brought Expo 67 and the 1976 Olympic Games to Montreal. If he could do that as a mayor, wondered one MP, what would he have done as a prime minister?

The most pressing item the Grits could find to talk about was what they would do six months down the road with the projected surplus in the new budget. As his highlight millennium project, Chrétien had introduced the $2.5-billion Millennium Scholarship Fund, which was to kick in at the start of the New Year. It would provide grants of $3,000 to students; students of special merit would get bigger prizes.

Some Liberals had hoped for something more striking. They thought Canadians needed a little poetry to go along with the plumbing. Allan Rock was an admirer of the prime minister, but he was also someone who had seen John F. Kennedy—"And now the trumpet summons us again"—inspire a generation. He hadn't come to Ottawa to do a good job of maintaining the status quo. "What vision do we have of the country in the next millennium?" Rock asked. "How do we see this country in the twenty-first century?"

Others in the party, like John Godfrey and Dennis Mills, were also tired of riding the soft mid-tides. They too wanted to aim higher, but they were up against a stodgy centre, where few creative notions were harboured. "One day, I was chatting with the prime minister," Mills recalled. "I said, 'Jean, the place is dead, the place is dead. And every time I try to do anything, I feel like I'm a fish out of water. I don't feel like I am welcome here any more.'" As Mills recalled, the PM responded, "Dennis, you make my insiders nervous with all these ideas. I like your ideas, but you make my people nervous."

"'I thought,'" Mills told him, "'that we were here to try to stimulate debate and ideas and maybe try a few things.'"

Chrétien had been interviewed earlier in the summer about the coming turn of the century. When he was asked his plans for the big moment, he tossed the question back at the interviewer. "What are you planning to do the last day of the millennium and the first day of the millennium?" he asked. "You probably stay home, have a beer, watch TV, see a show if there is one, and go back home." "Then," he added, "you have another beer or a bottle of champagne." The ultimate pragmatist had the last word. Canadians didn't need a sense of ambition. They had their booze.

He was fortunate that there was a division in his opposition not only on the right of the spectrum, but also on the left. It was scattered and in disarray. There was big labour. There was Maude Barlow and her 100,000-strong Council of Canadians. There was Naomi Klein and the anti-globalization throngs; there were remnants of Mel

Hurtig's National Party; there was another splinter group, Paul Hellyer's fiercely nationalist Canadian Action Party; and there was David Orchard, a leftist in a Tory cloak who commanded a big portion of the anti–free trade vote. If anyone could have pulled the various strands into something resembling a bloc, the left could have become a potent force. But the NDP was registering at a deathly 10 percent in the polls and couldn't seem to budge. The party was divided over whether to go moderate or radical, and it was lacking a leader of dynamism. Alexa McDonough, despite doing well enough in the 1997 campaign, couldn't move the numbers. No one discounted her dedication and good nature, but her old-fashioned style seemed to fit the tired image of her party.

The media tended to ignore the NDP, as well as the other left-leaning factions. The visibility of the right side of the political spectrum received a tremendous boost with Black's purchase of Southam and the creation of the *National Post*. The left could only dream that one from their own flock had come along to purchase those journalistic prizes and create a Canada-wide paper. Had that been the case, the national conversation would have been much different.

The Liberals governed Canada for two of every three years throughout the twentieth century. Their paramountcy was apportioned almost identically in the century's two halves—three and half decades in the first half, and three and half decades in the second. As the century closed, it looked as though their dominance could well be extended. Their lock on the centre of the political spectrum, where the mass of voters resided in Canada, was such that murmurings of a one-party state were beginning to be heard.

With the exception of Paul Martin, however, it was a government that lacked star power and a government that lacked intellectual heft. Late in 1999, the PM moved to fill that void. Roméo LeBlanc vacated the governor generalship and, like shining rocks through the Rideau Hall windows, came Adrienne Clarkson and her partner, John Ralston Saul.

Clarkson, a former CBC broadcaster and agent general for Ontario in Paris, brought a measured elegance, a precision with language, and a sensitivity to minorities to the post. Saul, an author and philosopher, was too imposing a figure not to be part of the package. He could rarely let a paragraph go by without mention of Boccaccio, Clausewitz, Dali, and Pitt the Younger. While giving a speech—with Saul in the audience—Allan Fotheringham observed that he was the only person he knew who could "strut while sitting down." He was also rumoured, Fotheringham noted, to own an alarm clock that applauded.

Some wondered how Clarkson came to be interested in the ceremonial post. When not exchanging pleasantries about meteorological conditions, governors general were supposed to be pinning ribbons on delegations from Bolivia and Chad. In the past when GGs had complained of having no power, they were accused of exaggerating their self-worth. But Clarkson, who was promoted for the job by Jean Pelletier, was keen on taking it. In a day when the air was fat with debate on tax cuts and the American agenda, in an era of dumb and dumber, when intellectuals were out of fashion, in an age of vulgarity, when sophistication was rarely to be found, she and Ralston Saul were a splendid, if arrogant, antidote.

With their left-of-centre tilt, they had been outspoken in the past on economic and cultural nationalism, and it was expected that they might have difficulty keeping their political passions in check. Clarkson had described Lucien Bouchard as a man of successive sincerities who was "emotionally on a wavelength that is not rational." Ensconced in the post, she grabbed headlines by making her first regal appearance in a designer ensemble that the press likened to a bathrobe. Meanwhile John "de Tocqueville" Saul, as someone called him, beat back his image as a tux-and-landau man by touring a homeless shelter in Toronto. The wealthiest city in Canada had streets crawling with too many of the destitute to count.

Clarkson was not the only major appointment in the fall of 1999. With the nomination of Beverley McLachlin, a self-described farm

girl from Pincher Creek, Alberta, Chrétien selected the first woman
to serve as chief justice of the Supreme Court. A pragmatist not
easily categorized, McLachlin was a widely respected consensus
choice. The court was entering one of its most controversial phases,
and the timing of her selection was fortunate. Judicial activism—
the tendency of the justices, with additional powers derived from the
Charter of Rights and Freedoms, to allegedly assume the role of
political legislators—had become one of the hot-button issues of the
day. In the West, the Reform Party had taken it up as a major cause.
At a Reform convention, the crowd erupted when Premier Ralph
Klein of Alberta lashed out at judicial overreach on cases involving
assisted suicide and abortion.

In addition to these appointments, Chrétien had made Sheila
Copps deputy prime minister in his first term, and Anne McLellan
was named the first female minister of justice. Women were reaching high station, and at the swearing-in ceremony for Chief Justice
McLachlin, Adrienne Clarkson remarked, "I think in the world
today there isn't a situation like this, with somebody in my place
and somebody in hers." It was a good omen, she said. In the glob-
alized economy, where men in red suspenders saw Canada as more
of a conglomerate than a culture, women, she sensed, had a deeper
sensitivity to the essence of the country. Copps, now in the heritage
portfolio, was a strong defender of the cultural ethic; Jane Stewart
in human resources had the Canadian flag stamped on her heart;
and Anne McLellan loved the country even more than she did her
dog, Susie.

But despite having made some good choices, Chrétien could not
escape the reputation of being a leader who played the patronage game
the old way, shamelessly awarding friends of the party and contributors to the party with plums aplenty. Modernizing the system was
never one of his priorities. Rather than looking for ways to devolve
some of his mammoth appointment powers to Cabinet committees or
the like, he opted for the status quo—power unto himself.

André Ouellet became head of Canada Post, Peter Donolo became consul general to Milan, Patrick Lavelle, his former Ontario campaign manager, became chair of the Business Development Bank and later head of The Canada Export Development Corporation. As chair of the bank, he was there when Jean Carle came aboard, not long after his bouncer's role at APEC, as a vice president. Carle was chosen by a headhunting firm for the bank job, but Lavelle, feeling Carle was a roughneck, tried to have the appointment blocked, going all the way up the ladder to protest to Chrétien himself. The PM, whose dealings with the bank would become a matter of major controversy, told Lavelle he thought it wasn't such a bad idea to have Carle there. Lavelle found himself with "no choice."

Under this prime minister, at least one Ottawa veteran, George Baker, found that nothing had really changed in terms of how the gravy train worked. If you were a backbench MP and you wanted a promotion of some kind, he explained, all it took was "some good old-fashioned ass-kissing." The colourful Baker appreciated the little guy from Shawinigan, in that he found him astonishingly straightforward. "With Chrétien, it's knock down, drag out. He says everything to your face, nothing behind your back, and I imagine because of that, he has very few close friends." But he also knew that like most everyone else, the PM appreciated a little buttering up. And so when Baker felt it was time to try to move up the ladder, he knew what to do. In the Trudeau years, he had been overlooked. "I'd been here for twenty-seven years, and there was something important, the extension of sea jurisdictions, that I wanted to get done. So I said to myself, What do I have to do to get into Cabinet? And I said, Well, I've got to start playing games. I've got to start praising the PMO."

And that's what Baker went about doing. "I was always standing up in the Commons and saying, 'We've got the best prime minister we've ever had,' and all this stuff they wanted to hear. I was doing fundraisers, and the PMO was hearing about my great work. Well, six months passed and guess what? I was in like a wet sock." He was appointed minister of veterans affairs in the summer of 1999.

The most important change of the time was one that didn't receive much notice. Peter Donolo had spent eight years with Chrétien as his spin doctor, and though times had got a little rough for him with the APEC fiasco and the Hussein funeral squabble, he had served the PM well. His sense of humour was always primed to defuse tensions, and he generally managed to avoid alienating the media. Conspiracy theories weren't part of his makeup. He had little time for lockstep Chrétien loyalists like Warren Kinsella, who, Donolo said, tended to see enemies around every corner.

Of great importance was the relationship he had carved out with Paul Martin's team over at the finance department. He had a long-time friend there in Terrie O'Leary, who was Martin's executive assistant. The two of them had worked to smooth over the cracks in the sensitive relationship between the two titans of the government. But now both Donolo and O'Leary were leaving, with O'Leary off to Washington as Canada's representative to the World Bank.

Stepping into Donolo's place as director of communications was someone of an entirely different nature. Françoise Ducros had worked for Stéphane Dion and Brian Tobin. Her father was a Montreal judge who knew Chrétien quite well. She had a razor-sharp mind, so quick it would sometimes outrun her speech pattern and she would have to back up. She was intensely partisan, a fierce loyalist ready to do battle with all comers.

Her appointment was curious, in that she had no experience in either public relations or journalism, two areas critical to the job. When he heard about the appointment, Brian Tobin recalled turning to his aide, Heidi Bonnell, and expressing a degree of shock. He thought Francie Ducros was a big talent, suitable for many jobs—with the exception of the post she had just received.

Donolo was among those who had recommended her for the job. Goldenberg had too, and Jean Pelletier made the final and hugely important call. Ducros and Pelletier talked about her lack of communications experience. "We came to the view," Ducros recalled, "that I had extensive policy experience, and the best communications was based on a good understanding of substantive policy."

The first controversy to involve her came at the end of the summer of 1999, a couple of months after Ducros took the communications job, when Chrétien made a minor Cabinet shuffle, dumping three ministers. One of the three, Christine Stewart, the low-key environment minister, was called over to 24 Sussex and found the prime minister out back, chipping golf balls. Between shots, he looked up to inform Stewart that she was no longer needed at the Cabinet table. Then, according to the story that made the rounds back at the PMO, he went back to his chip shots.

Along with Stewart, two other ministers, Fred Mifflin and Diane Marleau, were informed that they were out, while Marcel Massé, the Treasury Board chairman, and Trade Minister Sergio Marchi left to take up patronage posts. Jane Stewart moved from Indian affairs to human resources, Herb Dhaliwal from revenue to fisheries, and Pierre Pettigrew from human resources to international trade.

In the political optic, it was noticed that there was a left-of-centre tilt to the appointments, which wouldn't please Paul Martin. It was also noticed that his loyalists, some of whom appeared ready for promotion, had been overlooked. No one had to think too deeply to figure out why this had happened. It was obvious—and it didn't have to be publicly stated. But word leaked from the Prime Minister's Office, or someone close to it, that the shuffle was indeed meant to send a message to Paul Martin, a "shot across the bow," as *The Globe and Mail* put it. PMO sources were quoted as saying that the Martinites should curb their ambitions because the changes were a sign that Chrétien would be leading the troops into battle in the next campaign.

Donolo was taking Italian-language lessons to prepare for his posting in Milan when he saw the media reports. He was surprised and annoyed. He knew the Martin team had been organizing to have their man succeed Chrétien when the time was right, but the last thing needed, he felt, was for the clash to become too public. He drew an analogy to that of a spouse's infidelity. You can go on living with it and you don't have to deal with it. But the moment you call your spouse on it, you're bringing it to a head. You either have to stop it or split up.

He recalled receiving a phone call from Ducros, asking him what he thought about the spin, and he told her he didn't like the interpretation put on the shuffle. Don't bring it out into the open, he advised her. Don't go public with this stuff. Scott Reid, Paul Martin's spokesperson, was also in touch with Ducros. Why was she politicizing this thing? he wanted to know. Why was she airing dirty laundry in public? "It created a set of tensions," recalled Reid, "which were fundamental."

Ducros couldn't recall phoning Donolo or talking to him about the story. To Reid, Ducros said that she insisted that the spin was not her doing. She stared right at him, she recalled, and said, "Look into my soul. I swear to God, on the life of my family, I was not behind that spin." Years later, she explained that "the only spin that I put on that shuffle was that the prime minister was preparing to run again." There was nothing said, she recalled, about Paul Martin. But from the Donolo and Reid perspective, putting out the word that the shuffle meant the PM was preparing to seek a third term was damaging enough.

With Ducros's arrival, the mood began to change. Martin insiders complained about what they saw as her overly suspicious and combative nature. "I know that the way the Cabinet shuffle was spun was an important signal to us that the world was changing," said David Herle, one of Martin's key strategists. "We never felt that, up until that moment, the PMO felt it was at war with us. We were trying to succeed him, not get rid of him." Herle went public with the comment that the tension spilling over from the Cabinet shuffle was the result of "no adult supervision in the PMO." Ducros took that as a direct strike at her, and from that moment on, she and Herle were at war. By that time, Paul Martin had started to look warily at what he regarded as Ducros's tendency to escalate tensions. When asked several years later to describe the difference between her and Donolo in the communications job, Martin responded, "Night and day."

If access was power, Ducros was quickly becoming one of the most powerful players in Ottawa. "I think I spent as much time with the prime minister as anybody in that office," she said. No one, least of all the Martin crowd, doubted it.

The Liberals' big biennial convention was only half a year away. Martin and his supporters were hoping for a clear signal from the prime minister that he would be stepping down before the next election. If there was no such signal, they were prepared to make life difficult for him. Some Chrétien supporters saw the inevitability of a civil war between the two and advised the PM to cut Martin loose before hostilities deepened. One was Patrick Lavelle. Martin was too dangerous, he told Chrétien in September of 1999. He wouldn't stop until he got the job. But Chrétien said he feared that such drastic action would create a backlash in the party. What about financial markets? What about his Liberal caucus? What about Canadian public opinion? He was still of the view that Martin's ambition could be contained.

The finance minister's supporters were under the impression that there was a tacit understanding with Chrétien that he would serve only two terms. Martin had amassed great popularity in his party and across the country, and polls showed that a substantial majority of Canadians thought it was time for Chrétien, who had reached the standard retirement age of sixty-five, to step down. As he seemed to have no pressing agenda, many thought he was hanging around for the sake of hanging around—enjoying the exercise of power. He had almost blown the majority in the last election, and caucus members were afraid he would lose it this time.

But this set of arguments was met by another set, just as persuasive. Chrétien still had a commanding lead in the opinion polls, and he had won two straight majorities, the first Liberal since St. Laurent to do that. The country was in reasonably good shape from the point of view of the economy and national unity. No crisis was on the horizon, and the PM was in perfectly good health.

Nowhere in Liberal Party history was there a precedent for unseating a successful leader. Laurier had won four elections in succession, then lost in 1911, but even after that defeat, he was allowed to stay on into his late seventies as Opposition leader. Mackenzie King lost two elections but faced little in the way of party rebellion. St. Laurent, older than Chrétien, had scant internal opposition to running for a third term. Lester Pearson won only minority governments before setting his own retirement date, and Trudeau lost in 1979 to Joe Clark but was welcomed back with open arms.

Another problem for Paul Martin was that he had nothing significant in terms of policy or vision to distinguish him in the eyes of most Canadians from Jean Chrétien. The finance minister was viewed as being softer on Quebec, somewhat more pro business, a leader more in tune with the globalization trend and more forward-looking. But there was no single, compelling idea to set him apart. If he did have any bold new formulas, he was not in a position to let anyone know about them because to waver from the party line was seen as an act of disloyalty.

Martin had assumed new duties in the summer, becoming the head of a new group, the finance ministers of the twenty most economically powerful nations in the world. It was called the G-20, and it acted as a sort of board of directors of the evolving world economy; it had, as a specific goal, the establishment of ground rules to prevent wild currency fluctuations, which had set economies reeling through the 1990s. Not since the 1944 Bretton Woods Conference, which laid the basis for the creation of the World Bank and the International Monetary Fund, had anyone set out with such grand designs for reform. Martin was a big player, not just domestically but on the world stage. An optimist by nature, he sat one day in his office, pouring back the large quantities of coffee that kept him on high alert. "I am just really optimistic of what the next ten years will hold for us," he stated. The days of the big recession appeared to be gone. "I don't think we'll see in Canada something that we went through from 1990 to 1992."

What impressed his followers was his thirst for knowledge, a sense that he was genuinely intrigued more by policy than politics. Reg Alcock, a Winnipeg MP, had written a report about how information technology could be put to better use. Alcock visited various Cabinet ministers to explain his idea. He'd sit down and start buzzing on excitedly about his project, only to look across the room and see his host's eyes starting to glaze over. In Martin's office, he was told, "Reg, I don't have a goddamn clue what you're talking about." But then Martin added, "Help me understand this stuff." And from then on, Paul Martin bugged Alcock whenever he saw him to send him more materials on the subject. "Having the confidence to admit you don't know something allows you to learn," said Alcock. "Paul is just fabulous at it. Chrétien is just the opposite. Chrétien taught me a lot. But you can't teach him anything."

Martin was sixty-one. As he looked ahead, he had to harbour doubts. If Chrétien sought another term and won, it might be too late for him. He would then be older than sixty-five himself, and Canadians might start to look to someone else. He was in a hurry, and so were many of his caucus followers, who wanted to ride his coattails to higher stations, securing the promotions they weren't able to get under Chrétien. Impatient, they were sometimes hard pressed to stay quiet and said things that could be interpreted by suspicious minds as evidence of plotting to unseat the prime minister.

Eventually, there would be a leadership race, and there was a leadership review to come before such a race. It was logical that contenders for the crown would start to lay the groundwork. But there was a very fine line between making appropriate preparations and being disloyal. Much depended on who was interpreting the developments. Much depended on whether those who briefed the prime minister viewed what they were hearing as nefarious plots or just the predictable actions of ambitious people wanting to succeed him.

The situation became more difficult for Martin when major issues like the clarity legislation arose. His support and loyalty were required, even when he wasn't really sure he wanted to go along.

IT HAD BEEN A YEAR since the Supreme Court had rendered its decision on Quebec's right to secede in August 1998. For a year, Chrétien had pondered whether to enshrine the court's ruling, notably the message of the court on the matter of a clear question and a clear majority, in legislation. He had to weigh the odds. The demand for a clear question and a clear majority—say, 60 percent for a successful referendum—could significantly diminish the chances of a vote ever succeeding. But such a unilateral, in-your-face thrust by Ottawa could well backfire, mobilizing Quebecers to retaliate. The momentum in Quebec, even with Bouchard as premier, had continued to drift away from the secessionists. Bouchard seemed to lack the revolutionary fervour of years gone by. He couldn't do anger like he used to. He had thrown so many punches that his arms had become rubbery. If he couldn't find a new weapon with which to pummel Ottawa, a new humiliation card to play, it was over.

That was the argument put to the prime minister. Let sleeping dogs lie. Don't take a chance on reigniting the whole movement. Don't risk a repeat of the 1980s, when all seemed quiet after patriation until the Tories reopened the debate and put the country through years of constitutional quarrels. This song was played to Chrétien every day. It came not just from his political opponents but from the majority in his party, the majority in the media, the majority in his office, even the majority of his closest advisers, those cautious men who wished— sometimes advisedly so—to move ahead by inches instead of miles.

Chrétien took his stand. Rejecting the advice of them all, he revealed his firm intent to bring forward a clarity bill with rules set in stone. Having watched the other side frame the essentials of the referendum process for too long, he decided that now it was his turn. His government would soon set the rules for a clear question and a vote number of more than 50 percent.

Bouchard erupted. The Quebec government would make a unilateral declaration of independence if it won a referendum and Ottawa refused to negotiate, he vowed. The Liberals had already participated in two referendums in which 50 percent was good enough. How could they change the rules in the middle of the game? Pierre Bourgault, the firebrand separatist of days of old, came out of his bunker. "The little terrorist from Shawinigan, with what he considers a brutal law aimed at frightening Quebecers into submission, will soon find out that his bomb will explode in his hands. Mr. Chrétien's project forces the federal government, for the first time in our history, to admit that Canada is divisible. It's music to a separatist's ears."

Visitors came to urge caution on the prime minister, including many members of his caucus. His response was that if his plan backfired and there was an insurrection in Quebec, he would step down in good conscience and let someone else come in. But his visitors got the impression that he was determined and confident, and that this act would be the apogee of his career. He would leave a monument to his four decades of struggle for Canadian unity.

While he was laying out his intent, Chrétien, without divulging the specifics of the plan, enlisted the aid of President Clinton. At the 1999 G-8 conference in Britain, the prime minister approached the president and invited him to a conference on federalism planned for Mont Tremblant, Quebec, in October. That very night, Clinton called Gordon Giffin, his ambassador in Ottawa, and told him, "Jean wants me to come to this conference." Clinton had been planning to go to Ottawa to open the new American embassy. The dates were changed to accommodate Chrétien's wishes.

Ambassador Giffin got to work on Clinton's big speech. He worked hard, as it was a sensitive subject, and on the way to

Tremblant in the limousine, he handed over eighteen tidily typed pages. Clinton looked the script over, tore off the first page, which had the names of dignitaries to be mentioned, and gave the remainder back to Giffin. It's a good piece of work, the president told the ambassador, but "it reads too much like a legal brief." He'd give his own extemporaneous address, he said.

At Tremblant, Clinton delivered a magnificent historical treatise on federalism, articulating the principles under which there could be legitimate objection to inclusion in such a system. Without mentioning Quebec, he made it clear that the principles for objection did not exist in the Canadian system. What did exist, he suggested, was a celebration of diversity and common humanity that was a blessing for all.

Chrétien approached Giffin and expressed surprise that—since the speech came in a perfectly modulated and syntaxed structure—Clinton did not appear to have any notes at the podium. Was that the case? he asked. No notes? Indeed it was, the ambassador responded.

The president and the ambassador had scheduled a brief meeting with Lucien Bouchard. All week long, the separatists had dominated the conference headlines, scoring points against a weaker lineup of federalist speakers. But Clinton, whose address was the final one, had suddenly turned the tide in the other direction. As Giffin went into the meeting with Bouchard, he noticed that the premier wasn't the same. "Bouchard was shaken by the speech. You could tell he was visibly shaken. Clinton had just sucked all the oxygen out of the conference."

Later in the day, Chrétien and Clinton headed off to one of Tremblant's high-quality golf courses to engage in their most cherished outdoor diversion. They were different men in so many ways, but they were both political animals and they had the common bond of being avid golfers. Ruminating about golf one day, Clinton said that "it is like life in a lot of ways. The most important competition is the one against yourself. All the biggest wounds are self-inflicted. And you get a lot of breaks you don't deserve—both ways." It was an observation that could be applied to both men and their time in office.

When their round began, it was late, and with two holes left to play, it was dark. The president and the prime minister, both highly competitive, were determined to complete their game, and they got the Secret Service and the RCMP to line up their Jeeps—high beams shining down the fairways—for the last two holes.

It had been a splendid couple of days that began in Ottawa with the dedication of the new American embassy. Clinton attended a session of Chrétien's Cabinet and was treated to an esoteric question from Lloyd Axworthy on water diversion from Devil's Lake in North Dakota and its impact on the Red River. Axworthy thought he had caught Clinton off guard, but to his astonishment, the president spent the next several minutes explaining the entire history of the sedimentary basin. He told Axworthy why on one side of the lake there was one geology and on the other a different one. He then went into the difference between the river systems of the Missouri and the Mississippi, the depths of the water, and so on. He had maps out by now, and he was just getting warmed up when Chrétien looked over at Axworthy. "Well, Lloyd," he said, "I bet you wish you hadn't brought that one up."

Axworthy was dumbfounded. "The guy was phenomenal," he recalled. "I looked around the Cabinet table. Everybody was wondering what the hell we were talking about. They couldn't believe it. I mean, some pond in North Dakota."

The Quebec sovereigntists hardly appreciated Clinton's intervention at Mont Tremblant. It was their second bad bout with an American president in recent times. Not long before, they had with great fanfare unveiled a monument honouring Franklin Roosevelt in Quebec City. At the time, they were unaware of the contents of a note FDR had once penned to Prime Minister Mackenzie King. He advised him to rid himself of his French-Canadian problem through policies of assimilation. When the correspondence was made public, the sovereigntists, red-faced, tried to explain that all great leaders make mistakes, and that the view held by FDR was clearly one of his more pronounced errors.

In December, after weighing all the options of his clarity plan, Chrétien finally came forward with draft legislation. He sat at the Cabinet table in a sombre frame of mind and revealed the specifics of his plan. No debate this time, he said. He would consider technical changes only. As he had told Goldenberg, who was dubious about this enterprise, he wanted the bill tabled before Christmas because the holiday break was not a time that brought people to the streets to protest political action.

The final package marked a significant pullback. It didn't stipulate what percentage of votes was needed to win the referendum. Chrétien had concluded that putting up a marker of 55 or 60 percent would be too inviting a target for the separatists. Also, his lawyers had convinced him that such a specification might not survive a court challenge. The bill provided that the referendum question be referred first to the Commons to determine whether it was clear. The result of the vote would also be brought to the House, where members would decide if it was decisive enough. There would be no right to unilateral secession.

Chrétien called Trudeau. The former prime minister expressed some reservations at first—some of his friends had criticized Chrétien's plan—but by the end of the discussion, he was on board. *"Bon courage, bonne chance,"* Trudeau wished his old warrior friend. The Reform Party—a long-time proponent of clarity, though not, Eddie Goldenberg would later say, a significant factor in the PM's decision to go ahead with it—supported the bill. But the Bloc, the NDP, and the Conservatives all opposed it, as did Charest's provincial Liberals.

"People want clarity," said Chrétien. "It's absolutely unbelievable that people are objecting that the other side in a negotiation wants a clear question." Paul Martin had been hesitant to pronounce himself for or against; he kept dodging the question until finally the pressure built to the point that he came forward with a somewhat weak endorsement. "The prime minister speaks for Cabinet; he speaks for all of Cabinet, and I am a member of that Cabinet." He then added, "I think that matters ought to be clarified."

They weren't entirely clarified, however. Under the legislation, Quebecers would go to the polls having no idea what percentage would constitute victory. They would vote in a fog. You vote, Ottawa was saying, and then we will tell you whether you've won or not. In a way, it was claiming a kind of veto power.

Chrétien wished to send a message to the Quebec Liberals, as well as the sovereigntists. Aides remarked how he thoroughly enjoyed that aspect of the enterprise. It wasn't just the separatists he was nailing with the clarity bill but his own weak-kneed provincial cousins. The feds were asserting control. Guy Bertrand, the Quebec lawyer who was the trailblazer on the Supreme Court reference, was delighted as well, noting that "the cowards" of the provincial wing had been on their feet denouncing the Chrétien legislation even before Lucien Bouchard.

The Christmas season passed quietly. No rumblings in Quebec. Chrétien, fingers crossed, looked at polls. No rumblings in Quebec. The new year, the new century, the new millennium began. No rumblings in Quebec. Bouchard and Parizeau and the other big hitters of the sovereignty movement denounced the legislation as a raping of the free will of Quebecers. Quebecers were unmoved.

IN KEEPING WITH HIS INCLINATION to avoid grandstanding, Chrétien made no promises on the night the century ended. Tens of thousands came to Parliament Hill for what was billed as a grand Canadian celebration. What they got instead was a feast of the macabre, a wailingly grim musical score and a parading band of ghoulishly costumed puppets flinging themselves about in what seemed like some ancient tribal ritual. On the damp and frigid night, Chrétien shook hands with the onlookers and gave only a low-key boilerplate talk. While the country could have used something more, words of inspiration were not what the people had come to expect from this leader.

A few days later, Joe Clark could be found in his downtown office, addressing what he considered to be one of Chrétien's major failings. "There is an immense pride in Canada," he offered. "But there is no trigger to that pride." There was no Canadian dream. Unless you develop one, you have a problem, he noted. "You get a country that is less a country than an arrangement." This was the Clark who had been attacked for his small dreams once, his "community of communities" vision of Canada, and he recalled how Trudeau dismissed him as being the "headwaiter to the provinces." Now Clark was again advocating a strong community of strong communities as an alternative to the polarization that he believed the Clarity Act was nurturing. He had circumvented opposition in his caucus to stand against the clarity bill, causing much murmuring among his troops. But Clark recalled that he had opposed patriation in 1982, that he had been saluted for his courage then, and that he had correctly predicted it could lead to serious problems with Quebec in the future. He wondered whether the same might happen with the clarity legislation. Calmness at first. Backlash years down the line.

For the time being, it was indeed quiet. Chrétien had won the gamble. His caucus members marvelled at his political instincts, and even among Quebec Liberals and Quebec journalists, there was grudging respect. "We were sure that he made a mistake," said Liza Frulla, "and that here again they were scaring people and starting a battle, and we wondered, Oh my God, what is he doing? There I have to admit we made a mistake." Graham Fraser, the journalist who knew better than most the ill feeling toward Chrétien in the Quebec media, said this was one time where they had to give him his due. "The media, myself included, thought there would be a much more intense reaction."

With the success, it appeared that the way was clear for Chrétien to leave at the end of the term. Critics could not now complain that he had done nothing major, save balance the books, in his time in office. His chief purpose in politics had been to push back sovereignty and preserve Canadian unity. With the Clarity Act, he had created a monument to that goal. If he decided to go, he would be leaving on a high note. Everything was in place, even a highly regarded successor.

WITH THE START of the New Year came a series of miscues. Chrétien's government was being pressured to bring forward a financial salvation package for Canadian-based NHL teams. They were suffering because of the low Canadian dollar and their small markets. A highly reluctant Chrétien was persuaded to agree to a bailout package put forward by Industry Minister John Manley. The weaknesses of the plan were screamingly evident. How could any average Canadian countenance turning over tax dollars to millionaire hockey players whose driveways were covered with Porsches? "This," said the Liberal MP Roger Gallaway, "is a tremendously stupid move."

Dennis Mills, who was very active on the file, told Manley, "It'll be a bitch to sell, John, but I'll be there with you." He was right in his forecast. Within a few hours of the announcement, Liberals across the country were being bombarded with protests. Mills phoned Manley and bluntly told him, "John, we gotta bury this sucker."

"Can't we even get through the weekend?" asked Manley.

"John, if we let the media have at this thing through the weekend, your future will be dead. You've got to go into the press room Friday morning and bury this goddamn thing in a cement case and drop it fifty feet below the fucking ocean."

Manley did just that and did it well—and the matter was soon forgotten.

In the same week, the Liberals were pummelled for not acting quickly on a relief package for farmers. It was a bad year on the farms, and while critics suggested that the same bellyaching from farmers had been heard each and every year since the 1930s, the government was made to look miserly by not coming quickly to their rescue.

At the same time, the health care cutbacks from the 1995 budget were starting to take a harsh toll. In Ontario, ambulances were repeatedly turned away from overcrowded hospitals because there were no vacant beds. Reports said that Canadian cancer patients were pouring across the border to avoid long waits and receive better treatment. Health care delivery was inexcusably slow. Sophisticated medical equipment was in short supply, as were nurses, beds, and doctors. The Canadian system used to be an example for the United States, a model of sorts. Now *The New York Times* was publishing a big report on how Canadians were looking south.

In 1999 the government had brought in its so-called health budget, with its increased outlays of $2.5 billion. But in a system that was spending close to $100 billion annually, it was only a small dint. From Newfoundland, Brian Tobin came to Ottawa to denounce the feds for presiding over the death of medicare. Increasingly, there was talk from Ralph Klein and Reform, both encouraged by the newly dominant right-wing print media, about opening the system to more private care.

In the same dreary month of January, Jane Stewart, new in the giant portfolio of Human Resources Development Canada (HRDC), the department that handed out more grant money than any other, hurriedly released an internal audit of spending. The audit covered more than four hundred projects, and it revealed one example of gross mismanagement after another. According to the audit, 80 percent of the HRDC files sampled had "no evidence of financial monitoring." In a subsequent interview, not wishing to hide the seriousness of the problem, Stewart used a stark analogy. From an administrative point of view, the department was "in the Dark Ages."

Why, the opposition parties wondered, having been given the audit months earlier, was she so late in coming out with it? The Reform Party in particular was interested in that question. It had made an access to information request to get a copy of the audit on the eve of Stewart's making it public. Was that what drove her to rush it out— the fear that Reform would publish the audit and allege a cover-up?

Stewart had a lot of explaining to do. She asserted that the delay in releasing the report was unavoidable because the department needed the time to prepare a response to the audit. Reform's access request, she added, had had nothing to do with the timing because she didn't know of it until January 21, three days after her press conference. That sounded plausible, but then a strange letter from Stewart's office came to light. Dated January 20, the letter mysteriously stated that the access request wasn't received until January 21. How could that be? asked dumbfounded Reform Party members. This was the Gregorian calendar. Time moved forwards, not in reverse. Or maybe it was indeed the Dark Ages over at HRDC.

The minister's office said the mishap was simply a clerical error. A secretary forgot to change the date in the computer template that she used to prepare correspondence. A mere tempest in a template, they said.

Stewart was in high dudgeon. Time on the hustings had taught her to be sensitive to charges of the abuse of taxpayer money. "I was one of those politicians who knocked on doors in 1993 and had somebody spit at me because I was a politician," she said. The charge that she had rushed the audit out because of the Reform Party request, she claimed, was pure "bullshit." As for the poor administration of her department, she explained that the budget cutbacks had resulted in a substantial streamlining of personnel, and the traditional supervision was no longer in place. Canadians had complained about too much red tape. The department had tried to do away with some of it—and it didn't work.

Reformers didn't let up. They had three issues in one—abuse of taxpayer money; a possible cover-up by Stewart; and, it now seemed likely, a connection to the prime minister's golf course controversy. Some of the money that went into the prime minister's constituency had come from human resources programs in dispute in the audit. Wasn't it interesting, mused Reform's top strategist, Rick Anderson, that there turned out to be so few checks and balances in the same department that doled out money in such a haphazard fashion to the PM's riding? Anderson was beginning to see links. "There's too much of a pattern here for all this to be random ineptitude," he charged. It was all part of the great Liberal tradition of securing popular support. "We basically believe that the Liberals' regional development programs operated the same way as at HRDC and basically have for twenty-five years, and that the system is rotten."

The government took the position that it was a simple administrative problem that could be cleared up. As in the private sector, Goldenberg explained, human error occurs, money isn't always properly managed. Why the foofaraw? The important point, Chrétien argued, was that the money was recoverable. It hadn't gone missing, as the opposition charged in calling the story the billion-dollar boondoggle. He asserted that the random audit of 459 projects had prompted full investigations into only 37 of them, which carried a value of $30 million. "It's not allegations of big fraud there." But as HRDC officials confirmed, if the audit was extended to the 60,000 total projects, there would likely be 4,800 that had been badly mismanaged.

On Wednesday, February 2, 2000, the Liberal caucus assembled as usual, with the prime minister at the head of the table. Hec Cloutier, the MP from Renfrew who had been prevented by Chrétien from seeking the Liberal nomination in the riding in 1993, rose to tell a story that validated some of Reform's charges. Human resources had approved a $100,000 grant for job creation in his riding. But it wasn't being used for job creation, Cloutier told his colleagues. A company was using it to pay the rent on its building. Cloutier had taken the file to HRDC to lodge a complaint, but his complaint didn't register. No one would turn off the taps. The money kept pouring in. When Cloutier sat down, the prime minister looked over and, in his cement-mixer growl, said, "Good intervention, Hector."

The story was leaked to the media, and Cloutier, in his broad-rimmed hat, was on the front pages. At the next caucus meeting, he stood up and told his fellow caucus members that he liked them all. "But one of you sons of bitches," he charged, "went out and leaked everything I said here last week. . . . I still like you, but I'll wring your neck if I can ever find out who it was."

Reformers came up with more evidence indicating that Chrétien himself might have been abusing the system. They charged that he broke the rules to obtain funding for the construction of a big fountain in his riding. Documents revealed that the manager in his Shawinigan riding office sent a letter to HRDC authorities urging approval of the fountain project more than a month before an application for the grant had even been filed. What we have here, said Reform members of Chrétien, is "the little guy who shagged the taxpayer."

The Liberals fell back on dirty tricks, getting a party researcher, James Dykstra, to play the role of imposter. Operating under the false cover of a reporter for the *Ottawa Citizen,* he phoned the office of the Tory MP Jean Dubé. Dykstra was trying—unsuccessfully, as it turned out—to get examples of correspondence between opposition MPs and their constituents showing how grateful they were for the HRDC grant program. Dykstra was caught and, for his efforts, suspended for thirty days without pay.

Chrétien brushed aside accusations about the fountain and other alleged abuses, saying, "When there is a project in my riding, I do as Reform Party members do. I support projects in my riding that help to create jobs and make the area very attractive." But examples of government misspending and mismanagement continued to be uncovered. In one scrum, Jane Stewart, facing a relentless grilling by the media, appeared to be wilting under the strain. Chrétien was walking past, saw she was in trouble, and stepped before the mikes to deflect attention from her.

Stewart, who didn't translate well to the television medium, got pulverized to the degree that she contemplated resigning. Every day in the Commons became a "Get Jane" day. Pierre Pettigrew, who was the HRDC minister when most of the abuses actually occurred, didn't have to answer any questions. Mel Cappe, the deputy minister of the department through much of the "Dark Ages" period, got promoted to clerk of the Privy Council and later moved on to become high commissioner to London. Stewart, meanwhile, had medical problems people didn't know about, and her two sons, both in their mid-teens, were seeing their mother get beaten up on TV on a regular basis. Leaks from the PMO suggested that she wasn't doing a good job.

Thinking she might cave to the pressure, Chrétien telephoned and implored her not to resign. She listened and began a long march back up the hill. Female caucus members rallied behind her. She had been honest and up front, argued Toronto MP Carolyn Bennett, and this was a welcome contrast to the behaviour of some of the boys on the team. As an example, Bennett pointed to the performance of House Leader Don Boudria. Instead of admitting the truth, Binder Boy, as he was called, got down in the bunker and started hurling charges at the other side, Bennett alleged. "I just found it appalling that Binder Boy would be yelling across the House, 'You got this in your riding, and you be quiet because you got this. . . .' I just couldn't go into the chamber any more and watch it."

The HRDC controversy struck another blow against the Chrétien government's wish to be seen as a clean and ethical shop. In 1998, the Corbeil scandal surfaced. In 1999, it was the Grand-Mère affair. To begin 2000, the HRDC imbroglio.

Questions remained on all three controversies, and the opposition parties were coming straight at the prime minister. Preston Manning was leading the way, drawing on a graphic marine analogy to pillory the governing party.

"A fish rots from the head down," he said.

CHAPTER TWELVE

PRUDENCE AND PARANOIA

A S JEAN CHRÉTIEN LOOKED OUT across the landscape in the first year of the new century, he could find more unity in his country than in his party. A little-known confrontation with his Italian MPs was a reflection of the deteriorating condition of the governing group.

With only a handful of seats providing him a majority in the House of Commons, Chrétien had to guard against Paul Martin loyalists deciding to turn on him and vote with the opposition parties to bring down the government. Martin commanded the support of most of the Italian Canadians in the Liberal caucus, some of whom resented being overlooked for Cabinet positions. They were eager to see Paul Martin take over—the sooner, the better.

The PMO was closely watching their activities, especially at the Standing Committee on Transport, which was dealing with the collapse of Canadian Airlines and a possible sale of Air Canada. Italian Canadians on the committee, most notably Joe Comuzzi, were aggressively questioning Transport Minister David Collenette at hearings, and such was the level of tension in the Liberal Party that this prompted allegations that they were trying to undermine him because he was a Chrétien backer. The Toronto MP Carolyn Parrish, a strong supporter of the prime minister, made the charge in the media, saying the Italian MPs were doing Paul Martin's bidding. The allegation incensed the Italians who, wishing to set the record straight, organized a meeting with Chrétien.

At the session the prime minister sat facing seven or eight Martin supporters who said they were being slandered as an ethnic group for carrying out their normal parliamentary duties. Initially, Chrétien had wanted only one or two at the meeting, but the Italians insisted they all come.

Joe Volpe was one who showed up. He had been named by Parrish as one of the Collenette's attackers but claimed he hadn't even been at the committee meeting in question. "If you want to show leadership," he recalled telling Chrétien, "will you tell everybody in caucus to just stop this bullshit. 'Cause what you're doing is slandering each and every one of us, everyone who has an Italian last name. You're raising bogeymen and conspiracy theories where none exist."

Parrish, who liked to employ colourful language, said she at least had the guts to be quoted by name in the newspaper report about Collenette. Not so Volpe, she said. He was "one of the wimps and shit-heads" who hid under the cloak of anonymity when the controversy broke. Parrish had referred to the Italians as the "pasta caucus" in the newspaper report. That they tried to turn this into some kind of ethnic slur was ridiculous, she said. "They joked themselves about being the pasta caucus."

At the meeting, the prime minister tried to dismiss the suggestion that his office had orchestrated the criticism of the Italians' behaviour. He was nervous—so tense, so angry, his visitors recalled, that his knuckles were white. He had his top aides, Pelletier and others, stationed outside the door. They stuck their heads in every few minutes to say the meeting was running over the allotted time.

As the MPs made their case, Chrétien fidgeted impatiently with a little table stand beside him, eventually breaking the top panel of it. When he couldn't get it back on, the towering Comuzzi stood up, lumbered over, and said, "Here, let me fix the goddamn thing."

Sensing that the Italians were bitter about not getting promotions, Chrétien was not shy about letting them know why. He pointed at each of them in turn. "You supported Martin. . . . You supported

Martin. . . . You supported Martin." He mentioned Alfonso Gagliano and Maria Minna, two Italian Canadians who were his supporters and were in the Cabinet. "Why aren't they here?" he asked. He then pointed out that most of those present had received at least an appointment of a more minor nature, such as parliamentary secretary. "I've looked after all of you." Eyeing each one coldly, he said, "You got something. . . . You got something. . . . You got something." When he came to Comuzzi, he said, "I offered you something, but you didn't take it." Indeed, Jean Pelletier had pressed Comuzzi to take a parliamentary assistant's post, but the MP declined.

For most of the showdown, Chrétien held his ground. At every opportunity, he moved off topic and launched into one of his war stories—a favourite tactic of his—to try to run out the clock. He did. Nothing was resolved, and the Italians went away angry. "He never apologized or got Carolyn Parrish to apologize," recalled Joe Fontana. They were more annoyed when they saw how the story was being sold to the media. "The PMO was spinning it like they summoned us to the bloody meeting," Fontana said.

When he saw a TV report saying the Italians had been slapped around, Joe Volpe took after Francie Ducros, telling her that if she didn't get the report corrected, he would be in front of every camera and every newspaper reporter with the real story.

Some time later, Chrétien was in the Commons for a vote late at night. "We were voting around the clock on shifts on amendments to Indian Act legislation or something like that," Parrish recalled. "And Chrétien came traipsing in at around one o'clock in the morning and sat there and voted for a couple of hours. It was a smart move on his part because spirits were low. He was quite jovial and calling everybody to come down and have chats with him. It was wonderful. I felt had he done that more often, he'd still be in control."

Chrétien called Parrish down to his chair for a talk. He said, "Hey, the Italians don't like you very much?" She nodded. "Don't worry," he told her. Chrétien said his meeting with the Italians was private and he couldn't say much but then went on to say a lot. He told her how he went through them one by one pointing out their weaknesses and told them "you all get out of my office." He got a little flamboyant," recalled Parrish. He told her she was going a good job, that even Gagliano said so and that she didn't do anything wrong with the pasta caucus and they knew it. "I gave them hell and threw them out."

It was march in the capital, and the biennial convention for the natural governing party, the moment when the prime minister would finally speak of his future plans—plans that would have major ramifications for the country, the party, his likely successor—was only two weeks away.

There was speculation that if Chrétien didn't signal he was leaving, the Martin supporters would embarrass him at the convention. They would make it apparent that it was not the party's wish that he stay, and that it would be most difficult for him if he tried to. The mood was therefore testy at the PMO. The last thing they needed was for one of their own to come forward and say it was time to let the finance minister take over.

Maurice Chrétien, the prime minister's oldest brother, rarely spoke out. All the family members were scrupulous in this regard, keeping well in the background. Maurice had been a mentor to young Jean, the trailblazer, the one who had financed Jean's university education. Without him, Jean Chrétien might not have made it beyond his hometown.

Maurice was in his late eighties, but he was clear-minded and in good health, and he watched political developments closely. With the convention approaching, a journalist asked him whether he thought the prime minister should remain in office or call it a day. "He is my young brother," Maurice responded, "and, you know, he has done a lot for this country and a lot for the party, and I would suggest that he quits and comes home and has a good time."

His record was good enough, Maurice explained, although it hadn't been so good in recent months, with the controversies and all. In

Shawinigan, there were three separate police investigations underway because of the grants and loans controversies, and Maurice didn't get the impression that Jean was paying enough attention. "He doesn't seem to care much about that. But I would care." Still, Maurice felt that his young brother could be content to pass the torch. He had balanced the books, and with the clarity legislation, he had made it more difficult for Quebec to secede, an especially big accomplishment. So why get greedy, Maurice asked, and why push for more? Why not come home?

When Maurice's words—"Time to Call It Quits"—hit the headlines, there was consternation at the Prime Minister's Office. The anger was palpable. Maurice was pelted with calls, asking why he had said it. The prime minister's operatives tried to pretend that he was old and weak, and perhaps wasn't thinking clearly. They had raised no objections when he was quoted in other reports and in a biography of the prime minister. He had not said anything highly controversial then. But now that he had made remarks that were not in the prime minister's interest, they wanted to discredit the interview.

That they reacted so bitterly was revealing. If the prime minister really was planning to step down before the next election, Maurice Chrétien's words would not have bothered them. They would have been seen as setting the stage. Martin's advisers took note. They took note also of another statement Maurice had made in the interview. "I know that his long-term plan," he said, "is to be re-elected for a third time and step down after two years. That's what he would like to have." Maurice Chrétien, the straight shooter, wasn't the type of man who would make up such a story. He had obviously talked to the prime minister about it. Martin organizers had been in contact with one of Chrétien's top political honchos, David Smith. He told them the PM was staying as well.

Rumours began to circulate that if this was the case, Paul Martin might resign. He had accomplished most of his goals in the finance portfolio, and he did not possess a great hunger for any other Cabinet position. Instead of hanging around for a few more years, instead of having his every move interpreted as a political act, why not step down and bide his time—like John Turner and Chrétien himself had done before they won the leadership? Outside the tent, he would be free to enunciate his policy priorities and his ambitions for the country, things he couldn't do in the Chrétien Cabinet.

Given the developments, Martin strategists decided to call a meeting of some of his top supporters. They brought together important caucus members for a session at the Regal Constellation Hotel, near the Toronto airport, a few days before the conference. Joe Volpe, one of the party's better organizers, was in Edmonton working for Martin when he was summoned to the meeting. "I wasn't making any excuses for what I was doing out there," Volpe said. "I was recruiting for the next leadership campaign, which we all thought was coming." He asked the person summoning him what the meeting was about. Trends, directions, he was told, and Martin's recent budget. The budget? The budget, Volpe knew, had been a breeze. It was a budget straight out of the horn of plenty, a throwback to old Liberal juggernaut spending days. It was a budget so uncontroversial that the opposition parties forgot about it within a day and, much to the consternation of the Liberals, turned immediately back to the HRDC controversy.

Plans for the Constellation Hotel meeting seemed quite vague. But Volpe came, as did about twenty other close Martin supporters. David Herle, one of Martin's principal strategists, gave a presentation. He talked about economic trends and leadership qualities. Another presentation analyzed how Martin's budget had been received. There was talk of a coming campaign, and of how many seats the Liberals might lose with Chrétien as leader. Martin organizers released polling data showing that the finance minister would do better. All the while, Volpe was thinking, Okay, okay. This is fine, but what am I doing here?

John Webster, Martin's bagman, got more to the point. He told those gathered that it was now clear Chrétien would be seeking another mandate. "[They say] he's not leaving, and we're convinced that they're right. What does this mean? Well, it means that those of you who are recruiting will have to stop."

At the close of the meeting, Volpe approached Herle and Webster. He was hot. "You mean to tell me you don't want me to be involved in organizing for the leadership because of someone else's interpretation of what's going to happen?" he demanded. Others at the session weren't enthused. Albina Guarnieri came away thinking it was mainly a waste of time, just a review of things most people already knew. Joe Fontana had been told it was a meeting to encourage Martin not to resign. Nothing much happened, he said. Carolyn Bennett said the message coming out of it was to give the PM "the best convention he ever had because he wouldn't react well if cornered." Walt Lastewka made that same point to the group. They must respect the office of the prime minister, he explained. Any organized effort to undermine him wouldn't work. He thought he heard agreement around the table on this point. Judi Longfield, a strong Martin supporter from Whitby, Ontario, heard him, but she was upset. She had been told by her constituents that they wanted a leadership change, and she in turn had told them that Chrétien would likely be stepping down before the next election. Now she would have to eat her words.

The group dispersed. Later, they turned on their TV sets to discover that they had been at a secret meeting plotting the overthrow of the prime minister of Canada. The CBC aired the story, complete with pictures of some of those present. The pictures, Guarnieri said, made them look like plotters caught in the act of subterfuge. "CIA mug shots," she called them.

In the lobby of the Constellation, there had been signs pointing to the room the Martin meeting was being held in. That's how clandestine it was, Guarnieri explained sarcastically. And what about when Rock or Tobin or Chrétien supporters held political meetings? Weren't they held in hotel rooms?

Before the CBC aired its big story, the Prime Minister's Office was tipped off. Francie Ducros received a call telling her what would be reported. In room 228 of the Langevin Block, she huddled late in the evening with Goldenberg and Pelletier and others to see the report. They watched and concluded that this was a grave matter.

So did many others. Once the story had aired, there was no reversing the spin. Martin strategists could not make the meeting sound as innocent as they had claimed it was. They soon realized the optics of what they had done were disastrous. They should have known that news of such a meeting would leak, and they should have known how it would be interpreted—a conspiracy afoot, a *coup d'état* in the making.

"They completely took it wrong," said Carolyn Bennett. "Francie Ducros went ballistic. The damage was done by their reaction to it." Martin's spokesman, Scott Reid, said Ducros was running around telling people that a "coup" had been planned. She would later flatly deny she had ever said anything like this. Just as with the Cabinet shuffle in the summer of 1999, she claimed she was being blamed for things she did not do. She maintained that all she said about the Constellation Hotel was "We're not commenting on it."

Martin's problems were compounded when Stan Keyes, one of his top backers, was quoted in *The Globe and Mail* as saying, "It's time to pass the torch." If the meeting was so innocent, why would he say that? Other Martin supporters made statements of a similar nature. Chrétien could well imagine that the hotel meeting was set up to orchestrate disruptive activity—that in fact there *was* a plan in the works.

As the convention began, David Smith was approached by a PMO official and told that a car would pick him up at 11:30 to take him to 24 Sussex for lunch. He arrived to find the brain trust assembled around Chrétien, all of them in foul humour. "Chrétien was visibly shaken; he was hurt," Smith said. Smith had spoken to some of Martin's organizers, and he believed the hotel meeting was being blown out of proportion. He tried explaining this to Chrétien, arguing that while the meeting should not have happened, it hardly constituted a crisis. But no one around the table wanted to believe him. "The PM was sceptical," recalled Smith, "and sensed a plot."

One Martin supporter who had a chance to see Chrétien after the Constellation Hotel story broke was Walt Lastewka. He had a meeting scheduled with the PM on another subject. While there, he assured Chrétien that there was nothing nefarious about the Martin meeting. Chrétien didn't believe him.

In an attempt at damage control, Martin supporters fanned out across the convention floor. "I was walking up and down in the corridor like a prostitute talking to anyone in the media who would talk to me," recalled Guarnieri. But some Martin backers took the opposite approach, trying to avoid the spotlight. When the cameras caught up to Carolyn Bennett, she didn't know what to say. She looked guilt-ridden and appeared that way on television.

Martin had erred in allowing the hotel meeting to take place, especially since it came just before the big convention began. Now he erred in trying to explain it. Instead of meeting with reporters at a press conference and telling them exactly what happened, he got caught up in a cops-and-robbers-style chase across the convention floor and up and down escalators. He looked like a fugitive. "My staff meet with MPs on a regular basis," the finance minister tried to explain. They were meeting to discuss the recent budget, he said.

Scott Reid was angry at himself. He never should have let his minister wander into a scrum without an exit door close by. He had left his minister as bait for the media hounds. "I don't know whether the visuals could have been any worse," Reid recalled. "I turned it into a moving scrum. It was my fault."

Years later, looking back at the hectic day, Paul Martin said that the escalator scrum should have been a dead giveaway that nothing was going on. "If there had been a big plot going on, then I would have been better prepared. I had that escalator scrum. I was totally caught off guard." Of the hotel meeting, he said, "There was nothing in that. Not a thing. There was absolutely no big plot going on." Things were blown out of proportion by the mood of paranoia that had gripped the PMO, he explained. If the communications spinners had simply told the truth, instead of embroidering the hotel meeting with "coup" talk, "Nothing would have happened. They shouldn't have built it up."

To Paul Martin and PMO insiders like Percy Downe, the Constellation meeting was a prime example of the communications breakdown between the two sides. With O'Leary and Donolo gone, there were no highly effective emissaries to bridge the gaps. "Peter and Terrie leaving changed the dynamic," said Downe, who was soon to take over as Jean Chrétien's principal secretary.

Francie Ducros and Scott Reid got along to some extent. "In many respects, our relationship was effective," Reid would say. But there was a lack of trust. "She is very bright, but she is a very suspicious person. She would insist she wasn't behind this and she wasn't behind that, but there was so much evidence to the contrary that my trust was diminished."

At the convention, the prime minister was taking a Martin-forces-be-damned posture, signalling his intention to run for a third term. Entering the hall, he was greeted by the party's youth wing with shouts of "Four more years! Four more years!" He responded with thumbs-up rhetoric. "We still have a lot of work to do, and I intend to do it for the next four years. We have to build a country in the twenty-first century. It's going to be a fantastic campaign."

When it came time for the plenary session, where the prime minister fielded questions from the floor, the Chrétien forces heard that Martin organizers were planning to stack the microphone lineups with their supporters. Paul Sparkes, the prime minister's chief of operations, foiled the plan. He let the prime minister's sympathizers into the room via a separate route so that they could get to the microphones first. When the doors opened and the Martin people burst through, it was too late.

It was clear, however, that despite any bad publicity stemming from the Constellation episode, Paul Martin was the number-one attraction. His organizers feared he might hear some hisses when Chrétien introduced his Cabinet to the twenty-five hundred delegates. Instead, Martin's reception was thunderous. He received more good news when the convention elected a majority of his supporters to the party's national executive. As a headline in a Quebec paper put it, "They Like Chrétien, but They Love Martin."

For a long time, the finance minister had been coy about his desire to lead the Liberal Party. Now, for the first time, he decided to come out and say it. He did so in front of a sea of media, and although it was a statement of the obvious, it had the effect of clearing the air and making him and his entire team feel more at ease. There was nothing wrong with wanting the leadership, and there was nothing wrong with preparing for that end.

Eddie Goldenberg could have told him that. While he was campaigning to bring down John Turner in the 1986 Liberal leadership review, Goldenberg defended challenges to the leadership of the party. "It's your democratic right," he asserted. "If you're going to have a review—considering the fact that it's the democratic way of political parties—then it should not be considered almost subversive to take a side." Now, of course, Goldenberg's perspective had changed. The feeling that many MPs got from him and others in the PMO was that they were indeed just that—subversive—if they didn't toe the PM's line.

Chrétien, meanwhile, was facing polls showing that two out of every three Canadians wanted him to step down. He was under pressure to state his rationale for continuing in office. In his wrap-up address to the convention, he tried turning back the clock to old Liberal themes of standing up for the little guy and keeping Canada out of the hands of the Americans. The delegates reacted respectfully, but the standing ovation seemed more pro forma than enthusiastic. There was a sense of gratitude towards Uncle Jean, but no sense of anticipation. Martin and his closest allies sat in a darkened corner in the back of the hall. They had been quite sure before the convention ever began that the PM was going to stay on, and they were now receiving confirmation. But as the convention closed, they couldn't help thinking that the party members were trying to send Chrétien a message. They were saying thanks for a job done well, but it's time to move on.

The line in the prime minister's speech that touched off the loudest roar was his sarcastic reference, in attacking the right-wing hordes, to "the common touch of Conrad Black." It was clear from his tone of voice how much he enjoyed saying the line. He couldn't resist the shot, and coming from the blue-collar PM, it had a special connotation. His main challenge once again was from the bedrock conservatism of the Alliance, and he would be happy to make the next campaign an ideological struggle between left and right.

His broadside caught up with Black, who was in London. Over the telephone, the media magnate responded, saying that for many years, he had to "deal with this attempt to caricature me as some sort of right-wing extremist, which I am not and never have been." Then, with customary vituperation, Black lashed out. "If Chrétien is serious about this as an election theme, it will give me great pleasure to blow the wheels off it. But I can't believe that even he—petty and rather unintelligent man that he is—would try to inflict this kind of campaign on the country. The right thing to happen would be for Chrétien to go and Martin to take his place, because Martin is a competent man and Chrétien is basically an embarrassment." In the same phone call, Black hinted that he might soon be leaving Canada behind. Referring to a former Liberal Cabinet minister and governor general, he said, "I well remember when the late Jeanne Sauvé told me that if Chrétien became prime minister, she would emigrate. Well, fortunately, Jeanne Sauvé died and didn't have to face that conundrum. But those of us who survive do."

Though Chrétien left the convention more bitter towards Martin than he had been before, his staff found him more energetic than they had seen him in some time. The week had not been without its blessings. He had been searching for a rationale to stay in office—and now he had one. It would be a terrible precedent, he told colleagues, if the Liberal Party allowed a successful leader to be pushed out because of the naked ambition of another party member. He was not about to let that happen.

That he still looked upon the hotel meeting as a plot to get him was evident from a conversation he had with one of his young aides, Duncan Fulton, some time afterwards. Seated in his Challenger jet, skirting the skies, Chrétien was reflecting on the convention week. He mentioned how difficult it must have been for Paul Martin to be caught on the escalator, trying to dodge the media with their embarrassing questions. The young Fulton agreed. Yes, he told the prime minister, they really misfired on that one.

Chrétien pushed back in his seat as if he were to have a nap, put his hands on the armrests, and said, "Want to learn a lesson in politics, young man?"

"Yes, absolutely," said Fulton.

In a voice that was almost a whisper, Chrétien intoned, "If you plan a coup, don't miss." A look of great satisfaction swept over his face. He leaned back in his seat and closed his eyes.

Though Chrétien and his coterie had been assured that no *coup d'état* had been planned, it suited their purposes to believe otherwise. When he was asked years later if the PMO had exaggerated what happened at the Constellation Hotel, Jean Pelletier was candid. "That may, in fact, be right," he offered. "But in politics, it is not the facts that count, sometimes. It's the perception of the facts. . . . We read what we read, and we saw on television what we saw. It had been given a dimension, and that had created a problem for Chrétien."

Few could doubt the power of the media as the story played out. Spin was everything. The problem, Pelletier was saying, was that the media coverage had made it look like Prime Minister Chrétien was being pushed out of office, and he had to do something to correct that impression. He had to run again to prove that it was not true. He had to run again for the sake of his pride.

In the months before the convention, Aline had often told Maurice Chrétien that she hoped her husband would step down and come home. That all changed convention week. She was lying in bed one morning, leafing through the newspapers. She saw the headlines, put the paper down, and told her husband she had changed her mind. If you want to go again, she told him, do it. "They're not going to push you out."

With her endorsement, one of the last stumbling blocks was removed. Word quickly spread. Carolyn Parrish heard it from Public Works Minister Alfonso Gagliano, who had been edgy during the convention. He was an absolute Chrétien loyalist, and if the prime minister was going to step down, Gagliano was going to step down with him. After the convention, Parrish, who served as Gagliano's parliamentary assistant, noticed that the irritation was gone. "He came in one morning all buoyant, really happy, bouncing up and down, such a little round guy, and he announced, 'That's it. We're running again.'" He told the story of Madame Chrétien reading the newspapers. He had just seen the PM, who, he reported, was in a great mood. Chrétien had told Gagliano, "We're ready. We're going to war."

THEY WEREN'T SURE about the opponent yet. While the Liberals were trying to settle their scores, the promised new political formation of the right was born, but a leader for it still had to be chosen. The Reform Party, a regional enterprise throughout its thirteen-year history, officially transformed itself into the Canadian Alliance. The rebirth occurred with markedly little fanfare at Calgary's Metropolitan Centre. About three hundred party regulars came to hear the results of an internal party referendum. It passed with ease, ending a drawn-out process that had begun two years earlier. "I am giddy, actually," said Jason Kenney, the young Calgary MP who had done much of the grunt work involved in creating the new enterprise. "We've overcome so much scepticism, our own included, and it's a glorious moment to see it come to fruition." But while the idea had been to fold Reform and the Progressive Conservatives into one unit, there was no such coalescing. The Alliance was basically the old Reform Party in a new guise. Some provincial Tories had come over, most notably from Ontario; but at the federal level, the old Tory party remained intact.

The Manning team controlled the infrastructure for the new enterprise. He was the architect of the party, and he thought he could win the leadership of it. But some members were asking a pertinent question: Why go to the trouble of creating a new party if you're going to return to the old leader? Most thought it was time for Manning to pass the torch. It had become clear, over a dozen years and several elections, that he was unable to stretch his appeal beyond the West. But Manning thought that maybe with one more try, under a new label, he would succeed, and so he forged ahead, fuelled by every politician's weakness and every politician's strength—a surfeit of ego and ambition.

In some ways, his situation was comparable to Chrétien's. He could have made a triumphant exit at this time. He had created the Reform Party, built it into the official Opposition, helped set the national agenda, and now he had taken Reform to a new level with the launch of the Canadian Alliance Party. A hallowed place awaited him if he took the altruistic route of passing on the leadership. But, like Chrétien, Manning found the lure of continued power much too strong. Each leader came to the crucial crossroads in March 2000. Each had a secure and honoured place in history. Each set off on a dubious journey that risked dividing his party and debasing his reputation.

Chrétien had barely finished with the convention when he embarked on a Middle East disaster tour. A visit to a region so fraught with political land mines was a dangerous mission for any leader, and subtleties of diplomacy had never been the forte of the blunt Canadian leader. He was barely off the airplane before the problems started. His first questionable call was a decision to forgo visiting East Jerusalem, part of the territory annexed by Israel in

1967. Palestinian officials registered their annoyance that Chrétien would not tour the city's Arab section. As sometimes happened, the prime minister made an offhanded observation that compounded his difficulties. He said he didn't know where he was. "Some said I'm making a political statement in not going to East Jerusalem," he remarked. "I don't know if I am in West, South, North, or East Jerusalem right now. I came here to meet with the [Israeli] prime minister, and here I am."

Chrétien moved on to Gaza City, where he left the impression that he believed it was all right for the Palestinians to use the threat of a unilateral declaration of independence to force progress in their peace talks with Israel. Canadian officials explained later that he didn't really mean to suggest that he supported UDI (universal declaration of independence) or its use as a pressure tactic. In Nazareth, he was incautious again. He said it made sense to him that Israel wanted exclusive access to the Sea of Galilee, the freshwater lake in the Golan Heights. The observation came at a time of sensitive negotiations between Israel and Syria over the Heights.

Headlines bellowed the news of Chrétien's miscues all over the nation. In Ottawa, the opposition parties howled with outrage. Had he looked at precedent, the prime minister would have steered well clear of press conferences and scrums on this trip, realizing that words in the Middle East can be more easily misinterpreted than words anywhere else. He was furious at the media, as were the members of his entourage, for blowing his statements out of proportion. The contingent of scribes was a bad draw, they thought. With a different set of journalists, noted Ducros, it would have been a different reaction.

In the diplomatic slights department, Chrétien was joined by his nephew Raymond, the ambassador to Washington, who made remarks the media interpreted as meaning he favoured the Democrat Al Gore over George W. Bush in the presidential election. What Ambassador Chrétien had said was that Gore knew more about Canada than Bush.

But those words were spun into something more controversial than that—and the message was heard in Republican circles. Of course, there had never been much doubt that the Chrétiens favoured the Democrats. On an ideological level, they felt more comfortable with them than they did with Republicans. Chrétien saw the political ethos south of the border as far to the right of that in Canada. In Canada, Liberals were considered centrists, he said, but "a Liberal in the United States is almost a Communist."

In the summer, he lost his foreign affairs minister. Word leaked that Lloyd Axworthy was leaving before the next election to head up a think-tank in British Columbia. The standard-bearer for the left flank of the party wanted to have more family time and make more money. He was also no close ally of the heir apparent, Paul Martin.

With his soft-power agenda, Axworthy had left an imprint on Canadian diplomacy. The budgetary cutbacks had hit the foreign service hard, but despite these constraints, he was still able to give voice to a noble set of ideals. If Axworthy had not succeeded in many of his endeavours, he had at least tried to point the way. No one was going to be able to recreate the golden age of diplomacy, when, with Europe ravaged by the Second World War, Canada was one of the few powers left standing, and its word carried far more weight than in normal times. One of Axworthy's last major acts was to pointedly rebuke the United States for its announced intention to spend massively on a new missile defence program. With such an enormous lead in weapons stockpiles and a military budget seven times larger than that of the closest competitor, the Americans, Axworthy argued, had a historic opportunity to lead the world in the other direction, towards de-escalation.

Chrétien didn't enjoy losing one of his only political heavyweights from the West. But it wasn't a crippling blow. He could win the next campaign easily enough without much support in that region of the country, just as he had won the first two. He could leave the Alliance to its base as long as he held the centre of the country.

In the Alliance leadership race, it quickly became apparent that despite their respect for Manning, members wanted a new face. Stockwell Day quickly became the favourite, and he went on to beat Manning by a healthy margin. The Alberta treasurer, who could get by fumblingly in French, was articulate, telegenic, and national, in that he had lived in Ontario, down East, and out West. However, Day's social-conservative leanings—his views on abortion, gay rights, and the death penalty—were harsher and more out of line with the Canadian mainstream than anything the Liberals had faced from a major opponent in the past.

Chrétien knew that if he could bring on a quick election, he could catch Day totally unprepared. Day was new, his Alliance Party was new, and there was bitterness left over from the leadership campaign. Manning was not about to go gracefully in defeat. The Liberals looked at all these factors and could see that the mix was there for another election triumph. It would feature traditional values against those of the hard right. For students of history, Eddie Goldenberg drew a parallel. The election, he said, would be the closest thing Canada had ever witnessed to the 1964 presidential fight that pit Lyndon Johnson against Barry Goldwater.

To counter Day's youthful vigour, the Grits wanted to show that their sixty-six-year-old leader still had some vigour of his own. With TV cameras in tow, Chrétien went on a white-water rafting trip along the Ottawa River. He handled the athletic assignment artfully, so much so that he came to the rescue of a young woman in front of him who lost her balance. This followed his zipping around the Tarmac at Tokyo's Airport on a two-wheeled scooter, an event that was captured in a marvellous photograph that dominated front pages. These carefully orchestrated photo-ops cast Chrétien in a far more positive light than did a confrontation in Prince Edward Island. While he was making his way through a crowd, his security let him down again. A protester walked right up to him and smashed him in the face with a cream pie. Amid the shouts and mayhem, Paul Sparkes, his chief of operations, thought for a horrible second that there was acid in the pie mix.

Chrétien was hurried into a side chamber, cleaned off, and instructed to get back out and continue on schedule. The PM obliged, but he had been humiliated and, back in his car, cursed the lack of protection he had received. During the Flag Day ceremonies in Hull, he had taken security into his own hands. Maybe, he said, he should have done it here as well.

With his plan to call another early election, he faced concerted opposition within his own ranks. Autumn 2000 would mark just three and a half years into his second term. An early election call had almost backfired in 1997. Caucus members thought it would look doubly opportunistic to try it again, especially with no pressing issue on the table. But Chrétien was looking at polls in Ontario that showed his Liberals with a phenomenal 50-percent lead. He didn't like the thought of waiting, of giving more Canadians a chance to tire of him, of giving Paul Martin's boosters more time to disrupt things, of giving the newly created Alliance Party and its leader time to get on their feet.

Stockwell Day was having fun through the summer of 2000, a bit like Kim Campbell in the summer of 1993. He had been leader for only a few weeks when he decided he would bring some novelty to the art of the press conference. On a lake in his Okanagan riding in B.C., he climbed into a Sea-Doo, sped along the coastline, and pulled up on shore, muscles flexing in his skin-tight wetsuit. He took some questions, turned his ship of state seaward, and with a mischievous, male-mermaid grin, shot back off across the lake.

The caper netted huge coverage, delighting the new leader. The media jury was still out, however, on whether the stunt was novel and delightful or lightweight and goofy. Clark was ridiculing the Alliance as the "costume party," Mulroney called it the "Reform Party in panty-hose," and a headline writer captured the moment with "Premiering This Fall: Daywatch." Day looked on as media commentators made up their minds. They didn't know what to think, he recalled, "but then a decision was made by two or three of the lead ducks in the press gallery, and it was over. And the decision was, "'We're going to kill him.'"

The decision was, "You're no Trudeau." The Northern Magus could wear a Count Dracula cape to a Grey Cup game or break protocol and do pirouettes behind the Queen, but he had gravitas to go with the glitz. Stuntman Stock lacked that. He used the phrase "freedom train" to describe his movement, inviting Canadians to climb aboard. But what kind of freedom was he talking about? Chrétien wondered. Reform-Alliance had three big rallying cries: too much deficit, too much debt, too many taxes. The deficit had been erased, the Liberals were cutting the national debt at a faster rate than even Manning had recommended, and Paul Martin was poised to take the axe to taxes.

Health care showed up on all polls as the most pressing issue. Chrétien, while still not committed to the early election, called the premiers to Ottawa. His coffers loaded with surplus money, he was able to answer their complaints with a new funding arrangement, and they all appeared before the cameras to say what a fine day it had been. Health care professionals like Sharon Sholzberg-Gray, the president of the Canadian Healthcare Association, wanted a reform of the delivery system, not just an agreement on money. The Liberals, she charged, weren't getting at the root of the problem.

Tired of hearing these kinds of criticisms, especially from his own party members, Chrétien had a word with the wife of his deputy prime minister at a function a little later. "I understand you get paid to criticize me," he told her. "My wife does it for free."

Just as they had in the 1997 campaign, the Liberals had one fear. When their caucus held its annual meeting, this one in Winnipeg, members reported hearing rumours that the Alliance was going to trim back the GST. They all knew, as one of them put it, that "we'd get killed on that." The Alliance strategist Rod Love favoured a cut in the tax, and he began pushing the GST issue on Day and the party's finance critic, Jason Kenney. But mainly at Kenney's urging, they took a pass, letting the Grits off the hook. The Liberals were promising tax cuts of their own. The Alliance needed something to set its tax package apart, but they didn't take advantage of the opportunity.

IN SEPTEMBER OF THE YEAR 2000, as Chrétien prepared to make the election call, news arrived from Montreal that Pierre Elliott Trudeau had died. Chrétien was informed of the death on a flight between Central American countries. He took time to compose himself, then moved to the back of the plane to inform the journalists of his passing. Trudeau had been in declining health for some months. He had become smaller and his voice weaker. While on a ski trip, his son Michel had been carried by an avalanche into the freezing waters of a mountain lake. The loss had crushed Trudeau.

Trudeau had governed Canada with the logic of Socrates, the arrogance of a Roman emperor, and the vitality of a Cyrano. To many, he never fulfilled his full promise, but his dashing presence and diamond intellect separated him from ordinary mortals. Canada was a country "full of doubt," as the journalist Bruce Hutchison had written, and one that had "listened too long to timid men." But Trudeau rescued it from that plight. He stood up to everything he faced. He stood up to separatists, to presidents, to journalists, to big business. He stood up to Quebec and the West, and to constitutional accords. His arrogance was legendary, and after the surging Trudeaumania of the 1960s, people often found him too cocksure, too condescending, and too divisive to continue to accord him the admiration they once did. His capacity to separate reason from emotion and remain so long in a chamber of unfeeling logic deepened the fault lines. But he had shaped—with the Constitution, the Charter of Rights and Freedoms, official bilingualism, the indebted welfare state, the alienated West— much of the nation that Jean Chrétien came to govern.

He was a one-man cultural renaissance, taking a country that bordered on backwater status and giving it intellectual dimension. He worried in his final days about the weakening of the national will, but he thought more often of his three boys and the Saturday nights he spent reading to them when they were young. Every Saturday, he remembered, "I read them Rousseau, history books, poetry, Victor Hugo. Later, Stendhal and Tolstoy. We'd talk about what we read. Read out loud to each other." He recalled those days as being among the happiest of his life. His boys never had to worry—as Bruce Hutchison did—about timid men. In their presence was one of the most daunting leaders of the Canadian century.

In Ottawa, tens of thousands lined the lawns of Parliament and waited to pass by his coffin. Chrétien hugged Trudeau's two remaining sons and his distraught former wife, Margaret. In the Commons chamber, Joe Clark noted that it was ironic that a prime minister whose purpose was the unity of his country should have exacerbated the differences within the Canadian family. "I think there is a reason for that. His intellect guided him more than his intuition. In a sense, he was too rational for this country, which after all was formed and grew against logic."

Jimmy Carter and Fidel Castro came to his funeral. The dictator of Cuba was given prime place, a reminder to onlookers of the more leftist tilt that Trudeau once embraced and to which he had more recently returned. The idea of a world under the sway of the corporation appalled him, and in his final months, he had seen this type of world encroaching.

Chrétien never had a close or deep bond with Pierre Trudeau. One was an intellectual, the other a brawler. One was an artist, the other a working man. But they were joined by many of their attitudes towards the country. They shared a recalcitrance towards special status for Quebec; they shared suspicions about the United States; they each favoured pitting activist government against Bay Street's tenets.

Trudeau was able to see enough in Chrétien's Spartan strengths to reward him with ten Cabinet portfolios, including the top jobs of finance and justice. He was able to understand, while other leaders might not have, Chrétien's bond with the average Canadian. Chrétien, in turn, was unswervingly dedicated and loyal. To the quarterback with the razzle-dazzle, he was the old-fashioned fullback, the mudder who crashed into the line, advancing the ball a couple of yards at a time.

His brilliant field general was gone now and the mudder remained. In the Notre-Dame Basilica, as the hymns and requiems mourned his leader's passing, he could no longer sustain the hard edge of which he was normally capable. His face was a sheet of grief.

CHAPTER THIRTEEN

IDEOLOGICAL WARFARE

R EG ALCOCK, A WINNIPEG MP since 1993, had become so exasperated by the paranoia in his Liberal Party that he sat down in the spring of 2000 and wrote a letter. "Dear Prime Minister," he began. "I am absolutely amazed at the transformation that has come over your office lately. How three such experienced and intelligent people like you, Eddie, and Jean Pelletier can act like such jackasses is beyond me.

"Yesterday one of your employees was inquiring about my trip to rural Manitoba during the break. The clear intention of the questions was to determine whether my trip was 'leadership-related.' . . . Have you all become so paranoid that you view every concern as an attack on your leadership? Do you really believe that you are best served by your pom-pom chorus?"

The party was dividing up between the pom-pom chorus and the Paul Martin chorus, with much of the nation's business taking a back seat to the political feud.

Alcock's analysis, to which many subscribed, pointed to a bunker mentality at the all-controlling centre, a centre that had come to exert so much power in the Canadian system that the journalist Jeffrey Simpson was penning a book titled *The Friendly Dictatorship*. In his letter, Alcock expressed alarm over "the increasing influence of a small group of elites . . . who seem to have the ability to pre-decide issues for the government." The sense of entitlement, he noted, extended to several top bureaucrats, who appeared to enjoy a "certain impunity" and viewed the House of Commons "with disdain." This, Alcock stated in his letter, "is an affront to everything we stand for."

Imagining the knee-jerk reaction his letter would probably elicit from the PM, Alcock asked Chrétien not to dismiss what he was saying with the standard labelling. "I am not fronting for one of the putative leadership candidates. . . . I am not acting out of my dissatisfaction at not being in Cabinet. However, for the first time in my life, I am beginning to feel 'dirty' by association with our government."

The Canadian system imbued its prime minister with a surfeit of authority. As Donald Savoie meticulously chronicled in his 1999 book *Governing from the Centre,* the power had become all the more concentrated in recent decades, eventually reaching the point where, as he stated, "Cabinet has now joined Parliament as an institution being bypassed." That "centre," which was frustrating Alcock and so many others, had increasingly become Chrétien's fiefdom. The populist in power is less secure than the establishment man because while power is expected to accrue to the elites, it is not a natural fit for those from lower echelons. Chrétien always carried with him the knowledge that he had defied huge odds to reach the pinnacle. Having attained the hallowed ground—never quite sure he merited it, and always wary of being seen as unworthy—he was prepared to go to great lengths to protect his station. As Simpson noted, in Chrétien there lurked "a streak of terrible pettiness and vengeance directed against those who have crossed him."

His insecurities were magnified by the conditions of his stewardship, his hold on the office under threat from a popular and ambitious finance minister. Other long-serving prime ministers—Mulroney, Trudeau, Pearson, St. Laurent, King—didn't face such a constant challenge. Under siege, the holder of power can be expected to wield it more ruthlessly. He is more likely to resort to defiance and bullying, less likely to delegate power or trust anyone other than his closest loyalists. Threats, real or imagined, have to be stamped out. The writer Robert Fulford said of Chrétien that "he retains the raw, angry sensitivity of a man who grew up feeling like an outsider." Even as a success, Fulford wrote, he "feels scorned and mistreated." Fulford and others detected a curious strain in the Chrétien character. He was a sore winner.

While Chrétien showed no inclination to diminish central control, Paul Martin held out the promise of cleaning things up, of reforming the system to give members like Alcock and Roger Gallaway and others more respect and more influence. These MPs planned to bring the parliamentary reform issue to a head following the campaign, by pushing for the free election of Commons committee chairs and parliamentary secretaries, and for the curtailment of the power of lobbyists—reforms all favoured by Martin.

Jean Pelletier was getting letters and hearing objections not just from Alcock but from many in the party about the bunker mentality at the PMO and the suspicious attitude towards anyone having anything to do with Paul Martin. Sensing problems in communications, he went to the unusual length of inviting Martin's two communications specialists, Scott Reid and Ruth Thorkelson, to a meeting with him and Goldenberg.

Francie Ducros wasn't told about the meeting, which took place a few months after the heated biennial convention. Reid hadn't known what to expect, but he was relieved to discover that he was not being blamed for the divisiveness. Pelletier did ask Reid to do something, however. "I remember his exact phrasing," Reid recalled. "He said, 'Sometimes we can find the answer at the bottom of a good bottle of wine. So perhaps you and Francie should go out and empty a bottle of wine.'" Pelletier was saying, Reid recalled, that "we were still going to get this government to work and bring the temperature down." He had a long lunch with Ducros, though at the bottom of the bottle there were no magic answers. She denied things she had allegedly said and stories she had allegedly leaked.

In the months before a possible fall campaign, Martin was still giving half a thought to stepping down, a move that would have come as a heavy blow to the party and Chrétien. But quitting in a pre-election period, he concluded, would have been too divisive. It would have looked as if he was putting his own interests ahead of the party's. When Turner left Trudeau in 1975 and Chrétien left Turner in 1986, no elections were in the offing.

Most in the party, not just supporters of the finance minister, opposed the idea of an early campaign. But Chrétien had to silence the rebels, and he felt that winning another election would be a good way of doing it. He was confident of victory, and although many in his party were dubious, several people, even the likes of Fidel Castro, were advising the prime minister to go to the polls soon.

Castro had had a chance encounter with Stockwell Day following the Trudeau funeral. The Opposition leader had been advised to avoid the obvious bad optics of a conservative like him being seen with the dictator, so he tried to steer as far away from Castro as possible. At the church ceremony, he had done that successfully, but back at the hotel, he was about to get in the elevator when out stepped the Cuban leader, surrounded by a platoon of security goons.

"You are the leader of the Opposition," Castro announced.

Day nodded.

"How are you doing?" asked Castro.

"I think things are going very well, and I feel very positive. And if I have the opportunity to form a government, I'll look forward to talking to you," said Day. "But we will have some significant differences."

A grin came across Castro's face. The two men chatted for a moment or so on insubstantial matters, but the Alliance leader did not wish to linger.

Later that same day, Castro had a conversation with Chrétien. "I just met the new leader of your Opposition," he said.

"What do you think?" asked the prime minister.

"I think," said the dictator, obviously not impressed, "that you ought to call the election early."

Castro's advice was followed, a decision made easier when Day injudiciously issued an invitation for Chrétien to call the election. In the Commons, pummelling the prime minister over divisions within his party, the Alliance leader declared forcefully that he had to do one of two things: "Either resign because he has no support over there, or call an election based on his record as being the highest-taxing leader of the G-7 countries." Smiles lit up the faces of the Liberals along the front bench. How would Day be able to run around the country condemning the Liberals for calling an early vote when he had just stood up in the Commons and asked for one?

Looking on as the scene unfolded on television was a disbelieving Rick Anderson, Manning's old strategist. He was quickly on the phone to Rod Love, Day's top organizer. "Christ, Rod, what are you guys doing? Don't open this door for Chrétien. He'll walk right through it."

The Alliance Party wasn't ready for a campaign. "Absolutely everything for us was geared for the spring," Day would later say, revealing how shrewd Chrétien was to make the early call. "We didn't even have the nominations ready." He had been tense in his first month as Opposition leader, a job not easy to come to grips with, as Chrétien, despite all his experience, had learned in his disastrous first year in that position. "I knew I was going up against the most powerful and successful Liberal establishment in recent years, nationally or internationally," recalled the Alliance leader. "Not maybe as entrenched as Vincente Fox had to face in Mexico. But I was not naive about what I was about to embark on."

Being new, Day thought he might try to change what he viewed as some outmoded traditions. One idea was to bring some dignity to the proceedings by replacing the clamorous scrum after Question Period with a formal press conference in a separate room. He tried it for a while, but most journalists—who now had to interview the others outside the chamber, then scramble to the floor below to see Day— were put off. The advantage of the scrum was that the leader could march away from the mikes any time he wished, but in the formalized press conference, this was harder to do. Day quickly found himself under siege in the downstairs room. The pack was all over him. Before long, he abandoned his novel idea and the regular scrum was back on.

Day had trouble finding a strong election issue. For this campaign, the Liberals had money, mountains of it. The government's projected surplus was a roomy $20 billion, which meant that the Grits could shower Canadians with cash, mainly in the form of a healthy tax cut— the very one that the Alliance Party was to use as the basis for its campaign. Paul Martin rolled out a mini-budget that contained, he was delighted to boast, "by far the largest tax cut in Canadian history." The budget boosted his tax-reduction package—when combined with cuts already made—to a tidy $100 billion. Middle-income families would save $1,000 in the coming year alone. Business would keep more of its profits, as would stock-market investors.

The Liberals were opening the big umbrella, plying their trade with customary efficiency. They were moving, at election time, to take the meat off every opponent's plate. The NDP was targeting health care. But in September, Chrétien had arranged the new funding package with the premiers, taking a lot of the sting out of Alexa McDonough's attacks. Now, like wolves after bigger prey, the Liberals went right into the heart of Alliance land with the tax-cut promise.

But for Chrétien, it wasn't an easy entry into the third campaign. A week before the race began, John Reid, the information commissioner, released a report alleging that the PMO was trying to thwart the Access to Information Act with heavy intimidation tactics. Reid said that bureaucrats in his department were even being threatened with job loss if they strayed too far from the wishes of the PMO.

At the same time, the auditor general issued a report on the mismanagement of taxpayer money at HRDC. It didn't confirm, as opposition leaders had hoped, that vast amounts of tax money had gone missing. But there was ample evidence of widespread bungling of funding programs. The Liberals aggravated the situation by boycotting a scheduled committee hearing on the report, thus fuelling the impression that they had something to hide.

Having covered the right flank with tax cuts and the left flank with a health care package, Chrétien knew the abuse-of-power issue was his main point of vulnerability. Like the absent committee members, he appeared to be on the run himself when reporters tried to question him about the auditor's findings. On his way out of the Commons, in obvious foul humour, the PM bluntly told one scribe to get out of his way and, wearing that Flag Day Terminator look, pushed his way past another.

In previous elections, Chrétien had had a united Liberal Party behind him. But going into this third campaign, his party was a house divided. It was a Liberal Party that was unenthusiastic about having this leader at the helm and a Liberal Party that knew he was running again not so much because he had an important policy agenda for Canada but because he wanted to stop Paul Martin.

To bolster his election team and show some party strength, he persuaded Brian Tobin to return to federal politics. The Tobinator had only recently received a new electoral mandate in Newfoundland. To get him back, the prime minister promised him a big Cabinet seat— before he had even been re-elected in a federal riding. Tobin wanted the industry portfolio, where, it was understood, he could make the business contacts he would need to accumulate a war chest for an eventual leadership run. Giving industry to Tobin meant that a new post had to be found for the incumbent minister, John Manley. Since Axworthy was leaving politics, the foreign affairs slot was open. As a man on the right of the party—seven years in big business circles had moved him from his more activist ways of old—Manley hardly looked a suitable successor to "Pink" Lloyd. But if Chrétien wanted to accommodate Tobin, he had to find a big spot for Manley. Political priorities trumped other priorities, and Manley got the job.

The cynicism that greeted this shuffle was compounded by the removal from Cabinet of Veterans Affairs Minister George Baker, who had—after a quarter-century wait—just arrived at the table. One Cabinet minister from Newfoundland would do, and Tobin was the one. Reports were put out that Baker's wife, Avril, was very ill— though her health was no worse than it had been—and that this had necessitated the move. Baker professed not to be overly upset. He had found that he had little more power in Cabinet than he'd had as an MP. If MPs were a bunch of nobodies, as Trudeau had once put it, so too were most of the Cabinet members. The control by the executive branch, said Baker, was that tight.

In support of his point, he used the example of the appointment of his executive assistant, an appointment in which he had no say. It was the PMO's call, but Baker came to wonder if the people in that office knew what they were doing. He got three calls from different officials, he said, each one naming a different assistant for him. The calls weren't from small players—he got one from Percy Downe, who was in charge of appointments, one from Eddie Goldenberg, and one from Jean Pelletier. Baker knew something was wrong—he couldn't have three executive assistants. But each caller said the prime minister had approved the appointment.

"The last call," said Baker, "came from Pelletier, and he said the prime minister had decided who my executive assistant would be. I said, 'Jean, are you sure?' He said yes. I said, 'Well, that is the strangest damn thing, because I've been told by two other people that the prime minister decided to appoint somebody else.'"

Baker solved the problem by refusing to take an executive assistant. He found he had such minimal power that he didn't need one anyway. As a Newfoundlander, he wanted to work on the fisheries file, to extend Canadian jurisdiction in Atlantic waters. Because he was from the region, he felt entitled to some say in the matter. But he discovered that this was hardly the case. "I ended up in Eddie Goldenberg's office with the deputy minister of foreign affairs telling me to shut up about fishing."

At the Cabinet meetings, he also got nowhere. "You were expected to behave like a trained seal. You could no longer speak your mind. I mean, if you're not there to do something, why are all these men and women going around with their noses in the air?"

As THE CAMPAIGN BEGAN, the Liberals were in the mid-forties in the opinion polls, the Alliance was in the mid-twenties, and the other parties were stalled in the low-teens. Despite some painful moments in his first weeks in Parliament, Stockwell Day appeared to have momentum. On the day before the campaign officially began, he staged an attractive photo-op. On a sun-splashed podium, with the Gothic spires of Parliament as the backdrop, he stood before supporters looking much like a Ronald Reagan conservative, straight out of the Screen Actors Guild. "Jean Chrétien and his friends think they own that building over there," Day bellowed, arm outstretched to the tall grey tower. "Well, I have news for them. It is owned by the people of Canada—and we will take it back on November 27."

On his first day of campaigning, he chose another splendid backdrop, the infamous Human Resources Development Canada building, where he spoke of respect for the people and a restoration of real democracy. Alluding to the prime minister's defence of HRDC spending, he conceded that the grants had indeed created many new jobs—all those Mounties who had to be hired to probe the frauds connected with them.

But he made a puzzling decision to campaign on what he called "an agenda of respect." The high road was an odd route to choose when Jean Chrétien's plan was to impugn Stockwell Day as a right-wing nutbar at every opportunity. Observers wondered how Day could think that preaching honesty while the other guy savaged him would make up 20 percentage points in the polls. "Everybody was pushing me to call him corrupt every day," the Alliance leader recalled. "But I was saying I am not convinced the public likes to see this level of name-calling." He wasn't familiar with the credo of Chrétien's warrior, Warren Kinsella: In politics, half the game is "kicking the living shit out of the other guy."

That the Liberals were reliant on this game plan was evident with the release of their campaign Red Book, a policy document even more vacuous than the 1997 offering. But there was method to the meandering. "It was our intention to minimize the attention on our platform and keep the negatives on Stock," recalled Duncan Fulton. "We didn't have to try hard because when we launched the platform, the media looked at it, found no bullets, and dropped it. It was a one- or two-day story."

With the focus off himself, Chrétien could unleash his ideological warfare, his bid to turn Stockwell Day into a social-policy terrorist who would bomb abortion clinics, turf out immigrants, and send gays off to rehabilitation clinics. *Maclean's* magazine helped the Grits along with a cover story on Day headlined "How Scary?"

Chrétien's answer? "Plenty."

Day, in fact, was radical by Canadian standards. He was against abortion and for capital punishment. He favoured the deportation of non-Canadians who committed crimes, the end of regional development programs for poorer provinces, the end of big support programs for multiculturalism, and the devolution of responsibilities for health care, language, and natural resources to the provinces. Beneath the stereotyping and exaggeration, the campaign had many real elements of a left versus right struggle, a battle that pitted traditional centrist values against a new Canadian construct embodied in neoconservative principles.

To go after the Alliance leader, Chrétien's war room had at the ready not only its chief knee-capper, Kinsella, but also Francie Ducros and Duncan Fulton and the ace researcher Kevin Bosch. They performed effectively, lining up material that could contradict Day at every turn and getting it to the journalists on the buses. By the end of the first week, Day was already complaining about "a frightfully inaccurate blizzard of an attack." He was bashed with a particularly damning front-page headline in *The Globe and Mail* that said his party favoured two-tier health care with a big role for the private sector. The Liberals pounced. How scary? There it is!

The Alliance leader went to Niagara Falls, where, like the Bloc Québécois bus driver in the 1997 campaign, he experienced directional problems. Attempting to draw an analogy to Canada's alleged brain drain, he declared that the Niagara River ran north to south, instead of south to north. The mistake was one that journalists—who would hardly claim geology as one of their areas of expertise—would normally not have noticed. But as misfortune would have it, one of the CBC reporters following Day, the adept Eric Sorensen, was from the Niagara Falls area. He caught it instantly and pointed out the error. Instead of laughing it off, Day said he would have a serious talk with his researcher.

At first week's end, the polls indicated that the voters had been in a mood—perhaps were still in a mood—to consider an alternative. The Alliance was moving up, gaining four points to now stand at 29 percent. The Liberals held steady at 45 percent. It was clear that the Alliance had begun the campaign with the momentum. It was theirs to squander.

Liberal campaigners, meanwhile, were getting cool responses at voters' doorsteps. Many were saying that Chrétien had overstayed his welcome, and that if they voted for him, it would only be because there was no one else.

On the hustings, Chrétien was his usual self, stumbling along in his sometimes charming, sometimes alarming way. At St. Joseph's Catholic High School in Barrie, Ontario, a girl stood up in a packed auditorium to pose a question. In the United States, she said, students got wonderful opportunities via athletic scholarships. Wasn't it time Canadian universities offered the same?

The prime minister was nodding as she made her point. "I tend to incline with you," he blurted. Nervous, then raucous, laughter followed, whereupon the PM caught himself and amended his word choice. Eddie Goldenberg was watching from the back of the hall, amused and taking a great interest in the high quality of the questions from some of the students. "Isn't it great?" he said. "Forty years from now, these students will be telling their families about the time the prime minister came here and the question they asked him."

Another question touched on the delicate subject of abortion. Chrétien muddled along for a few seconds, and then—the prime minister of Canada talking to a sixteen-year-old questioner—he said, "I am not at the age any more to have my wife have an abortion." It took some time for the discomfort level to subside, but the PM seemed oblivious to having trampled on any sensitivities and answered the rest of the questions cheerily. By the end of the session, his folksy manner had won over many of the students.

At a training centre for carpenters in Toronto, he moved comfortably among the manual labourers, wedging in some strips of flooring and pounding nails into boards. The working men presented him with a jacket of black wool and leather, and he put it on, looking, despite the authoritarian lean he often displayed, much more at home in it than he did in his politician's suit. The carpenter's coat would have been a less comfortable fit for other leaders. For Brian Mulroney, a nightclub jacket, gold-sequined, would have been more becoming. For Lester Pearson an academic gown, Paul Martin a banker's suit, Pierre Trudeau a cape.

"For Aline and I, we're back at home," the ground-floor man of politics said of the experience of being among the carpenters. "It's because we're both coming from blue-collar families." He talked about the dignity of work. "You are learning skills, you young people here. It will give you something you will have all your life, the skill of working on construction."

He went to Regina, where he visited the training centre of the RCMP. Putting aside the assassination attempt at 24 Sussex, the pie in the face, the Airbus bungling, the Flag Day episode, and the pepper spray incident, he swallowed hard and told the recruits that they were joining the greatest police force in the world.

Though he made his usual number of head-spinning gaffes with the language, he still possessed enough clarity and alertness of mind—"I'm relatively young. I'm sixty-six," he reminded people—to handle the cut and thrust with journalists and campaign crowds.

With Day trapped in the two-tier medicare corner, he pushed universal health care as the big issue of the campaign, telling voters that he
had served in Parliament the day that medicare was introduced, and
that it had been "one of the proudest days of my life and never will I
let the Alliance destroy it."

In truth, though, there was no burning issue in the campaign. Just
as in the United States where a presidential election was underway, no
dire controversies marked the time either. All that was soon to change,
most notably in America, to a degree few could ever have imagined.
But on this rare occasion when elections in the two countries paral-
leled each other, the continent was comparatively calm. In the United
States, there was no great foreign foe, no war ongoing, no war on the
horizon. The economy was on one of its great runs, and poverty was
in decline, as was crime, as was racial tension. With the country
prosperous and at peace, Republicans had little to use to beat up on
their Democratic opponents, save sex in the Oval Office. George
Bush, Jr., a fresh face like Stockwell Day, ran a campaign that was
about pride and morality in America—Clinton without the stench.
Like the Chrétien Liberals, the Democrats should have been able to
win the election easily, but they had the preachy and stiff Al Gore
leading them, which meant that even the unseasoned and uninformed
Bush the Younger could compete. Gore didn't have a war room like
Jean Chrétien's. He didn't go after Bush like the prime minister went
after Day. In the debates, he had the opportunity, but he let it pass.

In the debates in the Canadian campaign, Chrétien's opponents
tried coming at him hard, just as they had in 1997. Joe Clark's Tories
were languishing and desperate to make up ground. To have official
status in the House of Commons, parties needed at least twelve seats.
The Tories were on track to fall short of that number, and the same
fate appeared to be awaiting the NDP, whose one-note health care
campaign was failing to connect.

In the English-language debate, Clark pounced. When Chrétien
was asked why he had called the early campaign, he hemmed and

hawed about needing a mandate to spend the government's new surplus monies. Clark glared at him. With conviction ringing from every trenchantly enunciated syllable, he declared, "The only reason was to prevent Paul Martin from getting your job."

Day, still reeling from charges that he would privatize health care, arrived with a prop. In the middle of the debate, he held up a sign saying NO TWO-TIER HEALTH CARE. He knew the picture would make every newspaper in the country. "We just had to stop the hemorrhaging," he said. But Clark nailed him too. What are you running for? he asked Day. "Game show host?"

The Alliance leader showed a good grounding in the issues, but he wore a cold and threatening look for much of the evening and lacked the sense of humour that he used on the campaign bus to keep reporters entertained. He looked a bit like what Chrétien had described him as—a man with a hidden agenda.

Day was overjoyed when a quickie CTV poll showed that he had won the English debate. But the feeling was temporary. "I remember very clearly all of us gathered in the bar when they announced the poll results," he said, "and we all went crazy. 'We won! We won!'" But the media wasn't prepared to go with that verdict. "From that moment on," Day said, "all the talking heads looked at each other and began the spin that Joe Clark won the debate."

Polling results showed only modest movement from the debates, mainly in Clark's favour, while the Liberals maintained a wide lead with time running out. Only a disaster could stop them—and for a moment, it looked like Chrétien had been hit by one. The *National Post*'s Andrew McIntosh revealed that Chrétien had actively lobbied the president of the Business Development Bank for the $615,000 loan to the hotel in Grand-Mère. The bombshell took the story on the golf course conflict to a new level. The PMO had previously denied that the government got "directly involved" in the lending decisions of the bank. But McIntosh's piece said that Chrétien had telephoned the bank's president, François Beaudoin, and also had him visit 24 Sussex.

Chrétien didn't try to deny the report. But in his offhand manner, he dismissed its significance. "You know, you call who you know and I know the president, so I called him once or twice. He came to visit me at my home with a group one day. Fine, it is the normal operation."

But it was hardly viewed as normal. The hotel owner who received the big loan had formerly paid the prime minister and his partners $200,000 for their part-ownership of the hotel. It was the transaction that Chrétien had said was made by his partners without his knowledge. It was the deal that had led opposition critics to charge that there was at least the appearance of conflict.

Chrétien later offered a candid explanation of his contact with the bank president. The third portion of the loan to the hotel was slow in coming, he explained, because the bank was "dragging its feet." So Chrétien made the call. "I called them, and I said, 'Make up your mind.'"

It was quite a blunt order coming from a prime minister, and the fact that he was showing such keen interest in a comparatively small file about the financing arrangements of a loan to a small hotel was bound to arouse suspicion. But he remained bitter that it had.

At the PMO, Duncan Fulton took a call from Campbell Clark of *The Globe and Mail*. He had, as Fulton recalled, about seventeen questions. "I got the phone call," he remembered. "I walked into Francie's office and said, 'This is what Campbell wants to know.' And I was given a line. 'The PM sold his shares and has no continuing interest in the golf course. That is your only line.'" Fulton phoned back Campbell Clark. "You have seventeen questions," he told him. "I have a one-line answer. Why don't we just save ourselves a bunch of time?"

More revelations soon surfaced. Beaudoin, it was revealed, had wanted to take legal action against Yvon Duhaime, the hotel owner, for failing to meet the schedule to pay off the loan. Beaudoin claimed that because he brought this matter to a head, he lost the presidency of the bank. In court documents, he spoke of the actions taken against him as constituting political interference in the affairs of the bank.

Another story that surfaced during the campaign concerned yet more money pouring into the hotel property, this time from the Immigrant Investor Program. In this program, immigrant entrepreneurs who want to obtain Canadian citizenship can ease their path with injections of capital. Yet again, Chrétien got trapped in a contradiction over his involvement. Early in 1996, just as it became apparent that he was not collecting on the debt owed him on the sale of the golf course, the prime minister held a meeting with an immigrant investor and a Montreal investment broker at his home. They discussed the financial situation at the Auberge Grand-Mère. But during the campaign, when he was asked about his role in obtaining immigrant investment in the venture, Chrétien denied involvement. He claimed that the Immigrant Investor Program was managed by provincial authorities. This was true, but provincial records revealed that investments were also managed by local brokers much like the man the prime minister had met with that February. "He had to have known," said Preston Manning, "that the broker was key to the arrangement." In all, $2.35 million came to the hotel from immigrant investors.

As the embarrassing revelations appeared, Chrétien and some in his circle began to wonder about the source. Their suspicions naturally fell on the Martin camp, whose members were not exactly making a show of standing up in support of their leader. Many MPs were also making it clear to Liberal headquarters that they wanted the finance minister campaigning in their riding instead of the prime minister. Chrétien stewed. He was on his way to yet another victory, and this was the appreciation he was getting.

The story on the Immigrant Investor Program brought to three the number of controversies surrounding government subsidies to the Auberge Grand-Mère. The other two involved the BDB loan and the Transitional Job Funds grant. Moreover, there was the whole business of Chrétien's friend Claude Gauthier and his purchase of the golf course lands while he was in receipt of government assistance for his companies.

With the campaign drawing to a close, opponents saw some hope. The hot-button issue had been two-tier health care, but now they could make it Chrétien's two-tier truth-telling. If, for example, there was nothing wrong, as he claimed, with his lobbying the bank president, why didn't his PMO make that clear earlier, instead of claiming that the prime minister did not involve himself in the decisions of the bank?

But the opposition parties were powerless to capitalize on the issue much further. The problem was referred to the prime minister's ethics counsellor, Howard Wilson, for adjudication. The Grits had been in power for seven years but had yet to fulfill their 1993 Red Book promise to appoint an independent ethics commissioner. Instead, they kept one who was dependent upon the goodwill of the PM to maintain his position.

Within just days of receiving the referral, Wilson brought in a verdict. He ruled that no regulation prohibits any MP, including the prime minister, from speaking to the head of a Crown corporation on behalf of a constituent. He did not look at any of the surrounding facts or any pieces of evidence connected with the Opposition's allegation of a conflict of interest. Indeed, it was not Wilson's role to do probes or investigations.

The opposition parties cried whitewash, trotting out a nickname someone had once given Wilson—"Ajax," as in the foaming cleanser. But the verdict was all that the PM needed. He could portray himself as the martyr again, as he had in response to other attacks on his integrity and intellectual well-being. This time, he maintained that Clark and Day had "overstepped the bounds of fairness and decency, which have been our tradition in Canadian elections. Instead, they have sought to destroy my reputation, and in so doing have demeaned the political process."

With Wilson's clearance, the bank story had virtually no impact on the campaign. Voters had, quite understandably, chosen not to wade into the thicket of detail on the complex story and were still prepared to give Chrétien the benefit of the doubt, especially when they had no one else to turn to.

That latter fact was becoming increasingly obvious as the Alliance campaign stumbled from day to day. The leader was unable to shake his regional and fundamentalist imprints. He had hoped to touch off a crusade of sorts, appealing to the young as Trudeau once had done. But the young gave up on Day early, and those he drew were mainly senior citizens from rural areas. At one point, a reporter asked Day, "So is this the freedom train or the fogey train?"

The media continued to bedevil him. A CBC documentary tracing his religious and creationist beliefs touched off jokes and ridicule that suggested he believed humans had walked with dinosaurs. Warren Kinsella, in an unforgettable gimmick, appeared on *Canada AM* with a gym bag containing a large stuffed animal, a purple Barney the dinosaur. Kinsella pulled it out in the middle of the show while intoning, "I just want to remind Mr. Day that *The Flintstones* was not a documentary."

Day was furious at the CBC's special segment. After the campaign, he visited the network's president. "We sat in his office," he recalled, "and I said that politicians always gripe about the media, but I'm telling you that was one of the worst pieces of sabotage I've ever seen, and your people didn't even call me."

While the Liberals were marching towards another victory, it was not enough to quell the unease within their ranks. The Martin wing of the party was becoming more entrenched in its belief that the country wanted the finance minister, not Jean Chrétien. Door-to-door campaigning continued to reveal a lack of enthusiasm for the prime minister. Herb Gray felt it in his hometown of Windsor. In Edmonton Southeast, David Kilgour could readily sense it. The Chrétien team wanted to send in the leader to give him a hand, but Kilgour resisted. "I was getting it at the door," he said. "Hundreds of people were telling me, 'We don't want your leader.' And so they were trying to send Chrétien in, and we were trying to keep him away." Eventually, he got Paul Martin to campaign in his riding instead, and he saw his numbers jump.

In the Toronto riding of St. Paul's, Carolyn Bennett felt the wrath of Eddie Goldenberg. The prime minister was campaigning there, at the Inn on the Park hotel, and Goldenberg noticed that something was missing from Bennett's campaign literature. "He took me aside," she recalled, "like I was being called into the principal's office, and demanded, 'Tell me why the prime minister's picture is not on your brochure.'" Bennett didn't have the nerve to tell him it was because she thought it would probably cost her votes.

In fact, brochures weren't necessary in her riding or most others. Voters told the Grits that they would be voted in because there was no alternative. Chrétien had gambled in going early, and he had played the winning hand again. The weakness of the opponent would do, just as it had in 1993 with Kim Campbell and 1997 with Manning. But he had also shown considerable skill in choosing both the timing for the campaign and the attack-dog strategy. In one survey, more than 60 percent of respondents said they believed Stockwell Day had a hidden agenda, just as the Liberals alleged. John Duffy, the author of *Fights of Our Lives,* studied the election performances of all the leaders and described Jean Chrétien as having "perfected the art of values politics." The 2000 election, he said, was a perfect example.

In the days before the vote, there was still talk of a minority government, but polling experts like Frank Graves were predicting a comfortable majority. Jean Pelletier and his wife spent the election eve in Shawinigan. They had settled into the hotel dining room for dinner just before the polls closed and other guests were approaching him, asking about the results. Pelletier forecast that the Liberals would win between 165 and 169 seats. "Oh, Mr. Pelletier, I think you're being too optimistic" was the frequent response.

But he was too pessimistic. The natural governing party won 172 seats, up 18 from 1997. The Alliance won 66 seats, up from 60 in the previous campaign. The Bloc dropped to 37. The NDP, with 13, and the Tories, with 12, both maintained official party status. "It's always the same with Chrétien," Pelletier concluded. "Always underestimated and finally he delivers more and surprises everyone."

Chrétien swept Ontario yet again, winning 100 of the 103 seats available. The Alliance made impressive gains in the popular vote, increasing its national tally by more than half a million over 1997. It was a bigger gain than that of any other party, including the Liberals, but it was small consolation. The critical question had been whether the party could build a base outside its region—and it had failed again to do so.

In Quebec, Chrétien won a special prize. As further proof that his Clarity Act carried no baggage, he increased his number of seats there from 29 to 37. The 37 equalled the Bloc tally, but the Liberals won a bigger slice of the popular vote.

Despite the charges of victory by default, the 2000 campaign was a sweet triumph for the man who believed election victories were the most enjoyable part of politics. He had been doubted by many in his party and beyond, and now he had achieved a record of sorts—a special place in the Liberal pantheon. All the celebrated Liberal leaders who won multiple majority governments had also suffered defeat. Sir Wilfrid Laurier lost in 1911. Mackenzie King was defeated in two general elections. Louis St. Laurent was brought down by Diefenbaker in 1957, and Trudeau lost to Clark in 1979.

Jean Chrétien was the exception. He won three majorities and never tasted defeat.

Campaign 2000 was hardly a stylish victory. He had captured a modest 41 percent of the popular vote. His timing, his relatively empty agenda, his levelling of Day with dubious calumnies, his absence of statesmanship—all won him few friends. A record low number of Canadians, only 62 percent, came to the polls, 5 percent less than had turned out in 1997.

In his hometown of Shawinigan, Chrétien told his followers, "We just finished a hard-fought campaign, a campaign that was, frankly, too negative and far too personal. The Canadian people expect us to carry out responsibilities with tolerance, openness, and civility, and that I will do."

But tolerance, openness, and civility were qualities with which Jean Chrétien and his team were becoming less familiar. Clark had told him in the debate that he was not the Jean Chrétien he used to know. Power, Clark said, had turned him into a callous man who wished to hoard it, not share it. Anthony Wilson-Smith of *Maclean's* described the campaign as "soul-deadening." The PM, he wrote, "emerges diminished, both in the eyes of his party, and in those of the voters." An Ipsos-Reid poll in the week after the campaign showed that 66 percent of those surveyed believed Chrétien "doesn't have what it takes any more to lead the country." Fifty-eight percent said the Liberals were arrogant and corrupt.

Just as in 1990, when Jean Chrétien won the Liberal leadership; just as in 1993, when he won his first majority; and just as in 1997, when he won his second majority, there was little sense of excitement or anticipation with this victory. The expectations for the little guy from Shawinigan remained low. Just where they had always been. Just where he wanted them.

CHAPTER FOURTEEN

CONTRADICTIONS

O VER THE COURSE of three elections, the Chrétien Liberals collected a staggering 298 seats from the 305 available in the province of Ontario. Nothing in the country's electoral history came close to matching that kind of performance in the Anglo heartland. The vote-splitting of the two parties on the right was a major factor, but even without that, the Liberals still would have won sizable majorities in the province.

Under Chrétien, the odds against a Liberal losing in Ontario were about one hundred to one. So when Hec Cloutier lost to a hairdresser, Cheryl Gallant of the Alliance, he was in total despair. His Ottawa-area riding, Renfrew-Nipissing-Pembroke, had gone Grit for sixty years. Cloutier had fought with Chrétien for the right to seek the nomination in 1990, and Chrétien had ended up stripping him of his Liberal Party membership. Cloutier had run as an independent in 1993, lost, then finally won the riding for the Liberals in 1997.

He spent a sleepless night and was in no mood to pick up the phone when it rang before sunrise the morning after the election. To his surprise, it was Jean Chrétien on the line.

"Don't feel so bad, Hector," the prime minister said.

"I let the team down," said Cloutier.

"You speak your mind, and sometimes you have to realize that people don't like that," the PM told him. "There's a way of telling the truth and getting your message across without being aggressive. I know you got in a fight up there with the hunters."

Chrétien had come to like Cloutier. He was a scrapper like the PM, and more important, he was loyal. That's why Chrétien made the 6:15 a.m. call. He was already thinking, in the middle of the night, immediately after his election victory, of the other fight he still had on his hands. Winning the country had been easy. Winning his party was another story.

"Come to Ottawa in a week," he told Cloutier. "I might have something for you." He wanted to put him in charge of caucus liaison. Normally not one of the most critical positions, it had become, with the Liberal civil war, a very important job. Chrétien wanted a battler and, like Chrétien, Cloutier was always in the combat zone.

With his government's 172 seats, Chrétien had performed beyond expectations for his party, especially in Quebec, and he had surprised even himself with the result. But he wasn't as happy as he might have been. The triumph seemed to earn him as much resentment within his Liberal ranks as admiration. When David Collenette visited him a few days after the campaign, he found Chrétien in foul humour. The prime minister sensed that many of his own troops hadn't been behind him in the campaign, hadn't stood up for him when the conflict-of-interest allegations surfaced. He was bitter. He had brought home the bacon again. These people couldn't take win for an answer.

The last thing on his mind, Collenette discovered, was policy, an agenda for the country. All Chrétien wanted to do was get away over Christmas and rest. Those who thought the Liberal Party was directionless were not going to be comforted. In his first two terms, he had been criticized for a rather passive performance. In the first, he had balanced the books. In the second, he had brought in the Clarity Act, but not much else. In the third, judging from the Red Book—which might better have been titled "Gentlemen, Book Your Tee Times"—it looked as though there could be even less to offer.

Challenging issues still faced the country. The health care system was in need of reform. The government had lagged behind on environmental problems. The military was in disrepair. Parliamentary reform had yet to be addressed.

But all this could wait. Chrétien was prepared to continue to let the motor idle while he fought a party war. In so doing, in failing to give the country and his party major policy goals, he was compounding his problems. Without a sense of direction, his caucus would grow more restless, more convinced that his governance was all about power for the sake of power. The media would have little to concentrate on, except internal party fights and scandals, petty or otherwise.

As THE NEW YEAR OPENED, the prime minister—still on his golfing vacation in Florida—received news that picked up his spirits. With a declaration that the sovereignty movement was sapped, Premier Lucien Bouchard announced he was quitting politics. It was an admission, in so many words, of defeat at the hands of the Chrétien federalists, and it marked a remarkable reversal of trends. Only a few years earlier, Lucien Bouchard had looked to be on the verge of winning the sovereignty fight.

Chrétien wasn't overly surprised to hear of the departure of the Quebec leader. A mercurial and proud man, Bouchard was never one for the long haul, never one to show patience in trying times. He could never be a true revolutionary because the fires burned in him only part of the time. Chrétien had watched his many turns. In the wake of the 1970 October Crisis, Bouchard left the Trudeau Liberals and moved to René Lévesque's Parti Québécois. When the sovereignty movement started to recede, he jumped on board the federalist bandwagon again, this time with Brian Mulroney. When the going got tough with Mulroney over Meech Lake, he backflipped again to the separatist camp. Now, faced once more with a challenge that looked too daunting, he made his final exit.

Bouchard was entirely unique in the country's history. No leader
had ever come so close to both unifying Canada and destroying it as
this brilliant, brooding colossus. He helped march the country to
the brink of a historic unity agreement, only to flee the Meech Lake
temple in the dying days. Then, with demagogic fury, he marched the
country to the brink of breakup, only to miss by a fraction. Having
failed as both the great healer and the great divider, Lucien Bouchard
left office in limbo.

Comforting for Chrétien was that his departure left the sover-
eignists without a tribune. Bouchard had a magnetism, an intellectu-
alism, an affinity for language, and a *profondeur* that was rare in
political men. Larger-than-life figures like him did not come along
often. With Bouchard and René Lévesque and Pierre Trudeau, Quebec
had produced three leaders of exceptional calibre, while in the same
time frame the rest of Canada had produced none.

Bouchard was the last great sovereigntist, Chrétien had outlasted or
beaten all the separatist giants who scorned him. He had helped stop
Lévesque in the 1980 referendum and had defeated his local Péquiste
arch-enemy, Yves Duhaime, in the 1997 election. He had outlasted
Parizeau, who was driven out in the wake of the 1995 referendum, and
now Bouchard had fallen before him.

On hearing Bouchard's announcement, Stéphane Dion declared, "He
was the best salesman for sovereignty." The problem, he added, was his
product. "Our strategy was to insist on clarity so that the people of
Quebec could see clearly what a bad product he was offering." Dion's
Plan B—taking the fight to the secessionists—had worked. While there
were many reasons for the decline of the sovereignty movement in the
six years that followed the referendum, the application of counterforce
figured prominently among them. For too long the Ottawa Liberals had
behaved like the provincial Liberals, cowering at sovereigntist onslaughts,
fearing that counterattack would only stir more indignation in Quebec.

Paul Martin wasn't so sure that Plan B had turned the tide. Instead,
he felt that the silencing of the sovereigntists ultimately had more to

do with progress on the economy. In Quebec, he noted in an interview in 2003, "the argument was made very strongly that we'd be better off without Canada, that we can make our own way. And what has happened as a result of the economic turnaround . . . is that Quebecers feel that in fact they can accomplish their goals far better within Canada than without."

The departure of Bouchard all but closed a chapter in Chrétien's political career. The Péquistes were still in power, but they were no longer an immediate threat. The prime minister's focus switched to the United States, where a new Republican administration was finally installed after the heavily politicized U.S. Supreme Court voted strictly along party lines to finalize the 2000 election verdict in favour of George W. Bush. It was hard for the Liberals to see the Democrats leave, and it was difficult for Chrétien to lose his friend Bill Clinton. After serving the maximum two terms, Clinton departed seemingly as buoyant, as mischievous, and as full of potential as when he arrived. Here was a mind as glittering and bountiful as any president's since Theodore Roosevelt. But for all his potential, Bill Clinton could never fulfill it. As the first president of the post–Cold War era, he entered office lacking the authority that the leader of the free world had once had, and he further diminished that authority with his adolescent sexual escapades. He left the White House as a starlit talent to be filed away in the category of opportunity missed.

Chrétien's final goodbye came when he visited Washington for a last round of golf with Clinton in December. After the game, he was to fly to North Carolina to speak at Duke University, but just as he was leaving, Clinton looked over and said, "Jean, why don't you come back to the house for a Scotch?" Gordon Giffin, the U.S. ambassador to Canada, was looking on. "It was just sort of like Joe and Tom playing golf with each other Saturday afternoon, and one says, 'Come back for a beer.'"

At "the house," about three hundred workers were putting up Christmas decorations, and the president and the prime minister wandered through the rooms, sipping their drinks and putting up the odd bulb. Chrétien phoned Aline to tell her, "I'm just helping the president with the Christmas decorations." During the tree-trimming, he got Clinton's version of how the Republicans stole the election.

The prime minister was indebted to this president for his assistance in the 1995 referendum, for his intervention at Mont Tremblant, for the status he accorded Chrétien at international gatherings. He was also going to miss Giffin, an ambassador with whom he had developed such a good rapport that the PM would routinely call him out of the blue and chat about any number of things. A Duke University graduate and close follower of the school's powerhouse basketball team, Giffin was hunched over watching a game one night when Chrétien phoned to make a couple of observations on how the Blue Devils were playing.

Giffin had been working to try to correct the record on Raymond Chrétien's remarks allegedly suggesting that Canada had wanted Gore to win the election. This was no easy task because of Brian Mulroney's relations with the new White House. The Tory crooner was a close friend of George Bush, Sr., so close that the former president attended the wedding of Mulroney's daughter, Caroline, in Montreal. He was also getting to know Bush the younger quite well. Given Airbus, Meech Lake, and the other blows he took from Chrétien, only the naive could believe that Mulroney was not relishing the opportunity to inflict a little damage of his own.

He was so tight with the new American administration, in fact, that he briefed the Bush team on what to expect from the Chrétien government. It was one of the more extraordinary developments in a long bilateral history. A former Conservative prime minister was becoming, in effect, Canada's main interlocutor with the White House while a Liberal government held power. Mulroney had a closer relationship with the Bushes than the new Canadian ambassador, Michael Kergin. After talking to the Bush team, he showed the courtesy of telling Kergin the content of his discussions.

In his values, George W. Bush was far to the right of the Chrétien Liberals. A neophyte in the world of foreign affairs, having hardly travelled abroad, he tended to view complex subjects in black and white, and was dependent to a large degree on the word of hardline advisers like Vice President Dick Cheney and Defense Secretary Donald Rumsfeld.

At Bush's inauguration, demonstrators who were not amused at how he had won the election held signs saying HAIL TO THE THIEF. Under dreary skies, he tried to sound a temperate note, using words like "compassion" and "civility" repeatedly, while vowing that the citizens of his great nation who had been left behind would not be forgotten under his stewardship. As a Texan, Bush had an understandable affinity for Mexico, and he dispensed with the usual presidential practice of making Canada his first foreign stop, giving his southern neighbour the honour instead. His national security adviser, Condoleeza Rice, not well schooled in Canadian affairs either, spoke of Mexico as America's "largest trading partner." Richard Nixon had once announced that Japan was America's largest trading partner. Now it was Mexico. In fact, as even Ronald Reagan was aware, it was Canada by a healthy margin.

Big tax cuts and large increases in defence spending, traditional Republican priorities, were the major Bush themes. His agenda clashed with Canada's in a number of areas. He was proposing a missile defence shield, Arctic resource development (which involved drilling in the ecologically sensitive Arctic National Wildlife Refuge), and a better energy-sharing arrangement with Ottawa. He and Chrétien had an encouraging first meeting in Washington, with the prime minister steering clear of his usual pet subjects, like the neighbour's barbaric gun culture. "We don't want to be the fifty-first state of America, and he understands that," Chrétien said of the new president. Briefed on the prime minister's quip about not wanting to go fishing because he was afraid to end up, like Mulroney, on the end of the hook, the president announced with a mischievous grin that the two of them should go fishing together soon. Making his debut as foreign minister was Axworthy's successor, John Manley, who sat down for post-dinner talks with Secretary of State Colin Powell. Bush later trundled by in his jogging suit, offering an aside to Manley that would have its credibility well tested over time. "You've got a hell of a boss," he said.

Chrétien followed the Washington visit with a return trade mission to China. He had taken the first such mission to the Middle Kingdom in 1994, and now he was back with six hundred business leaders. Commerce between Canada and China had more than doubled in the intervening years, from $6 billion in 1994 to $14 billion in 2001. But the figure was short of the goal of $20 billion that Ottawa had set during the first visit. More controversial was the eternal question of trade versus human rights. In 1994, Chrétien had favoured giving trade priority. Why lecture the Chinese on human rights? he'd argued. They wouldn't listen anyway. But he had been harshly criticized for his position, and human rights advocates like the respected Irwin Cotler, now a Liberal MP from Montreal, were making their voices heard. Before he stepped down, Axworthy had several sessions on the question with Chrétien and noticed him "moving over." When the prime minister first came to office, his foreign affairs agenda was tied to economics, noted Axworthy. By late in his stewardship, it was more humanitarian. This time in China, Chrétien delivered a stronger admonition than had been anticipated, saying that reports of the persecution of religious groups offended some of the most deeply held principles of Canadians. "No one can be above the law," he told Chinese students in a rebuke of their government. "And no one can be forgotten by the law or denied its protection."

In his eighth year as prime minister, he was becoming a senior statesman among Western leaders, and while prone to missteps, he had gained knowledge and confidence. Like many prime ministers, Chrétien viewed the foreign trips with relief because they took him away from domestic hostilities. Through the first few months of 2001, he might well have wished he was away all the time.

THE ATTACKS OVER what by now was commonly referred to as Shawinigate were intensifying. Joe Clark had made the issue his passion. The Reformers, led by top-quality researchers like Laurie Throness and Commons critics like Diane Ablonczy, had initially brought the abuse-of-power story to the fore, but the Tory leader, seconded by aggressive caucus members like Peter MacKay, gradually took the lead on the file. Clark was still one of the best questioners in the House. His voice shook with rage, his cheeks burned orange, and he managed, though relegated to a seat miles from the main players, to command attention.

He had been busy over the Christmas period. He went to the unusual extreme of meeting with the RCMP about what he regarded as conflict-of-interest breaches by the government, specifically on Shawinigate, and he followed up with a letter to Commissioner Giuliano Zaccardelli in mid-January, pointing out more avenues the Mounties might pursue on the case.

Chrétien looked on coldly. As the Commons resumed sitting, there was the usual exchange of post-holiday well wishes before business began, and Clark thought he would extend the courtesy to the prime minister. No sooner had he begun his "welcome back" small-talk routine than Chrétien lit into him with a stern warning that Clark was pushing too hard on the corruption file. The prime minister was obviously referring to his trip to the police. "I'm not going to forget about this," he threatened. Clark fired back, "I'm not going to let you forget about it."

The usually cool-headed Jean Pelletier buttonholed a Tory senator, demanding to know what was behind the attacks. "I had never seen him like this before," the senator recalled. Chrétien's House leader, Don Boudria, had a meeting with his Tory counterpart, Peter MacKay, who wanted a bigger parliamentary budget for his small Conservative caucus. Boudria told him if he laid off on Shawinigate he might get it. MacKay told Binder Boy to forget it. The Tories then reported mysterious interceptions of their communications and the theft of a computer from their offices. The strange developments convinced them that they were on to something. "A couple of times during Shawinigate," recalled MacKay, "we were up all night, and we thought, This is it. We've got him."

Stockwell Day's continuing woes spurred the Tories to take the lead on the story. The official Opposition was collapsing under the strain of leadership infighting. Though Day tried to treat Manning with the degree of respect the elder statesman was entitled to, the former Reform leader could not get beyond the bitterness of defeat. Perhaps dreaming of regaining his lost title, Manning let the dogs loose on Day, encouraging a rebellion of his loyalists.

Meanwhile old history caught up to Day. While serving in Ralph Klein's Cabinet in Alberta in the 1980s, he had written a letter to a newspaper editor in Red Deer, criticizing a lawyer there for taking up the defence of a man accused of possessing child pornography. The lawyer sued, and Day's legal fees were still being paid for by Alberta taxpayers—to the tune of $700,000. The controversy dragged on through the winter months, until Day finally put it to bed by apologizing and announcing that he was taking out a $60,000 mortgage on his Alberta home and sending it to the treasurer of that province to help compensate taxpayers. The revelation not only gave the Manning rebels ammunition but also neutralized Day on Chrétien's conflict file. Whenever he stood up to criticize the Liberals for the squandering of taxpayer dollars, Chrétien threw the $700,000 right back at him.

But the Alliance was far from being shut out in the drama. Its members knew that the Liberals were still vulnerable on their 1993 Red Book promise to create an independent ethics counsellor. The promise, like the one on the GST, was hanging over the Grits like the sword of Damocles. In a savvy piece of political theatre, Day and company got the sword to fall.

Over the years, Reformers had lashed out frequently on the issue. But they needed something more, and what better way to make the Liberals eat their words, they reasoned, than by tabling a motion calling upon them to implement their original Red Book promise. It was the perfect squeeze play. The Liberals couldn't vote yes and bring in an independent arbiter with so many conflict files on the ledger. But they also couldn't be seen to be voting down their own Red Book promise.

In the end, the PMO chose the latter course, instructing caucus members to stand bolt upright on the vote and draw an X through their campaign vow. Only two on Chrétien's team, Paul Steckle and Ivan Grose, voted with the opposition parties in favour of an independent ethics counsellor. Four Liberals abstained. Many others complained of having to stand there, as one put it, and "look like goddamn hypocrites."

Paul Martin was among them, hating the moment. Desperate for some rationale to explain the about-face, House Leader Boudria said he voted against the motion because the opposition parties were trying not to reform the system but to embarrass the government. Others made the same claim. Rarely had they looked so lame. Eddie Goldenberg was normally the last one to admit a mistake. "But I've got to tell you," he later reflected, "that was one of the biggest embarrassments we've had in the government for ten years. In hindsight, we probably should have made it independent from the very beginning."

Issuing campaign pledges in Red Book form had its advantages. But Chrétien was learning there were drawbacks too. Two promises—the GST and the ethics counsellor—had come back to bite the Liberals hard. Better news came with the announcement by the RCMP that it had rejected Clark's request for an investigation of the prime minister, saying there were no grounds to proceed. Delighted with the police clearance, Chrétien was prompted to pin a new label on Clark. "Somebody said to me that he started out as Joe Who," said the PM. "Now he's Joe McCarthy."

But Clark and other opposition critics kept exposing gaps in the government's case. On a complex dossier, the occasional misstatement by the prime minister or a Cabinet minister was understandable. But so many contradictions, zig-zags, and falsehoods kept turning up that even Chrétien's most loyal supporters wondered if something was being hidden.

Chrétien had claimed, for example, that his former aide, Jean Carle, was not involved in the controversy over the bank loan the PM had helped arrange for the Auberge Grand-Mère. But Joe Clark produced documents that proved Carle had helped the PMO come up with a response strategy for dealing with media questions about the loan. The PM was then caught contradicting his own ethics counsellor. Chrétien said that he told Wilson when he took office in 1993 that he was owed a debt on his sale of the Grand-Mère golf course. In a newspaper interview the same day, Wilson said the opposite. "There was no detail provided on the fact that there was an outstanding debt obligation." Asked later about it, Wilson did his best to shield his boss, saying it was probably not an intentional omission on his part.

The PM and the ethics counsellor were often unable to get their stories to coincide. Chrétien kept insisting that his dealings on the golf properties were in a blind trust, and that he had nothing to do with them. "It's a blind trust, and blind means blind," he said in Parliament on June 8, 1999. "From the day I became prime minister, I have had no decisions to make on it."

But blind didn't mean blind. Wilson told a parliamentary committee that "in January 1996, when he [Chrétien] said he was not being paid, we discussed the options." By options, he meant the choices Chrétien had to try to recoup the debt owed him on the sale of the golf course. Still, Chrétien and his surrogates continued to tell Parliament that the debt was in a blind trust. And the contradictions didn't end there. Chrétien claimed that he had informed Wilson of the $300,000 owed to him in 1994. But in testimony before the Industry Committee, Wilson said he had not heard about it until 1995.

The maze of discrepancies did nothing to still the growing animosity of PMO officials towards the media and parliamentarians who kept up the watch on the Shawinigan file. Despite the swarm of erroneous statements in their boss's recounting of events, Eddie Goldenberg and others held to the line that the media was on a witch hunt and the prime minister was being subjected to terribly unfair treatment.

Facts kept emerging, however, which made their case harder to sell. They claimed that there was no substantive financial tie between the hotel and the golf course. This was a significant claim. If indeed there was no connection, Chrétien could well argue that by sending government money to the hotel, he was in no way enhancing the financial position of the golf club itself, and thus he wasn't increasing his chances of recouping the $300,000 owed him.

But the prime minister's position was again undermined—and again by someone on his own side. Yvon Duhaime, the owner of the hotel, testified before Quebec's liquor and gaming authority that his business depended in a "major" way on clients from the golf club. Golf tournaments with corresponding dinners were arranged sometimes a year in advance, Duhaime testified. "Agreements, accounts, and contracts were made between the Auberge and clients. You can understand that this represents a major part of the receipts, since it is a clientele of tourists and also buyers of golf packages."

The opposition parties were claiming that a calculator was needed to keep track of the number of times the PMO story didn't square with the facts. Chrétien's office had, for example, said it didn't get involved in the decisions of the Business Development Bank, only to have the prime minister's lobbying of the president of the bank revealed. There were the misleading statements Chrétien had provided on his dealings with the Immigrant Investor Program. Then there was the PMO's insistence that Chrétien didn't stand to gain or lose from his sale of the golf course property. PMO staffers argued that there was a fixed price—the $300,000 owed him—and he could not collect more or less than that, so the government subsidies were irrelevant. But Howard Wilson himself contradicted this point, telling Southam News that if the golf course property substantially decreased in value, Chrétien obviously had less chance of getting his full debt paid. As it turned out, he did in fact collect substantially less than $300,000.

The strongest PMO line of defence was that the prime minister could always have sued the buyer, Jonas Prince, to get the repayment.

Since he had that option, Goldenberg and others argued, why would he go to extremes to pump money into the properties? But he never chose that legal avenue. According to Prince, such a suit would have been a tough sell. He didn't view the terms of sale in the same light Chrétien did.

The *National Post* was doggedly pursuing the story, and Conrad Black was keen to see the pursuit continue. But Black was now only half-owner of the *Post*, having sold the remaining interest and the major papers from his Southam stable to CanWest Global's Asper family. The Aspers took an entirely different view of the story. Chrétien, at least at that time, had good relations with Israel Asper, and there was little doubt the two men had had some interesting exchanges on the Shawinigan file. In a development that rocked Canadian journalism, David Asper, chair of the publications committee of CanWest, launched a blistering attack on the media and Joe Clark for their focus on the story.

In a column distributed and published in Southam papers and the *National Post*, Asper, who had little experience in print journalism, said the media and Clark were remarkably unfair and irresponsible, particularly since reports from both Wilson and the RCMP had cleared the prime minister. The headline on his column in the *Post* read, "To Chrétien's Accusers: Put Up or Shut Up." He spoke of unfounded fishing expeditions and of crossing the line that delineates solid investigative reporting from adjective-driven innuendo. He waved the possibility of a lawsuit at reporters, citing the crime of public mischief for those who make false accusations. "Our national political affairs," wrote Asper, "have been hijacked by mischievous, unfair scandal-mongering as opposed to things that really count."

Canadian journalism had rarely been subjected to such a frontal assault from a major media owner. Asper's outburst was widely viewed as an attempt to intimidate reporters. Much of the Shawinigate reporting was based on government documents obtained through the Access to Information Act. Many of the stories, such as those about the lobbying of the Business Development Bank, had been confirmed by the PMO itself.

The response to Asper was fast and furious. Ken Whyte, the editor of the *Post*, wrote a lengthy editorial in which he essentially told the young Asper, "We've put up—now why don't you shut up?" Whyte chronicled how Chrétien had stonewalled MPs and journalists at every turn, how it appeared that he had misled the House of Commons, how the PMO had even threatened the jobs of employees in the information commissioner's office who sought to release material unflattering to the government. His editorial said that the RCMP review was narrowly focused and overlooked interviews with key officials, and that Wilson's review was anything but credible.

Given that the Aspers owned 50 percent of the *Post*, Whyte's rebuttal took courage. In a direct hit at David Asper, he said, "The only observers who do not see this as serious are partisans or people unaware of the basic facts that have been on the public record for some time. In such circumstances, it would be a dereliction of duty and a national embarrassment if media were to ignore the story."

Asper's outburst appeared to be part of a two-pronged counter-attack at journalists. In the same time frame, Francie Ducros began a letter-writing campaign, with missives sent to several papers denouncing their coverage of the controversy. Many other ridings were getting just as much money as the PM's in grants and loans, she argued, yet they were hardly mentioned in reports. But the reasons the other ridings were not the focus of media attention were because they were not the subject of several police investigations and there had been no allegations of mismanagement of funds or contradictions from the local MP. Ducros also maintained that all Chrétien could receive on the debt owed him was a fixed amount of $300,000, but in fact he ended up receiving less than that. In her letters, she disputed the word of the auditor general, who had said that the Transelec company, owned by Claude Gauthier, a close friend of the prime minister's, should never have received a grant from the Canadian International

Development Agency (CIDA). Two weeks after her letters appeared, CIDA's senior vice president admitted that the agency had been wrong to allow Transelec to bid on the contract.

Ducros maintained that she was perfectly comfortable with the prime minister's comportment on all the files relating to the grants and loans for his riding. "The people of Saint-Maurice, and the prime minister as their MP, have availed themselves of perfectly appropriate government assistance to fund legitimate projects designed to bolster economic development," she wrote.

The "deny, deny, deny" strategy of Ducros and others at the PMO was not without impact. The abuse-of-power file was too complex to generate much public interest. With the PMO not giving an inch, people had to decide whether they wished to believe the opposition parties or the government. The public had come to know Jean Chrétien. He had been around since 1963. Most were not prepared to believe he could be engaged in such underhanded behaviour.

JOE CLARK TOOK AN EXTREME STEP. On March 23, he demanded that Chrétien step down until an inquiry had settled the conflict-of-interest question. No prime minister had ever stepped aside for an inquiry or resigned amid scandal since Sir John A. Macdonald in 1873. Clark summed up his case this way: "It is now clear the prime minister was simultaneously involved in lobbying to secure a loan for the Auberge Grand-Mère and in negotiating the sale of shares in an adjacent golf course whose value could be affected by those same loans."

Chrétien was not in the House, so Herb Gray spoke on his behalf. He was rarely presented with as difficult a case as this one to defend—and it showed. Gray was cornered several times. All he could do was evade the questions and stonewall, accusing the opposition parties of smear tactics.

For months, Chrétien had been criticized for not bringing forward documentation to prove his case. His office held to the line that a prime minister should not have to stoop to revealing his personal finances when he has done nothing wrong. But another revelation had brought the matter to a head. Newspaper reports suggested that Chrétien's name was still on the books as an owner of the golf course shares after 1993, the date he was said to have sold them. If this was in fact true, if he was still an owner, the opposition parties would have a clearer case of conflict of interest than the one they believed they already had.

The PMO brass met all day with Chrétien on Sunday, March 25, to debate the pros and cons of releasing the private papers. Some still felt that he should tough it out. When Mitchell Sharp told the *Ottawa Sun*'s Anne Dawson the papers would be released, the PMO's press office contradicted him. But Sharp turned out to be correct. The green light was given for some—though not all—of the documentation to be made public. Included was a handwritten agreement, on a scrap of paper dated 1993, between Chrétien and Jonas Prince, the Toronto developer. In it, Prince agreed to buy the newly elected prime minister's interest in the golf club for $300,000 plus interest.

The opposition parties wondered how someone about to become prime minister could be so cavalier as to do a business deal on a scrap of paper. But the release of it was of some importance. It cleared up the latest allegation, and those not following the case closely could conclude that it cleared up the whole matter. That's how Chrétien chose to interpret it, demanding an apology from his accusers and saying he had been smeared on the basis of innuendo. "They have refused to recognize the truth. They have it now. They are embarrassed and what they should do is apologize, turn the page, and deal with the problems of the nation."

But the release of the bill of sale settled—ostensibly, at least—only the one issue. The other accusation that had led to Clark's demand that the PM step aside still remained, as did many other conflict-of-interest allegations related to Shawinigate. In his defence, Chrétien simply kept repeating that all he had done was try to help his riding. How on earth could they call him a criminal for that? he asked.

Sometimes he would make light of the whole issue, trying to reduce it to a joke. How could this be a scandal, he would say, when there was no sex and he had lost money? Critics pointed out that many a scandal has come from people trying to cut their losses—and the prime minister had a lot of potential losses to cut. The release of the documents confirmed that when Chrétien finally did collect on his debt in 1999, he had to settle for $45,000 less than the $300,000 owed him—and none of the more than $100,000 in interest.

The prime minister's case was an especially tough sell because of the matching time frames. It had become clear early in 1996, as Howard Wilson confirmed, that Chrétien's original deal with Prince was falling through and he was not going to collect full payment on the debt. He then had two options, according to Wilson. He could sue Prince for payment, or he could try to have his lawyer work out a negotiated settlement over time. He chose the latter, which meant that the opposition parties could make the case that he had an ongoing financial interest in the properties. The same time period, 1986 and 1987, was when the highly controversial loans and subsidies were granted to the hotel and when Claude Gauthier purchased the golf course land. "He knew he was losing money," alleged Joe Clark. "He wanted to do something that would increase the value of his own interests." It was also interesting, added the Tory leader, that the prime minister did not choose, with his release of documents, to include papers from 1996 to 1999. Why was that? Clark asked.

Clark never believed Chrétien felt guilty about his behaviour. "I think he thought he might get caught, and that's different. Did he think he was wrong? No." The matching time frames, which raised suspicions, might well have been coincidental—just as the PMO tried to argue. The mass of contradictions in the PM's story could also have been the result of his sloppy memory on a highly complex dossier.

The money, Eddie Goldenberg would claim years later, getting heated in a discussion of the subject, was never a matter of concern to the prime minister. It wasn't something he would have even thought of. He had enough money to be comfortable in his retirement. The loyal aide also rejected the contention that there was even the appearance of a conflict of interest. Goldenberg argued correctly that the press had overlooked the fact that Chrétien had always fought to get government help to locate a hotel in his riding. He maintained that despite Duhaime's testimony before the liquor and gaming commission, the value of the golf course had nothing to do with Chrétien's ability to collect his $300,000. Jonas Prince was very solvent, he said, "so you could collect on that debt by seizing one of Mr. Prince's assets in Montreal, Toronto, Vancouver, anywhere else."

Jean Pelletier, the keeper of Chrétien's store, held to the same view. "I've been working with Chrétien long enough and close enough. Shawinigate is an invention of the opposition parties. Chrétien never benefited, never wanted to benefit. They mix two files. They mix the file of the golf course and the file of the hotel."

Chrétien himself would hold to the line that it was all nonsense or, to use his word, "bullshit." His wife, Aline, was reading a book on the Clintons that examined the long and fruitless pursuit of the president and his wife by political opponents and the media over alleged financial improprieties relating to Arkansas land development schemes. Aline Chrétien told her husband, "Jean, it's very familiar." The prime minister liked the Whitewater comparison. The Clinton critics spent millions and "they proved nothing," he said. "It was harassment."

Chrétien was wealthy enough, and it wasn't crucial that he collect on the debt owed him. But even if there was nothing in all the circumstantial evidence, in all the suspicious timing and the stream of contradictory and misleading statements, the prime minister's behaviour had certainly been reckless. He left himself wide open to charges of inappropriately helping friends, if not himself. Having been in the political game so long, he knew of the dangers of conflicts of interest, particularly involving Cabinet ministers and prime ministers. He had watched as so many Pearson Cabinet members resigned. He had watched the depths into which the

Mulroney government plunged over alleged abuse of power, and he had promised to do better. As prime minister, he should have been setting the highest example of probity.

Several factors could explain his careless actions. One was that he had never been scrutinized by the media for his dealings in his own riding, and since no one was watching, he might have felt that he could cut corners. A second explanation is that the separatists were a legitimate threat to him in his riding, particularly in the 1997 campaign, and he needed every advantage he could muster; therefore, he opened the vault and indiscriminately let the subsidy money pour.

A third possibility, and the one the opposition parties preferred to believe, was that he was returning favours. He had made promises to friends who had helped him—Claude Gauthier, for example—and once in power, he kept his pledge to help them in return. And if in helping them along with government subsidies, he improved his chances of recouping the debt owed him, then all the better.

The opposition parties compiled a lot of evidence but did not put forward an airtight case. In the end, the public believed the prime minister. Polls showed that Chrétien's popularity was hardly affected by the Shawinigate allegations. To make a big breakthrough, the opposition parties needed a whistle-blower. But by 2001, they still hadn't landed that type of source to help them along. Wilson remained in his boss's corner and the Mounties did not appear overly enthusiastic about following up on leads the opposition tried to provide them.

In British Columbia, another political leader wasn't so fortunate. Glen Clark, the former premier, faced conflict-of-interest allegations over matters of marginal consequence. The charge was that in exchange for lobbying to get a friend a casino licence—a licence that wasn't granted—Clark got some free contracting work done on his home. As inconsequential as the allegations may have been, they were enough to push the B.C. premier to resign. He faced police charges, and after a long process, the courts exonerated him. To Chrétien critics like Gordon Gibson of the *National Post*, the evidence against Glen Clark was not as damning as that against the prime minister. But the B.C. premier did not have the right people supporting him.

For Chrétien, Howard Wilson was the key. He always gave the prime minister the benefit of the doubt, a benefit that a more independent ethics counsellor might not have provided. The prime minister was strongly criticized for failing to abide by his Red Book promise to appoint that independent counsellor. His fellow party members were humiliated when they had to vote that promise down. But as it turned out, it may have been one of the best decisions Jean Chrétien ever made.

CHAPTER FIFTEEN

A COOL HEAD

SEPTEMBER 2001 was still months away. The affairs of state had their usual rhythms. The Summit of the Americas was bringing together all the hemisphere's powers, thirty-four leaders, in Quebec City, where Chrétien had attended law school. He was to host the summit, which would be George W. Bush's first major international outing, and try to make progress towards a hemispheric free trade agreement.

It was only a remote possibility, free trade expanding so far. It was something that could come about in decades, perhaps, but not at this time. Besides, there wasn't all that much benefit in such an accord for Canada. Forty percent of the country's economic activity resulted from trade with the U.S. and Cuba. The other thirty-one countries in the hemisphere accounted for only 2 percent. "There may be a huge market down there," said the Ottawa trade expert Michael Hart, "but four hundred million poor people are still four hundred million poor people. Just like the Chinese market, with its 1.2 billion. We keep waxing about it, and we keep sending about 1 percent of our exports there."

But the symbolism of having free trade with other nations, not just the United States, appealed to the Chrétien government, as did the opportunity to take a lead role in fostering better relations with Latin America. Mulroney laid the basis for the expansion of interests with his much-criticized decision to join the Organization of American States in 1989. Many feared the move would make Ottawa a puppet of American interests, but the Tory prime minister often sided with

Latin American states against Washington. The Liberals had come to accept the wisdom of the Mulroney decision.

In Quebec City, Chrétien moved comfortably among the leaders, gaining the expected consensus on the idealistic measures, but much of his work was drowned out by the legions of anti-globalization demonstrators. They weaved their way through clouds of tear gas, charged the fences that separated them from the leaders, clashed with six thousand police, and—worst of all from the point of view of the assembled politicians—hijacked the media coverage.

In emphasizing the need to protect labour, the environment, and human rights as a precondition for free trade, Chrétien hoped to ease their concerns. But he wasn't surprised his offerings didn't. Many of the demonstrators were showing up, he said, just for a lark. "They say to themselves, 'Let's go spend the weekend in Quebec City. We'll have fun, we'll protest, and blah, blah, blah.'"

Chrétien got on well with Bush, better at least than he did with the new Quebec premier, Bernard Landry, who hadn't endeared himself to the federal government when he sniped at the Canadian flag as "a piece of red rag." Before the summit, the president had sent Chrétien a picture of the two of them together in Washington, and he had written at the bottom, "This could be the start of a great friendship." Chrétien placed it front and centre in his entrance hall at 24 Sussex, so that it was one of the first things visitors noticed.

But the Bush administration then struck hard at Canada, imposing big duties on softwood lumber, a major Canadian export. With his country experiencing one of its temporary energy crises, Bush was also talking up the need for a new continental energy regime. No one was quite sure what that meant. On a more minor matter, his country had levied duties against Prince Edward Island potatoes. In Quebec City, his Canadian hosts served him red snapper and spring vegetables—with a large helping of PEI spuds.

While the two men seemed to get along, there was an unease among Canadian officials about Bush. Anyone being briefed by Mulroney was not likely to have a favourable impression of the prime minister. Moreover, there were too many basic ideological differences, "an attitudinal difference," as Percy Downe, the prime minister's new chief of staff, put it. "They are a Republican right-wing administration. We are a left-of-centre—in their mind, probably way left—but a centre-left party. When they talk about abortion, when they talk about guns, when they talk about health care, there are a whole range of issues where we are not on the same page at all."

Downe, a mild-mannered fellow from PEI, had replaced Jean Pelletier, who became the chair of VIA Rail. Pelletier's departure was a critical moment for the government—he slipped away quietly, generating scant notice. If the PMO ran the show, which it did, then the loss of the smooth executive who ran that office should have merited banner headlines. But while the real power in Ottawa lay in the executive branch, which was based in the Langevin Building, across the street from Parliament Hill, the media focus was on Parliament, the secondary power.

As a result, many of the biggest power players, like Pelletier, were barely known to the public. When he left, the prime minister no longer had his voice of calm, of reason, and of strength at his side. Eddie Goldenberg now took up even more space, as did Francie Ducros. That brought more edge, more combativeness, a more testy approach. Downe was competent but lacked Pelletier's authority, experience, and intimacy with Chrétien. "It's always easier to come in after somebody who made a mess of things," said Downe. "That was not the case here."

Pelletier's departure naturally heightened speculation that the PM would be soon to follow. So did Chrétien's decision to increase his own salary and pension package. His salary went from $184,000 to $262,000. His pension, because of all his years as an MP, would be $175,000. MPs got a 20-percent pay boost, from $109,000 to $131,000. To make his increase more palatable to a public that was always sceptical about politicians giving themselves raises, Chrétien made the case that his salary was now at the level of that of the chief justice of the Supreme Court of Canada. Why shouldn't the prime minister make the same?

Chrétien had given his troops another majority election victory and a nice pay raise. A leadership review was scheduled to be held at the beginning of 2002, less than a year away. But in keeping with the prime minister's wishes, the Martin forces, who controlled the party's national executive, pushed the date back a year. They agreed that Chrétien should be allowed a grace period for winning his third majority in a row. They also thought that by that time, 2003, it would be easier for the PM to signal that he was leaving, thus avoiding a confrontation within the party.

Martin was letting it be known that as party leader, he would initiate significant parliamentary reform that would give more powers to MPs. As well, he wanted a cleanup of the patronage-laden, top-down system of governance, a thorough democratization, including the appointment of an independent ethics counsellor. PMO officials were hardly amused to hear of his plans. A few days later, John Turner came to Ottawa for the unveiling of his prime ministerial portrait in the halls of Parliament. With protocol demanding that Chrétien make the introductory speech and a detectable tension in the air, the PM stayed strictly to the high road, reliving none of the unhappy past. But not so Turner. He couldn't restrain himself, and after a few nice words, he took up the theme of the vital role of Parliament and the respect that must always be accorded the institution. He took several undisguised shots at Chrétien's poor record in the area. The prime minister looked on glumly.

The rumblings in Chrétien's caucus hardly compared to the insurgency confronting Stockwell Day. Several of his MPs had split ranks to form what they called the Democratic Representative Caucus. The rebel group included such leading lights in the party as Deborah Grey, Monte Solberg, and Chuck Strahl. All had been strong Manning loyalists, and their move had the look of a well-orchestrated plot, long in the works, to bring down the leader. Cathy Smith, a former campaign manager for Monte Solberg, told the media, "This has all been set up from the very beginning. This has all been cooked up." For anyone "to say now that it was based primarily on something Stockwell did, or didn't do, is garbage." As a result of the pressure, Day promised to resign and call a leadership convention—where he would try to win back his job.

The summer passed quietly enough. Chrétien got past a nettlesome moment in August when Judge Ted Hughes tabled his 453-page report on the APEC affair. In it, he accused Jean Carle, Chrétien's chief of operations, of improperly bullying Mounties into moving protesters out of the sight of leaders attending the summit. Chrétien wasn't personally named for any wrongdoing, but the report raised an obvious question: If the boss's right-hand man had violated Canadians' rights to free speech, had the boss himself created an atmosphere in the PMO that encouraged it? The young Carle was setting quite a pace for himself. After his work at APEC, he had moved on to the Business Development Bank, where, it was alleged, he was involved in a backroom plot to oust the president—the same president who was causing the prime minister headaches on the Auberge Grand-Mère file. In court documents, François Beaudoin said he was forced out after Carle led an investigation into his pension and use of bank resources.

Shortly before the APEC report was issued, it was announced that Carle was leaving the bank to join the Just for Laughs comedy festival in Montreal as vice president and chief of operations. He wasn't long in that position before he faced more allegations. The festival began receiving large infusions of government largesse, much more than it had received in the previous year. Public Works Canada, which was run by Alfonso Gagliano, doubled its sponsorship of the festival in the same month that Carle was hired. A few months later, the festival received a rare retroactive grant of $100,000. Officials promptly denied there was anything untoward in the decision-making process.

As the month of September began, the prime minister played golf with Tiger Woods. The Royal Montreal Golf Club was hosting the Canadian Open, and using his business contacts, Chrétien hitched himself up with Woods in the pro-am. He telephoned Mike Weir, Canada's pre-eminent player, to tell him he was sorry he wasn't able to play with a fellow countryman. On the first tee, he bashed one straight down the middle. But with the pressure of thousands watching his every shot, he played below his usual standards the rest of the way. Once, he mistakenly stepped on Woods's line, a no-no in golf, though hardly important in a warm-up round. With Woods, he couldn't find the comfort zone he could with some other celebrities, and at game's end, the golfing phenom was hard pressed to issue the compliments usually reserved for such occasions.

Soon there were other preoccupations.

ON THE SUNNY MORNING of September 11, 2001, the mood was breezy at the prime minister's breakfast table as he met with Lorne Calvert, the successor to Roy Romanow as premier of Saskatchewan. Goldenberg was there. They were talking about a drain road on the prairies when Bruce Hartley, the PM's veteran aide, stepped in to say that an airplane had crashed into a tower in Manhattan. They continued their discussions, and had moved from the drain road to the province's unusually dry weather when Hartley alerted them that something horrendous was happening. Chrétien saw the second hijacked plane hit the World Trade Center. He and Goldenberg discussed strategy while watching the appalling situation unfold. President Bush would be too busy to take a call, but Chrétien reached Ambassador Paul Cellucci to express his sorrow and support.

There was a possibility, the Mounties warned Chrétien, that Ottawa was also a target for the terrorists. From his living room on the second floor of 24 Sussex, the prime minister could see across to the Gatineau Airport. If terrorists wanted to use a plane from there, he reasoned, it would take them only a moment. If they wanted to get him, he recalled thinking, it would be easy. His wife, he felt, would be safer up at the residence at Harrington Lake. He pressed her to go there, but she insisted on staying close by.

Recommendations came to him to close down Parliament Hill and send all government workers home. But in crisis situations, Chrétien, aides noticed, had a tendency to underreact. He wasn't about to go along with the pack until he had stepped back and taken a long look. His initial instincts were often to go in the opposite direction. He told Percy Downe, "No, let's not create a panic. People are very upset. If they want to go home, let them. But we have not been attacked. Let's carry on."

Against the wishes of his security detail, he went to Parliament Hill. During the short ride in the limousine along Sussex Drive, the phone in the back seat rang. Chrétien picked it up, and right away, from the blank, frozen look on his face, Percy Downe, who was in the back seat with him, could tell it was something grave. A South Korean airliner had gone beyond its Alaskan destination. It was headed towards Canada with possible terrorists aboard. Another plane was arriving from Madrid, and contact had been lost with it as well. U.S. authorities wanted the prime minister's permission to shoot those planes, with hundreds of innocent people aboard, out of the skies. Chrétien hung up the phone. A chill swept over him. He told Downe that he had just given the go-ahead—if necessary—to kill everyone aboard.

Chrétien had had an experience of this nature before, but on a much different scale. In 1999, a small plane carrying the golfer Payne Stewart and a few passengers was flying on automatic pilot, with everyone aboard presumed dead. It was on target to crash in Winnipeg, and Chrétien gave instructions to shoot it down before it reached the Manitoba capital. It came down before it crossed the Canadian border.

On September 11, the question was whether he should give a speech to the nation, one that would seek to comfort people and assure Americans that Canada would do everything to help. Chrétien rejected the idea in favour of a routine scrum in the Commons lobby. He didn't say much, mainly that there did not appear to be a direct threat to Canada, and that he had offered Americans any support they needed. A major speech, he felt, was unnecessary. "I had to talk to the nation in a very informal way—the way they know me."

Two hundred and twenty-four planes carrying thirty-three thousand passengers were prevented from landing in the United States and diverted to north of the border, where Canadians put many of them up in their homes. At the transport department, David Collenette was directing operations. Like others, Collenette was struck by the even-tempered response he was getting from Chrétien. He had expected to be on the phone to him every minute. But without much instruction, he went ahead on his own. "I took decisions that the prime minister never knew about. If I screwed up, I would have been out." Collenette didn't screw up.

In the Eastern Townships of Quebec, Finance Minister Paul Martin, having just returned from a trip to China, had been resting at his country estate when his wife, Sheila, told him to turn on the television. "I suddenly realized," recalled Martin, "that, my God, this is the centre of the world's financial district. My biggest concern, apart from the human tragedy, was the fear of economic paralysis, so I spent the next day and a half just working the phones, phoning all around the world." As chairman of the G-7 group of finance ministers, Martin had special responsibilities, and he worried, with the collapse at the nerve centre, about a liquidity crisis.

Bush called the morning of the twelfth to thank Chrétien for the help with the displaced passengers and to ask for his support in building an anti-terrorism coalition. "You go tell the Canadian press that the United States is very grateful to Canadians," he said.

Since Parliament was due to reconvene at the start of the next week, Chrétien decided against calling it back right away. He did not call a full Cabinet meeting either, feeling that only ministers with direct responsibilities, such as Collenette, needed to be involved. Many contrasted him unfavourably with Britain's Tony Blair, America's biggest admirer, who called emergency Cabinet sessions, gave grandiose speeches, and vowed to go to the ends of the earth to stamp out terrorism. Chrétien's colleagues in Cabinet didn't expect that kind of reaction from the PM. Fine for Blair, said Anne McLellan, but it wasn't the Chrétien style to grandstand.

Suspicions surfaced that some of those behind the attacks in New York and Washington had entered the United States through Canada. It was no secret that some terrorist groups had cells in the country. Ward Elcock, then Canada's leading intelligence official, had said during 1998 testimony before a Senate committee that "with perhaps the singular exception of the United States, there are more international terrorist groups active here than in any other country in the world." Within a couple of days of the catastrophe, Ambassador Paul Cellucci was suggesting that Ottawa should bring its immigration laws into line with those of the U.S. He talked about establishing a North American perimeter, which would apply more rigorous controls to people landing from overseas. Chrétien wasn't interested.

At the PMO, his policy adviser, Paul Genest, was preparing to throw all his old plans overboard to deal with the new exigencies. But Chrétien told him that he didn't want all hands running to one side of the ship. "My instructions were to keep working on the policy agenda," recalled Genest. "He was cooler than I was, that's for sure."

Though he was alarmed by the catastrophe and sympathetic to his ally, Chrétien never saw the Americans as family, as many of his conservative critics did. He was moved, but he was not moved to the extent some wished him to be. He didn't have many close friends in the United States or a genuine intimacy with the country. He admired its freedoms, its economic engine, but he thought the size of the underclass was a disgrace for a country with so much wealth. His heroes were men like Nelson Mandela. He had come up in politics under Lester Pearson, the internationalist, and Pierre Trudeau, whose doubts about the United States were well known. He'd given Lloyd Axworthy, hardly America's foremost admirer, a long run in the foreign affairs portfolio.

In preparing to host the 2002 G-8 summit in Alberta, Chrétien had already chosen to make the plight of Africa the focal point. Late in developing a big interest in foreign policy, he had become more sensitized to the staggering inequalities between the Third World and the First, and while he was stunned that a calamity of such magnitude had happened in Manhattan, he wasn't surprised that the deep animosity many felt towards the world's only remaining superpower had found expression.

It took some convincing, in particular by Brian Tobin, but Chrétien decided, wisely, to have an outdoor memorial service on Parliament Hill for the September 11 victims. Initially, PMO staffers and others wanted a smaller chapel service, similar to what other countries were doing. Some raised objections to an outdoor service. What if it rains? Tobin was asked. "If it rains," he replied, "people will bring umbrellas."

It didn't rain. The skies were beautiful and close to a hundred thousand people stood on the lawns as the band struck up "The Star-Spangled Banner" and the American ambassador tried to maintain his composure. The prime minister, never known to evoke the required eloquence for these types of occasions, struck appropriate chords this time. He said his country would go "every step of the way" with the United States to defy terrorism. "Even when we weep for our own dead, the message we send to our American friends is equally clear: Do not lose courage. You are not alone in this. We are with you. The entire world is with you."

He told the ambassador, "As your fellow Americans grieve and rebuild there will be no silence from Canada. Our friendship has no limits. Generation after generation, we have travelled many difficult miles together side by side. We have lived through many dark times, always firm in our shared resolve to vanquish any threat to freedom and justice, and together with our allies, we will defy and defeat the threat that terrorism poses to all civilized nations."

The moving service, which inspired the U.S. ambassador to say, "You truly are our closest friend," eased some of the criticism directed towards Ottawa for allegedly not showing enough support. Foreign Affairs Minister John Manley announced that Canada would stand "shoulder to shoulder" with the United States. Immigration and security laws would have to be re-examined with a view to closer co-operation with America. Every effort had to be made, noted Manley, because "we have simply too much at stake economically in our ability to access the United States market—over $1.3 billion U.S. dollars per day in trade. We can't have them build a wall around the United States and us be on the outside of it."

In the nation's newspapers, Manley was hailed for showing clarity of purpose while Chrétien was pilloried for a halting and muddled performance. No strong speech, no visit to Ground Zero in New York, no dramatic action. The criticisms caused some concern in the PMO, but Chrétien was unperturbed. He knew much of it could be attributed to the change in media ownership, which had resulted in far more criticism from the right than in the days of Trudeau and Pearson.

Everybody was looking for quick fixes to September 11, he told aides, but "we'll deal with it in the right way, and we'll take criticism in the short term for not acting boldly and swiftly enough. But in the long term, people will look back and say we did the right thing." Six months later, he was showing aides polls saying that the Canadian people agreed with how he had handled the crisis.

He was angry at suggestions that Canada should share responsibility for the failure to prevent the terrorist attacks. It was the American defence/intelligence system that had suffered an appalling breakdown. Washington spent $30 billion annually on intelligence, almost three times Canada's entire military budget, but stories circulated that the CIA and FBI had fouled up communications with each other and allowed the terrorists to infiltrate the country. At a flight-training school in Minnesota, an Arab man was reported to have told his instructor that he wasn't too interested in learning about takeoffs and landings—just how to do mid-air turns.

Chrétien wasn't blunt enough to ask Washington for an explanation of the security breakdown that had cost many Canadian lives, but he didn't feel there should be much criticism hurled at Canada. Though an enemy had made a mockery of his nation's defences, Bush was riding high in public esteem in the wake of the disaster. Polls showed that the most murderous attack in American history had resulted in a phenomenal jump in support for the president—his approval ratings shot from the mid-fifties to almost 90 percent in little more than a week.

In the weeks following the disaster, Bush laid on a bravura performance. He showed a resilience of purpose, a reasoned caution against going on the attack before discovering the perpetrators of the deed, and he found the right words to express a nation's anger and sorrow and strength. "We will not falter; we will not fail," Bush told his Congress and country. "We are a country awakened to danger and called to freedom." He had Tony Blair in attendance, but not the prime minister of Canada. Looking up to Blair, Bush said that America had no greater friend than Great Britain. "Thanks for coming, friend."

Blair, Chrétien would explain in an interview in 2003, was in Washington that day anyway, though it may have been planned that way. Chrétien wasn't invited, and he said he hadn't been interested in seeking an invitation. "I never thought of going to Congress to listen to a speech by the president. You know, it's not a normal thing to do." If he had been in Washington and had been asked to come over, he probably would have. But "we're an independent country and, you know, things have to be done according to that."

After the speech, Bush talked to his father, the former president, on the phone. In the room with Bush, Sr., was Brian Mulroney. He had watched the historic address with him, and he also got on the phone to offer his congratulations to Bush, Jr.

There was no mention of Canada in the speech. Other countries received special thanks from Bush, including Britain, Germany, Korea, Egypt, Australia, Pakistan, Israel, El Salvador, Iran, Mexico, and Japan.

But America's biggest trading partner, the country that presidents had customarily considered its closest friend, had been left out. This despite Canada's help in taking in planes and putting up stranded Americans, despite the outpouring of emotion at the memorial service, despite the Canadian lives lost in the tragedy.

Washington put out mixed messages in trying to explain the omission. David Frum, a Canadian who worked as one of Bush's speech writers, maintained that there wasn't time to mention Canada because if Bush had done so, he would have had to spend a moment mentioning several European allies as well. In addition, noted Frum, Canada had just not done enough to be noticed by Bush. Some in the PMO suspected that Brian Mulroney had had an influence on Bush's thinking. It was clear from his public utterances on bilateral affairs that he was hostile to the Chrétien approach, and it could only be assumed that he was hostile in the presence of the Bushes as well.

When Chrétien flew to Washington for a quick meeting with the president, Bush had another explanation at the ready. "I didn't necessarily think it was important to praise a brother," he told reporters. "After all, we're talking about family." Why, then, thought some in the Chrétien entourage, did he go to such lengths over family member Britain? "I suggest," Bush continued, "that those who try to play politics with my words and drive wedges between Canada and me understand that at this time, when nations are under attack, now is not the time for politics."

After the visit, Chrétien had to dash back to Toronto, forgoing another opportunity to see Ground Zero in favour of attending a long-planned Liberal Party fundraiser. He gave a speech to the party faithful without dwelling on the tragedy in New York. He "set the bar low," remarked *The Globe and Mail* columnist Margaret Wente. "And under he went. . . . It was a profoundly weird moment. It was almost as if September 11 hadn't happened."

In an interview, Chrétien explained his decision not to go to Ground Zero sooner. "I didn't think I wanted to have a photo-op over dead bodies." To go sooner would have offended the sensibilities of New Yorkers. Some world leaders who went earlier, he noted, were viewed as exploiting the moment for political gain.

Because of the intense focus on the issues of defence and security, a spotlight was shone on the deterioration of Canada's armed forces. Influential voices, such as that of Jack Granatstein, a specialist in war history, gave power to the argument for greatly increased defence outlays. Early in their governance, the Liberals had had reason to cut into defence. The Cold War was over, there was no significant challenge to American paramountcy, and at home, there was the crushing deficit burden to contend with. Over time, when asked why he didn't now want to devote more of the budget to the military, Chrétien held to the line that helping poor people was more important.

In a special budget brought in after September 11, it was assumed defence would get a major boost, but Chrétien granted only a middling increase. A good chunk went instead to intelligence spending. As Chrétien saw it, terrorism, suicide bombers, and the rest could best be fought by intelligence agencies. Canada faced a threat, he reasoned, that at least in hard military terms was much smaller than that faced when the Soviet Union had ringed the globe with nuclear weapons capable of erasing North America in a matter of minutes. Eggleton, the defence minister, didn't try pushing the prime minister hard. Pounding the table wasn't a tactic that worked with Chrétien, he found. One had to rationalize clearly and make the case as briefly as possible. As for Paul Martin, Eggleton found that his friend the finance minister was just about as lukewarm towards defence spending as the prime minister. It was an opportunity missed.

With the lack of funding, Eggleton was in an even weaker position than normal in his dealings with Washington. Not that he got much of a hearing there anyway. As trade minister, he had found that he had some clout south of the border. "They would actually listen to me," he said. But on defence, Eggleton provided a candid assessment: "Nobody in Washington gave a damn what we said."

EIGHTEEN DAYS AFTER the terrorist attacks, the prime minister finally journeyed to the site of the horror. He took the opposition leaders with him, which was a good way of neutralizing the sting of their criticisms of him for not having gone earlier. But ever the politician, Chrétien had more than Ground Zero on his mind as he flew to New York. Spotting Stockwell Day on the plane, he tapped him on the shoulder and asked him to come and sit with him. Day was surprised. He hadn't exactly got on well with Chrétien. What was this all about?

The prime minister sat him down and gave him a lesson on politics. Some advice from an old pro, a sharing of the secrets of political war. "He saw me as his junior," recalled Day, "sort of the sorcerer's apprentice. It was a unique time, and he shared with me some personal things." Personal things like how he had kicked Day around the block in the previous election campaign. "It was like, 'Look, I know you have problems. Here's how I would deal with them,'" Day recalled. That the PM would give advice to his principal opponent surprised him. "He was very transparent and very human. He didn't move me. It was not a case of the Stockholm syndrome kicking in. But I was surprised at how transparent he was."

Chrétien later recalled the discussion with Day. "You know, what is amazing is you give good advice, but they don't believe you. . . . Sometimes I will be candid enough to tell them, 'If I were you, I would do that.' But I have noted a few times they did exactly the contrary."

When they finally arrived in New York, Chrétien and his entourage boarded a boat on Manhattan's Upper West Side and headed south to the biggest crime scene in American history. Two and a half weeks had passed since the attack on the World Trade Center, but the burning, acrid smell from the debris and the bodies remained. The tour was short, about fifteen minutes. Day, Clark, Gilles Duceppe, and Alexa McDonough, who choked back tears, walked in stony, stunned silence. Chrétien's face and his red-tinged eyes said more about the way he felt than he could put into words with his limited vocabulary. "It's an unbelievable sight," he said. "This attack is unbelievable. We have to work, all the nations together, to make sure that terrorism is destroyed."

He met with Mayor Rudolph Giuliani, who, like Bush, saw his approval ratings shoot to record highs for his valour. Chrétien gave him a religious message: "We are all brothers and sisters. We have to tell everybody that whatever the language, the colour of the skin, the religion that you profess, you know we're all together and that terrorism will be defeated."

The messages of peace, togetherness, and equality were hardly in vogue at that moment. Understandably, the United States was in no mood for that kind of talk. Any criticism of America had become politically incorrect, and Bush enjoyed virtual immunity from attack for months. When the comedian Bill Maher made cracks about Americans calling terrorists cowards while their own soldiers were sitting on aircraft carriers sending in cruise missiles to blow up targets, his TV show *Politically Incorrect* was cancelled and he was nearly branded a traitor. The anthrax scare added to the climate of paranoia. The lethal powder was being sent through the mail, though authorities didn't think it was part of an overseas terror campaign.

Though Canada did not appear to be a target, the anthrax scare resulted in yet another assault on Allan Rock. This time, he was pilloried for the bungled purchase of drugs needed to treat Canadians in the event of a biochemical attack. Rock's department had decided to buy the drugs from a generic maker, Apotex Inc., instead of from Bayer Inc., which held the patent for the pill. Health Canada had ignored its own patent rules in the rush to get the drugs and ended up having to pay both manufacturers.

The media hysteria was producing the kind of fear that terrorists thrive on. The White House contributed to it by repeatedly issuing terrorist alerts for attacks that never came. Hugh Segal, president of the Institute for Research on Public Policy, urged that some perspective be brought to bear. "Long before September 11, Canadian, American, Japanese, Spanish, British, French, and South American experiences have included subway bombings, acts of mass murder, letter bombs, and allegedly toxic mail deliveries," he pointed out. The theme was developed in an extraordinary way by Adrienne Clarkson. Tradition dictated that the governor general, like the Queen, avoid engaging in political commentary, but Clarkson gave a speech to the country's journalistic elite to challenge the oft-repeated line that September 11 had changed the world. It's too easy, too facile, to say that, Clarkson observed. "The world seems to be in as much danger as it always has. . . . Working yourself or other people into a frenzy believing that what we're living through is something new and completely different is futile." History was full of anarchists and revolutionaries and terrorists. Of the overreactors she said, "I wonder if they actually remember any history or do not know it."

THE PRIMARY TARGET for the American response to September 11 was Afghanistan, which harboured terrorists and was run by the Taliban, an archaic, repressive regime. Since it was one of the world's weakest and most impoverished nations, the United States required little help in this campaign, but it was thankful for the assistance Canada provided. Two thousand Canadian service personnel were sent, mostly to help with surveillance, support and delivery of food, and humanitarian relief. Screaming "Off to War" headlines made it sound like the country was entering another Second World War.

With the Afghan campaign supported around the world, Chrétien had no difficulty getting backing for it from Canadians at large or in his caucus. He took aside Bonnie Brown, one of the dissenting members, and told her that he had no choice, that all the allies were on board. Brown recalled Chrétien telling her that the post-September situation would require a judicious approach, something that wasn't exactly the Americans' strong suit. She rose in caucus to make a more general and important point: that the government had to keep a close eye so that people with long-held agendas didn't take advantage of the crisis situation to further their own career goals. She noted that several presidents, dating back more than a hundred years, had wanted a unified continental defence system. "Previous prime ministers have resisted these efforts," she told Chrétien, "and I trust that you will as well."

Canada's contribution in Afghanistan eased the strain in the bilateral relationship, a strain aggravated by finger pointing from Attorney General John Ashcroft, who had made reference to Canada's "porous borders." Given the porousness of his FBI, which had allowed the terrorists to infiltrate the U.S., Chrétien and Manley showed admirable restraint in keeping their responses in check. But through this period, Manley was quick to point to glaring inadequacies in Canada's intelligence and defence capacities and its contributions to foreign aid. "You can't just sit at the G-8 table," he told the *National Post*'s Paul Wells, "and then, when the bill comes up, go to the washroom." Canada, he said, was "still trading on a reputation that was built two generations and more ago—but that we haven't continued to live up to." While quickly becoming the darling of the right, Manley vowed to be no pushover for the Americans, describing Ambassador Cellucci's idea of a common continental security policy as simplistic.

Though Chrétien challenged the view that Canada was not carrying its own weight, he was hardly on terra firma in so doing. His critics could point as an example to the government's astonishingly inept and politically driven handling of the purchase of new military helicopters. It was a file that put Chrétien's legendary stubbornness repeatedly on display.

Back in 1993, Chrétien had cancelled Kim Campbell's plans to outfit the military with new helicopters, forty-three EH-101s. The price tag, $5.8 billion, was considered beyond the fiscal capacity of the day. That meant that the old helicopters, Labradors and Sea Kings that first saw action when John Diefenbaker was prime minister, would have to do.

In cancelling the Tory contract, the Liberals cost taxpayers roughly $500 million, the result of a judgment for breach of contract with the firm originally chosen by the Mulroney government to supply the helicopters. That was a heavy blow—half a billion dollars for nothing in return—but the bigger fiasco was the endless chicanery of the governing party when it came time for them to purchase new choppers themselves. Having dispensed with the company that had made the agreement with the Tories, the government could not be seen to be putting out tenders that might have allowed that same company to win the new contract. That would have been as embarrassing as voting down its own Red Book resolution. And so what followed was a decade-long marathon of indecision, unconscionable delays, and political meddling in helicopter procurement requirements so the government would not be embarrassed. Anything and everything was done to avoid giving the impression that the Tories had been right.

At the end of a decade in power, the Liberals had no choppers on the assembly line. The Canadian military was still using forty-year-old whirlybirds described by pilots as "ten thousand nuts and bolts flying in loose formation." And it was costing the taxpayer a fortune—$60 million a year just in service costs to keep the duds operating.

Defence Minister Eggleton was candid enough to call the helicopter saga "the file from hell." Though no new contract was worked out for the old Sea Kings, the Labradors were replaced. The same company that the Tories had hired, Team Cormorant, was awarded that contract in July 2000, worth $790 million. Chrétien was furious. Eggleton broke the news to him, saying that nothing could be done. They had won the bidding fair and square. "There was no doubt he was unhappy," recalled Eggleton. "It didn't sit well with him." The PM "had a suspicion of the military" with regard to the first contract, Eggleton said, and he couldn't shake it. With the delays replacing the Sea Kings, it was estimated that it would be the second decade of the new century—almost twenty years after the initial contract was signed—before the new helicopters were ready.

Through it all, Chrétien dug in, hiding behind lame rationales. It was another example that showed that on matters he saw as affecting his personal standing, he could not concede error. When trapped, Jean Chrétien would not admit to being trapped. In a sense, it was the appendicitis story all over again. Only in this case, it was the military that lost a body part because of his mule-headed intransigence.

In an interview in 2003, he was still running from any guilt on the chopper fiasco. He claimed that he didn't care which company won the contract. "We want to have a competition. We want to have three or four companies bidding. We want the best price possible for a helicopter that can do the job. The notion that only one helicopter can do the job is a bit too much for me." The Americans, he said, had different helicopters, as did NATO. "There's only one that can fit Canada. It's a bit surprising. So let's have the best helicopter at the best price. The best deal for the taxpayers, and if it is one or the other, I don't mind. I don't give a damn whoever gets it."

RESPONDING TO THE NEW SECURITY DEMANDS, Justice Minister Anne McLellan tabled in October a far-reaching anti-terrorism bill containing 146 new provisions, including one allowing the police to carry out "preventive arrests." People suspected of planning terrorist acts could be detained for seventy-two hours and compelled to appear before a judge. Bill C-36 also placed limits on the right to remain silent and allowed for life imprisonment for the leaders of any terrorist groups directing plots. Since there were no deterrents for people prepared to commit suicide for their cause, McLellan wanted the emphasis to be placed on preventive measures.

The justice minister was acting in keeping with the get-tough atmosphere of the period. The harder you looked, the better you looked. But Privacy Commissioner George Radwanski, considering the broader perspective, argued that the bill could "gut all the privacy protections that Canadians now have." Herb Dhaliwal, the natural resources minister, was sensitive to human rights issues and demanded a sunset clause. McLellan "went bananas," as Dhaliwal recalled, appealing to the prime minister to shut him down. Chrétien did just that, castigating Dhaliwal in front of the Cabinet. Dhaliwal wanted to respond, but he held his tongue. After the meeting, the PM took him aside. "You didn't mind, did you, Herb? You're my friend."

But Dhaliwal didn't back down. He continued to apply pressure, and with criticism building in other quarters, McLellan and Chrétien eventually gave way. Her bill had been prepared in haste, and as a result, had to undergo several revisions to soften the more draconian elements.

It had been a year since Chrétien's election triumph of November 2000. At that time, the government appeared to have little to do except contend with its internal battles and alleged scandals. But the catastrophe of September 11 had given it a new sense of purpose. From species-at-risk legislation and free trade with Costa Rica, there came a dramatic new set of imperatives. The Liberals faced a war abroad, a domestic economy imperilled by September's aftermath, the redrawing of the Canadian security apparatus, and the fear that sovereignty had been dealt a telling blow by the need to come together with the southern neighbour to secure the continent.

For Chrétien there was a whole new set of priorities. Paul Martin's challenge to his job security and the abuse-of-power controversies seemed, at least for a few months, to be far away.

CHAPTER SIXTEEN

THE SOUNDS
OF CIVIL WAR

THAT THE CONTINUING RAMIFICATIONS of the terrorist attacks would be the overriding concern of the government seemed self-evident. But in Ottawa, it was hardly the case. After Black September, it took only four months for the Chrétien Liberals to be engulfed again in internecine political turmoil and convulsions related to the abuse of power. Government in Ottawa, as the Liberal consultant John Duffy put it, had become all about "the politics of retaining power rather than exercising power."

If it wasn't all politics all the time, it was close to it, and it was debilitating. Previous Liberal governments hadn't behaved this way. Pierre Trudeau was only occasionally preoccupied with the political ramifications of the decisions he made. Lester Pearson had to be more concerned, because he presided over delicate minority governments. But he was no political animal like Chrétien. Louis St. Laurent had come to politics late in life, was handed a safe governing majority, and rarely had to ponder the political equation to the neglect of other priorities.

Over the decades, political infighting had been the reserve of the Tory Party, not the Liberals. But that had changed when the relentlessly combative Chrétien became a leadership candidate in 1984. From that time on, through the Turner years and into his own, the party was frequently at war with itself—with Jean Chrétien at the centre of the storm. The year 2002 would arguably represent the worst of it. It was a year when the party's civil war reached a fever pitch, when the prime minister and his finance minister were like scorpions in a bottle, when Cabinet ministers resigned or were forced out, when evidence of corruption and abuse of power reached heights unscaled in other years of the Chrétien stewardship.

The government had already suffered through the "Dark Ages" rumpus at HRDC and the ongoing Shawinigate drama. To begin the year, a slew of new charges landed. *The Globe and Mail's* Daniel Leblanc and Hugh Winsor located a whistle-blower, a civil servant who worked under Public Works Minister Alfonso Gagliano and was appalled at what he saw. Gagliano, one of the Cabinet members who was closest to Chrétien and Jean Pelletier, had been hit with allegations of impropriety and influence-peddling the previous year. Now Jon Grant, the former chairman of Canada Lands, a Crown corporation overseen by Gagliano, described how the minister had pushed to have friends put on the government payroll. Worse was Grant's accusation that Quebec had become a Gagliano fiefdom. Canada Lands was created to sell off surplus government-owned property. As an indication of how politicized the operation had become, Grant recounted instructions he'd received from Gagliano's chief of staff, Jean-Marc Bard. "The rest of Canada is yours," Bard told him. "Quebec is ours."

Gagliano denied the statement and other claims by Grant, but taxpayers soon learned more about Canada Lands deals. *The Montreal Gazette* revealed that Canada Lands sold one of the city's most valuable residential properties to a prominent developer for less than half of its assessed value. The property was sold to the Entreprises El-Pine Inc., which was owned by a Montreal developer who was a Liberal Party contributor. The price paid to Ottawa was $4 million. "That price was a joke," said the real estate agent Sheila Weitzman. The property, she said, had been appraised at $9 million.

Before Jon Grant stepped forward, the opposition parties had been hounding Gagliano over millions of dollars in contracts issued from his department to a company owned by Michèle Tremblay, one of his friends and supporters. Then came an intriguing revelation about Gagliano's relationship with an Italian senator. Maurizio Creuso was convicted of fraud in Italy, but he parachuted to Canada, where he found his comforts. He obtained Canadian citizenship in the mid-1990s and was awarded contracts with federal agencies under Gagliano's jurisdiction. Creuso said he had been a friend of Gagliano's for two decades and had accompanied the minister on trips. Not so, Gagliano protested. Creuso was more like an acquaintance.

Carolyn Parrish, who was the parliamentary assistant to Gagliano, got a close-up view of the roly-poly minister in action. She didn't think Gagliano would have acted wrongly, she said in an interview in 2003. And one other thing was certain. He would never, ever do anything of a significant nature, she said, without clearance from above.

For his part, Gagliano felt that he was the likely victim of an inside job. The dissension, the infighting in the Liberal ranks, was so intense that someone was out to get him because they envied his power as regional minister for Quebec. He suggested that it could even be a fellow Cabinet minister. "I mean, naturally, sometimes for somebody to move up, you have to bring somebody down."

The PMO tried for a time to defend the public works minister, issuing a letter Grant had once written to him complimenting him on his "frank insight, advice and counsel." But Gagliano had become too hot. Chrétien decided to dump his close friend—and so began the Liberals' year from hell.

Wrapping the Gagliano send-off in the nicest package possible, the prime minister was able to say, without choking on his words, what a wonderful public servant and friend the minister had been. He gave him the cushy diplomatic post of ambassador to Denmark.

Other friends or acquaintances of the prime minister's also found themselves in trouble. In Shawinigan, the RCMP caught up to a former campaigner who ran a business group that distributed government funds. Paul Lemire admitted defrauding two groups, Groupe Forces and the Canadian Institute of Tourism and Electronic

Technology, which had received HRDC grants, as well as money from other government sources. Lemire, whose office was once right next to Chrétien's constituency office, liked to boast about his connections, telling friends he was so close to Chrétien that during the PM's trade mission in 1996, he had taken him by the arm on the flight and got him to sit with Lucien Bouchard to talk things over. The PMO distanced itself from Lemire, saying there were no close links. Lemire was fined $10,000 and ordered to serve two years of community service.

His story captured only modest attention compared with a report by the new auditor general, Sheila Fraser, a no-nonsense woman who had replaced the debonair Denis Desautels. Fraser had an attention-grabber to kick off her term. She revealed that the government sent rebate cheques for heating expenses during the previous winter to thousands of dead people. Unfortunately, no amount of heat could help them. And if the dead weren't receiving the cheques, it was the incarcerated. Another sixteen hundred cheques went to prisoners. A further 40 percent of the recipients were not the needy Canadians the money was intended for. It was clear that the rebate program had been hastily put together, and those who probed further found a possible explanation for all that apparently unintentional government largesse: A few days after the rebate program was announced, the 2000 federal election was called.

Each year, Ottawa doled out $16 billion in discretionary grants. Fraser found that while there had been some improvement at HRDC, the system was deficient in program design and measurement, and the monies were at risk of being used for purposes other than those intended. The opposition parties chimed in, charging that the loose management suited the government of the day perfectly. The political arm could direct the grants and loans where the votes were most needed.

OVER THE CHRISTMAS HOLIDAYS, a political drama had been brewing. Brian Tobin had been back in federal politics for little more than a year. In that time, he had performed ably enough in the industry portfolio, while making sufficient contacts with the rich and powerful to build a campaign war chest. The experience had helped him round out his resumé, giving him some support on the right as well as the left. In polls, he had emerged as the biggest threat to Paul Martin in a leadership race. It was also believed, though the prime minister had never tipped his hand, that the Tobinator was Chrétien's preferred choice to succeed him. Martin organizers feared that on a second ballot, he could bring together the votes of the party activists, supporters of Allan Rock and Sheila Copps.

To respond to the post–September 11 exigencies, Martin was bringing in a special budget. Looking for a showcase program for himself and his department, Brian Tobin came up with a plan to connect every corner of the country to a broadband Internet network. It would cost $1 billion. From the budget, he wanted a good chunk of that amount for start-up costs.

He pushed hard before the budget came in but wasn't getting the positive feedback he'd expected. Percy Downe, Chrétien's chief of staff, had spoke with Tobin and got the impression that he was highly frustrated. During a trade mission to Dallas, Downe informed the prime minister that the finance department was resisting Tobin's ambitious proposal, and that something had to be done or Tobin might resign. Phone calls were made from Dallas to the clerk of the Privy Council and to Eddie Goldenberg. The problem was presumed to have been fixed.

But with the unveiling of Martin's budget, the money for Tobin's prized Internet plan was nowhere to be found. He got only $105 million—and that was over a three-year stretch. Tobin and his staffers were furious. They suspected that Goldenberg had "screwed" them on the broadband project. They suspected that he and Paul Martin had quietly scuppered it, even after the instruction from Dallas.

Everyone knew about Tobin's acrimonious relationship with Goldenberg. They began quarrelling during the 1990 leadership campaign, when Tobin came aboard to help with communications, and they rarely stopped sniping after that. They disagreed on Tobin's approach on the fish wars and the referendum rally. The Newfoundlander was right on both counts, but that didn't make relations any warmer.

Goldenberg didn't want either Tobin or Allan Rock to succeed Chrétien. When Rock made his ambition known, his staff noticed a cooling in their relations with Goldenberg's office. His choice was Paul Martin—only not right away. Not for several years yet. "Goldfinger" naturally enjoyed having his hand on the power levers, on making history, and he was in no hurry to give that up. He had kept up good relations with Martin while at the same making sure he let the PM know who was number one.

The way Goldenberg told the story, Paul Martin simply did not want to provide the funding for the broadband project. He was the minister of finance, and he did not like having his hand forced—especially by someone intent on giving him a run for the leadership. Goldenberg was only too happy to support Martin. Then the word went up to the Prime Minister's Office—after Chrétien had returned from Dallas—and, said Goldenberg, "the prime minister backed the minister of finance."

Chrétien knew how critical the issue was to Tobin—Percy Downe had told him that Tobin would resign. But thinking that Tobin was probably just bluffing, he went ahead and undercut him anyway. He believed Tobin was just bluffing. Most around the PMO believed that after a couple of days of blowing off some steam, Tobin, the great blarney boy, would settle down and be a good Chrétien soldier once again. But this wasn't the minister of fish anymore. This was a Tobin who had served as premier and who had more pride. Chrétien and Goldenberg miscalculated—and it was one of their most costly blunders.

Tobin wasn't bluffing. He was angry not only about the broadband issue but about another matter. With his control of the Liberal executive, Martin had set up the campaigning mechanisms in a way that made it difficult for Tobin and others to sign up new party members and thus nominate delegates to a leadership convention. Tobin had spoken to the prime minister about this and hadn't received—in his mind at least—a satisfactory response.

In early January, Tobin phoned the prime minister, who was golfing in Florida. He set up an appointment and went to 24 Sussex shortly after Chrétien's plane landed. He put forward his side of the story and told Chrétien: "You can't hit me from behind like that." It was over, he told the PM. He had thought about it, and he wasn't changing his mind. Chrétien protested, saying he had told his staff to fix the broadband financing. But Tobin had a hard time believing that. If that was really the case, he said, "You have a problem on your hands, Prime Minister." It meant, Tobin pointed out, that he wasn't in control, that someone else—namely, Eddie Goldenberg—was running the country.

The two men had a Scotch and were able to find refuge in other areas of discussion. But Tobin was gone—and the repercussions would be felt for months to come. Chrétien was, in effect, stripping himself of armour. He was losing one of the government's ablest communicators, one of his fiercest defenders in Cabinet, and the one candidate who could perhaps put up a strong fight against Paul Martin for the leadership of the party. One of the big storylines for the media had been the developing Martin–Tobin clash. Now that there would be no real leadership race to focus on, the media's attention turned back to Martin and Chrétien, and it remained there, tormenting the government, week in, week out.

Reverberation number one from the Tobin desertion came quickly and hit hard: Chrétien had to make a major Cabinet shuffle. His long-time colleague Herb Gray, thinking it was business as usual in Ottawa, returned home from a trip to the Middle East. Most everybody still liked Gray. He was the grandfather clock that had kept his party ticking. He was glue for a party that was coming apart like a model airplane. When he landed in Ottawa, someone handed him a message that said, "Go straight to 24. The prime minister wants to see you."

Gray had barely sat down when Chrétien, notes in front of him, came quickly to the point: "I don't think you should continue in Cabinet." Gray, having spent four decades in the trenches with Chrétien, couldn't believe it. He wanted to challenge the decision, but he could see from Chrétien's face—expressionless, nothing but frozen tundra— that it would be pointless. This wasn't a request. It was an order.

They talked about what Gray might do next. A Senate seat didn't interest him. Leader in the Senate, maybe, but the PM wasn't even offering that. Gray's old friend Paul Martin, Sr., who had served for so long, had been rewarded with that position before going to London as high commissioner in 1974. Gray was the government's longest-serving member, but the PM had nothing of significance in mind for him.

There was no reminiscing, no soft talk. Gray racked his brain to think of something he might have done wrong. He thought he had given added value to the government, and to Chrétien. He had tried to defend him on the Shawinigan file. If he had looked weak in doing so, it was because some days there was just no good rebuttal to what the opposition parties were throwing at him. Gray also had had to deal with the Airbus mess and Conrad Black's peerage case, which even his wife had given him hell about.

Gray didn't realize that some around the PMO had been pressuring Chrétien to drop him from Cabinet for a long time. Goldenberg had wanted him to go, as had David Zussman. Percy Downe was hearing grumblings from the Ontario caucus, of which Gray was leader. Much of Paul Martin's support was coming from that caucus. But if there were good reasons for moving Herb Gray—and most in the caucus did not think there was sufficient cause—the boss, everyone felt, could have found a better way of doing it. He didn't have another position at the ready for Gray, and he didn't even have a day of tribute in mind. Was this any way to treat a pillar of the party?

So now Tobin, one of his best blockers, was out and Gray, another stalwart defender, was also gone. In those unruly weekly caucus meetings, there would be no unifying wrap-up from Herb Gray any more.

None of what Joe Comuzzi called the "We're all one family" speech that always sent the troops away feeling a little better.

The Cabinet shuffle was the biggest Chrétien had made since coming to power. The stolid John Manley took Gray's slot as deputy prime minister and as head man for the Ontario caucus. Manley retained his role as head of the national security file and was also made minister responsible for federal infrastructure programs and Crown corporations. Chrétien was sending a message that Paul Martin could well understand. There was no doubt who was number two in this government—and who was Jean Chrétien's man.

Allan Rock finally got out of the health portfolio, where he was replaced by Anne McLellan, and slid smoothly into industry. The Quebec star, Martin Cauchon, became minister of justice, while the foreign affairs portfolio went to a first-time Cabinet member, Bill Graham. Don Boudria was moved into the patronage portfolio of public works, from which Gagliano, all set for six-course meals in Denmark, had been ousted. Seven backbenchers—all men—became junior members of Cabinet, or secretaries of state, as they were called. With so much in play, those male appointments didn't receive much notice—except from the women.

Any Cabinet shuffle left behind a lot of tortured egos. But this one was much more delicate because of the hundred-member Ontario caucus. Many of its members had been waiting a long time—three terms—and those who didn't get rewarded now knew it was over for them. They would never make it to the big table under Chrétien. Martin was their only hope.

Dennis Mills went to see Chrétien. "What the hell happened?" he asked. "You put in Graham! You put in Graham, for Christ's sake!" Chrétien said he had only one slot open from Toronto. "I don't care if you had no slots," Mills fired back. "You should have created one for me." Mills, many believed, at least deserved a junior Cabinet spot, but he had had a run-in with Goldenberg some time ago, and Goldenberg had a long memory.

"Jean," Mills said. "This is bullshit. I'm one of your best work-horses."

Chrétien protested, saying they should still be friends.

"We're still friends," Mills replied. "But I want to tell you something: I've done my part for you. . . . Now I have to start looking out for what I have to do to gain some respect around here before I leave."

Among the women shut out for promotions were the two Carolyns, Bennett and Parrish. Bennett was the strong-willed chair of the women's caucus. Parrish was equally feisty. She was the one who had taken on the Italian rebels on Chrétien's behalf, and she had thought her chances of getting into Cabinet were good. Before Christmas, she visited the prime minister. She wanted to point out the lack of Cabinet representation from the area surrounding Toronto, where she was from. She had approached Percy Downe before the meeting and given him maps to prove her argument. "Percy's a stats geek," she recalled. "So he was just thrilled with it."

At the meeting she chatted with Chrétien for a few minutes and then broke eye contact as she began to pull out her maps. She looked up to see Chrétien pulling the same charts from under his desk. He proceeded to give chapter and verse on the political history of the whole area, whereupon Parrish started laughing and remarked, "Well, I guess I don't have to say anything."

"I know it all," said the PM. "It's very impressive what you've brought. But I already know it."

Parrish sat speechless while he toyed with her. "He did it with such glee and joy," she recalled. She tried extending the conversation, hoping the PM would talk about the pending Cabinet shuffle. Then he got her hopes up. He couldn't make her any definitive promises, he said, but he noted that she had been a loyal and excellent MP. "I know it hasn't been easy at times," he said. Then came the topper. The PM was usually formal with women, "not a huggy guy," as Parrish put it. But as she was leaving, he gave her a hard grip and a kiss on the cheek. "He winked at me and he laughed, and he said, "'You know, I haven't ever had anyone Polish in my Cabinet before.'"

Parrish left feeling elated, her expectations soaring. All she wanted was a junior spot. She waited anxiously for shuffle day. When it came she got nothing. The big zero. The Martinites were closely monitoring these proceedings, and now they started swarming around Parrish like bees. Within days, she had signed on with the finance minister.

The other Carolyn, Carolyn Bennett, was already a Martin supporter. Noting the male, male, and more male makeup of the new appointments, she told the media it was an unfortunate message for the women of Canada. The next morning, she saw a quote from an anonymous PMO official in the papers. It said, in effect, "What do you expect from a Martin supporter?" Bennett was seething. There it was again—the PMO giving every single act a political motive. It was the very reason Reg Alcock had sent that letter calling them a bunch of jackasses.

Bennett got on the phone to Francie Ducros. "I have too much important work to do around here to turn around and see you putting everything through that lens, Francie!" she said angrily. Ducros claimed she wasn't the one quoted, but Bennett said it was perfectly obvious that it was her or someone who reports to her. "So stop it," she demanded and hung up.

When the Liberal caucus met, Bennett stood up and made a cutting point about party financing. Party central was tithing the individual ridings, she charged, and yet the party was still in debt and no one knew where the money was going. She took dead aim at two executives, Stephen LeDrew and Terry Mercer. Anne McLellan looked on, fascinated. She recalled Bennett saying, "If you guys were in the private sector, you'd be fired." Quite a shot, but, noted McLellan, that was what everybody was thinking.

Then Bennett changed course. She started talking about how all the men in suits got Cabinet promotions, but the women were shut out. What was the prime minister thinking? This wasn't right, she said. "We have to know what the party is doing for us." With that broadside, Chrétien had had enough. He snapped forward in his chair. "It got you elected, madam." The look on his face was frightening. "He just blew up," recalled McLellan. "Right off the Richter scale! And there was stunned silence. I had never seen that from him before. Right off the Richter scale!"

He went through the list of all the female appointments he had made—and there had been many. The GG, the chief justice, Copps as DPM. He had a point, but many onlookers thought that even so, this was no way to treat a lady. "It was like," said one caucus member, "he turned a firehose on her."

All he had done for the party! All he had done to get everyone elected and re-elected and re-elected again! As the venom kept coming, Stéphane Dion began to notice something strange. The prime minister was trying to stop himself, but he was so angry that he couldn't do it. On three occasions Stéphane Dion could see him trying, but he couldn't stop.

Initially, Bennett was alarmed. But then she thought of her time as a delivery room doctor, when she had faced crises worse than this, and she steeled her resolve. When she sat down, however, she was browbeaten and in tears. "Any of us would have been in shock," McLellan recalled. "I mean, we would have been destroyed, any one of us. . . . I don't believe there was a person in that room who had seen that kind of anger displayed by him."

Some Chrétien loyalists thought Bennett had it coming. Not for the point she had made about female representation, which was fair enough, but because, said Bonnie Brown, "at every single cocktail party she was at, Carolyn Bennett was bad-mouthing the prime minister." She should have known it would get back to Chrétien, Brown felt. Others should have known it too, when they did the same thing. That's why they didn't get promotions. "You can't have people in your Cabinet who don't have respect," said Brown. "He is very big on respect."

Most women in the caucus got the sense that Chrétien had an old-fashioned Roman Catholic shyness towards them. He struggled to understand the female perspective, said McLellan, "and it's almost a palpable, physical struggling that is reflected on his face sometimes." He often doesn't get it, but the difference, she said, is that he tries. "Lots of guys these days wouldn't bother."

After the caucus meeting, members went to Bennett to console her. She broke down completely then, tears falling like rain. Meanwhile, journalists were waiting outside. Caucus members weren't supposed to repeat a word of what went on in their weekly sessions, but this time they were almost running to the microphones to spill the story of the great tongue-lashing and how the prime minister was losing it.

Bennett suspected that the ire had been prompted by Francie Ducros. "Francie was probably telling him what a bitch I was." More likely, however, something that had happened that morning had turned the PM's mood sour. He had received word that his adopted son, Michel, was in trouble with the police again. In addition, Chrétien had seen an overheated headline in a Montreal paper about his poor performance on women's issues, and that had set him off.

Late in the day, both Bennett and the PM showed up at a cocktail reception in the parliamentary restaurant. Bennett was being consoled when Chrétien walked in. Dennis Mills told the prime minister that he could not allow what he had done to stand, that he had to apologize to Bennett. He steered Chrétien by the arm towards her, and the PM issued a statement of regret, of sorts, saying he might have been a bit harsh.

With a considerable degree of interest, Paul Martin had been watching the story unfold. His caucus supporters were the ones who were giving chapter and verse to the media. Martin himself called Bennett after the caucus meeting. That same night, he took her out to dinner.

WHEN PARLIAMENT REOPENED at the end of January 2002, leadership quarrels consumed the headlines. Reeling from the Cabinet overhaul, the resignations, the Bennett blow-up, Chrétien warned that the infighting had to stop or the Liberals would soon look like the

Canadian Alliance. But as if to send him a message that his grasp was slipping, the caucus elected a resolute Martin supporter, Stan Keyes, as its chair. Keyes had made headlines at the party's biennial convention when he said that Chrétien ought to consider stepping down. He was a towering, outspoken Hamiltonian whose favourite expression was "Politics is a whore's game," and who couldn't find many who could cogently counter the point. He defeated a Chrétien loyalist, Steve Mahoney, for chair in a secret ballot. Chrétien had been confident his man would win. When the result was read out, he turned white. Martin now controlled the party executive and the caucus chair. Many of Brian Tobin's supporters were heading his way. Herb Gray, who had many allies, had lost a lot of faith in the PM, and he was letting that fact be known.

The spring came—and with it came yet another round of malfeasance from the party that was supposed to clean up government. Auditor General Sheila Fraser issued a catchy line in detailing the latest breach of ethics. She declared that bureaucrats broke "just about every rule in the book" to award three contracts, worth $1.6 million, to the Quebec firm Groupaction Marketing Inc. The company was to produce reports on how to boost the visibility of the federal government in Quebec. Two of the reports appeared to be almost identical, a case of double-dipping, while the third couldn't be located. To make matters worse, it was revealed that Groupaction had donated a reported $70,000 to the Liberal Party since 1998. Senior civil servants "demonstrated an appalling disregard" for the government's financial administration laws, the auditor said. "This is a completely unacceptable way for government to do business."

The department at the centre of this controversy was public works. The abuses happened while Alfonso Gagliano, lauded by the prime minister as a great public servant, was in charge. Fraser referred the matter to the RCMP, while vowing to conduct her own probe into Ottawa's advertising, polling, and sponsorship programs. In the Commons, MPs demanded Gagliano be recalled from his diplomatic post just as the prime minister was thinking of giving him a better one.

Chrétien and company could be shockingly cynical on these occasions. Every allegation was met with defensiveness and denial. On the Groupaction matter, Chrétien declared that if money had been lost, even great sums of it, it was all for a good cause. By promoting federalism, the government was pushing back separatism. "Perhaps there was a few million dollars that might have been stolen in the process," he told a fundraising dinner in Winnipeg. "It is possible. But how many millions of dollars have we saved the country because we have re-established the stability of Canada as a united country?" He had no regrets. "If somebody has stolen the money, they will face the courts. But I will not apologize to any Canadians."

If fraud and corruption were the means to an end, the prime minister appeared to be saying, no apology was necessary. The end justifies the means. Don't get in Jean Chrétien's way. If winning meant abusing, so be it. His unity minister, Stéphane Dion, didn't seem to share his opinion about the effectiveness of the lost millions. The sponsorship program, Dion ventured to say, had only a marginal impact on the unity debate.

Brian Mulroney couldn't contain himself. He declared in Halifax that the Chrétien government would be remembered for little else but "squalid conduct and stunning hypocrisy." Normally, Mulroney's favourite word for describing foul behaviour was "odious." For Chrétien, the former PM had turned it up a notch. "Squalid" was the new adjective.

What Mulroney found particularly galling was a revelation that the prime minister had rushed through the $101-million purchase of two new luxury Challenger jets for his own use, overcoming opposition from senior government officials who said the new planes weren't necessary. Having made such political hay of his humble old-Chevy style, Chrétien was now leaving himself wide open to charges of hypocrisy. When Mulroney spent $2.5 million for the refurbishment of his Airbus jet in 1993, the Liberals ridiculed him, calling it a flying Taj Mahal. While Chrétien tried to argue that he needed the upgrade, reporters were quick to point out that the Canadian Forces were still flying around in forty-year-old Sea King helicopters. The press was in high dudgeon. Earlier, *The Globe and Mail*'s Margaret Wente had dissected the PM's authoritarian bent in a piece titled "Come to Me with Respect; I Am Still the Godfather." Now, Andrew Coyne of the *National Post* diced up Chrétien in a searing column titled "Bossism Rules." Having pointed out that there was no public tender, that the jets' purchase had been rushed through public works over the objections of three senior officials in three departments, that it was made without the approval of Cabinet, that the contract went to Bombardier, a generous donor to the Liberal Party, Coyne wrote, "So let's see. That's abuse of process, contempt of parliament, grievous waste, pork-barrelling, multiple counts of aggravated policy failure [a reference to the helicopter file] and rank hypocrisy, all driven by the prime minister's *droit de seigneur* philosophy of public finance."

Trying to bring efficiency to his much-criticized public service, a public service in which he had invested so much faith at the outset of his stewardship in 1993, Chrétien moved out his top bureaucrat, Mel Cappe, sending him off to the posh post of British high commissioner in July 2002. Since Cappe had experienced a tough run, first as deputy minister at HRDC (though the problems there were not revealed until after he left), then as clerk, it was a nice reward. In a rare admission, Chrétien said in a 2003 interview that his public service had let him down. "They made mistakes. And you, the press, were trying to blame the politicians for the mistakes made within the system. . . . You're not interested to find a bureaucrat's mistake."

In Cappe's place, Chrétien put Alex Himelfarb, a widely respected veteran bureaucrat with a cigarette hanging eternally from the corner of his mouth *à la* René Lévesque. Himelfarb, who had a left-of-centre reputation, immediately set about coordinating an activist platform and helping the prime minister focus on policy as much as politics.

With polls now showing that almost half of Canadians thought the government was corrupt, Chrétien rushed forward with an ethics reform package, which included new rules on how ministers should deal with Crown corporations, new rules for fundraising by Cabinet ministers, and a stipulation that the ethics counsellor issue an annual report to Parliament. The government wanted to show that it was turning the proverbial corner on the abuse-of-power morass into which it had fallen.

As it turned out, the timing could not have been more unfavourable. Two days later, the *Ottawa Citizen* revealed that Defence Minister Art Eggleton had put a former lover, Maggie Maier, on his payroll with an untendered contract worth $36,500. It was to study stress and other health issues related to defence personnel. At the time, a more extensive study was already being conducted by the department.

Though Maier and Eggleton denied that the contract had anything to do with their relationship, the timing of the revelation—which had appeared in *Frank* magazine months earlier—proved disastrous for the minister. With all the recent evidence of unethical conduct, Chrétien felt he couldn't let this episode pass without a response. When Howard Wilson, the ethics counsellor, decided there had been a breach of conflict guidelines, it was all over for Art Eggleton. He was a Martin supporter as well, and he had been caught up in an embarrassing imbroglio earlier in the year, when the prime minister was kept in the dark for a week on the Canadian Forces' capture of al-Qaeda prisoners in Afghanistan. The captives were handed over to U.S. troops, who neglected to declare them prisoners of war, which would have meant they were protected by the Geneva Convention. Chrétien was left confused, and Eggleton was pummelled from all corners.

Tobin had left, Gagliano had been ushered out, Herb Gray forcibly retired, Eggleton dismissed. Now Don Boudria joined the rogues' gallery. He had been in public works as Gagliano's successor for only a few months. It was revealed that in March, he had held a family reunion at the posh Quebec estate of Claude Boulay. Boulay was the president of Groupe Everest, a Montreal public relations firm that had received a tidy $55 million in federal advertising and sponsorship contracts since 1993, when the Liberals took power.

Whether Boudria intended to pay for the family holiday was an open question. The opposition parties found out that an $800 cheque from Boudria for payment was cashed the very week the controversy broke, which was May, two months after his stay. The timing was too much for even some in his own caucus to swallow. As the Grits stumbled, once again the old Mulroney Tories could take delight. In the 1980s, Boudria had been a member of the fabled Rat Pack, which handed a "patronage of the week" award to the Tories every Friday. Now his own play on patronage cost him his job. Chrétien removed him from public works, put him in his old House leader's job, and gave the earnest and highly competent Ralph Goodale the public works hot seat. "Perhaps after almost nine years, people got a bit too comfortable," Chrétien reasoned. "So that will be a lesson to all of us."

If the PM was firing ministers for offences like those of Eggleton and Boudria, some journalists were cheeky enough to wonder if he shouldn't be looking in his own backyard. Don Martin noted that Howard Wilson had come running forward on a moment's notice to finish off Eggleton. "But what would you call," asked Martin, "the prime minister's chat with a Crown corporation banker to bail out a hotel linked to a golf course he may still have had an interest in? Funny, ethics counsellor Howard Wilson was in a 'see no evil' monkey mode on that score."

The *National Post* and *The Globe and Mail* led the media assault on the ethics file. Ever since CanWest had condemned journalists for pursuing such stories with little evidence, so much evidence of malfeasance was becoming public that few could keep track. Being fired at from all sides, Chrétien might have assumed he would be spared embarrassment from his own close ally, John Manley. But Manley, who had an admirable habit of blunt speaking, criticized the prime minister while unveiling new rules of conduct for Cabinet ministers in their dealings with Crown corporations. The new rules, said Manley, were a result of the prime minister's interference with the Business Development Bank. In reference to that meddling, Manley told Jack Aubry of Southam News, "I think we went into this on the presumption that that had offended people, and therefore it was something that probably he shouldn't do again." The headline in the next day's *Ottawa Citizen,* translated to an editor's shorthand, shouted: "Manley Says PM 'Offended' Canadians." Manley, so furious with the headline writer that he almost had to be scraped from the ceiling, had to face Chrétien that very morning.

If almost every other member of the Cabinet team was falling into the conflict-of-interest trap in one way or another, why not Paul Martin as well? He had sat looking on dispassionately as the prime minister bore the brunt of the allegations day after day in the Commons. But now he was sideswiped himself. James Palmer, a Calgary lawyer, sent a $25,000 cheque that was intended for Martin's leadership campaign. But the cheque went to the wrong office, turning up at Liberal Party headquarters, which of course was full of Chrétien devotees. They took considerable interest in this cheque because the same James Palmer was being paid by Martin's finance department to provide advice on taxation in the energy sector. It had the look of a clear conflict. That the news of it was leaked to the media by Liberal headquarters surprised no one in Martin's entourage, and the finance minister quickly severed ties with Palmer.

THROUGH THE LIBERALS' UGLY WINTER and spring, the Alliance Party was in the throes of a leadership campaign that was won handily by Stephen Harper, who had been out of Ottawa for several years, working as head of the National Citizens Coalition. Vowing not to stab the new leader in the back, Stockwell Day—with the wounds still fresh in his own—stayed on as a regular MP, becoming the party's foreign affairs critic. He had lasted as leader less than two years, and barely a day of it had gone by without his being ridiculed in some fashion or another. The old saying about the cup being either half empty or half full didn't apply to the Alliance leader. With Day, it was completely empty. The fact that he could step down with any of his dignity intact was an accomplishment in itself.

The youthful, clean-cut Harper had depth on some files and could be expected to bring intellectual discipline to the party. But he was camera-cold, weak at the political art of glad-handing, and too far to the right of most Canadians to give the Liberals much cause for concern. He showed unusual warmth his first day as official Opposition leader. "I was four years old when the prime minister first took his seat in the Commons," he declared. "I recall turning to my mother, who is here today, and saying, 'Someone has to do something to stop that guy.'" But he was quick to find trouble, playing into the narrow, intolerant stereotype of old Reformers with belittling comments about the defeatist attitude of eastern Canadians and derogatory shots at Ottawa's Official Bilingualism program. Under siege in the Commons, he lost his cool and mistakenly addressed the Speaker as "Mr. Question."

In the Liberal camp, the upheaval and intrigue continued. Late one night, Chrétien's aide, Duncan Fulton, was at his girlfriend's house when he received a phone call from a Martin strategist. The caller accused Fulton of plotting to get a Martin supporter fired from a job in the private sector. He told him, "Fix it, or there will be consequences." Fulton wondered how the fellow even got the phone number. "My first response," he recalled, "was general surprise, because I had no idea what he was talking about. My second response was 'Fuck off!'"

Since the Cabinet shuffle, the prime minister had been aware that he was bleeding support. Caucus members were abandoning his team, and Hec Cloutier, the man responsible for keeping the soldiers happy, found there wasn't much that he could do about it. There weren't enough rewards in the system to keep the egos satisfied. The electoral sweeps in the province of Ontario were remarkable successes, but the re-election of the same one hundred people from the province was also the cause of instability in the party. They weren't advancing, and they blamed it on the guy at the top, the prime minister. They wanted a change. "And if it wasn't someone like Paul Martin," said Cloutier, "they would be looking someplace else."

THE PM WAS ISSUING MORE WARNINGS about all the unofficial campaigning for the leadership. Though the previous year he had agreed to let candidates start to organize, now he was clamping down. He didn't really care much about Rock and Copps. The target was Martin.

At earlier Cabinet meetings, Chrétien had made his views known to the finance minister. He wouldn't address Martin directly, but everyone knew who he was talking about. They knew because he would sometimes fix Martin with a cold stare. He would come in—everyone could tell his mood from his look—and he would talk about a newspaper story that indicated disloyalty. He would remind everyone around the table that this was not good for party solidarity and that they had to show unity under him. After the spiel, Chrétien would turn to his ministers for their approval, and like trained seals, everyone would agree with him.

By the time the finance minister was allowed to speak, Chrétien, as someone in the room described him, was in full "schoolyard bully" pose. Martin would argue that he could not possibly control the voices of all his supporters in the party or across the country. He grew red-faced on a couple of occasions, such was the prime minister's air of censure, and being such a competitive man, it was clear to everyone that he hated being embarrassed like this and that he was not about to forget it.

Members admired Martin for the restraint he showed in not brutally rebutting the prime minister. The finance minister, after all, was the government's pillar of strength. He was the most popular federal politician in the country, and he had the most support in the party. Yet here he was being treated like a truant at a boarding school.

Always with a ready answer to any charge, Chrétien's people would explain that he was not trying to target Martin specifically but was sending a message to all candidates. "Paul had one view—that he was being singled out—and the PM's view was that he never singled him out," Goldenberg explained in an interview. "He said [the PM] looked straight at him, but he also sat right across from him."

On Thursday, May 30, 2002, the stare across the table was longer and harder than ever before. Chrétien issued a direct order to Paul Martin to shut down all his campaigning activities. Martin had not anticipated the directive. He said he had had "no idea" it was coming. "I went into Cabinet on Thursday, and the prime minister came in and was really upset and basically said, 'No more campaigning. Stop fundraising, stop organizing.'" Martin paused as he recounted the story. "I don't know what the hell happened." Later that afternoon, he recalled, the calls started coming in to his office from the press. Reporters were telling him that "Francie's out there saying the prime minister stared you down in Cabinet." Then the next day, said Martin, "the whole thing blew up."

Both men were scheduled to speak in Toronto on Friday. Martin was also speaking to the Federation of Canadian Municipalities early in the day in Hamilton. Then he had a fundraiser in the evening, not far from the Ontario Liberal Party convention that Chrétien would be addressing.

David Smith, his key Ontario organizer and a strong loyalist, drove with Chrétien from the airport. He got the impression that the PM was moving the issue to a head, and that if Martin stepped down as a result, all the better. Smith's account gave credence to Martin's contention that the pushing was coming from the prime minister's side. Smith, in fact, told Chrétien that maybe it wasn't wise to push so hard. "I just think you're better off to have Martin in the tent," he advised.

But Chrétien was not in an accommodating frame of mind. "I don't think it was his intention to fire him," Smith later said, "but I didn't think he would do anything to stop him from walking." This was unfortunate, thought Smith, because "I think it could have been managed."

Intent on showing who was in command, the prime minister's staff tried to have parts of Martin's Hamilton speech changed. It wasn't a controversial speech, but they wanted Martin to delete references to a "new deal" between Ottawa and the municipalities. He refused, saying that he had never had his speeches vetted before. "I was supposed to make all kinds of changes to my speech, and I said no."

There had been two strikes: the Cabinet edict and the order on the speech. Now came a third. "Then they said I could not speak to the fundraiser in Toronto that night," recalled Martin. "And then after my speech, Francie [Ducros] sent the press over and said, 'Scrum him after the speech because he is being disloyal to the PM.'"

Goldenberg had a different take. "He was making a speech in Toronto at exactly the same time the PM was to address a different group, and didn't tell us. When we found that out, we tried to figure out what to do because we didn't want stories written that Chrétien had a thousand people and Martin had fifteen hundred. . . . I think his office was playing games. I think there were people on his side that wanted him out, and it was just a question of when."

Martin delivered his fundraising speech, met with strategists, and prepared a statement for the few reporters who were waiting downstairs in the hotel. "Some time ago," he said, "the prime minister stated that it was fine for people to organize for the leadership. In fact, he even encouraged some candidates to present their candidature. . . . Now it would appear that he has changed his mind. That's his prerogative." But, he added, "I just really don't know how this is going to work. I don't know what it means." Was it really true, he asked, that prime ministerial candidates couldn't go to riding meetings and fundraisers and party functions? Then Paul Martin dropped the bomb. "Let me just say that I am obviously going to have to reflect on my options."

He would have to reflect, he said, "given the events of the last couple of days, on my capacity now as a member of Cabinet, as a member of the government, to have an impact on those decisions, matters that I feel very strongly about. And the question is, Will my continuation in the Cabinet, given these events, permit me in fact to exercise the kind of responsibility and influence that I believe a minister of finance must?"

The reporters were stunned. If he was announcing his intention to quit, shouldn't he at least have informed the prime minister? Chrétien had gone to John Turner when he left the Liberals in 1986. Turner had visited Trudeau when he was about to resign as finance minister in 1975. What kind of way was this to do things? A basement scrum with reporters?

But Martin had not decided to leave yet. He said it would have been obvious to anyone who looked at his schedule that he didn't want to leave his finance post. "I sure as hell didn't want to resign. . . . I had the G-7 finance ministers' meeting in Halifax two weeks later. I had spent two years working on a massive education package for Africa and I really wanted to put it through, and I had a number of other things that only as chairman could I put through. The last thing in the world I wanted was to have this happen."

When the prime minister's camp got the news of the scrum, Goldenberg quickly concluded that Martin wanted to leave. "The first thing that happened," he recalled of the weekend, "was that Paul went on television and said he wasn't sure he could remain in Cabinet. That is effectively resigning. I think he would have liked to resign and keep his job at the same time, because he loved his job."

On Saturday, Chrétien appeared at one of the big social events of the year, the annual Parliamentary Press Gallery dinner. He woke up that day to headlines about Martin's threat and to a four-page spread in the *Ottawa Citizen* titled "The Collected Untruths of Jean Chrétien." Painstakingly, the article went through his version of events on Shawinigate, pointing out a barrage of contradictory and misleading statements he'd made. An editorial in the paper, in keeping with many editorials across the land, said that it was time for the PM to step down. Izzy Asper, the head of CanWest Global, happened to be in town for the dinner. The Aspers had made it known that they wouldn't tolerate criticism of the prime minister's activities in his own riding. Russell Mills, the popular publisher of the *Ottawa Citizen,* would be gone from his post before the month was out. His departure prompted a storm of protest against the Aspers over freedom of the press. Four thousand disgusted *Citizen* readers cancelled their subscriptions.

At the dinner, which Martin did not attend, the prime minister got off a few jokes, in keeping with the tradition of the event, and left to tend to the crisis. He had asked Eddie Goldenberg, who had known Martin for decades, to speak to him. But discussions did not proceed far. Goldenberg found that there was no room for compromise, that Martin was prepared to leave and there was no trust left in the relationship. He wanted a statement from Martin clarifying his position and declaring his loyalty to the prime minister. That was not possible. Martin's team wanted a statement from Chrétien clarifying his support for the finance minister. That was not possible.

Cabinet members and Liberal MPs were urging both parties to act like adults and patch things up. Anne McLellan told Paul Martin that she couldn't believe the immaturity. Had the situation involved two women, she told him, they would have been able to resolve it easily. Goldenberg spent a lot of time on the phone with Martin. At one point, he recalled him saying, "The link of confidence between the prime minister and the minister of finance has been broken." Goldenberg responded, "'Paul, is there anything more? I don't want to read tomorrow that if only you'd had a phone call or something, you would have stayed. Is there anything?' And he said no."

On Sunday, Martin was en route to Ottawa from his farm in the Eastern Townships when his car phone rang. It was the prime minister, ostensibly wanting to know if Martin had made up his mind about his future. The finance minister still had not decided. He needed more

time, he said. The prime minister was concerned about the reaction of
the markets. He wanted a decision in a hurry. Sensing that Martin was
noncommittal, he handed the phone to Eddie Goldenberg, who began
reading a letter that said Martin had decided to leave, by mutual
consent with the prime minister. Martin said he was not prepared to
sign any such letter.

Later in the afternoon, Martin heard on Rex Murphy's *Cross
Country Checkup* on CBC Radio that there was to be a Cabinet
shuffle that afternoon. He couldn't have been terribly surprised.
Earlier in the day, finance department officials had been called to his
office to prepare a speech for the new minister of finance, who was
to be John Manley.

Martin went to the National Press Theatre on Wellington Street
and, without putting it in specific words, implied that he had been
fired. The Martin strategists had figured out that Chrétien would
come across as the bad guy if he was seen to be dismissing the highly
popular minister. Much better to have the story portrayed that way
than for Martin to be seen as a quitter. Percy Downe and others in
the PMO sensed that the story was turning in this direction, and
they sent out Goldenberg for a rare television appearance to try to
set things straight. But there was not much media pickup on what
he said.

Looking back almost two years later, Goldenberg remained angry
about Martin's portrayal of events. He said he knew that Martin had
phoned Manley earlier in the afternoon to wish him well in his new
job. Then, recalled Goldenberg, "he said he was fired, and I found that
a little hard to stomach."

Nonsense, Martin would later say. "I spoke to Eddie and said,
'The situation is pretty serious. It's very hard to see how there is
going to be a reconciliation, but I'm not resigning now. I haven't
made up my mind.' I made that very clear. I had not decided." As
for Goldenberg's claim he had called Manley, that was dead wrong,
said Martin. "Manley called me. I didn't call Manley. And I returned

his call, and what I said to him was, 'If I go, then I hope you replace me.' And I was very, very clear to everyone that I had not made up my mind."

Martin came to a rock-hard conclusion—that the prime minister had organized a plot to get rid of him. He and his supporters wanted to force him out—and they did. "I thought it was very clear that some plan had been put in place," Martin said in an interview in 2003. "What happened in Cabinet . . . I mean, there are Cabinet leaks, but this one took about three seconds. Then all of a sudden— bang!" He went on, "I'm not playing any games here. This thing started on Thursday . . . then I reacted on Saturday. Look, I'm not saying that I would have stayed in the job the next twenty years, but the fact is, I learned about John Manley's appointment on the radio. If I was going to resign, I would resign to the prime minister. I wouldn't resign to John Manley."

Chrétien, looking composed, named Manley his new minister of finance that afternoon at Rideau Hall. "Mr. Martin and I agreed for the good of the governance of the country that it was better that he was not to be the minister of finance," he told the assembled journalists. "I said to him that I was very sad."

The next day's headline in *The Globe and Mail* read, "Chrétien Fires Martin." It was spun just as the Martin team had wanted it— Chrétien as the villain, Martin the martyr. Some took an opposing view. The historian Jack Granatstein noted at the time that "Martin has worked against Chrétien and organized against Chrétien continuously. Frankly, I don't blame the prime minister for being angry with him. The way Chrétien has pushed him out is pretty rough but quite understandable."

"I think Martin was ready to leave and it was just a matter of timing," Goldenberg reasoned. "I don't think it should have been done the way it was done, but I think it was done with the best of intentions." It was probably a long time in coming, he added. "The fact that it didn't happen for eight years was pretty good."

Chrétien had long been advised to move Martin aside. He had resisted, fearing the potential backlash. Now he was about to see if that backlash would come. The prime minister had pushed Martin out. Now the question was whether Martin would push the prime minister out.

Jean Chrétien is embraced by his wife, Aline, upon winning
the Liberal leadership in Calgary in June 1990.
By permission of Jean-Marc Carisse, www.carisse.org.

On a plane to Ottawa, the day following his 1993 election
victory, Chrétien meets tête-à-tête with Eddie Goldenberg
(senior policy advisor) and Jean Pelletier (chief of staff).
By permission of Jean-Marc Carisse, www.carisse.org.

By permission of Jean-Marc Carisse, www.carisse.org.

A study in glares: Jean Chrétien monitors Paul Martin (top) at the Red Book launch in Ottawa during Election Campaign 1993; and (bottom) Liberal caucus chair Stan Keyes, a Paul Martin supporter, gets the look from Chrétien at a press conference in Chicoutimi in August 2002, where—under pressure from his caucus—Chrétien announced his decision to eventually step down.

Photograph by Diana Murphy. By permission of the Office of the Prime Minister.

Chrétien meets privately in Montreal with Daniel Johnson (Quebec
Liberal leader) and Jean Charest (federal Conservative leader)
prior to the referendum on October 30, 1995.

Photograph by Jean-Marc Carisse. By permission of the Office of the Prime Minister.

The infamous Shawinigan Chokehold of 1996: The PM's wife,
Aline, thought her husband would have to resign after being
filmed grabbing a protester by the throat in February 1996.

Photo courtesy of Global Television Network, A CanWest Company.

With U.S. President Bill Clinton following
a round of golf during the June 1995
G-7 Summit in Halifax. Chrétien's
final score was a "state secret."

Photograph by Jean-Marc Carisse.
By permission of the Office of the Prime Minister.

Prime Minister Chrétien
offers a farewell handshake
to Fidel Castro in Cuba
on April 28, 1998.

Photograph by Jean-Marc Carisse.
By permission of the Office
of the Prime Minister.

Jean Chrétien stands on a desk and addresses his caucus in the
Government Lobby (prior to Question Period) following
a meeting with the provincial premiers on February 4, 1999.

Photograph by Jean-Marc Carisse. By permission of the Office of the Prime Minister.

Chrétien, with "Blues Brother" Dan Aykroyd, playing "Let the Good Times Roll" at 24 Sussex Drive on April 15, 1999.
Photograph by Jean-Marc Carisse. By permission of the Office of the Prime Minister.

The key players making their way to Parliament in 2001. From left, Jean Chrétien, Françoise Ducros, Percy Downe, and Eddie Goldenberg.
Photograph by Diana Murphy. By permission of the Office of the Prime Minister.

Following the death of Pierre Trudeau in September 2000, his son Justin is greeted by Prime Minister Chrétien in the lobby of Parliament.
Photograph by Jean-Marc Carisse. By permission of the Office of the Prime Minister.

In the heat of the Shawinigate controversy in January
of 2001, Chrétien has a cold Commons exchange
with Bloc Québécois leader Gilles Duceppe.
*Photograph by Diana Murphy. By permission of the
Office of the Prime Minister.*

Britain's Tony Blair receives a round of applause during
his visit to the House of Commons in February 2001.
Photograph by Diana Murphy. By permission of the Office of the Prime Minister.

Meet and greet in the Oval Office: Jean Chrétien has his first
official sit-down with George W. Bush in February 2001.

Photograph by Diana Murphy. By permission of the Office of the Prime Minister.

In the wake of the September 11 attacks, Chrétien and other Canadian
political party leaders view the catastrophe from close up
at Ground Zero in New York City.

Photograph by Diana Murphy. By permission of the Office of the Prime Minister.

By permission of Reuters News Picture Service. Photograph by Jim Young.

Two types of prime ministers: Jean Chrétien (top) looking thuggish with his entourage in January 2002; and (bottom) the PM embraces one of his heroes, Nelson Mandela, in September 2002.

Photograph by Diana Murphy. By permission of the Office of the Prime Minister.

CHAPTER SEVENTEEN

"WE WERE BEING STUPID ..."

T HREE DAYS AFTER Paul Martin left the Cabinet, the Liberal
Party caucus, its unity shredded, sat down for its weekly session
with the prime minister. Normally, the prime minister listened to all
the comments from the floor, then closed with his own observations.
Past prime ministers had rarely veered from this routine. Mulroney
was known for his soothing strokes, Trudeau was a study in patience,
Mackenzie King was famous for his incisive summations. But in the
past couple of years, Chrétien had been dispensing with the convention and interrupting members along the way. Herb Gray and other
veterans, believing this was the time when members were supposed to
have their say, were unimpressed.

At this particular caucus, Chrétien didn't wait for any of the
others. Tense but trying to stay calm, he opened with a twenty-
minute speech of his own. He acknowledged having made a mistake
a year earlier by giving ministers the green light to start organizing
leadership campaigns. The whole business had got out of hand. They
were raising money for themselves, not the party. Discipline had to
be restored.

He praised Paul Martin for having been a strong minister of
finance. It was not a matter of firing him, he told his troops, but he'd
needed a quick answer from Martin because David Dodge, the governor of the Bank of Canada, had told him that the situation had to be
resolved before the Asian financial markets opened on Sunday
evening. It was clear that some in the room were sceptical about
Chrétien's version of events, and when he began talking of how he had

tried to prevent the final break with the finance minister, the guffaws were almost audible. "Horseshit," one Martin supporter whispered in another's ear. "Absolute horseshit."

Chrétien's spiel concluded with an obligatory ovation. A couple of his loyalists then stood to defend what he had done, but the large majority spoke out against him, including members he wouldn't have expected, like Raymond Bonin and Roy Cullen. The Ontario caucus had met earlier in the day. John Manley, the new finance minister, had appealed for calm, saying that members should refrain from criticizing the prime minister because they would damage the brand of the office. He was shouted down.

In the full caucus, the Martin backers took their turns at the microphone. Anger spilled from their every phrase. They told the prime minister that his move against the finance minister was inexcusable. He had forced out the party's one big star. He was labelled a bully, a dictator, a man so power hungry that he was placing his own welfare ahead of everything else. Dan McTeague, a bulldog for Martin, called on Chrétien to step down. "You made a decision for Paul Martin," McTeague said. "You should make the same decision for yourself."

Watching in amazement was Carolyn Parrish. She was disappointed that Chrétien hadn't put her in Cabinet, but she still couldn't believe the treatment he was receiving from "these ungrateful sons of bitches." She had never witnessed anything quite like it. "They purposely went in there, every single one of them, and slowly stuck in another knife. It was a concentrated effort to destroy him." She watched Chrétien's reaction. "His face was evil. His eyes were like a shark's eyes." She couldn't understand why he didn't just get up and walk out. "Any other person would have," she said, "especially knowing that most of those assholes telling you this couldn't get elected dog catcher if they weren't on a Liberal ticket on your coattails."

Caucus members attacked Francie Ducros as well, complaining about her abrasive style. With reference to her predecessor, Peter Donolo, they started chanting, "Bring back Peter! Bring back Peter!"

There was no chance of that. By standing up so vigorously for the prime minister, Ducros had endeared herself to him—and to Aline Chrétien. Ducros sometimes spoke on the phone to the prime minister's wife several times a day. Any complaints about Ducros, or Chrétien's other pit bull, Warren Kinsella, didn't get past Aline's door. She treasured loyalty. Her husband was under siege, and if Ducros and Kinsella were going around throwing hand grenades at his adversaries, well, then, all the better. Let those "ungrateful sons of bitches," as Parrish called them, have it right between the eyes.

Goldenberg was hearing angry reports about Ducros and Kinsella as well. The changes in PMO personnel had hurt, Goldenberg recalled. "I think Peter Donolo did a fabulous job, and I think Terrie O'Leary did a fabulous job. I think we lost a lot with both of them. . . . But I don't think Paul left the Cabinet because of Francie."

Chrétien's staff anxiously awaited the polls after Martin's exit. They wondered if this would be the moment when Jean Chrétien finally experienced the great free fall. The year had featured one dreadful piece of news after another—resignations, scandals, firings—all culminating in the loss of the government's number-one star.

He did lose some support, but not much. One poll showed that 46 percent approved of the way he was handling his job. While it was rare that he dipped below the 50-percent mark, 46 percent was still respectable. Brian Mulroney had languished in the teens. Pierre Trudeau had fallen into the twenties. More important, the loss of Martin had not had a substantial impact on his party's standing. The Liberals maintained their customary thirty-point lead on the nearest rival.

Again, Chrétien was fortunate. Again, he had a weak opposition to rely on. On the day Martin left, Stephen Harper, who should have seen it coming, was caught unawares. He appeared before the cameras in the Centre Block wearing a drab brown golf shirt, looking like he had just climbed out of his hammock. In the next few days, his shirt received more press than did his reaction to the news.

Voters weren't warming to Harper, nor were they excited about the return engagement of Joe Clark. It was clear he wasn't moving the yardsticks for the party. The Tories' support level was in the teens, just as it had been for many years. With the Alliance firmly on the right flank, Clark moved to the centre. He aimed to keep the Conservatives a "big tent" party because he understood that in Canada only that kind of party could win. But no one knew what Clark and the Tories stood for, what set them apart from the Grits. The country already had one political war dog in the middle, offering the politics of pragmatism. Why have another? Moreover, Clark's fight with the Alliance over the concept of a united right had been debilitating. He looked like he was about to benefit when a few Alliance rebels split with Stockwell Day and then sat with the Tories, but the disaffected soon returned to their party after Harper took over.

Clark had been uncertain whether he would lead the party into another election. He now decided to hand over the reins, announcing a leadership convention for May 2003. Day had fallen, Clark was leaving, and now the NDP's Alexa McDonough made it three. Like Clark, McDonough had earned a degree of respect from the public, but, also like him, she couldn't light a spark under her party. The media paid her little heed. She seemed forever the provincial leader from Nova Scotia.

While the failures of the others sustained the Liberals' ranking in the polls, there was a downside to having a pusillanimous opposition. The spectre of an enemy unites. The lack of one divides. The Liberals had lingered too long without having someone to rally against. "We didn't have a common enemy," said Senator Sharon Carstairs. "So we started fighting among ourselves."

The mix was too explosive to contain—no common enemy, no bracing policy agenda, a caucus full of men and women who hadn't found political reward, and an heir apparent ready to reward them.

Paul Martin was free now to organize for the February 2003 review of Chrétien's leadership. He maintained his status as an MP, returning to the House a few days after his resignation to a resounding ovation. Now he could travel more, spend more time on organization and platform development. He was still not in a position to speak out on major policies. The official leadership race had not begun yet. Also, he had been a central part of the government and its policy-making machinery for almost nine years. He couldn't suddenly turn around and start advocating policies that were radically different.

Because of Chrétien's indecisiveness about running for another term, members had started wandering off. He hadn't tended to the flock. They hadn't been kept in line. Chrétien would later admit that he had let things slide. "I wasn't going to run again myself, so the organization and who is president of what riding was my last preoccupation."

He had lost touch. Early in 2002, on a Saturday evening, a consultant who was an occasional golfing companion received a call from the PM as he was preparing for a dinner party. "So," Chrétien began, "how would I do in a review vote?" Before his friend could respond, the PM estimated his strength at about 80 percent. The consultant was shocked. "Ah, Prime Minister, I think it would be a little less than that." The PM tried 70 percent. After all, he'd received 90 percent in his last review vote. Even John Turner, after being trounced in the 1984 election, won a 76-percent endorsement from the party. The consultant knew Chrétien was a man of sound political instincts. How, he wondered, could he be this far off? He finally got around to telling him that he thought he would be lucky to hit 60 percent.

After Martin's resignation, it became clear that Chrétien would have to campaign hard if he was to avoid defeat in a leadership review. The prime minister had planned to spend much of the summer on the golf course. Instead, he had to suffer the humiliation of phoning back-bench MPs to beg them for their support so he could survive the review. No one could imagine Trudeau or Pearson or St. Laurent going through such a degrading exercise. Opposition leaders sometimes had to do this. But this was a prime minister who had won three majorities in succession and was sitting on a thirty-point lead in the

polls in a country where the economy was performing well, unity
was intact, and the people were relatively content.

Walt Lastewka, the MP from St. Catharines, Ontario, was a
supporter of Martin's, but he liked Chrétien, and until recently he had
been loyal to him. He had seen Martin and Chrétien work together,
and he had been impressed. As a former senior executive at General
Motors, he knew how difficult it could be to get things done when
there were differences at the top. But they had done it, and he gave
them credit for it. He began to notice a change at the PMO, however.

One day in June, he was driving with his wife and daughter near
Toronto when the PM called him. Right away, Lastewka could tell that
something was wrong. Chrétien "wasn't himself." Lastewka had chaired
the Industry Committee meeting the previous day, a difficult assignment because Howard Wilson, the ethics counsellor, had appeared. The
thought initially crossed Lastewka's mind that Chrétien was calling to
compliment him on handling the job well. But then, hearing his tone
of voice, he thought, Who the hell put him up to this? There was no
banter, just a direct question: "How are you voting on February 19?"

Lastewka told Chrétien that he had been the right man for the
job up to that point, but, he said, "I think it's time for a change."
At first, it seemed as if the PM understood. But then he launched
into an attack on Paul Martin, one that Lastewka felt "just wasn't
warranted." Chrétien even questioned Martin's competence. Finally,
it got so bad that Lastewka cut the conversation short. He didn't
want to hear any more.

The Hill Times newspaper, a feisty tabloid that reports on
Parliament, published a survey of Liberal MPs. It was devastating
for the PM. It showed only fifty-two members supporting him,
ninety-four for Martin, others undecided. Caucus support was crucial
for the coming review. The PM got hold of the list—he was a great
list-keeper himself—and set about trying to have it redrawn. Calls
went out to people in the Martin column and pressure was applied,
particularly to the Cabinet ministers. In a sign that the centre still

exercised considerable power, several Martin backers, including Anne McLellan, Ralph Goodale, and David Anderson, had their names moved to the Chrétien column.

The PM continued to express confidence that in the crunch, his Liberal family would support him and he would be around to celebrate his tenth anniversary in power in the fall of 2003. "I will be prime minister in November—no doubt about it," he told CBC Newsworld's Don Newman, "because I know the Liberal Party, and the Liberal Party will show confidence in the leader who has won three majorities for them."

THE G-8 SUMMIT in Kananaskis, Alberta, on June 26 and 27, 2002, gave him the opportunity to move the focus off politics and onto real matters of governance. Chrétien had adroitly carved out his own agenda for the summit, turning the focus on poverty in Africa. In exchange for commitments to democratic and economic reform from African states, he was pushing the G-8 members to come up with large infusions of aid, a quasi Marshall Plan for Africa. To critics, it had the desperate look of a Chrétien-come-lately effort to salvage some respect, especially given the heavy cuts in foreign aid in his early years in power. "All of a sudden, Jean Chrétien discovered Africa," wrote the journalist Andrew Cohen in his book *While Canada Slept*. "It held no attraction for him in his first eight and a half years of stewardship. . . . So behold Saint Jean of Dakar and Addis Ababa, saviour of Africa's struggling masses."

Chrétien had done some homework, travelling to Africa to get a first-hand look, meeting with many of the leaders there, and lobbying all the G-8 leaders in preparation for the summit. As the leader with more seniority than them all, as the host of the event, he had at least a semblance of authority. What he was lacking was a big push from the Americans. At the time of the summit, Ottawa and Washington were feuding over the softwood lumber issue and George W. Bush's farm subsidy policies, which Chrétien called stupid. The omission of

Canada from Bush's big speech to Congress, the Bush friendship with
Mulroney, and Canada's opposition to American unilateralism were all
part of the mix. To make matters worse, four Canadian soldiers were
killed by an American F-16 pilot in a live-fire training exercise in
Afghanistan. The great euphemism of the time for such dumb and
deadly incidents was "friendly fire."

There was another problem. While Bush's efforts in Afghanistan
following September 11 had received the full support of the Canadian
government, the president had begun to worry Ottawa with his talk of
expanding the war on terrorism to other countries. Iraq had suddenly
moved front and centre, although there was no evidence the country
had had anything to do with the events of September 11. Chrétien
made his position clear at the end of 2001. Unless some firm link was
established, he was not interested in having Canada participate in any
war against Iraq.

The prime minister didn't feel he had to take any lessons from the
new boy in the White House. His own experience in the world, after
so many years as PM, was far deeper, far broader. He came from a
Liberal tradition wherein the party leaders had often acted as a voice
of restraint against American adventurism—and many did just that
with some degree of vindication. Lester Pearson had courageously
challenged Lyndon Johnson, warning him against the escalation of the
Vietnam War. In the early 1980s, Pierre Trudeau had launched an
idealistic and much-ridiculed world peace tour to try to encourage
the Soviets and the Americans to meet at the bargaining table. While
Washington ignored him, the spirit of what he and his top adviser,
Tom Axworthy (brother of Lloyd), were advocating was later picked
up by Mikhail Gorbachev and Ronald Reagan, who brought about
the great thaw that led to the end of the Cold War.

Just as the Kananaskis summit was about to begin, Bush veered off
in a direction Ottawa could hardly appreciate. In a major speech on
the Middle East, the president called for the election of a new
Palestinian leadership, with a proposal for an independent Palestinian

state to follow. It became the early focus of the summit, steering attention away from Chrétien's African initiative. Bush had earlier promised a broad increase in foreign aid, but he wasn't about to do Chrétien any favours by turning the African initiative into a landmark moment. There were nice words but no ironclad commitments from America or the other participants for the billions of dollars a year in new aid that Chrétien wanted. He put the best face on the loose pledges. "We have a deal," he said, "a deal that represents a new beginning and a fresh hope for the African continent. We have acted collectively to make sure globalization benefits all the citizens of the globe, and that no continent is left behind."

He could well boast that Kananaskis was a stylistic triumph. Having seen previous summits get bogged down by massive delegations of bureaucrats, Chrétien limited the numbers, and the streamlined summit was talked about as a model for others to come.

Then it was back to full-time survival politics. The Chrétien team that had brought him victories in the past was pulled together and told to go thermonuclear if necessary to prevent Paul Martin from bringing down the king. John Rae, David Smith, David Collenette, Jean Carle, and a host of others at the PMO went to work. Chrétien kept *The Hill Times* list in front of him and continued to work it over and move wayward Liberals into his column. He even invited the author of *The Hill Times* article, Angelo Persichielli, to 24 Sussex to sound him out.

But while the arm-twisting gradually increased the numbers in his column, he could instill no momentum in his campaign. Since he was not committed to running for a fourth term, why, his friends asked, was he putting himself through this?

The Chrétien character held the answer. It was yet another example of the man whose pride would not let him give way—even when caught, even when trapped, even when there was virtually no way out—to an admission of error or defeat. Better a charade. Better to put himself and the government through hell than to be seen to be giving in to the natural successor at a natural time for transition. Chrétien was losing Cabinet ministers, his caucus was in revolt, the nation's business was on hold, all because he would not say he would step down. Had he made such a declaration a year or even a few months earlier, the war with the Martin wing would have ended, the party could have reunited, and Canadians would have admired Jean Chrétien all the more.

The defiant prime minister would say repeatedly that he couldn't announce his intention to leave early because he then would be a lame duck and it would be hard to get the work of government done. But, eventually, when he did become a lame duck, he would claim that there was no problem whatsoever with carrying on as usual. Why, every American president, he would say, was a lame duck for his entire second term.

IN JUNE 2002, he went to Stratford, Ontario, home of the Shakespearean theatre festival, for a photo-op with some of the actors. His staff hadn't realized that the players were rehearsing *Richard III*, a tragedy in which the king is slain. The optics were not the most favourable, and his communications team alerted him to this. But Chrétien told his staff to go ahead and invite everybody in. After watching the rehearsal, the prime minister jumped to the stage and took a sword from an actor. He explained that in the House of Commons, there was a reason why the governing and Opposition desks were across the floor from one another. "It's so you can't do this!" he cried, lunging at the man and pointing the sword to his neck. Then, sabre in hand, Chrétien spun around, looking playfully at the others in the cast, and demanded, "So who wants to go?" He spotted the lead player—"So, you're the king?" he asked—and, showing off his amateur fencing skills, almost knocked the sword out of his opponent's hands. He then stuck his sabre to the king's chest and announced, "Thank you very much."

On the airplane on the way home, Chrétien was sitting with Duncan Fulton, reliving the moment. "He was trying to kill me," the prime minister explained, "so I had to kill him first." Then he looked at his staffer and said, "That's politics, young man."

Politics was war, and his former warriors continued to desert him. The Toronto MP Jim Karygiannis was the dedicated, fiercely competitive worker who had stuck gum in telephone slots to sabotage Martin's campaigning in the 1990 leadership race. Now the PM wanted him to repeat the performance, and he told his campaign managers to call Karygiannis. But Jimmy K was one of the many in the Ontario caucus who had never been rewarded for their service. He hadn't even come close to a Cabinet seat. Funny thing, he said, when they called him this time, "You've never had the time of day to call me before." During the 2000 election, Chrétien came to Toronto and was in his riding telling people, "You know, Jimmy's a great friend of mine and has done a hell of a job." At that, one of Karygiannis's friends piped up, "Well, if he's so good, why didn't you appoint him to Cabinet?"

Hearing now of Jimmy K's hesitance, Chrétien reached into the bag of political tricks and pulled out an old one. Karygiannis's father was gravely ill at home in Greece. Chrétien had never met the man, but got his phone number and reached him on his sick bed to wish him a full recovery. The phone call and all the other lobbying didn't help, however. Karygiannis told Chrétien that he could no longer support him, and that he should leave while he could still do so with his dignity intact.

Pressure came from the old party establishment as well. Tom Kent, an architect of Liberal policy in the Pearson and Trudeau years and still a voice of some gravitas, told the media that Chrétien had grown too fond of power and was listening to sycophants. "You tend, of course, to get surrounded by toadies who won't say anything other than you're wonderful. . . . The present Cabinet is looking pathetic in those terms." He asked that those Cabinet members consider how loyal Chrétien had been to John Turner.

Martin had collected a big campaign war chest over four years. In 2002, the prime minister brought in Cabinet guidelines requiring members to publish the names of campaign contributors. Technically,

since Martin was out of Cabinet, he didn't have to adhere to the regulation. Chrétien supporters suggested he had something to hide—
namely, the identities of people who had donated to his campaign
while getting business from his finance department. But Martin had a
one-word reason for not wishing to release the names yet: retaliation.
Those seen as Martin supporters risked losing their positions. To
bolster their argument, Martinites pointed to the case of Raymond
Garneau, who had been sitting on the board of the Bank of Canada
since March 1996. Garneau had made the mistake of saying it was
time for Martin to take over. His seat at the bank board was not renewed.

In late July, Pope John Paul II visited Toronto for World Youth Day
celebrations. The event had been organized by Dennis Mills. He spent
the weekend with Chrétien, the two of them sitting for hours through
outdoor masses and addresses by the pope to hundreds of thousands.
One night, Mills met Sister Yoshim, the successor to Mother Teresa.
She told him that Mother Teresa had never really liked politicians. And
why was that? asked Mills. "It's because," she said, "she always thought
they did things for the love of power rather than the love of people."
The words stuck in Mills's memory, and he repeated them to the PM,
who didn't react.

Aline was present at the papal extravaganza too. She knew that
although he had not made it to Cabinet, Mills was still quite loyal.
"Jean has told me you're always with us," she said, thanking him. But
she didn't seem to realize how bad the situation had become. "Aline,
I'm with you," Mills said. "But I want to tell you that we have a gap
here that we can't fix."

Mills was a politician who tended to ham things up, who never
met an overreaction that he didn't like. But he was convinced that the
weekend in the presence of the pope, away from political combat, had
a significant impact on Chrétien. He thought it had restored the
PM's inner compass, got him thinking more about his old activist
beliefs and less about ego-driven survival. By coincidence, Chrétien
was seeing the pope in the same week that his adopted son was

brought up on more sex-related charges. Michel, thirty-three, was charged with sexual assault by the RCMP in Yellowknife after a preliminary investigation into a complaint filed by an eighteen-year-old woman. The victim's mother had originally contacted the PMO about the alleged attack, and she later spoke of pressure not to press charges. Hurt by the big play the media gave the story, Chrétien released a statement saying it appeared that Michel had relapsed into his long-standing troubles with substance abuse. "We have been heartened at the progress he has been making, and we're deeply discouraged by his apparent relapse."

In 1971, when he and Aline took the boy from an orphanage in Inuvik, Michel was only eighteen months old. There was no way they could have known the problems that awaited them. Later, there were suspicions that Michel suffered from fetal alcohol syndrome. The prime minister was raised in a strong Catholic environment, and Michel's crimes cut deeply. Friends say he poured out as much kindness and understanding as he could. Though the media didn't know it, the prime minister had made quiet trips to Saskatchewan to visit Michel when he was incarcerated for previous offences.

After attending the papal mass, where he could offer prayers for his son, Chrétien met with Peter Mansbridge. The CBC anchor was preparing a big special for the first anniversary of September 11. Mansbridge had interviewed Chrétien from time to time over a twenty-year stretch, but he had never seen him in such a vulnerable, sensitive frame of mind. The son, the pope, the suffering he saw in Africa, the political rebels at his gate—it was all taking a toll, and the more he and Mansbridge talked, the more reflective the PM became. When the conversation turned to September 11, he was drawn out on the question of what might have motivated the terrorist attacks.

Mansbridge left knowing he had a fascinating segment on his hands—and he also knew something else. In the months before the interview, he had been telling colleagues that Chrétien would fight on, say to hell with Paul Martin, and run for a fourth term. But now he sat down and wrote an e-mail to the Ottawa bureau chief, Keith Boag. Something is different now, Mansbridge told him. "Forget my earlier prediction. There will be no fourth term."

Chrétien's organizers, meanwhile, had been taking hard politics to the limit. John Rae, Don Boudria, and others had come up with the idea of cementing support from caucus members by having them sign letters pledging their undying commitment to Jean Chrétien. It was tantamount to a blood oath, and when the calls started going out, the reaction was swift.

Dennis Mills was among those approached. "So I get this call from Collenette at my cottage, and he says, 'Look, we've got this letter that we want you to sign.' I said, 'I'm not signing any fucking letter.' Collenette replied, 'Well, will you at least listen to me read it?' 'You can give it a try,'" Mills recalled saying. "'But [whoever] has come up with this idea has got to have shit for brains.'" Collenette read it. Mills said forget it.

Liza Frulla, the one-time member of the Quebec legislature, had been recruited by the federal Liberals and won a by-election in May 2002. She had always been a friend of Martin's, and she saw her future in the party with him. But it was Chrétien who had invited her to join the team, and the PMO was angry that she was not declaring her support in return. They came after her, threatening reprisals and even trying to get the president of her riding association to discredit her.

Frulla put in a call to Quebec's justice minister, Martin Cauchon, who was involved in the strong-arming. "I picked up the phone," recalled Frulla, "and I said, 'Don't do this. Don't fuck with me like this. You guys, you're kids. What we've lived through politically in Quebec, you're kids.'" She then arranged to replace the riding president with her friend Francis Fox.

Carolyn Parrish was appalled at the blood-oath campaign. "You scratch your head and wonder. It just showed a certain desperation with the people surrounding Chrétien. It was like someone had come in with a giant vacuum and sucked the brains out of their ears. Pelletier would have slapped them about the head and shoulders had they tried coming up with this."

It was backfiring. "Tactical stupidity" was how Joe Fontana, the former caucus chair, described it. Chrétien had never been so heavy-handed early in his governance. "He used his natural instincts," said Fontana. "But then they took them away from him." Members were coming to Chrétien's caucus liaison, Hec Cloutier, to say that it was downright insulting. Cloutier had never liked the plan, but as part of the team, he had to play the game. "I want to make it clear," he later said. "It wasn't my idea."

Only about 55 percent of caucus signed the letter, a heavy embarrassment, particularly given that Cabinet members and their parliamentary assistants didn't have much choice but to sign—even if they were Team Martin members. The numbers sent a clear message to Chrétien. Diehards like Collenette and John Rae told him that in the crunch he would still win the review, that the party wouldn't turn around and vote against a sitting prime minister with such a winning record. Others, a large number of others, made a different argument. If he was determined to run for a fourth term, they told him, then he should push ahead. If he wasn't keen, however, it made no sense to fight a review, to further split the party. Why do it if you're going to step down anyway?

The more pertinent question was, Why do it if he was going to lose or win by a fifty-plus-one vote, a margin not good enough even for the separatists? The party's annual caucus meeting was scheduled for mid-August in Chicoutimi, Quebec, Lucien Bouchard's home region. A few days before they were to leave, Eddie Goldenberg had lunch with the prime minister. Their partnership in power had lasted almost thirty years. They had had over a thousand of these lunches. At this one, Goldenberg got directly to the point. "I asked him if he was going to run again in the next election," he recalled. Chrétien said no. Well, then, Goldenberg said, in reference to the review vote, "Why go through with it?" Why not stake out what you want to accomplish with the rest of your mandate and say you'll be leaving when that is done? In other words, leave on your own clock, not when Martin wants it.

There was no possibility of a Chrétien–Martin summit meeting, a head-to-head session where the two of them could thrash out their differences and sign a treaty for the remainder of Chrétien's term. Goldenberg would have been the one to bring them together, but he had concluded "it wasn't doable." If their personal animosity towards each other wasn't enough, there was the problem of the people around them. "I remember reading a piece," said Goldenberg, "that said they don't hate each other, but that they have 'designated haters,' and I think we went through a lot of that."

Mitchell Sharp, who had been at Chrétien's side even longer than Goldenberg, called Susan Delacourt of the *National Post* to his office a few days before the caucus gathering was to begin. He told her that the prime minister wasn't interested in seeking a fourth term. He just wanted to complete his work, then leave in a graceful way. He expressed puzzlement that the two men were so far apart when no significant differences on policy separated them. It was all about Martin's determination to be prime minister, he concluded. Yes, but is it a bad thing to have such an ambition? asked Delacourt. "Not particularly," answered the elder statesman. "It could have been difficult for the prime minister if the person concerned put that ahead of his responsibilities. That's a different matter. I never heard that [Martin] did that."

The PMO played down Sharp's remarks about Chrétien's lack of interest in a fourth term. But some remembered that Sharp had been the one who had announced that the PM would release the documentation on the Shawinigan controversy. Though that too was denied, Chrétien later did that very thing.

Meanwhile, the battle of the lists continued. Senators Laurier LaPierre and Sharon Carstairs released one showing that a huge majority of Liberal senators backed the PM. Chrétien loyalists then called a press conference to say that they had 94 of the 170 MPs onside. But the next day, desertions began. Five MPs came forward to say their names shouldn't be on the list and ask that they be withdrawn.

Chrétien would explain later that he had planned on announcing in December that he would not be seeking a fourth term. When the pressure continued to build, he changed his mind. He decided he would announce his intention to leave on September 10, his wedding anniversary. But then he switched plans again. His team was scheduling fundraisers so he would have the money to fight the review campaign. But since he had decided he wasn't going through with the review, he didn't want to do those events. "When they said, 'You have to raise money,' I said the hell with it," he recalled. He would make the announcement in Chicoutimi in August.

At Chicoutimi's Hôtel Le Montagnais, he delivered a major speech that gave every indication he planned to stay for a long time to come. The policy agenda he was laying out would probably require two more budgets to complete, he said. The agenda was popping with activist stuff, plans that had been sidetracked by the deficit, the terrorist attacks, and the Liberal Party civil war. There were announcements on aboriginal policy, child poverty, infrastructure for cities, the environment, health care, research and development.

"I confess that our agenda may not meet with the approval of Bay Street or the *National Post* or even *The Globe and Mail,*" said Chrétien. "But it is an agenda for Main Street, for Saguenay–Lac St-Jean, for the east side of Vancouver and the interior of Newfoundland, for Regent Park in Toronto and Market Square in Winnipeg, for the east end in Montreal and for one-industry towns scattered throughout Canada."

The Martin contingent looked on in dismay. The fight was going to be even bloodier than anticipated.

Martin himself was miles away at a barbecue in Roberval. The PM had taken aim at him earlier in the day, comparing him to Kim Campbell. "Remember in 1993," he said, "we had a great star all summer that we called at that time a shooting star. She had a summer job. It was Kim Campbell." When the remark was relayed to him, Martin said, "It's been a long time since the PM referred to me as a star, shooting or otherwise."

The next morning, on his way into the hotel, Chrétien saw a journalist he knew and pantomimed a golf swing, signalling, the journalist thought, a certain intent. He was smiling when he made the swing, looking relaxed. When he returned to his suite, he started calling staff members and his closest friends in caucus to his room. Some came in groups, some one at a time. He told them that he would serve out the bulk of his term, then leave. Downstairs in the lobby, CTV's Mike Duffy was breaking the story to the nation. The news, though not unexpected, was jolting nonetheless. After Chrétien's speech of the day before, his loyalists had started thinking they were in it for the long haul. Now they knew that it was over, that one of the greatest fighters Canadian politics had ever produced was laying down arms.

Chrétien was calm as he told those he'd assembled of his verdict. His visitors sat quietly and didn't try to make him change his mind. Then he went down the hall and stood before his caucus in a dimly lit room. "This summer we have not been focused on governing," he began. "We are not doing our job. Canadians don't like that. Liberals don't like that. I have reflected on the best way to bring back unity, to end the fighting, to resume interrupted friendships. I have taken into account my duty to protect for my successors the integrity of the office I hold from the Canadian people, an office that is non-negotiable. Here is my conclusion: I will not run again. I will fulfill my mandate and focus entirely on governing from now until February 2004, at which time my work will be done, and at which time my successor will be chosen."

The Martin backers had been buzzing around the lobby of the Hôtel Le Montagnais for two days, telling scribes that the party was theirs and it was damn well time the prime minister realized it. Now they weren't sure what to think. Chrétien had produced a masterly counterpunch, announcing his intention to both go and stay. It was as if he'd said, "You want me to go? Fine. I will be here for another year and a half. I will be serving out most of my term, just like I originally planned. And I'll be bringing in a sheaf of legislation to put my stamp on the party before I leave."

The review convention was six months away. Now there would be no need for a review vote—and Chrétien would be staying on as if he had passed that vote.

In losing control, the prime minister was reasserting himself. The media in Chicoutimi wasn't focusing on defeat, humiliation, how he lost the party, how he was, in effect, fired. Instead, the story was about eighteen more months in power, his new policy agenda, and how tough it would be for his rival. Here was Paul Martin, hiding away in the wings of the Hôtel Le Montagnais while the trumped incumbent piled one remarkable page of fiction atop another.

No, he hadn't been driven from office, Chrétien told a press conference. Despite all those pleading phone calls he'd made to MPs asking for their support, he had planned on retiring all along. No, there weren't problems with caucus. He had its "full support," he said, for his new policy agenda. No, his final eighteen months wouldn't be a problem. Nothing wrong with being a lame duck, even though he had often pointed to how difficult it was for Lester Pearson to govern after he announced he was leaving. Yes, the Liberal Party constitution calls for a leadership convention to be held within a year of a prime minister setting a retirement date. But he, Jean Chrétien, was dispensing with that rule. He'd be leaving in eighteen months.

Paul Martin had triumphed in the spin wars on his leaving. Chrétien was doing the same with his departure.

Martin was restrained in his response, stating no objection to the eighteen months. He didn't want to wait that long, but his camp was relieved that the party would avoid the bloodbath of a review convention, and that Chrétien was not going to seek a fourth term. Many were doubtful the PM would be able to last as long as he thought. On announcing their departures, most prime ministers called for a leadership convention five or six months down the line.

The Liberals had, in effect, already put themselves through a leadership fight that lasted nearly eighteen months. Did they really want another year and a half of waiting?

As for the prime minister's big agenda, how could he expect to have the moral authority to impose it after having been drummed out by his caucus? How could he get the votes in that caucus when Martin had a majority on his side? The word from on high now carried much less weight. Intimidation tactics didn't have as much effect. The days of Tony Soprano, as one Martin rebel offered, were over.

Chrétien still had to face the likelihood of more embarrassing revelations on the abuse-of-power file. Auditors' reports and police reports were forthcoming. More evidence of malfeasance could lead to pressure for an early departure. Who was to say the party wouldn't just ignore him, leaving him looking like a foolish old man stripped of power?

HIS ANNOUNCEMENT WAS UNPRECEDENTED. Chrétien was the only leader among all the great Liberal prime ministers to have an undefeated electoral record. At the same time, he was the only sitting Liberal prime minister to lose the support of his party and effectively be ordered out. He had never been defeated by an opposing party. Instead, it took his own to bring him down. He was Thatcherized.

Eddie Goldenberg, who knew the history of the Liberal Party, offered three reasons for Chrétien's predicament. The first was that he had had a powerful Cabinet minister organizing against him almost since he lost the leadership to him in 1990. The second was that the same caucus members kept being re-elected and there weren't enough rewards to hand out to keep them content. Third, because Chrétien was not planning to run again, he failed to put in place an organization to keep the party rank and file in line.

A fourth reason, offered by Paul Martin and Peter Donolo, as well as several others at the PMO, was the change in Chrétien's communications strategy. For years, the notion of peaceful coexistence had prevailed. Paul Martin's ambition was known. Jean Chrétien's enmity toward Paul Martin was known. Efforts were made by strategists to overcome the tensions and adhere to the agenda of governance. But in 1999, when hostilities broke out, the strategy changed, mainly at the bidding of the Prime Minister's Office, from one of peaceful coexistence to something approaching open warfare.

Chrétien could not keep the instincts of youth in check. And when he was presented with what looked like evidence that Paul Martin was taking the challenge to a new level, he responded by moving onto the field of battle. The critical question was whether Paul Martin actually had been planning a campaign of aggression or whether some imaginations in the PMO were working overtime. It required quite a leap to interpret Toronto's Constellation Hotel meeting of March 2000 as meaning that a takeover or *coup* of some kind was being planned.

The key players in both camps believed that the departures of Terrie O'Leary and Peter Donolo had been costly for both sides. They would have been unlikely to interpret the Constellation Hotel meeting so dramatically. But if in fact Ducros was playing to the PM's warrior instincts—if in fact she was escalating tensions, as Paul Martin and many others claimed—it was still the prime minister who made the final call. A man of his experience and savvy should have been able to see beyond the advice of one person. He had been in the game long enough to separate distortion from reality.

In an interview in 2003, Chrétien said the Constellation Hotel meeting had changed everything. Before that event, he'd made up his mind to leave at the end of his second term. But he felt they were trying to push him out, and that wouldn't do. "So I arrive at the convention, and everybody starts to shout, 'Four more years.' Fine. And I stayed four more years."

Chrétien's brother Maurice didn't believe this version of events, nor did many in the Martin camp or even some in Chrétien's own circle. Maurice Chrétien said the plan all along had been to go for a third term and step down after two years of it. Others held a similar view.

Jean Chrétien had planned to run again, they believed, no matter what happened at that convention.

No one knows what was going on in Chrétien's mind. But being the great political craftsman, he was certainly capable of exploiting the Constellation Hotel meeting to win sympathy and momentum for staying in power.

In the interview, Chrétien said that any talk of Paul Martin's being able to stage a *coup* was nonsense. "One thing you're missing," he said. "A prime minister in Canada who has the confidence of the House, there's no danger of a *coup d'état*." And if, Chrétien added, he had lost the confidence of the House, he would have gone to the governor general to call an election—an election he knew he would have won. There was no great danger, but being the ultimate political warrior, Chrétien contrived one, because it fit his political purpose at the time. He needed a reason for staying on, and nothing so motivated him as the sight of an enemy, real or imagined. Seduced by the lure of the fight, trapped inside his own character, Chrétien had wanted a war, and he got one. He could have called a truce many times. In the end, the war brought him down, but he was staying on the battlefield anyway. It was his way of not admitting defeat. In Chicoutimi, he spoke as if he was not being pushed out, as if it was what he had wanted to do all along. He didn't show any pain, but all who knew him realized how deeply it must have hurt to lose to Paul Martin.

Reflecting on that moment ten months later, he did not go so far as to say he had been hurt by it. "I was disappointed, but I understood that some were getting impatient. You know, the minute you become prime minister, you start to make enemies because you cannot have 172 Cabinet members. So those who are not there get mad at you." He even conceded that maybe it was a mistake to have waited so long to announce his retirement. He and Aline had made up their minds that "we were not to stay in politics forever," the prime minister said. "And we were being stupid in a way.

"You know, and I want to enjoy life. And, you know, I have had enough of it."

CHAPTER EIGHTEEN

THE RESURGENCE

T HE ODDS WERE STACKED HIGH against his lingering another year and a half, but Chrétien was nothing if not a testament to endurance. The separatists thought they had him in the 1995 referendum—until the campaign's last week, when the numbers turned back in his favour. John Turner thought it was over for Chrétien after he defeated him in the 1984 leadership convention, but Chrétien turned around and published *Straight from the Heart,* which vaulted him to national prominence once again. The opposition parties thought they had him pinned down on Shawinigate and other alleged scandals, but they weren't even close. Despite being trapped in contradictions too numerous to mention, the PM blew off the allegations as if they were nothing.

Never conceding defeat was still a cornerstone of his character. When he had been kicked out of boarding school in Trois-Rivières, instead of returning home to Shawinigan to face his father, he went to Montreal, hid away at a friend's place, then returned home at the end of the school year as if nothing had happened. Not much had changed. The Liberals had now sent him home. But Jean Chrétien planned—and a hideaway could well be necessary—on getting there in his own sweet time.

He felt a sense of liberation in the wake of announcing his retirement. When Sheila Copps accompanied him to Shawinigan a few days later, he took her to the house where he was born. Copps could sense the relief he felt in these surroundings. With his wife, Aline, proudly looking on, Chrétien told a crowd, "I'm really home here. It's the real people here."

In Ottawa, he prepared for the first anniversary of September 11. George W. Bush was using the occasion to build support for an attack on Iraq. Unable to tie Saddam Hussein's regime to the terrorist attacks, he was now arguing that Iraq was a dire threat because it possessed weapons of mass destruction. Before a scheduled meeting with Bush in Detroit, Chrétien, in so many words, said, "Show me." Ottawa, he announced, wanted proof that Iraq had such weapons, as well as the capacity to launch them and the intent to terrorize others. His foreign minister, Bill Graham, pointed out that many other countries have such weapons and "You can't, presumably, attack them all." Under international law, proof of an imminent threat of an attack would be required to justify a pre-emptive strike against Iraq.

When he met Bush in Detroit, Chrétien repeated the arguments and told the president he should get the approval of the United Nations before he moved on Iraq. He told Bush of Lester Pearson and Canada's preference for the multilateral approach. Bush applauded the PM's plain-speaking style, saying he would make "a great Texan." There were a lot of smiles and chuckles, though much of it seemed forced.

The motivation for the new American militarism and muscle-flexing was understandable, but it was hardly looked upon with favour by the prime minister. During a trip to South Africa, he had conferred with his hero, Nelson Mandela, and the champion of the struggle against apartheid had let him know his views on Iraq. Mandela had tried calling Bush to state his opposition to plans for a war without the sanction of the United Nations. Bush wouldn't return his calls.

On September 11, the interview the prime minister had taped much earlier with Peter Mansbridge was aired. In retrospect, it was a mistake for Chrétien to do the show in advance, because he was not able to feel the emotion of the day itself and was less sympathetic to the United States than he might have been had he waited. In the interview, he made two observations that suggested the West had to bear some responsibility for the attacks. "You cannot exercise your powers to the point of humiliation for the others," he told Mansbridge. "That is what the Western world—not only the Americans, the Western world—has to realize. Because they are human beings too. There are long-term consequences." He then added, "And I do think that the Western world is getting too rich in relation to the poor world and necessarily will be looked upon as being arrogant and self-satisfied, greedy and with no limits. The eleventh of September is an occasion for me to realize it even more."

The remarks prompted a rash of criticism, most notably from conservative politicians and like-minded commentators. Alliance Leader Stephen Harper termed the performance "shameful." Brian Mulroney said Chrétien had delivered "a uniquely disgraceful statement." The media brouhaha stretched over several days, but Chrétien was reading the polls and the polls showed that more than two-thirds of Canadians thought the U.S. was at least partly to blame for the September 11 attacks and that similar numbers supported the way the Chrétien government had responded to September 11.

Canada's relations with Washington were on a downward spiral, but Chrétien didn't appear overly concerned. He had fundamental differences with the right-wing Republican administration and was prepared to express them. As he headed down the long road towards retirement, he abandoned the politics of caution. He brought in a Speech from the Throne that was noticeably more left-of-centre than previous ones. Back in May, before Martin was ousted and Chrétien himself was pushed towards the exit door, he had sat down with Alex Himelfarb, his newly appointed clerk of the Privy Council, and spelled out what he wanted to do in his final stretch in office. Himelfarb knew then that Chrétien was not intending to run again, and that his focus instead would be on a major policy agenda. The day after Chrétien left Chicoutimi, Himelfarb got a phone call from him. He had thought the prime minister would be licking his wounds. Instead, an intense discussion of that agenda followed. Much had to be done to fill the policy vacuum that had been left by all those years of political infighting and warding off scandal. Chrétien was freer now because he didn't have to worry about facing voters again. Moreover, he had a retirement deadline to meet, and nothing focuses the mind like the end game.

His government had been slow to address environmental issues, and he hated to see reports saying that the Tories, with their acid rain treaty with Washington and a host of other measures, had a better record in this area. Responding, Chrétien pledged to create ten new national parks and five marine conservation areas. More importantly, he made a final and firm commitment to ratify the 1997 Kyoto accord on global warming. The accord bound countries to deeply reduce their greenhouse gas emissions, which are believed to upset the earth's climate balance. Canada had been dragging its feet on whether to give it the go-ahead. The deadline to meet Kyoto commitments was 2010.

Alberta was heavily reliant on fossil fuels for electricity, and its huge oil sector stood to suffer if industry was compelled to get clean fast. The province put up a big hue and cry, led by Ralph Klein and Peter Lougheed, the premier who had fought Ottawa over the National Energy Program twenty years earlier, and said the province was now being penalized in a similar draconian manner. The U.S. rejected Kyoto, and now with the West coming at him, Chrétien had a huge fight on his hands. "I tell you," recalled his policy adviser, Paul Genest, "there was a lot of nervousness in the Cabinet, especially after the Americans bailed." Chrétien made a forceful statement in Cabinet, however, saying that he did not want to be identified with the American position. "He was very clear, and he startled a lot of them," recalled Genest, "because some felt, given how tightly our economies are linked, that we had to go along with them." Corporate Canada was against him, as was Republican America, and, recalled Genest, "It tickled him to be aligned against very powerful big business interests." He knew he had the support of most of the provinces—and of public opinion across Canada. It was not a gamble comparable to the one he took on the clarity legislation, nor was it anything like the National Energy Program. Paul Martin, who had more power to block Kyoto than did the opposition parties, wanted to see more details on how the plan would be implemented, but he generally favoured moving ahead with ratification.

Trying to refocus the agenda on policy, Chrétien was derailed again by ethics transgressions. First came a new patronage storm involving Solicitor General Lawrence MacAuley, his close political ally and friend from PEI. MacAuley was accused of steering federal funds to operations from which political friends could be seen to benefit. In one case, MacAuley had lobbied for a plan to create a police training project at Holland College, where his brother, Alex, was president. Howard Wilson ruled that, in so doing, he was in breach of some obligations. The ruling angered Chrétien and Goldenberg, who were of the view that the charges were Mickey Mouse. "Do you want us to be eunuchs in our jobs?" Chrétien had protested earlier in the year. He didn't seem bothered by the prospect of Cabinet members pushing bureaucrats to direct funds to people in their ridings. The question was complicated because in some small-town jurisdictions, a minister knew almost everyone and could be accused of favouritism no matter where he or she turned.

MacAuley resigned, insisting he had done nothing wrong. He became the fifth Cabinet minister of the year to be forced out by some controversy or another, which left historians to wonder if there ever had been another year with as much Cabinet carnage in Ottawa.

But the Islander's resignation was less embarrassing than Chrétien's tumble on the question of parliamentary reform. His stubbornness when it came to surrendering even a pinch of his prodigious power had always been hard to fathom—but it was even harder to understand now that he was planning to leave anyway. Paul Martin had been scoring points with Liberal MPs by pledging to address what he called the "democratic deficit" by awarding them more influence in the system. He intended to support an Alliance motion stipulating that the chairs of Commons committees be selected by secret ballot rather than by the Prime Minister's Office. Chrétien decided to fight the motion, and in so doing, to fight the Martin wing of the party. Giving in to the Alliance demand, he felt, would imperil the government's ability to ensure regional and gender balance among parliamentary chairs. What's more, Liberals in committee could split their votes, allowing opposition members to win chairmanships and endanger legislation.

But since it was a small concession that Chrétien's likely successor, Paul Martin, would have to deal with, many thought the PM would be willing to compromise. Agreeing to long-demanded democratization of the system would soften his dictatorial image, undercut the critics, secure him more respect in his own party, and—on the matter in question—save him from a major embarrassment.

Paul Martin's growing strength had just been demonstrated in the summertime. How could Chrétien believe that he could defeat Martin in this showdown? But with his stubbornness getting the better of him, the prime minister appealed to caucus members to support him in maintaining the status quo. Headed for another defeat, he was persuaded by Hec Cloutier, his caucus liaison chief, and others to at least make it a free vote, meaning members were allowed to vote their conscience. Losing a designated free vote was considered less embarrassing.

It was rare that Aline Chrétien came to the Commons, but she showed up on voting day. First she appeared at the top of the stairs when her husband was about to take questions from the media after a Cabinet meeting. Then she sat in the Commons gallery for the vote. Even though the PMO maintained that she wasn't trying to influence anyone, her presence could only be interpreted as a signal that this vote meant a great deal to her husband.

It didn't help. Fifty-six Liberals voted along with Paul Martin in support of the Alliance motion, which was easily enough to carry it. As he turned from his front-row bench to watch member after member vote against him, Chrétien wore a pale, disbelieving look. Each vote must have been like an arrow entering his body. In his nine years as prime minister, they had never done this to him.

When the Speaker called out Paul Martin's name, the former finance minister stood in support of the motion, buttoned his suit jacket, and projected an air of confidence. "I voted for this measure because I believe it represents positive change," he later told reporters. "It speaks to the independence and the authority of members of Parliament."

A day after the defeat, Chrétien met with his caucus. The man who once told an MP that his suit was just as expensive as Paul Martin's now demonstrated the same small-town insecurities in front of his members. In a gratuitous defence of his self-worth, he said, "Don't worry about me. I've got seven job offers from seven different law firms."

To rub it in, to pulverize him some more on the issue of parliamentary democracy, Brian Mulroney came to town for the unveiling of his prime ministerial portrait. The PM spoke first and kept the script light, as he had with John Turner at his unveiling, trying to inject some goodwill into the proceedings. When Mulroney came forward, a protester ran behind him waving an American flag over his head. The former prime minister, in his deep, honey-filled baritone, got off a few one-liners, then turned serious. In hushed tones, he started in on the fundamental, overriding importance of showing caucus respect and how he had been able to do that and how others had not. He didn't mention Chrétien by name, but it was obvious to everyone who he meant—and it was obvious from Chrétien's grim, frozen countenance that the blows were hitting the intended target. It was a masterful display on a subject that Mulroney could address with credibility. Few disputed his smooth handling of his large caucus. In his later years, his ability to keep his crew members on board his sinking ship was astonishing, particularly as they went right ahead and sank with him. With Chrétien, the caucus had abandoned a winner. With Mulroney, they had remained loyal to a leader who was at 15 percent in the polls.

TRIPS ABROAD WERE USUALLY A RESPITE from problems at home, but when Chrétien journeyed to Prague for a NATO summit, there was no such relief. John McCallum, his defence minister, took a swipe at the Americans, telling them to quit lecturing Canada on defence spending. The nation's military budget was a decades-old subject of derision in the White House. Ronald Reagan's hawkish defence minister, Caspar Weinberger, once said that you could fit the entire Canadian military on a football field and still have room for the game. McCallum firmly made the point that he was quite capable of doing his job without advice from the Pentagon. But his offering was soon overshadowed by a casual remark made by Francie Ducros to a CBC reporter in the media centre. In discussing Bush's push to have the NATO summit focus on Iraq, which was annoying Chrétien, Ducros exclaimed, "What a moron!" Bob Fife of the *National Post* overheard her. He decided her remark should be reported because of her important position in the government, because she was in the media centre at the time, and because the friction between Bush and Chrétien was an ongoing story. He assured Ducros before the story appeared that he would not use her name in his report. Instead, he attributed it to an unnamed Canadian official, as was customary practice. But when the *National Post* played up this aspect of his story with a front-page headline that screamed, "Canadian Officials Call Bush Moron," there was little chance of the remark remaining anonymous. In fact, in the PMO, where Ducros had few supporters, one official was delightedly telling reporters it was Ducros who had said it.

Asked about the insult the next day, Chrétien made matters worse by injudiciously repeating the offending phrase. Bush is "a friend of mine," said Chrétien. "He's not a moron at all." The normal diplomatic response would have been to say that his aide had made an inexcusable, insulting remark and that she would be disciplined. Instead, he fed a new raft of headlines—"Chrétien Denies Bush Is a Moron"—and the like.

Pressure built for Ducros's dismissal, but Chrétien stalled. He and Aline had many reasons for wanting to defend their fiercest loyalist.

They owed her that. They didn't want to see the media, most of whom disliked her, get their way. Moreover, the Chrétiens knew that the Martinites loathed her—a *Toronto Star* story had recently said they "spit out" her name at every turn—and they hated the idea of handing them her scalp as well. Aline Chrétien was furious. When she and Fife crossed paths, she gave him a porcelain glare that almost cut him in half.

Back in Ottawa, the PM was under growing pressure from Washington to take action, and seeing that the story was not going away, he cut Ducros loose, saying she had done a very good job. The Martin camp tried to conceal its glee, as did many PMO staffers who had been pressuring Chrétien to fire her well before this episode. In the media, Ducros had established close ties to a few leading female journalists, who felt she was a victim of male bias. But outside this group, Ducros had few supporters, and as a result, she got a rough going-over. "A Style That Grates on Enemies—and Friends" ran a pitiless headline in *The Globe and Mail.* The veteran columnist Hugh Winsor described her as having "a prickly personality and a strident manner," while Susan Delacourt of the *National Post* subtly picked her apart in a piece that concluded she was "her own worst enemy."

Ducros, perhaps the most critical player in the Martin–Chrétien wars outside of the combatants themselves, lived by the sword and died by the sword. As Brian Tobin had once remarked, Ducros had a wealth of talents, but an appreciation for the nuances of public relations never ranked among them. With one of the sharper minds in Ottawa, she could have performed brilliantly for Chrétien in many other positions, but she was too combative and territorial and defensive to fulfill the vital communications role. She went away believing, as she would say in an interview months later, that so many of the things attributed to her were simply untrue. "The notion of undermining others was not part of the way I functioned." During a trip to Boston, she visited the Kennedy library. "I was particularly intrigued," she recalled, "by Kennedy saying there's only one thing more dangerous than lies—and that's myth. Because they're persuasive and you can't denounce them and you have to live with them."

Her replacement was the veteran TV reporter Jim Munson, who had abundant experience among media people and set about trying to ease tensions with reporters and with the Martin wing of the party. Martin soon reported that he noticed a big difference with Munson in the role. Relations would never be mended, but a slow healing had begun.

There was much to mend. The year 2002 had already become the worst Chrétien had experienced as prime minister. Five Cabinet ministers resigned, the Liberal caucus rebelled, Paul Martin was pushed out, the prime minister was forced to declare a retirement date, his close aide was bounced, and he was humiliated on the committee chair vote. But there was still more to come, a hammer blow that was summed up in a gigantic headline in Scott Anderson's steadfastly conservative *Ottawa Citizen:* "The Largest Cost Overruns We've Ever Seen." It was a capsule summary of Auditor General Sheila Fraser's analysis of overspending on the firearms registry.

When gun-control legislation was announced in April 1994, the government forecast that the net cost to taxpayers would be only $2 million. The $119 million needed to implement the program over five years was supposed to be offset by $117 million in fees. Instead, by 2002, the firearms registry, still not complete, had cost $800 million—with the fees taken into account. For irresponsibility in the handling of the taxpayer dollar, the government had climbed a new mountaintop.

Some of the problems stemmed from several provinces' refusal to administer the program. This meant that Ottawa had had to establish its own bureaucracy to issue firearms' licences in five provinces. Developing a computer system for the program cost no less than $227 million. A third problem involved revenues from fees, which the government routinely reduced or waived to encourage owners to license their guns.

The public service that Chrétien had so touted had let him down again. Bureaucrats had failed, Fraser noted, to keep Parliament abreast of the cost overruns. As early as 1993, Dennis Mills and Percy Downe had worried that Chrétien was making the bureaucracy too independent, too free of political oversight. Much had happened since then to substantiate their fears. The Liberals were finally responding with a plan for public service reform. But as the one-time MP and long-time columnist Doug Fisher noted, no one could get their hopes up. He had counted thirty-seven initiatives designed to reform the public service in the forty-five years he had been around.

The registry spending scandal touched off a blame game among Liberal Cabinet ministers. Allan Rock, who brought in the program, said that the problems began after he left the portfolio, and that attempts to target him were the work of people who wanted to undermine his Liberal leadership campaign. In defending the program, he cited a decline in gun deaths in the 1990s, but critics said this had more to do with Tory legislation stiffening rules for gun acquisitions. Anne McLellan, whose justice department oversaw most of the cost run-ups, admitted there was a basic government deficiency. "This government has had a sorry history—not only this one but the one before it—with major information technology projects. Once they get involved they start realizing that it is more complex, and the specifications change and cost run-ups go wild," she said.

The fiasco sparked new calls for Chrétien to face reality and leave office before his announced deadline of February 2004. But just as he seemed to be reaching the nadir, just as it appeared his leadership of the country would end in bitter disappointment, he somehow summoned up new strength and new purpose.

To be able to leave on a credible note, he had to find a way to reassert control of the party and implement a far-reaching policy agenda, which could rebut critics who said he had little to show for all his years in power. Formalizing Canada's commitment to the Kyoto accord was his first test. To placate the West and corporate Canada,

Ottawa revamped its plan and allowed businesses to push back deadlines for reducing emissions. It also offered caps on the burden big business would bear. The prime minister then rammed through a motion to cut off parliamentary debate on the issue after eight days, a move that prompted objections from Paul Martin, who said a longer debate was required to establish a national consensus.

Chrétien signed the agreement without having spoken in the Commons on the issue, other than in Question Period. Ratification, wrote Don Martin, the biographer of Ralph Klein, "comes at a time when bureaucratic audits have questioned Kyoto's spending practices, provinces are declaring their refusal to implement the accord and Opposition warnings that billions are about to be squandered are dismissed." Martin foresaw another gun-registry fiasco in the making. Klein was holding his nose until Paul Martin took over, wrote the columnist, because then the pact wouldn't be worth the paper it was written on. Chrétien waved off the critics, however. "It's a great day today, I am passing Kyoto. All you guys some weeks ago were telling me that I was going to hit the wall."

Drubbed repeatedly for his ethics lapses and his refusal to democratize the system, Chrétien announced a broad plan to severely limit corporate and union donations to political parties. The parties would now rely primarily on individual donations, and the government would pick up the slack, pouring millions more into election campaigns. Eligibility for government funds would depend in large part on a party's most recent campaign performances—thus providing the Liberals with a built-in advantage. Nevertheless the plan sparked another internal Liberal row, with Stephen LeDrew, the party president, calling the Chrétien move dumber than a bag of hammers and predicting a backlash from both taxpayers and party members.

The backlash never came.

Defiantly, as he had on Kyoto, Chrétien forged ahead. To keep the Martin rebels at bay, he used the threat of a snap election. If they teamed with the opposition parties to defeat him on a major vote in the Commons, the prime minister said, he would gladly go to the polls and win again. The Martinites suspected he was serious. As unlikely as it sounded, Chrétien's worst year had still left the Liberals at 41 percent, twenty-six points ahead of their nearest rival, the Alliance. The Martin wing knew he stood a good chance of winning a fourth election, and if that happened, Paul Martin would be history.

Now the PM moved on health care. Roy Romanow, the former Saskatchewan premier, had concluded a one-man commission into health care and Senator Michael Kirby had also weighed in with a large study. With money in the bank from his high-performing economy, Chrétien was able to spend, spend, spend. Not all of Romanow's reforms could be funded, but the bulk could be put in place. First, Chrétien needed an agreement with the premiers. He was well experienced in this form of compromise and manipulation, and he leaned to the latter tactic in this go-round. Premiers complained of his bullying approach in negotiations. Klein talked of seeing "a dark side" he had not seen in the past, forgetting perhaps Airbus and Somalia and the Black peerage case and the Shawinigan chokehold. As the premiers told the story, Chrétien laid out the deal, declared he would be back in a few minutes, and left, saying, "Sign, or you'll get nothing."

If it was blackmail, it worked. PMO staffers would be talking for weeks about how their prime minister ran circles around the premiers. If he had been so weakened by the party rebellion against him, the premiers should have had him for lunch. Instead it was the other way around.

Like the Kyoto accord, the health care agreement had the look of an eleventh-hour compromise. It met some of the needs outlined in the Romanow report while skirting others. The provinces got an estimated $237 billion in new health care spending, spread over five years. The money was tied to an expansion of the system to cover needs not covered before. There were pledges to tackle three issues that had dominated much of the health care debate: primary care, home care, and pharma care. Highly important was tracking how the money would be spent. To this end, a Health Council of Canada was to be put in place to do the monitoring. While emphasizing that there was still much to be done, Romanow was generally supportive of the pact. Saying the country was on the road to progressive reform, he cited the agreement's measures for catastrophic drug coverage, a fund for diagnostic machinery, and support for home care programs. Maude Barlow of the Council of Canadians, generally impressed by some of Chrétien's other work, took a contrary view, saying the accord still left the door open to privatization.

But for the Liberals, big government was back in vogue, this becoming all the more evident when John Manley, the new finance minister, delivered a horn-of-plenty first budget, one straight out of the 1960s. Manley had said a couple of weeks before his budget that "what Canadians don't want is a laundry list of new spending." He then went on the biggest single-budget spree since the Trudeau era, a whopping 11-percent spending increase over the previous year. Health care, Kyoto, municipal infrastructure, aboriginals, official languages, the National Child Benefit, foreign aid, and a raft of other Liberal favourites all got large new infusions. The military got a boost of $800 million, which, while large by comparison to previous years, was far short of what critics were demanding.

By now the spending cuts from Paul Martin's landmark 1995 budget had been almost entirely reversed. Martin, who'd wanted a more focused budget, was annoyed at Manley's big-spray act. But the great difference between the 2003 budget and the ones in the Trudeau and Mulroney years was that none of this new spending would have to go on the credit card. The economic fundamentals were in place, and the economy was outperforming that of the United States.

CHAPTER NINETEEN

"NO" TO WAR

C HRÉTIEN'S DOMESTIC AGENDA was soon overshadowed by
America's rush to war and the question of whether to take part.
This was a tougher decision than the one Ottawa had faced in the
1991 Persian Gulf War. Then, there was clear-cut aggression by a
foreign adversary of Washington's. This time, there was no such aggression. There was only speculation about what that foreign power, Iraq,
might do.

In 1951, Prime Minister Louis St. Laurent had talked about bilateral
relations with President Harry Truman. "We have been negotiating
many times with our American neighbours," the Canadian said. "Never
have we been made to feel that we were obliged to agree to something
because they were bigger and stronger than we were." Washington was
annoyed at the time that Ottawa had provided only three destroyers for
standby duty in the Korean War. "That's no mere token," External
Affairs Minister Lester Pearson claimed. "Okay," replied an American
diplomat. "Let's call it three tokens."

In 2003, St. Laurent's thesis was about to undergo a severe test. No
modern Canadian prime minister had been subjected to so much
pressure as Jean Chrétien was on the war against Iraq. In the two world
wars in the first half of the century, Canada entered before the United
States. In Korea, Canada did face U.S. pressure, but it was middling by
comparison. In Vietnam, Pearson received a tongue-lashing from Lyndon
Johnson, but it was for a speech decrying the increased bombing, not for
staying out of the conflict. In the 1991 Gulf War, Mulroney was there on
a moment's notice. And in Kosovo, Chrétien went in of his own accord.

With Iraq, Chrétien faced an unusual set of circumstances. Britain, Canada's other great ally through history, was George W. Bush's biggest war supporter. For Chrétien to turn down one ally was tough. To turn down both was politically unfathomable. Canada now had an official Opposition party, the Alliance, that was staunchly pro-American in its values. It could be counted upon to shout down the prime minister every day of the week for not backing the Pentagon. Another factor was the media. With its turn to the right, Canada's print media—the *Toronto Star* being one of the few exceptions—was adamantly pro-war, this in contrast to the Canadian public.

In the run-up to the war, the Grits were already suspect for their management of the American relationship. Chrétien was still viewed as having been too lukewarm in his reaction to September 11. There was the ruckus over the "moron" comment, there were a host of prickly bilateral disputes, there was Chrétien's paltry performance on defence spending and at base was a lack of trust between the president and the prime minister.

Chrétien knew the Bush family's obsession with Iraq. He was dubious about some of the fear-mongering coming out of the White House, and he stood strongly opposed to Bush's apparent willingness to run roughshod over the United Nations. While not trying to defend Saddam Hussein's tyranny, he challenged Bush's wish for regime change. "Where do you stop?" he asked. He wondered how many bad guys and dictators you go to war against, and how you decide who to invade and who not to invade. What kind of precedent would it set for nations with different values looking at Western countries? He wondered if they might want a regime change also.

For all his ugly history, Hussein had not caused trouble outside his border in a dozen years. The Western policy of containment seemed to be working. He hadn't used banned weapons since the 1980s, and when he used them then—while he was on better terms with the U.S.—Washington had turned a blind eye.

But conservatives on both sides of the border were making their case forcefully—and they had a good case to make. Saddam was a proven menace to the region. He was an obstacle to peace in the Middle East. His totalitarian dictatorship had oppressed his people for decades. He was in possession, or so they said, of the horror weapons. Why, in a post–September 11 world, should the United States tolerate such a danger?

But Bush's case was being undermined by the failure of United Nations arms inspectors in Iraq to find evidence of weapons of mass destruction. This prompted Secretary of State Colin Powell to appear before the world body and lay out a welter of charges, accusing Saddam of hoarding great stocks of chemical and biological weapons, of having unmanned aerial vehicles and the makings of a nuclear program.

Powell was effective in his sales pitch, but many in Ottawa remained sceptical. The United States had a history of exaggerating threats. It often played to a president's political agenda to cast himself as the great protector of the people. Among the many examples of threat inflation used by the Americans were the McCarthyist red scare of the 1950s, the so-called missile gap with the Soviet Union in 1960, the domino theory used to justify the Vietnam War, the continued exaggerations of Soviet military strength during the Cold War, Ronald Reagan's casting the Sandinistas of Nicaragua as a military threat to the American mainland, and the highly inflated tallies of horrors in Kosovo prior to that war.

But few were looking at past history. The Powell performance found many believers and the pressure on the Canadian government intensified. Experts argued that if Canada stayed out of the war, it would suffer serious economic retaliation from Washington. Canada's economic health was tied so tightly to the Americans, some critics said, that it had no choice but to follow the U.S. into war.

Chrétien wasn't buying one bit of this. The suggestion that Canada was so dependent on the U.S. that it couldn't exercise freedom of choice riled him. One evening, he rhymed off how dependent the Americans were on Canadian energy supplies. "They won't retaliate," he told reporters. Again, there was history to go by. Canada opposed the Vietnam War, and a short time later, in 1965, the historic Auto Pact was signed. Pierre Trudeau alienated the Americans on several fronts and, though there were threats, he escaped retribution of major consequence. Historically, the biggest American measures impacting the Canadian economy, the Smoot-Hawley Tariff of 1930 and Nixon's 10-percent import surcharge in 1971, were measures taken against all foreign trading partners, not just Canada.

In February, Chrétien went to Chicago to speak to the Council on Foreign Relations. He urged the United States not to act alone. This wasn't quite the equivalent of Lester Pearson's going to Philadelphia in 1965 and asking Lyndon Johnson to halt the bombing, but it took some courage to do this in Bush's backyard.

"War must always be the last resort, not only because of the human suffering it produces, but because of the inevitable unforeseen consequences," Chrétien stated. "But if it must come to war, I argue that the world should act through the United Nations. This is the best way to give legitimacy to the use of force in these circumstances." He also warned the United States against arrogance. "Great strength is not always perceived by others as benign," he observed. "Not everyone around the world is prepared to take the word of the United States on faith."

At home, he faced a strange dichotomy. The opposition parties and the media were pressuring him to go to war. The Canadian public and Chrétien's left-leaning Liberal caucus wanted him to stay out unless an invasion was approved by the U.N. Outbursts from caucus members, these following the "moron" remark, were giving him the look of an anti-American. The colourful Carolyn Parrish, walking away from a reporter's microphone one day, got picked up blurting, "Those damn Americans. I hate those bastards." Parrish always spoke in graphic terms and was frequently given to cursing. But she got caught at the wrong moment. Herb Dhaliwal, citing Bush's failure to abide by the democratic will of the United Nations, said he was not acting like a statesman. In light of some of the epithets laid on Trudeau by Nixon and Diefenbaker by Kennedy,

Dhaliwal's slight wasn't even a candidate for the B list. But a great bally-hoo followed his comment as well. Chrétien was then denounced for not coming forward to discipline his caucus members.

Dhaliwal was supposed to lunch with American ambassador Cellucci the day after he made the remark. The lunch was promptly cancelled. In the days following, Goldenberg told Dhaliwal he should apologize for his remark. He worded an apology for him, sending a paragraph to be inserted in a coming speech. Dhaliwal stuck to his guns. He didn't use it.

Looking ahead, Chrétien had to know that the Americans would win the war in short order. Their military budget was pushing $400 billion, while Iraq's was less than Canada's. With victory, Bush and Tony Blair would be pounding their chests while frowning upon the allies who didn't join in. That would be embarrassing for Ottawa, and if weapons of mass destruction were found or Saddam detonated them, Canada's stand would look all the more cowardly.

The Canadian business community was avidly pro-war and Chrétien could feel pressure coming from that quarter. But, as in the case of the Kyoto accord, he relished the opportunity to thwart the establishment class. His instincts were on the other side, which explained, in part, his attitude toward military spending.

During the heat of the Iraq debate, he telephoned a friend, George Young, who reminded him of the voices of the powerful who were arrayed against him. "Don't worry," Chrétien said. He then made a remark to the effect that after having stood up to these people for forty years, he was not going to let them force a decision on him now. Meanwhile in Cabinet he was reminding ministers, as he often had done during his stewardship in matters relating to Bay Street, that "those guys aren't going to vote for us anyway."

He was still quickly to challenge "those guys." When it was suggested to him in an interview that they were saying he should put more money in the military, Chrétien replied curtly. "Of course. When you put more money in that, you put less money in the children."

He was more comfortable in his position on the war than on other tough decisions he'd made during his tenure, aides reported. The majority of nations were on his side, and precedent was on his side as well. The criterion for Canada's taking up arms with the United States and other allies had always been blatant aggression by another power. This was the case in the two world wars, in Korea, in Iraq in 1990, and to some extent, in Kosovo in 1998. But Canada had never entered a war on accont of an American president's fixation with overthrowing a foreign dictator.

In mid-March, Chrétien stood in the Commons and read a brief statement saying Canada would not join the war effort. Even though he had been leaning in this direction all along, it was a dramatic moment. His caucus erupted in support. MPs talked of it being a signal display of Canadian sovereignty. On the way out of Parliament later in the day, Chrétien told a reporter, "I've been saying it for months."

But he hadn't been saying it effectively, and he hadn't made the case the way he should have on this day either. Such a significant foreign policy decision required an in-depth speech outlining the reasons for the decision, the ramifications, the thread of Canadian history on participation in foreign conflicts. But Chrétien was not in the habit of providing intellectual ballast for his decisions. He was a leader who let the big moments pass. "You know," said Lloyd Axworthy, who was much in support of his decision, "if we were bringing in a budget, we'd have ministers fanning out across the country to sell it. Why didn't we do it on something like this?" Paul Martin supported Chrétien's decision but felt it should have been handled better as well. Chrétien was always contrasted unfavourably with Tony Blair, who, if insufferably sanctimonious, was mellifluous, pointed, and dramatic when the occasion required it.

The war, as expected, was all but over in less than a month, the Super Bowl champions making short work of a third-rate power. The utter collapse of the Iraqis appeared to belie the suggestion that their leader had been building any terror machine. Of relief to the Canadian government was the failure of the Iraqis to deploy any weapons of mass destruction (WMDs). This appeared to be vindication for Ottawa's stance at the United Nations. If Hussein had the weapons stocks, as Powell had so forcefully argued, surely, in his last stand, he would have used them. Nonetheless, the Americans could well glow triumphant for ridding the world of a dictator, and when a few hundred Iraqis came out to celebrate the destruction of a huge statue of Hussein in Baghdad, it was interpreted as a sign that all of Iraq would welcome the Americans with open arms.

But within a few weeks of the conquest, Chrétien's position gained more favour. There was still no evidence of WMDs, and Bush and, especially, Blair found themselves facing charges they had lied to the world to justify their war. They asked for more time to find the weapons, prompting PMO staffers to point out that this was all that the U.N.'s chief arms inspector, Hans Blix, had wanted before the conflict began. A little more time.

Bush and Blair were in a nettlesome position. Even if they found some evidence of banned weapons in Iraq, the question of why Hussein hadn't used them still remained. An additional problem was that the Iraqis were not welcoming the liberators as hoped. Iraqi forces and outside agents continued to protest the American occupation, killing more U.S. soldiers with every week that passed.

Time would tell if the military action, which took more than two thousand civilian lives, was justified. The opportunity for freedom in Iraq and peace in the Middle East would be measured against the cost in lives, the sidelining of the U.N., and the possibility that the war would generate such animosity towards America that it would create new Osama bin Ladens.

Bush cancelled a scheduled visit to Canada for early May. It was for the obvious reason, said a Canadian official, that on the war, "we told him to go get stuffed." But there were no economic reprisals, as some had feared. Chrétien argued that his position on the war had strengthened Canada's image abroad. As evidence, he pointed to the number of European leaders who asked how he had the nerve, as

America's neighbour, to say no. They, or so he reported, told him that his stance had emboldened them to stay out of the war themselves.

In an interview after the war, Chrétien was blunt, full of the bricklayer pragmatism that was often his trademark. "Was it one of your toughest decisions as prime minister?" he was asked.

"Probably. But you don't look at it as 'I have to make my tough decision.' You make a decision when you have to make a decision. You should never measure the toughness of a decision. You make a decision, that's it. One after the other. You don't classify decisions. You make decisions. Otherwise, you get confused."

His roundabout way of expression never failed to amaze. During the war, he unintentionally entertained the masses with a statement he made in favour of U.N. inspectors returning to Iraq to find evidence of banned weapons. When asked what kind of proof would be needed, Chrétien responded, "A proof is a proof. What kind of a proof? It's a proof. And when you have good proof, it's because it's proven."

JUST AS TEMPERATURES from the conflict were cooling with Washington, the prime minister walked to the back of his plane for a chat with reporters. Knowing from experience that such conversations were often reported, he took aim at Bush's "right-wing" administration, saying that if Ottawa was spending money at the rate Bush was doing, Canada would have a deficit of $75 billion. "The Americans will have a deficit of $500 billion this year, and it is a right-wing government," he said, adding that Canada's economic performance was the envy of the G-8 nations. He then outlined his differences with right-wingers, saying that Bush was pro-gun, pro–capital punishment, and anti-abortion, and that he, Chrétien, was none of those. At home, newspaper headlines blasted him for lecturing Bush. Editorialists were given to wonder why he felt this was necessary at the point when relations were starting to pick up.

But as the war story played out through the summer of 2003, it began to appear that on the most important foreign policy decision made by his government, Jean Chrétien had good ground on which to stand, and that he had correctly reflected Canadian sentiment.

The goal of the Americans and the countries supporting them was indisputably a good one. Ottawa wasn't arguing that Iraq wouldn't be better off without the Hussein regime, or that the entire region wouldn't benefit in the long run. The Chrétien government was not challenging the notion that one less tyrant was one step better. But the invasion of Iraq was based on misinformation—if not outright lies—and the way the aggression was then carried out violated so many judicial and democratic principles that the Liberals' decision began looking better by the day.

The United States went to war to disarm the Hussein regime. Once in, it found essentially nothing to disarm. The publicly stated basis for the attack—the threat of weapons of mass destruction—did not appear to exist. But that didn't prevent Washington from proceeding with the arrest or killing of anyone tied to the Hussein regime. The concept of due process was savaged.

In a further irony, the American and British invaders employed—at least in the eyes of the other side—their own form of WMDs. Thousands of cluster bombs were dropped by U.S. and British planes, some in civilian areas. Cluster bombs are small bomblets that detonate from a large canister in mid-air. Each canister carries as many as two hundred bomblets, and these scatter over a wide area, each single fragment powerful enough to cause intestines to explode. Many fragments fail to detonate for days, months, or years. They remain on the ground as lethal land mines. The staggering military superiority enjoyed by the Americans cast grave doubt on the need to overplay such weapons.

Several months passed and the news kept getting worse for the United States. Still no WMD. Still no substantial link of Iraq to September 11. The Bush–Blair argument that Iraq represented an imminent danger that had required an immediate attack was collapsing all around them. Canadians supported an anti-terrorist campaign but it was hard to support the killing of thousands of Iraqis for reasons that were turning out to be bogus.

With more killing and chaos in Iraq, more killing and chaos in the Middle East, the euphoria of the quick victory in the war had disappeared. Opposition in the United States mounted as Bush continued to amass huge deficits and his economy continued to stall. At summer's end the same George W. Bush who had spurned the United Nations and multilateralism now had to turn around and ask that body for financial and military help in trying to rebuild Iraq. It was a stunning reversal. In Britain Tony Blair faced an inquiry at which it was alleged his government had purposely exaggerated the threat from Hussein in order to create support for the war. His popularity tumbled.

Chrétien meanwhile faced increased approval for his war position. Wisely this time he chose not to have any airplane scrums with reporters in which he sounded vindictive. No final verdict on the war was in. In the coming months it was possible that the tide could turn the other way with the war looking better.

Chrétien had hardly performed smoothly or articulately in opposing the war and had been unable to rein in his caucus. His stance could have been taken with much more sophistication. But, in looking at the polls, he could see that he made the right call. Though Canadian elites had been more in favour of war, the masses had been more inclined to the nay side. One of the secrets to Chrétien's enduring popularity was that he was seldom entrapped by establishment theology. His ear was more reflexively cocked to average Canadians and it was average Canadians who had triggered his decision on the war. It would have been easy for him to go the other way. He would have been saluted by Bay Street, the Alliance, the national newspapers, the United States— all the places, he knew, where the voters weren't.

At home, Chrétien's good friend Alfonso Gagliano was in trouble again. In January 2002 *The Globe and Mail* reported that his son Vincenzo had benefited from controversial printing deals with the public works department when Gagliano was minister. The paper also reported that a $63,000 donation from the company of a Liberal fundraiser was followed by a $492,000 contract to the fundraiser's brother. The contract was also from public works.

Ralph Goodale, the department's new minister, rose in the House to say, "Both the prime minister and I have made it absolutely clear that we will not defend the indefensible." But PMO sources revealed that Chrétien had been paving the way for his good friend to become Canada's representative to the Vatican, an even cushier assignment than that of ambassador to Denmark. The new revelations came just in time to stop the planned move—and to save Chrétien a good deal of embarrassment.

It was then revealed that Privacy Commissioner George Radwanski, who had ties to the Chrétien team, was forgiven almost $540,000 in unpaid taxes just one day before his appointment to the $210,000-a-year privacy job. Radwanski was forced to resign after his lavish spending of public money became the talk of the town. But questions about the tax deal and the appointment to the high-paying position remained.

The evidence of Liberal ethics transgressions wouldn't go away, but Chrétien remained unapologetic. He was especially intransigent about the sponsorship program, which he maintained helped sell federalism in Quebec. "This is what is important. And if people committed mistakes in the process, too bad."

As a mark of how federalism was faring, Jean Charest's Liberals came from well back to upset the Parti Québécois in the provincial election in the spring of 2003. The turning point came when a buoyant Charest—"The guy in the best mood wins," wrote the journalist Paul Wells—shredded Premier Bernard Landry in the campaign debate. Though he was hardly on the best of terms with Charest, Chrétien was delighted by the victory. For him to leave office with the separatists out of power in Quebec was a cherished prize, and further confirmation of the wisdom of his Quebec strategy. "The Liberal victory spells more than the end of the PQ's decade-long hold on the National Assembly," wrote Chantal Hébert, one of the nation's leading commentators on

Quebec. "This morning, Quebec's sovereignty movement is effectively in shambles." In his final Liberal fundraising dinner in Montreal, Chrétien was able to boast, "My friends, in all modesty, I think that we can state without hesitation that when it comes to the important file of national unity, we can say, 'Mission accomplished.'"

In Ottawa, the Bloc Québécois was still a substantial force but that had never bothered Chrétien because the Bloc further divided up the opposition by taking seats that would normally have gone to a federalist party. He even concocted strategies to help the Bloc along, so they would remain a viable force. As much as he loathed separatists, Jean Chrétien would do what he could to assist them if their presence was of political benefit. "You have to work on these things," he said, without revealing what measures he had taken.

In what was supposed to have been a dreadful year for Chrétien, with Paul Martin's supporters dictating his every move, good news continued to overturn the expectations. Despite all the threats from caucus rebels to make him pay if he pushed ahead on it, Chrétien passed his plan for campaign finance reform. It was something to offset the many black pages in his ethics record. He also had in the works legislation to create an ethics counsellor who, while not fully independent, would be far freer than the system he had thus far allowed.

In a landmark decision, dictated in large part by the courts, his government decided to change the definition of "marriage" to include gays and lesbians. Chrétien opted not to appeal rulings by provincial courts that said banning same-sex marriages was unconstitutional. "Rather, we will be proposing legislation that will protect the right of churches and religious organizations to sanctify marriage as they define it," he announced. "At the same time, we will ensure that our legislation includes, and legally recognizes, the union of same-sex couples." Extra attention was paid to the way his statement was drafted. Chrétien flipped the sentences around so that the phrase "protecting the rights of churches" came first.

Initially he was relieved and surprised that the plan did not touch off a highly divisive debate across the country. But the debate soon erupted. The Church went on the attack, with a Calgary bishop going so far as to say that the prime minister's "eternal salvation" was in grave danger because of his stance. The Toronto MP Charles Caccia rallied to the PM's cause, declaring, "I will go to hell with you," while Chrétien brought back memories of the days of John F. Kennedy in delineating the separation of church and state. In 1960, Kennedy said, "I do not speak for the Church on public matters, and the Church does not speak for me." Chrétien echoed the statement when he said, "I am the prime minister of Canada. When I am prime minister of Canada, I am acting as a person responsible for the nation. The problem with my religion—I deal with it in other circumstances."

But the decision on same-sex marriage was not an easy one for the prime minister to take. "Believe me, for someone of my generation, born and brought up in the Catholic, rural Quebec of my youth, this is a very difficult issue. But I have learned over forty years in public life that society evolves, and that the concept of human rights evolves more quickly than some of us—and sometimes even in ways that make some feel uncomfortable. But at the end of the day, we have to live up to our responsibilities."

His caucus was balkanized on the issue, and a rancorous nationwide debate was shaping up over not only the power of gays but also the far-reaching power of the courts to make the decisions that counted. Some in caucus and on the opposition benches wanted a compromise that would endorse gay relationships as "civil unions" rather than marriages. But Justice Minister Martin Cauchon rejected such a plan, saying it would still leave same-sex couples with unequal status. An emotional national caucus meeting in North Bay, Ontario, in August 2003 showed the divisions among Liberals on the issue. Again, Chrétien was accused of showing little sensitivity to the voices of his backbenchers. He had referred a draft bill to the Supreme Court for a ruling on its constitutionality without even having a debate on the issue in Parliament. The court's recommendation was not likely to come down until Chrétien was out of office, thus leaving the hot potato in the hands of his successor.

Some proposed having a national referendum on the issue, but Chrétien won applause this time with a firm declaration on the rights of minorities. "To have a referendum to decide the fate of a minority, it's a problem," he stated. "It's why we have constitutions to protect the minorities. It's why you have the Charter of Rights. So if it is always the majority vote by the referendum, who will defend the minorities?"

Though he favoured more time for parliamentary debate on the issue, Paul Martin took a position close to Chrétien's. Opinion polls showed Canadians split over the issue, which meant that the Liberal Party was not in serious danger of finding itself out of sync with a huge majority. Like other storms, it was likely to weather this one.

CHRÉTIEN'S POSITION on same-sex marriages fit the leftward lean of his policy-making throughout his last year in office. He was putting a stamp on his stewardship, defining himself more graphically than in the many years preceding.

Few could have imagined that his final phase would be so critical. Had he not been so defiant—had he opted to leave a year earlier, as most in his caucus and in the country had wanted—his legacy would have been greatly diminished. He wouldn't have been around to chart Canada's position on the war. He wouldn't have had the Kyoto accord on his ledger, or the health care pact, or the campaign finance reform, or his groundbreaking initiative on same-sex marriages. He had resurrected the big-L Liberal tradition of Pearson and Trudeau. He could be viewed as a prime minister who got things done, as opposed to one who wallowed in political combat and idled on the policy front, content with the status quo.

The war and gay rights did not stop the string of endless controversies. Severe Acute Respiratory Syndrome (SARS) hit Toronto with a vengeance in early 2003, almost shutting down the city's tourist industry. Chrétien faced a torrent of criticism, especially from the Ontario government, for offering insufficient financial support, but he was bailed out of the mess by the pluck of one of the most enterprising men in his caucus, the irrepressible Dennis Mills. Mills engineered a massive concert headlined by the Rolling Stones, a Woodstock-style event that attracted 400,000 people and that sent a message to the world that Toronto was open for business.

A tiny outbreak of mad cow disease got Canadian beef exports banned from the United States and other countries, a move that threatened to cripple the Alberta beef industry. In reflection, perhaps, of the rocky relationship that still existed between the president and the prime minister, Washington took its sweet time in lifting the ban.

Then, as Chrétien was putting his feet up at his cottage in the late summer, a power breakdown in Ontario and the American Northeast landed him in controversy again. Instead of returning to manage the crisis from Ottawa and address the problem on national television, Chrétien stayed low-key throughout and was derided by his own MPs for blacking out in the blackout.

As the Ottawa media relations guru Barry McLoughlin put it, in crises leaders were expected to be out front, as Rudy Giuliani was after September 11. "If you're not there, you don't care," quipped McLoughlin. But as Chrétien reminded his blackout critics, his style was never to be the grandstander. And as he looked at his polling numbers, he could well argue that Canadians appeared to be comfortable with that style. They realized that Chrétien was no Cicero, that his speeches rolled off his tongue as if they'd been written in a morgue, and that, as the late Dalton Camp put it, he was "agony on television." Moreover, there was perhaps something innately Canadian about Chrétien's self-effacement—a character trait that Tory prime ministers like Mulroney, Diefenbaker, and R. B. Bennett never enjoyed in abundance, but Chrétien had.

As he prepared for his exit, everyone—or so it appeared—was tired of him. They had been tired of him for three or four years. Strangely, however, it wasn't a sentiment that showed up in assessments of Liberal Party popularity or his own polling numbers across the country. The appeal he had always had with working-class Canadians was still there. The other parties were still on the mat. The Tories had hoped to bring in Bernard Lord, the promising premier of New Brunswick, as their leader, but the Liberals got lucky again when Lord backed away from the race, leaving the lesser-known Peter MacKay to take up the challenge. Under Stephen Harper, the Alliance was still in the mid-teens in the polls—and still anchored far to the right of the Canadian mainstream. The political map hadn't changed much since the earthquake that was the election of 1993. The party that was in the centre enjoyed the support of 50 percent of the population. The smallish regional parties were all below 20 percent. No change was in sight. As fatigued as the population was with Chrétien, he was in a position—had he wished to stay on—to win yet another mandate.

When his own party gave him the signal to leave in Chicoutimi in August 2002, the game plan, recalled Jim Munson, became to change the image of the prime minister from lame duck to mighty duck. Few believed this was possible, given the beating he had taken. But as he headed to his tenth anniversary as Canada's prime minister and his final days in power, Jean Chrétien was no longer being described in terms akin to wounded waterfowl.

His own party thought it had killed him off, but he had come back from the dead. The final word would be his own.

CHAPTER TWENTY

"I AM AN IRON MAN. YES."

H E ONCE TOLD A STORY to a Cabinet colleague about a farmer standing in a field covered in cow dung. The farmer, Chrétien explained, didn't try to wipe the manure away. He knew that if he tried that while it was still fresh, he'd only spread it around and make matters worse. Instead, the farmer was patient and stood very still. He realized that the excrement would eventually dry and start falling off. Then he could brush the rest away and move on.

Chrétien liked telling this tale. You get hit with so much in life, he'd say, that the best thing is to do as the farmer did. Remain standing. Be patient. Persevere.

That's what Chrétien had always done. He'd been covered head to toe in abuse since his earliest days, but it only served to harden his resolve. He'd weathered it, and if further evidence was needed to show that he was one of the toughest men ever to occupy the Prime Minister's Office, it came when his own Liberal family "showered him in shit," as a friend of his indelicately put it, ordering him to leave. Chrétien defiantly stood his ground, doing more in his final year and a half than in the several shameful seasons that preceded it.

He had outlasted them all, and he'd done it, by and large, without changing with the times. At the end of his career, he seemed just as enamoured of the old values as he had been when he arrived four decades earlier. He still saw himself as the commoner, the anti-establishment man, and he took great pride in it.

In an interview in his home in his final summer at the helm, he explained that when he played golf at the Grand-Mère Club, he lined up with about thirty average guys at the first tee at 8:30 in the morning and put his ball in the hopper just like the rest of them. He would be randomly assigned a group to play in, and he might tee off with a barber, an engineer, a clerk—people he didn't know. "The Prime Minister of Canada!" he exclaimed. "I put my ball with them, and I start when it is time to start. And I have a great time. I am happy doing that."

Chrétien never liked the rich because the rich, he said, always wanted more. He never liked ideology because "when you're doctrinaire, you're always looking for things to justify your doctrine." He liked Ralph Klein because, like him, the Alberta premier was close to the people. "It's very dangerous," Chrétien maintained, "when you find comfort with the big shots."

His goal as prime minister, he explained, had been to bring "more social justice" to the country. "You have to be fiscally responsible and socially progressive," he offered. "You have to be able to know that the quality of a nation is the happiness of the individuals. So I always wanted to have the unhappy people a bit more happy." If some of the rich people were complaining, so be it.

The elites didn't like him or the job he had done. The average Canadian thought more of him, but it wasn't as if there was any great love affair. If he golfed with the regulars on Saturday, it didn't mean he listened to them on Monday. Canadians suspected that Chrétien's leadership was more about catering to his own needs than to theirs. It was chiefly—and in this respect he was like most political leaders—about himself. "I went for my values," he said in a revealing moment as he sat on his couch in 24 Sussex Drive. "No doubt about it."

His governance was about his priorities and his vexations. It was about the range of forces that played and preyed upon his self-esteem. It was a one-man show, a cult, so to speak, of the Jean Chrétien personality, not just because the Canadian political system imbued him with so much power, but also because of his defensive nature. When cornered—and he saw himself as cornered much of the time—the thuggish side would emerge.

Chrétien's reign was much about protecting what he had surprisingly achieved in life. Given the traits he'd displayed as a youth, it was to be expected he would turn national politics into an alley fight. That type of fight was one he was confident he could win.

It was said of him that power always interested him more than the uses to which it could be put. Politics, as he cynically defined it, was like sport. It was about winning, scoring points. The attitude perhaps explained why policy, through much of his stewardship, looked like an afterthought, a sideshow to the main action, which was political warring.

He acted only when circumstances compelled him to act. The deficit problem reached critical mass, then he finally moved. The referendum campaign reached a crisis point, then he finally moved. A Quebec lawyer took the separation issue to court, and Chrétien turned those court rulings into his Clarity Act. Re-elected in 2000, he was idling again when September 11 spurred him to action. Then his engine stalled once more, to the point that his own party issued him an ultimatum to leave. This final affront—no one had ever subjugated Jean Chrétien—goaded him to greater levels of output than in any other year.

He went for his values, and in essence, he got them. In his first speeches to Parliament in the mid-1960s, he scorned the beliefs of the right and talked about building a country different from the United States. He warned of the growing dangers of nationalism in Quebec, and he emphasized the necessary role of big government in taking care of the disadvantaged and bringing about equality. As prime minister thirty years later, he pushed back the separatist tides, repelled the challenge from the conservatives, stood up to the United States, erased the deficit, and brought compassionate government back to the table. In launching his final activist spurt, he quoted Franklin Roosevelt: "The test of progress is not whether we add to the abundance of those who have much. It is whether we provide enough for those who have too little." In the era of globalization, it seemed like a quaint notion. But Chrétien, one of the last of the great Liberal dinosaurs, still viewed it as vital.

HISTORIANS TEND TO LOOK at the biggest policy boxes, the economy and national unity, when assessing prime ministers. Any analysis of those two themes would serve Chrétien well. Brian Mulroney had put in place some of the building blocks for economic recovery, but the Chrétien government nevertheless inherited a grave fiscal crisis and was able to restore economic health to the point where, as the columnist Jeffrey Simpson put it, "we are now the best-governed country [economically] in the Group of Eight." Something quite unexpected happened on Jean Chrétien's watch: Canada became a nation where deficits would no longer be tolerated. Chrétien, a relic from the profligate Trudeau years, had ushered Canada into the deficit-free era. No prime minister was going to get away with plunging the country into red ink for some time to come. That it was the Liberals who had done this—while to the south the Republicans were neck-deep in deficit—was an irony to be noted.

Chrétien had arrived in power at a perilous moment in the nation's history, when Canada was facing the double threat of the crushing deficit burden and Quebec sovereignty. As he was leaving, each danger had been swept away. Having courted disaster in Quebec with his weak performance in the 1995 referendum, he had altered strategies and watched the tides turn to the point that there was hope the country could look forward to as long a respite from the separatist wars as it could from budgetary red ink. He had begun his years as prime minister with rock-bottom approval ratings in his native province, but by the end, he had earned a measure of respect.

He was gaining a measure of respect as well for his courage in saying no to Washington on the Iraq war. If Brian Mulroney had blurred the border with his integrationist tendencies, Jean Chrétien had put the stakes back in the ground.

His record on the great issues of the day was buttressed by his electoral victories and other achievements. On the environment, he compiled a weak record through his first nine years in power, but in the final stretch, he put forward plans for national parks and marine conservation, and he rammed through a patched and porous Kyoto Protocol. On health care, his cuts in 1995 were probably more savage than they had to be. He watched as the system fell into disrepair, and then he dawdled some more. Finally, in his last year in power, Chrétien put together an agreement with the provinces that addressed at least some of the systemic problems. On the social side, he was also proud of the progress his government made in reducing child poverty with the Child Tax Benefit and other initiatives.

Although he was dismissive of the alleged brain drain, maintaining it was a ploy by big business to get tax cuts, Chrétien was pragmatic enough to realize that the tax burden was too much, and he brought in notable reductions. To prepare Canada for the knowledge economy, he made a flurry of investments in universities and in research. They included the Millennium Scholarship Fund, an endowment for the Canadian Foundation for Innovation, the Canada Research Chairs Program, and the networks of Centres of Excellence—all programs that won the praise of the critics and would serve as inducements to keep ambitious Canadians at home.

But for all its achievements, the Chrétien government was leaving a bad taste in the mouths of many Canadians. Leading academics like Jack Granatstein, Michael Bliss, and Norman Hillmer were unimpressed. Many respected voices rated even the Mulroney government as superior. The media gave Chrétien middling reviews, and Canadians themselves were suspected of re-electing him only because of the lack of alternatives.

His government lacked a landmark achievement. It had been a government for Ontario and Quebec, one that failed to make progress against the nagging problem of Western alienation. Chrétien had overstayed his welcome by several years, which created the impression that he was all about power for the sake of it. His bumbling ways were often embarrassing, and he could never articulate a clear sense of direction for the country. In a time of international peril he had left the nation's defences in deficient condition. His government's record of ethical malfeasance, of misspending, of truth shaving had eroded Canadians' trust in government and soured their taste for politics even more. He was so weak in managing his caucus that despite his glowing electoral record, it rebelled against him.

In his youth, Chrétien sometimes went to wild extremes to avoid conceding error. In office, the modus operandi was often the same. Joe Clark described it as "deny and bully." In 1994, Chrétien had talked of the trust Canadians had in their institutions as being as vital to democracy "as the air we breathe." The time had come, he said, "to put an end to the politics of cronyism and backroom deals." But his government, much of the time, was an ethical embarrassment, a government that, as the *Toronto Star* columnist Jim Travers put it, too often "mistook the public purse for its own."

Any government in power for a decade will suffer its share of scandals and blunders and spending mishaps. But the degree of folly in the Chrétien years was egregious. There was Airbus, the gun registry, the sponsorship program, the military helicopters fiasco. There was the Somalia shutdown, the GST flip-flopping, APEC, and Shawinigate. There was Pearson Airport and tainted blood and the department that was in "the dark ages," HRDC. There was a government voting down its own Red Book resolution on an ethics counsellor. There were no less than five Cabinet resignations owing to one controversy or another in the course of a single year.

Investigations into several of the ethics files were still ongoing as Jean Chrétien prepared to relinquish power. His reputation could well be tarnished some more with the results of those probes. Not all the files involved the man at the top, but there was some truth to the observation of Preston Manning about the fish rotting from the top.

For those who thought of public service as an altruistic or ennobling pursuit, the endless power struggle between Chrétien and his finance minister was distressingly juvenile. Chrétien had made the public interest such a personal game that he chose to let a meeting of opponents in a hotel room become his ostensible reason for staying in power for four more years. Never mind the broader interests of Canadians or whether that decision was right for the country—his ego was being challenged. He had to stay in power for the sake of a few more grams of self-esteem. The standards—and the rhetoric—of the schoolyard bully prevailed.

This was a word-challenged prime minister who failed at every turn to give the country a sense of ambition. Canada trudged along in the Chrétien years, accompanied by little but the thud of routine endeavour and lowly political combat. He was a prime minister who couldn't lead a national conversation, who could never say to Canadians, "This is our time."

There were moments when elegance was required, and in these moments, Chrétien wasn't there. He wasn't there with a moving plea for unity during the 1995 referendum. He wasn't there at the turn of the millennium, the perfect moment to put forward a new vision for the country. He wasn't there with soothing words for his neighbour and his own people on September 11, and he wasn't there to cogently explain why Canada stayed out of the war against Iraq.

Canada's twentieth prime minister was a triumph of instincts, a failure of words.

His successes, critics argued, were as much the result of good fortune as anything else. Other prime ministers had always had a major opposition party to fight, but Chrétien's major opposition all but disappeared the moment he came to power. In addition, he became prime minister when the country was emerging from a deep recession and entering a period of sustained growth. The combination of a divided opposition and a healthy economy made a practically unbeatable mix. Chrétien's 1997 campaign was weak, and he still won a majority. His 2000 campaign was a policy-free zone, and he still won a majority.

When a government experienced the kind of dismal year the Liberals did in 2002—five Cabinet resignations, Martin pushed out, the party racked by civil war, scandal upon scandal, civil servants breaking every rule in the book—and still could end up with a 25-percent lead in the polls, it was a signal that something was wrong with the system.

BUT WHILE JEAN CHRÉTIEN had many of his successes handed to him, it would be churlish to deny him his due. Compared with the country he'd inherited in 1993, the Canada he was leaving behind a decade later was in measurably better condition. To find a time when the country was more unified and in better shape economically, one had to go all the way back to the Centennial year of 1967. Though he did not have a glowing monument for the history books—a new Constitution or a free trade agreement or a Canadian flag—Chrétien had stabilized the country and readied it to move forward.

Compared with his predecessors, he was leaving on a high note, his party poised to win yet another majority. Brian Mulroney was a reviled figure when he stepped down, his support level in the teens. When Pierre Trudeau left in 1984, his Liberals were low in the polls, the country was in deep deficit, and he was being crucified for his spate of last-minute patronage appointments. In four attempts, Lester Pearson was unable to win a majority government, and the party was not prepared to let him try a fifth. John Diefenbaker was driven out, and Louis St. Laurent departed on a dispirited note, the country having turned against him in his 1957 campaign.

Chrétien's political success was singular. All the other great Liberal leaders had tasted defeat at least once. Chrétien remained unbeaten. He had never even experienced a big fall or an extended slump in public approval since his arrival in Parliament in the 1960s. His bond with the regular people was so strong that as prime minister he was always above 40 percent in the approval ratings—and usually much higher than that. With all the controversies that greeted his final years in power and all the drubbing he took in the press and from members of his own party, it seemed hard to imagine, but the statistics didn't lie. Jean Chrétien was arguably the most popular prime minister in Canadian history.

The public likes underdogs, but underdog status is a temporary phenomenon. It disappears with winning. What was entirely unique in Chrétien's case—and what helped explain his high approval ratings—was that he won every time out, and still remained the underdog.

His infirmities were his strength. The "terrible kid" from the streets of Shawinigan had defied the odds. Those who had dared suggest he was peasant stock had witnessed the revenge of peasant stock. The separatists, with their intellectual pretensions, fell before him. The establishment and the monied classes took a beating. The neo-conservatives and their values were trounced by Chrétien in election after election. Chrétien had overcome the scorn of them all.

In the end, wrote the author Peter C. Newman, "a politician's greatness must be judged as much by its impact on the country's conscience as by what he did or left undone."

Chrétien, a consolidator, not an innovator, left much undone. His impact on the conscience of the nation was often more numbing than inspiring. But he did leave an imprint, one that would endure. His career and record in office stood as a symbol of the strength of the common man and the common man's values. Chrétien tended to see life in the old-fashioned optic of a class struggle. He backed the values of the masses against the classes—and, by and large, the masses won.

In his living room at 24 Sussex Drive in his final summer as prime minister, he talked about his long career and how he had fought off all the doubters. Leaning forward on his chesterfield, he said, "I am an iron man. Yes."

He reflected for a moment, then he added, "You have to be an iron man to see it through. . . . We wanted to restore the economy, and we wanted to build back the unity of the country and have a country that is independent. . . . I delivered the goods. Canada is in good shape today. So I'm going home. My job is done."

Paul Martin, the one man Chrétien could not defeat, stood primed to take over. The country was ready for him. His arrival promised to bring peace to the party and a fresh voice to the nation. Chrétien had re-anchored the country to its traditional pillars, but now it was time for Martin to create a more modern Liberalism, a more modern party, a more modern democracy.

Jean Chrétien could move on in peace—though he would probably never find it. The eternal fighter could never be happy outside the ring.

Outside the ring, there was no one left to fight.

NOTES

Each entry is preceded by a page number or range that indicates where text references are located.

Prologue: "The Terrible Kid"

1 The interview with the prime minister at 24 Sussex Drive was done by the author in the presence of Jim Munson, Chrétien's director of communications.

2 Chrétien talked of being ridiculed in an interview for *Chrétien,* Volume 1, *The Will to Win* (Toronto: Lester Publishing, 1995).

3 The prime minister felt that he sounded somewhat harsh about his father, Wellie, in Volume 1. But in his interview for Volume 2, he again made the point about his father's emotional distance. Never a hug. In those days, he explained, fathers didn't do that.

3 Garceau quotation: Author interview with Pierre Garceau for Volume 1, *The Will to Win.*

3 The anecdotes about his school years are from interviews with Chrétien for Volume 1.

5 The stories of Chrétien at the Liberal leadership convention and meeting with Louis St. Laurent are from volume 1.

5 "I could have become a snob": "Man of Contradictions," *Toronto Star,* June 24, 1990.

Chapter One: Welcome to the 1990s

10 "It's the arrival of the Chrétien era": *Toronto Star,* January 24, 1990.

11 Guarnieri quotations: Author interview with Albina Guarnieri.

12 Broadbent quotations: Author interview with Ed Broadbent.

12 Collenette quotations: Author interview with David Collenette.

12 Zussman quotations: Author interview with David Zussman.

13 Martin's meeting with Fotheringham: Author interview with Allan Fotheringham.

13 "You know the mountain?": John Sawatsky, *Mulroney: The Politics of Ambition* (Toronto: Macfarlane Walter & Ross, 1991).

14 "I came back into politics for one reason": *Toronto Star*, February 1, 1990.

14 "Canada now needs a vision": *Toronto Star*, April 1, 1990.

16 Shelving slogan for "Policy Matters": Author interview with the Martin strategist Tim Murphy.

16–17 Analysis of the Chrétien style: Author interview with David Zussman.

17 "I don't think Chrétien had any warm feelings about Martin—ever!": Author interview with Patrick Lavelle.

18 But "how about not getting your nomination papers signed": Author interview with Joe Comuzzi.

18 "I needed a tough guy": Author interview with Lavelle.

18 "I signed up anything that moved": Author interview with Jim Karygiannis. Other quotes from same interview.

19–20 "Jean did two things": *Toronto Star*, April 23, 1990.

20 "The shit had hit the fan": Author interview with Dennis Mills.

20 "Nobody is going to force you to get in line": Author interview with Sharon Carstairs.

21 ". . . as a Quebecer": *The Globe and Mail*, March 26, 1998.

22–25 The account of the leadership forum in Montreal is based on author interviews with Jean Chrétien, Paul Martin, Eddie Goldenberg, Mark Resnick, and Scott Reid, and on press reports in *The Globe and Mail* and the *Toronto Star*.

25–28 The account of the Calgary leadership convention is based on author interviews with Chrétien, Goldenberg, Martin, Carstairs, Lavelle, and Resnick, and on reports in *The Globe and Mail* and the *Toronto Star*.

27 "But, you know, it had nothing to do with Meech": Author interview with Jean Chrétien.

Chapter Two: The Wrong Job

29 "A doer, a person who loves action": *Toronto Star*, June 24, 1990.

30 "Chrétien is the invisible man": *Toronto Star*, August 12, 1990.

31 "To have credibility, you've got": Author interview with Herb Gray.

32 "I'm here to put a spin on the defeat": Author interview with Dominic LeBlanc.

33 "The worst government in our history": *Toronto Star*, November 7, 1990.

33 "At the moment, we in Canada": *Toronto Star*, November 22, 1990.

35 "I made up my mind": Author interview with Joe Comuzzi.

35 "For me, it is a new job": *Toronto Star*, February 23, 1991.

36 "I have opinions of my own": David Olive, *Political Babble: The 1,000 Dumbest Things Ever Said by Politicians* (New York: John Wiley and Sons, 1992).

36 Anecdote about being taught how to say the word "the": Author interview with George Young.

37–38 "He didn't know it was": Author interview with Sharon Carstairs.

39 "How do we work together?": Author interview with Eddie Goldenberg.

39 "It wasn't a question of working to keep": Author interview with Paul Martin.

39 "In politics, one half of the job": Warren Kinsella, *Kicking Ass in Canadian Politics* (Toronto: Random House, 2001).

40 "But we are not filling it now": *Toronto Star*, February 16, 1991.

40 "I think Mr. Martin's position": *Toronto Star*, February 16, 1991.

40 "We have a party position": *Toronto Star*, February 16, 1991.

40 "It's not only a mistake, it's political stupidity": *Toronto Star*, May 7, 1991.

41 "Liberal Strategists Hope Chrétien Will Quit": *Toronto Star*, May 9, 1991.

41 "He can barely read it": *Toronto Star*, June 22, 1991.

41 "Everyone knows my language problem": *Toronto Star*, June 22, 1991.

42 Interview with Michel Chrétien, *The Globe and Mail*, May 19, 2003.

42 "It was pretty damn blunt": Author interview with Joe Fontana.

42 ". . . the bunch of gadflies": Author interview with Fontana.

42 ". . . and he just stood up and walked out": Author interview with Warren Kinsella.

43 "I had confidence in him": Author interview with Jean Pelletier.

44 "I never forced anybody to go": Author interview with Jean Chrétien in 1995.

44–45 Holt Renfrew story: Author interview with Peter Donolo.

45 "This is the only way it can add up": Author interview with Donolo.

46 "The problem with the Opposition party": Author interview with Eddie Goldenberg.

46 "There were a series of things that were difficult for me": Author interview with Jean Chrétien.

47–49 The account of the Aylmer conference is from author interviews with Zussman, Chrétien, Pelletier, Goldenberg, and John Duffy, and from accounts in *The Globe and Mail* and Edward Greenspon and Anthony Wilson-Smith, *Double Vision: The Inside Story of the Liberals in Power* (Toronto: Doubleday, 1996).

Chapter Three: The Only One Left Standing

51 Chrétien's response to the Dubuc letter first appeared in the *Toronto Star* on January 17, 1992.

52 "One of the greatest assets of Chrétien": Author interview with Jean Pelletier.

56 "We were trying to bring everybody into the tent": Author interview with Joe Clark.

57 "I predicted this would happen": *Toronto Star,* November 30, 1992.

57–58 The account of the raucous encounter between Chrétien and Hec Cloutier is based on the author's interview with Cloutier.

58 "He saw a more targeted government": Author interview with David Zussman.

59 "I asked for it and nobody else": Author interview with Paul Martin.

61 "New Tory, same story": *Toronto Star,* June 15. 1993.

63 "I remember I was with Eddie Goldenberg": Author interview with Peter Donolo.

53 ". . . you know a balloon": Author interview with Jean Pelletier.

63 "I went back to her high school": Author interview with Warren Kinsella.

63 The Fogo Island story: Author interview with George Baker.

63 ". . . a very real understanding of what ordinary people need to have": Author interview with Joyce Fairbairn.

64 "I can say how many jobs I'd like to create": For the inside Tory perspective on the campaign, see David McLaughlin, *Poisoned Chalice: The Last Campaign of the Progressive Conservative Party* (Toronto: Dundurn Press, 1994).

65   "This has got to be the easiest campaign": *Toronto Star*, September 18, 1993.

66   "Be like Billy Graham": Author interview with Peter Donolo.

66   "This magical weapon of accountability": Author interview with John Duffy.

67   "My wife is a member": *Toronto Star*, October 9, 1993.

68–69   For a thorough account of the controversial face ad, see Ken Whyte, "The Face That Sank a Thousand Tories," *Saturday Night*, February 1994.

69   "I thought this was going to hurt him": Author interview with Sharon Carstairs.

Chapter Four: Bare-Boned Pragmatism

72   "Politics, for me, it's a sport": Author interview with Jean Chrétien.

72   "Once you have the look of a losing campaign, it gets worse": Author interview with Peter Donolo.

74   ". . . driven by forces which he himself doesn't seem to understand": Author interview with John Ralston Saul for his book *The Antagonist: Lucien Bouchard and the Politics of Delusion* (Toronto: Penguin Canada, 1997).

74   "I came to think there are about eight Lucien Bouchards": Author interview with Arthur Campeau for *The Antagonist*.

75   "Our deficit, our debt": Author interview with Walt Lastewka.

75   "I'm really grateful to be back": *The Gazette* (Montreal), October 24, 1993.

76   "All I was thinking": Author interview with Eddie Goldenberg.

76   ". . . the people are fed up with lies": From David Zussman, cited in Greenspon and Wilson-Smith, *Double Vision*.

77   "Martin wants industry": Author interview with David Smith.

79   Changes to authority of the bureaucracy: Author interviews with Jean Pelletier, Percy Downe, and Dennis Mills.

81   "I remember the discussion clearly": Author interview with Zussman.

81   "The beauty of it": Author interview with Peter Donolo.

82   "We've got to kick the shit out of the banks": Author interview with Mills.

83   ". . . we have a certain number who you could tell": Author interview with Bonnie Brown.

84 Discussion of Cabinet appointments: Author interviews with Sheila Copps and Anne McLellan.

85–89 Paul Martin's first budget: Author interviews with Martin, Chrétien, Goldenberg, Pelletier, Zussman, and others.

87 Story of confrontation between Martin and Coyne at *The Globe and Mail:* Greenspon and Wilson-Smith, *Double Vision.*

88 Chrétien's lack of expertise in the finance portfolio is drawn from author interviews with Tommy Shoyama and Gerald Bouey for Volume 1, *The Will to Win.*

91 "That land you people occupy up there . . .": Author interview with Doug Roche.

92 "In Bosnia, there is no peacekeeping because there is no peace": *The Globe and Mail,* January 8, 1994.

92 "I'm the prime minister of a country of 28 million people": *The Globe and Mail,* March 19, 1994.

93–95 Analysis of the Dupuy affair: "Chrétien Turns Blunder into Ethics Lesson," *The Globe and Mail,* November 1, 1994.

Chapter Five: Perilous Times

97 "Chrétien is a counterpuncher": Author interview with Torrance Wylie.

98 Paul Martin's reflections on the run-up to his landmark budget: Author interview with Martin.

99 "What gives you the right to act as judges?": Recounted in Greenspon and Wilson-Smith, *Double Vision.*

100 "Chrétien let you run your department": Author interview with Anne McLellan.

100 "The senior statesman told his son": Peter Newman, *Maclean's,* March 13, 1995.

102 Goldenberg's mediation on budget dispute: Author interviews with Martin and Goldenberg.

104 ". . . a watershed document": Peter Newman, *Maclean's,* March 13, 1995.

105 For a comprehensive analysis of the plight of Lloyd Axworthy's social reform plan, see Greenspon and Wilson-Smith, *Double Vision.*

106–7 "Chrétien didn't understand the file": Author interview with Giles Gherson.

107 "Axworthy was encouraged to move": Author interview with Goldenberg.

108 "There was a real appetite to back off": Author interview with Reg Alcock.

109 ". . . there were no hospital closures": *National Post,* November 16, 2002.

110 "The feds just walked away from this responsibility": Author interview with Rick Anderson.

110 "It wasn't just that he had none of the extravagances and pretensions of Brian Mulroney": Ron Graham, *All the King's Horses: Politics Among the Ruins* (Toronto: Macfarlane Walter & Ross, 1995).

111–113 The fish war: From Brian Tobin, *All in Good Time* (Toronto: Penguin Canada, 2002), and from author interview with Tobin.

Chapter Six: To the Brink of Disaster

115 "I think the president is reaching the people through his infirmity": Lawrence Martin, *The Presidents and the Prime Ministers: Washington and Ottawa Face to Face* (Toronto: Doubleday, 1982).

118 "The offer was status quo and shut up": *National Post,* September 28, 2002.

118–19 "What would happen was that Gagliano would give us a report": Author interview with Art Eggleton.

119 "We've had a crash course": Author interview with Liza Frulla.

119 "I said, 'Wait a minute'": Author interview with Sheila Copps.

121 "Quebecers like negotiation": Author interview with Eddie Goldenberg.

122 "For me, you are Quebec's Gandhi": Cited in Martin, *The Antagonist.*

123 "We were fifteen to twenty points ahead in the polls": Author interview with Goldenberg.

123 ". . . everything was going along just tickety-boo": Author interview with Copps.

124 "It was marked, the division": Author interview with Dominic LeBlanc.

124 "The relations were not good": Author interview with Jean Pelletier.

125 "I remember being absolutely stunned": Author interview with Paul Martin.

126–27 ". . . a two-week stretch of nausea": Author interview with Peter Donolo.

127 "We muscled in": Author interview with Pelletier.

129 "I don't want to be the last prime minister of Canada": Author interview with Dominic LeBlanc.

130 "How can a person from a small town in Quebec": Author interview with Bonnie Brown.

131 "I hated that": Author interview with Jean-Claude Rivest for *The Antagonist*.

132 "They stopped on Thursday!": Author interview with Chrétien. The prime minister raises here one of the great unsolved mysteries of the referendum: Why did they stop campaigning? A huge gap in the country's history has been left by the lack of a major book on the referendum campaign. The story of how the country was almost lost warrants several such studies.

133 "You better go back to your country": Author interview with Liza Frulla.

133 "We'll win by 1 percent": Author interview with Chrétien.

133 "Chrétien recalled having a 'fatalistic' attitude": Author interview with Jean Chrétien.

133–36 Scene at the prime minister's home on the night of the referendum vote: Author interviews with Chrétien, Goldenberg, Pelletier, Zussman, and others.

135 "You know, at fifty plus one, I was not about to let go the country": Author interview with Jean Chrétien.

Chapter Seven: Hitting Back Hard

137 "A cold shower": Author interview with Jean Pelletier.

137 "Don't worry, I'll back it up": Author interview with Peter Donolo.

138–40 The assassination attempt: Author interviews with Donolo, Dominic LeBlanc, and Chrétien.

141 "For the first time in my life": *The Globe and Mail*, November 29, 1995.

142 "If it wasn't for that bastard": From André Pratte, *Charest: His Life and Politics* (Toronto: Stoddart, 1998).

145 "He shouldn't have been there": *The Globe and Mail*, February 20, 1996.

146 "I don't want to tell you, Prime Minister": Author interview with Peter Donolo.

147–54 The account of the Airbus affair: Author interviews with Herb Gray, Peter Donolo, Jean Chrétien, Eddie Goldenberg, officials in Allan Rock's department, and William Kaplan. Also from press reports and from Kaplan's book *Presumed Guilty: Brian Mulroney, the Airbus Affair, and the Government of Canada* (Toronto: McClelland & Stewart, 1998).

155 "If the GST is not abolished": *The Globe and Mail*, April 24, 1996.

155 Martin blames Mike Harris on GST: Author interview with Martin.

155 "And that Red Book stinks": *The Globe and Mail*, April 25, 1996.

156 "I was the minister stuck with this": Author interview with Paul Martin.

157 "I don't think when he was a little boy": Author interview with Carolyn Bennett.

157–61 The shutdown of the Somalia inquiry: From author interviews with David Collenette, Peter Donolo, Eddie Goldenberg, and Peter Desbarats, as well as press reports and Desbarat's book *Somalia Cover-Up: A Commissioner's Journal* (Toronto: McClelland & Stewart, 1997).

Chapter Eight: The Second Majority

164 "The first thing everybody wanted to know": Author interview with Art Eggleton.

166 "Fearing that French Canadians will create a separate state": Cited in Martin, *The Antagonist*.

167 "Mr. Bouchard could make a sharp turn": Author interview with Jean Pelletier.

167 "Stéphane is brilliant": Author interview with Liza Frulla.

168–69 Quotations from Chrétien's appearance at the CBC town hall are from various reports in *The Globe and Mail*, December, 1996.

169 Scene backstage after town hall: Author interviews with Peter Mansbridge and Peter Donolo.

170 "If I and others left the impression": *The Globe and Mail*, December 17, 1996.

170–71 Donolo's phone call to Mike McCurry: Author interview with Donolo.

171 Incident at Camp David: Cited in Martin, *The Presidents and the Prime Ministers*.

171 "Good and not too cozy": *The Globe and Mail*, April 10, 1997.

171   "You're the big guy from Little Rock": Chrétien in conversation with reporters, June 2003.

172   "We have recently enacted": *The Globe and Mail,* April 10, 1997.

173   "Would you like to move to Washington?": Author interview with David Smith.

173   "Because for me it is very important that we go to the people": *The Globe and Mail,* April 28, 1997.

173   "Some birdbrain": Author interview with Sharon Carstairs.

174   ". . . symbol of an unnecessary election": Author interview with Peter Donolo.

174   For analysis of the debate within the Liberal party over whether to have big visionary goals, see Edward Greenspon, *The Globe and Mail,* July 5, 1997.

176   "I'd like to get you on TV": Author interview with Andy Scott.

178–84   Unless otherwise indicated in text or notes, all quotations on these pages are from reports in *The Globe and Mail.*

178   "In hindsight, it was a mistake": Author interview with Peter Donolo.

179   "If there's one commitment I have made to my children": Cited by Preston Manning in his book *Think Big: My Life in Politics* (Toronto: McClelland & Stewart, 2003).

180–81   "I think Preston tended to be one of those people": Author interview with Rick Anderson.

182   "Mr. Chrétien has a little bit of an African side": *The Gazette* (Montreal), May 30, 1997.

183   Yves Duhaime's reaction to the loan from the Business Development Bank: Author interview with Yves Duhaime.

Chapter Nine: Soft Power, Hard Power

186   "In 1997, we were regaining control of public finance": Author interview with Jean Pelletier.

187   "We used to watch him in the summer": Author interview with Dominic LeBlanc.

187   "We were different from Paul Martin": Author interview with Donolo.

187   "You see these two guys here?": Author interview with Donolo.

189   "Have you thought about defence?": Author interview with Art Eggleton.

190 "There's a fairly steep learning curve": Author interview with Sheila Copps.

191 ". . . believed in the dignity of the human person": *The Globe and Mail,* June 28, 1997.

192 "Chrétien was foreign affairs critic under Turner?": Author interview with Joe Clark.

192–93 Quotations from the open microphone incident are from *The Globe and Mail,* July 10, 1997.

196 "Oh, everybody takes too much credit all the time": Chrétien in an interview with the CanWest columnist Don Martin. Martin graciously shared his transcript of the interview, some of which—like this quotation—did not appear in his columns.

197 "I always thought Turner was a very nice man": Author interview with Bonnie Brown.

199 "I could have killed him": Author interview with Peter Donolo.

200 Chrétien's days as a student protester are recounted in volume 1, *The Will to Win.*

200 "I am sorry that some people had a problem": *The Globe and Mail,* September 23, 1998.

201 "I felt completely supported": Author interview with Andy Scott.

203 "They just talk money": Chrétien interview with Don Martin.

203 "I suspect what I heard was a simultaneous grinding": *The Globe and Mail,* March 20, 1998.

203 "Here comes the sun": Cited in Greenspon and Wilson-Smith, *Double Vision.*

205 "You should be ashamed": Author interview with Carolyn Bennett.

206 "It's not that I don't bleed for the people who have problems": *The Globe and Mail,* September 18, 1998.

Chapter Ten: Signs of Trouble

208 "On account of my name, they would not accept me": Author interview with Gabriel Chrétien.

210 "Two things happened to me": Author interview with Joe Clark.

210 ". . . it will be damaging to him": *The Globe and Mail,* January 9, 1999.

212 "Nobody knows what I read, sir!": Author interview with Chrétien for Volume 1, *The Will to Win.*

212 The backbenchers' brass band: Author interview with Joe Fontana.

214 "There is an instinct in the Liberal Party towards central control": Author interview with Joe Clark.

215 "Get that statement corrected": Author interview with Brian Tobin.

218 "Why we are there is because of the cleansing": Author interview with Chrétien in June 1999.

219 "After the NATO bombs began to fall": "The Tragic Blunder in Kosovo," *The Globe and Mail,* January 10, 2000. After he published his critique of Ottawa's position, James Bissett tried to pay a courtesy call at the Canadian embassy in Belgrade. As a former diplomat, he would routinely do this when visiting foreign countries. He was told that no one wanted to speak to him.

219 ". . . the propaganda was unbelievable": Author interview with Eggleton.

219 Lloyd Axworthy didn't contest the notion: Author interview with Lloyd Axworthy.

219 "But the problem is when you use bombs": Author interview with Chrétien, July 1999.

223 "A friend of the prime minister took a money-losing hotel": *The Globe and Mail,* March 19, 1999.

223 "That was all run by my friend. I was busy": Author interview with Jean Chrétien.

224 "You know everybody in Shawinigan": *The Globe and Mail,* March 24, 1999.

226 "He has received both personal financial": *The Globe and Mail,* June 2, 1999.

227 "If they have any decency, they will make": *The Globe and Mail,* June 2, 1999.

227 ". . . do everything that is legally possible": *The National Post,* June 23, 1999.

228 "No, no, everything is done according to the rules": *National Post,* June 23, 1999.

228 "I was only trying to help my riding": Author interview with Joe Fontana.

231 "I remember being really annoyed at Herb": Author interview with Sharon-Sholzberg Gray.

232 ". . . a revolution in U.S.–Canadian affairs": This material is from documents obtained by the author through the U.S. Freedom of Information Act.

Chapter Eleven: From the Head Down

235 "Jean, the place is dead": Author interview with Dennis Mills.

235 "You probably stay at home, have a beer": Author interview with Jean Chrétien.

237 "emotionally on a wavelength that is not rational": Author interview with Adrienne Clarkson for *The Antagonist*.

239 ". . . some good old-fashioned ass-kissing": Author interview with George Baker.

241 "We came to the view": Author interview with Francie Ducros.

241–42 The spin on the Cabinet shuffle: Author interviews with Peter Donolo, Ducros, and Scott Reid.

242 ". . . no adult supervision": *National Post,* November 23, 2002.

243 "I think I spent as much time with the prime minister as anybody": Author interview with Ducros.

245 "I don't think we'll see in Canada": Author interview with Paul Martin.

245 "Having the confidence to admit you don't know something": Author interview with Reg Alcock.

247–49 Description of Mont Tremblant conference: Author interviews with Gordon Giffin and Lloyd Axworthy.

251–52 "But there is no trigger to that pride": Author interview with Joe Clark.

252 "We were sure that he made a mistake": Author interview with Liza Frulla.

253 Controversy over NHL support: Author interview with Dennis Mills.

254 ". . . in the Dark Ages": Author interview with Jane Stewart.

255 ". . . somebody spit at me because I was a politician": Author interview with Stewart.

255 "There's too much of a pattern here": Author interview with Rick Anderson.

256 "But one of you sons of bitches": Author interview with Hec Cloutier.

258 "I just found it appalling that Binder Boy": Author interview with Carolyn Bennett.

Chapter Twelve: Prudence and Paranoia

259–62 The story of Chrétien's meeting with the Italian caucus has been pieced together from author interviews with Joe Comuzzi, Joe

Fontana, Joe Volpe, Albina Guarnieri, Carolyn Parrish, Francie Ducros, and David Collenette.

262 Maurice Chrétien was interviewed for the newspaper column by the author.

264–66 The account of the Constellation Hotel meeting is based on interviews with Jean Chrétien, Paul Martin, David Smith, Joe Volpe, Scott Reid, Francie Ducros, Joe Fontana, Albina Guarnieri, Walt Lastewka, Judi Longfield, and Carolyn Bennett.

268 "Peter and Terrie leaving changed the dynamic": Author interview with Percy Downe.

269 "It's your democratic right": Author interview with Eddie Goldenberg for Volume 1, *The Will to Win*.

270 "If Chrétien is serious about this as an election theme": Author interview with Conrad Black.

271 "Want to learn a lesson in politics?": Author interview with Duncan Fulton.

271 "But in politics it is not the facts that count": Author interview with Jean Pelletier.

272 "They're not going to push you out": Author interview with Jean Chrétien. He also related the story of Aline's change of heart to several other people.

272 "He came in one morning all buoyant": Author interview with Carolyn Parrish.

276–77 Pie in the face: Author interview with Paul Sparkes.

277–78 ". . . but then a decision was made": Author interview with Stockwell Day.

Chapter Thirteen: Ideological Warfare

282 "Dear Prime Minister": Alcock provided the author with copies of some of his letters. The exact wording of those sent to the PMO might have been a little different, he admitted. He couldn't recall, for example, whether the one quoted here went through another rewrite. But the overall message, he said, was the same.

283 "He retains the raw, angry sensitivity of a man": *National Post*, June 3, 2002.

284 "I remember his exact phrasing": Author interview with Scott Reid.

285 Day meeting with Castro: Author interview with Stockwell Day.

286 "Christ, Rod, what are you guys doing?": Author interview with Rick Anderson.

286 "I knew I was going up against the most powerful": Author interview with Stockwell Day.

289 The account of the trials and tribulations of getting an executive assistant was provided by George Baker in an interview with the author.

290 "Everybody was pushing me to call him corrupt every day": Author interview with Stockwell Day.

292 The author accompanied the Chrétien campaign to the high school in Barrie, Ontario; to the Toronto training centre for carpenters; and elsewhere.

295 "I remember very clearly we were all gathered at the bar": Author interview with Stockwell Day.

296 "I called them, and I said, 'Make up your mind'": Author interview with Jean Chrétien.

296 "You have seventeen questions": Author interview with Duncan Fulton.

299 Day's visit to the CBC after the election was revealed by him in an interview with the author.

300 "Hundreds of people were telling me": Author interview with David Kilgour.

300 Bennett's encounter with Eddie Goldenberg: Author interview with Carolyn Bennett.

301 "It's always the same with Chrétien": Author interview with Jean Pelletier.

Chapter Fourteen: Contradictions

303 Chrétien's phone call to Cloutier: Author interview with Hec Cloutier.

304 These people couldn't take win for an answer: Author interview with David Collenette.

307 ". . . the argument was made very strongly": Author interview with Paul Martin.

308 "It was just sort of like Joe and Tom": Author interview with Gordon Giffin.

308 Brian Mulroney's briefing of the Bush administration was first revealed in a *National Post* report by Bob Fife.

311 Clark's confrontation with Chrétien: Author interview with Joe Clark.

312 ". . . we were up all night": Author interview with Peter MacKay.

313 ". . . one of the biggest embarrassments we've had": Author interview with Eddie Goldenberg.

314 "Joe Who, and now he's Joe McCarthy": *The Globe and Mail*, February 21, 2001.

316 The Asper editorial, "To Chrétien's Accusers: Put Up or Shut Up," ran in the *National Post* on March 7, 2001. On the same day, the *Post* ran an answering editorial titled "Putting Up."

319 "It is now clear the prime minister was simultaneously involved in lobbying": *The Globe and Mail*, March 24, 2001.

320 "They have refused to recognize the truth.": *The Globe and Mail*, March 28, 2001.

321 ". . . so you could collect on that debt by seizing": Author interview with Eddie Goldenberg.

321 "They mix two files": Author interview with Jean Pelletier.

322 "They proved nothing. It was harassment": Author interview with Jean Chrétien.

Chapter Fifteen: A Cool Head

324 "There may be a huge market down there": Author interview with Michael Hart.

325 "Let's go spend the weekend in Quebec City": *The Globe and Mail*, April 16, 2001.

326 "They are a Republican right-wing administration": Author interview with Percy Downe.

326 "It's always easier to come in after somebody": Author interview with Downe.

329–44 The account of the government's response to the September 11 catastrophe was put together from author interviews with Jean Chrétien, Paul Martin, Eddie Goldenberg, David Collenette, Paul Genest, Herb Gray, and Brian Tobin.

336 "I didn't think I wanted to have a photo-op": Author interview with Jean Chrétien.

337 "Nobody in Washington gave a damn": Author interview with Art Eggleton.

338 The odd development that saw the prime minister giving the Opposition leader political advice was described by both Chrétien and Stockwell Day in their interviews with the author.

341 "Previous prime ministers have resisted these efforts": Author interview with Bonnie Brown.

341 The problems of getting new helicopters: Author interviews with Eggleton and Chrétien.

344 "You didn't mind, did you, Herb?": Author interview with Herb Dhaliwal.

Chapter Sixteen: The Sounds of Civil War

346 "The rest of Canada is yours": *The Globe and Mail,* January 9, 2002.

346 "That price was a joke": *The Gazette* (Montreal), January 15, 2002.

347 Alfonso Gagliano's relations with Maurizio Creuso: *The Globe and Mail,* November 5, 2001.

347 The victim of an inside job: *The Globe and Mail,* December 20, 2001.

348 The convictions of Lemire and Pépin: *National Post,* January 10, 2002, and March 7, 2002.

349–51 The account of Brian Tobin's departure is drawn from author interviews with Eddie Goldenberg, Tobin, Paul Sparkes, and Percy Downe.

352 "I don't think you should continue in Cabinet": Author interview with Herb Gray.

354 "What the hell happened? You put in Graham!": Author interview with Dennis Mills.

355 "He winked at me": Author interview with Carolyn Parrish.

355 "So stop it": Author interview with Carolyn Bennett.

356 "He just blew up. Right off the Richter scale!": Author interview with Anne McLellan.

357 "Every single cocktail party": Author interview with Bonnie Brown.

360 Purchase of luxury jets: *The Globe and Mail,* April 12, 2002.

361 "They made mistakes. And you, the press, were trying to blame": Author interview with Jean Chrétien.

366 The description of the treatment of Martin at the Cabinet table is based on interviews with other Cabinet members.

366   "Paul had one view—that he was being singled out": Author interview with Eddie Goldenberg.

366–72   The account of Paul Martin's resignation is based on author interviews with Martin, Chrétien, Goldenberg, Percy Downe, Francie Ducros, Anne McLellan, and others.

Chapter Seventeen: "We Were Being Stupid . . ."

374   "These ungrateful sons of bitches": Author interview with Carolyn Parrish.

374   "Bring back Peter! Bring back Peter!" *Ottawa Citizen,* June 6, 2002.

375   "I think Peter Donolo did a fabulous job": Author interview with Eddie Goldenberg.

376   "We didn't have a common enemy": Author interview with Sharon Carstairs.

378   Chrétien "wasn't himself": Author interview with Walt Lastewka.

379   "So behold Saint Jean of Dakar": From Andrew Cohen, *While Canada Slept: How We Lost Our Place in the World* (Toronto: McClelland & Stewart, 2003). Cohen makes a compelling case that the Chrétien government was unable to live up to Canada's high traditions in foreign diplomacy.

382   The prime minister on the stage at Stratford: Author interview with Duncan Fulton.

383   "You've never had the time of day": Author interview with Jim Karygiannis.

384   The Chrétiens and the pope at World Youth Day: Author interview with Dennis Mills.

386   "Forget my earlier prediction": Author interview with Peter Mansbridge.

386   "I'm not signing any fucking letter": Author interview with Dennis Mills.

386   "I picked up the phone": Author interview with Liza Frulla.

386   ". . . sucked the brains out of their ears": Author interview with Carolyn Parrish.

387   "I want to make it clear. It wasn't my idea" Author interview with Hec Cloutier.

387   "Why go through with it?": Author interview with Eddie Goldenberg.

389 "When they said, 'You have to raise money'": Author interview with Chrétien.

394 "I was disappointed, but I understood": Author interview with Chrétien.

394 "And we were being stupid in a way": Author interview with Chrétien.

Chapter Eighteen: The Resurgence

395 "I'm really home here": Author interview with Sheila Copps.

396 "You cannot exercise your powers to the point of humiliation": *The Globe and Mail,* September 12, 2002.

398 "He was very clear, and he startled a lot of them": Author interview with Paul Genest.

402 "What a moron!": Although Francie Ducros gave an interview to the author, she declined to discuss the controversial name-calling incident.

405 "This government has had a sorry history": Author interview with Anne McLellan.

Chapter Nineteen: "No" to War

409 "That's no mere token": An analysis of bilateral relations in the St. Laurent–Truman period can be found in Martin, *The Presidents and the Prime Ministers.*

412 "War must always be the last resort": *The Globe and Mail,* February 14, 2003.

413 Chrétien's phone call: Author interview with Chrétien. He delivered the message to a friend who was in hospital.

414 ". . . if we were bringing in a budget, we'd have ministers fanning out": Author interview with Lloyd Axworthy.

416 "You make decisions. Otherwise, you get confused": Author interview with Chrétien.

416 "The Americans will have a deficit of $500 billion": *The Globe and Mail,* May 28, 2003.

419 "And if people committed mistakes in the process": Author interview with Chrétien.

Chapter Twenty: "I Am an Iron Man. Yes."

425 One of the Cabinet ministers to whom Chrétien related the story of
     the farmer in the field was Brian Tobin.

426 "When you're doctrinaire, you're always looking for things to justify
     your doctrine": Chrétien's interview with Don Martin.

426 "So I always wanted to have the unhappy people a bit more happy":
     Author interview with Chrétien.

428 ". . . we are now the best-governed country in the Group of Eight":
     The Globe and Mail, April 30, 2003.

INDEX